A History of Crimea

A History of Crimea
From Antiquity to the Present

Kerstin S. Jobst

Translated by John Heath

BLOOMSBURY ACADEMIC
LONDON • NEW YORK • OXFORD • NEW DELHI • SYDNEY

BLOOMSBURY ACADEMIC
Bloomsbury Publishing Plc
50 Bedford Square, London, WC1B 3DP, UK
1385 Broadway, New York, NY 10018, USA
29 Earlsfort Terrace, Dublin 2, Ireland

BLOOMSBURY, BLOOMSBURY ACADEMIC and the Diana logo are trademarks of Bloomsbury Publishing Plc

First published in 2020 in Germany as *Geschichte der Krim: Iphigenie und Putin auf Tauris* by De Gruyter

First published in Great Britain 2025

Copyright © Kerstin S. Jobst, 2025
English translation copyright © John Heath, 2025

Kerstin S. Jobst has asserted her right under the Copyright, Designs and Patents Act, 1988, to be identified as Author of this work.

Cover image: Vorontsov Palace in the town of Alupka, Crimea, Ukraine, 1950s. Reproduction of antique photo. 11th Oct, 2014. © Igor Golovniov/ZUMA Wire/ZUMAPRESS.com/Alamy Live News

All rights reserved. No part of this publication may be reproduced or transmitted in any form or by any means, electronic or mechanical, including photocopying, recording, or any information storage or retrieval system, without prior permission in writing from the publishers.

Bloomsbury Publishing Plc does not have any control over, or responsibility for, any third-party websites referred to or in this book. All internet addresses given in this book were correct at the time of going to press. The author and publisher regret any inconvenience caused if addresses have changed or sites have ceased to exist, but can accept no responsibility for any such changes.

A catalogue record for this book is available from the British Library.

A catalog record for this book is available from the Library of Congress.

ISBN: HB: 978-1-3503-2800-6
PB: 978-1-3503-2799-3
ePDF: 978-1-3503-2801-3
eBook: 978-1-3503-2802-0

Typeset by RefineCatch Limited, Bungay, Suffolk
Printed and bound in Great Britain

To find out more about our authors and books, visit www.bloomsbury.com and sign up for our newsletters.

CONTENTS

List of Illustrations viii
List of Abbreviations x
Maps xii
A Note on the Translation xiv
Orientation: Terminology and Spelling xv

Introduction 1

1 Crimea in Myth and Legend 7

2 Greeks, Scythians and Others 23

3 New Actors: Sarmatians and Others 31

4 The Mithridatic Wars: Crimea under Roman Rule 35

5 Goths, Huns, the "Great Migration" and Its Impact on Crimea 39

6 Crimea as a Site of Early Christianity 43

7 Crimea between the Eastern Roman Empire, Crimean Gothia and the Khazar Empire 47

8 Crimea between Kyivan Rus', Byzantium and Eurasian Semi-Nomadic Groups 53

9 Kumans, Polovtsians and Kipchaks 57

10 The Fourth Crusade (1202–04) and Its Consequences for Crimea 61

11 The Pax Mongolica, Trade, Slavery and the "Black Death" 65

12 The Principalty of Theodoro and a Lithuanian Intermezzo 71

13 The Crimean Khanate: The Beginnings 75

14 The Establishment of the Crimean Khanate 81

15 The Crimean Khanate: Ottoman Suzerainty and the Balance of Power in Eastern Europe 89

16 Slavery and the Topos of the Crimean Tatar Warrior 97

17 The Nogai as a Factor in Early Modern Crimean History 103

18 Cossacks as a Factor in Early Modern Crimean History 107

19 Inside the Crimean Khanate 111

20 The Lead-Up to Annexation: The Strengthening of the Russian Empire, the "Greek Plan" and the Treaty of Küçük Kaynarca of 1774 117

21 The 'Independent' Crimean Khanate and Russian Annexation (1774–83) 127

22 The First Decades of Russian Rule in Crimea 133

23 Multiethnic and Multireligious Crimea under Tsarist Rule: The Tatar Population – Gender Relations 141

24 Multiethnic and Multireligious Crimea under Tsarist Rule: 'Old' and 'New' Inhabitants – Economic Development 149

25 The Crimean War: A 'Modern' War? 157

26 The Crimean War: The Events in the Peninsula 163

27 After the War: Crimea between 1856 and 1905 169

28 The Crimean Tatar Population after the Crimean War 175

29 The Revolution of 1905 and its Impact in Crimea 181

30 The First World War and the Revolution on the Periphery: The Crimean Peninsula, 1917–20 187

31 The Crimean Peninsula, 1920–41 199

32 Crimea in the Second World War 207

33 The Deportations of 1944/45 and Their Background 215

34 Crimea after the Second World War 221

35 After the Dissolution of the Soviet Union: Crimea as Part of Independent Ukraine 235

36 Russian Again?! Crimea after the Annexation of 2014 241

Postscript 251
Notes 255
Bibliography 303
Index: People 351
Index: Places 357

ILLUSTRATIONS

1.1 *Portrait of Alexander Pushkin*, painting by Orest Kiprenskii, 1827   17
Photo: Elton Luz, public domain
(https://www.wikiart.org/ru/orest-kiprenskiy/portret-a-s-pushkina-1827)

1.2 The Fountain of Tears in the Khan's Palace, Bağçasaray   20
Photo: Andreas56; licence: Creative Commons Attribution-Share Alike 3.0 Unported
(https://creativecommons.org/licenses/by/3.0/deed.de)

2.1 Scythian archers, Panticapaeum, 475–450 BC   25
Photo: PHGCOM in Musée du Louvre; licence: Creative Commons Attribution Share Alike 3.0 Unported
(https://creativecommons.org/licenses/by/3.0/deed.de)

2.2 The ruins of Chersonesus   26
Photo: Dmitry A. Mottl; lizenz: Creative Commons Attribution Share Alike 3.0 Unported
(https://creativecommons.org/licenses/by/3.0/deed.de)

8.1 *The Baptism of Rus'*, painting by Viktor Vasnetsov, 1890   55
Photo: Shakko; license: CC BY-SA 4.0 DEED Attribution-ShareAlike 4.0 International
(https://creativecommons.org/licenses/by-sa/4.0/deed.en)
(https://commons.wikimedia.org/wiki/File:Baptism_of_Vladimir_(N._Novgorod)_01_by_shakko.jpg)

19.1 The Khan's Palace of Bağçasaray   114
Photo: Fluid70; licence: Creative Commons Attribution-Share Alike 3.0 Unported
(https://creativecommons.org/licenses/by/3.0/deed.de)

25.1 The Battle of Sinop on 18 November 1853 (*The Night After the Battle*), painting by Ivan Aivazovskii, 1853   160
Photo: xenexx, public domain
(https://www.wikiart.org/ru/ivan-ayvazovskiy/originalnoe-nazvanie-sinopskiy-boy-18-noyabrya-1853-goda-noch-posle-boya-1853)

25.2	*The Defence of Sevastopol' 1854–1855*, panoramic painting by Franz Rubo, 1904	160
	Photo: Rumlin; licence: Creative Commons Attribution 3.0 Unported	
	(https:// creativecommons.org/licenses/by/3.0/deed.de)	
28.1	İsmail Gaspıralı (İsmail Gasprinskii)	179
29.1	The battleship *Panteleimon* (formerly *Kniaz' Potemkin-Tavricheskii*), in a photograph from 1906	182
33.1	Amet-Han Sultan – two-time hero of the Soviet Union, photograph from 1945	219
34.1	Group photo at the Yalta Conference, 1945 (Winston Churchill, Franklin D. Roosevelt and Joseph Stalin)	224
34.2	The Artek Pioneer camp, 1986	228
	Photo: FORTEPAN / Györgyi Dóra; licence: Creative Commons Attribution-Share Alike 3.0 Unported	
	(https://creativecommons.org/licenses/by/3.0/deed.de)	
35.1	The flag of the Crimean Tatars	238
36.1	The Crimean Bridge under construction, 13 October 2017	248
	Photo: Rosavtodor.ru; licence: Creative Commons Attribution 4.0 International	
	(https://creativecommons.org/licenses/by/4.0/deed.de)	

ABBREVIATIONS

BdCh	Biblioteka dlia chteniia [The Reading Library] – (1834–65)
BSÈ	Bol'shaia Sovetskaia Èntsiklopediia [Great Soviet Encyclopedia]
IIRGO	Izvestiia Imperatorskogo russkogo geograficheskogo obshchestva
	[Letters of the Imperial Russian Geographic Society] – (1865–1924)
ITUAK	Izvestiia Tavricheskoi uchennoi arkhivnoi komissii
	[Letters of the Taurida Scholarly Archive Commission] – (1887–1917)
KOL	Kolokol [The Bell] – (1857–67)
KS	Kievskaia starina [Kyivan Antiquity] – (1882–1906)
ÖZG	Österreichische Zeitschrift für Geschichtswissenschaften
RS	Russkaia starina [Russian Antiquity] – (1870–1918)
SIRIO	Sbornik Imperatorskogo russkogo istoriechskogo obshchestva
	[Collective Volume of the Imperial Russian Historical Society] – (1867–1916)
SOV	Sovremennik [The Contemorary] – (1836–66)
VE	Vestnik Evropy [The European Messenger] – (1802–30; 1866–1918)
ZhRVIO	Zhurnal Imperatorskogo russkogo voenno-istoricheskogo obshchestva
	[Journal of the Imperial Russian Military-Historical Society] – (1846–1917)
ZhMNP	Zhurnal Ministerstva Narodnogo Prosveshcheniia

[Journal of the Ministry for the People's Enlightenment] – (1834–1917)

ZIOOIiD   Zapiski Imperatorskogo odesskogo obshchestva istorii i drevnostei

[Notes of the Imperial Odessa Society for History and Antiquities] – (1844–1916)

MAPS

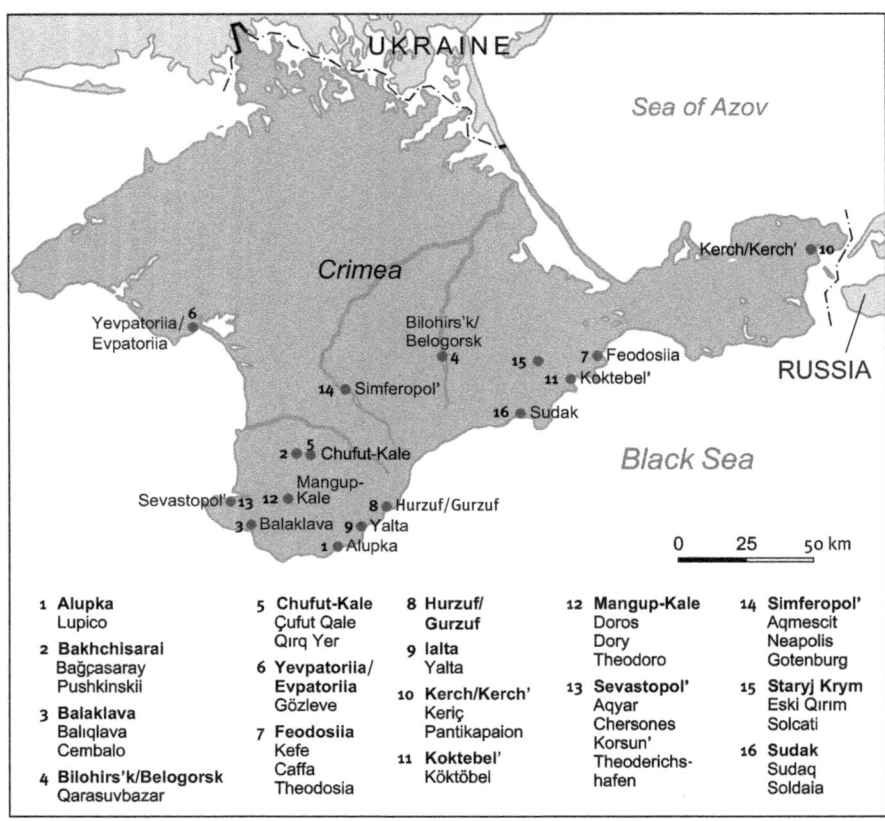

Map of Crimea

Map of the Black Sea region

A NOTE ON THE TRANSLATION

When citing sources in foreign languages, the book uses published translations wherever possible (see the bibliography); in all other instances, the translations are the translator's own or, in the case of Russian, Turkish, Romanian and French sources, the work of the author, Ninja Bumann and Anna Guboglo. I am most grateful to the latter two, as well as to Oleksandra Krushynska, for their tireless assistance in sourcing the published English quotations.

For direct quotations, the book uses double quotation marks. Single quotation marks, when not indicating a quotation within a quotation, denote the author's desire to distance herself from certain terms.

ORIENTATION: TERMINOLOGY AND SPELLING

From time immemorial, "incomparable" Crimea, as the Soviet poet Vladimir V. Maiakovskii (1893–1930) described it, has held a unique status from manifold perspectives:

> And the stupid call her "The Red Nice"
> And the bored call her "The All-Union Sanatorium"
> With what is our Crimea comparable?
> Our Crimea is incomparable.[1]

The peninsula has been traversed, conquered and settled by countless peoples. This has not only shaped its multiconfessional and multicultural character, but is also manifested in the different geographical names and terms; there are various names and spellings for places, people and technical terms, in Crimean Tatar, Russian and Ukrainian, but also Greek and other languages.

The original edition of this book, published in 2020 in German, used the predominant variant of each era and context under discussion; that is, when discussing the Ancient Greek colonies in Crimea, I used the Greek Pantikapaion, for instance, and this English edition follows suit. In the context of Russian rule over Crimea after 1783 and the Soviet era, however, I now give preference to Ukrainian spelling. There are exceptions: in the discussion of the city of Bağçasaray, I use Crimean Tatar spelling, reflecting the name's Crimean Tatar origins (as the "Palace of the Garden"). Upon first mention of a place, I also provide, when the context requires, the other variants in the official languages of Crimea today (Crimean Tatar, Russian, Ukrainian). The same holds for names of people.

Ukrainian and Russian names, terms and titles are rendered following the ALA-LC transliteration scheme. An exception is made for the names of people for which Anglicized versions have long been established: Pushkin, for instance, appears as "Alexander" rather than "Aleksandr". In the case of ethnonyms too, the common English term is used (for Khazars and Kipchaks, for example). Crimean Tatar and Ottoman terms, with the exception of place names, are generally rendered using the Oghuz-Turkic forms of modern Turkish. Hence the variant Giray is preferred to other common forms such as Geray or Kerey.

Here it is worth mentioning the etymology of the name "Crimea", the origins of which are not entirely clear. Essentially, there are two variations on the term's derivation: it might come from the Turkic term "kerim", meaning "fortress", or from "qrım" (rock). An alternative explanation points to the Cimmerians mentioned by Classical authors such as Herodotus, who are said to have lived in eastern Crimea.

The present volume also examines ideas and concepts prevalent at different times in different cultures, such as 'civilization', the 'Orient', 'exoticism' or 'barbarianism'. Since these constructs require contextualizing and historicizing, strictly speaking one would have to place them in inverted commas. In the interests of readability, I have largely refrained from doing so.

Russian distinguishes between the terms *russkii* (Russian) and *rossiiskii* (belonging or pertaining to Russia). While the former denotes Russian ethnicity, language and nationality and is generally translated into German as *russisch*, the latter generally refers to the supranational state – today the Russian Federation (*Rossiiskaia Federatsiia*). While in German the neologism *russländisch* is becoming increasingly established in order to do justice to this distinction, English does not have such neat options, although the expression "Russia's Muslims" has been used for disambiguation. Dates relating to Russia before the switch from the Julian to the Gregorian calendar at the end of 1918 are generally given according to the former.

This book was intended to provisionally bring a close to my longstanding study of the study of Crimea. When I first took up the subject, many considered it somewhat exotic, and not only due to the peninsula's Mediterranean climate and the Muslim influence. However, events since 2014 and 24 February 2022 have shown that "incomparable" Crimea has again taken on global political significance – it would appear indefinitely.

I thank my colleagues, friends and students who have contributed to the development of this history of Crimea in one way or another. Above all, mention must be made of Ninja Bumann, who has cast such a trained eye on my writing. The same goes for Ana Guboglo and Oleksandra Krushynska. It would be impossible to list the names of all of those who have contributed to the book's genesis, but I am particularly indebted to Christoph Augustynowicz, Marija Wakounig, Andreas Kappeler, Ulrich Hofmeister, Kirsten Bönker, Christiane Strobl and Anja Freckmann. Special thanks are due to my translator, John Heath, not only for the present translation, but also for his patience with an at times somewhat wavering author. The responsibility for the deficiencies I nevertheless fear will be found in this book on over 2,000 years of Crimean history rests solely with me. I also thank my father, Ernst Jobst, and his partner, Elisabeth Pust, for their steadfast support, and my daughter, Elisabeth, who was not born 'in Crimea' but has 'grown up' with it, for her understanding and wonderful humour; she has been a constant source of inspiration. This book is dedicated to her.

Kerstin S. Jobst, Vienna, December 2018/June 2023

INTRODUCTION

A cursory inspection of the following lines, notwithstanding (anachronistic) terms such as "Supreme Soviet of the Union of Soviet Socialist Republics", which disappeared along with the rest of the USSR in 1991, might give the impression they are taken from a dialogue connected to the Russian Federation's takeover of the Autonomous Republic of Crimea from Ukraine in 2014:

> "Try to get through to General Staff and ask what has caused the invasion."
> "Invasion??" Chernok smiled. "What invasion?"
> "What are you talking about?" shouted Sabashnikov without a trace of his former buffoonery.
> "Turn on the Moscow channel."
> Fofanov found Moscow on the television set. [. . .] "As is well known," (to whom and on what basis was unclear, since the Soviet population had been kept totally in the dark) "broad segments of the originally Russian territory" (not a word about the State Duma; it might just as well not exist) "of the Eastern Mediterranean Region" (even in this context the name Crimea was out of the question) "have appealed to the Supreme Soviet of the Union of Soviet Socialist Republics for inclusion in one of the Republics." (Another little fib, an off-white lie; that was not quite how the request was worded). "Yesterday at a meeting of the Presidium of the Supreme Soviet the appeal was approved in principle. It must now gain the confirmation of the Supreme Soviet as a whole. [. . .]"[1]

It was of course in the late March of 2014 that the Kremlin intensified its announcements concerning Crimea's future, following months of protests by the Euromaidan movement and the Ukrainian government's resignation in the late January of the same year. The fact that the peninsula belongs to Ukraine by international law had been a thorn in the side of the majority of people in the Russian Federation and their political representatives. Russian military officials in Crimea attempted to convince local politicians to collaborate with Russia's representatives; at the same time, Federation troops stationed in the peninsula began covertly taking strategically important positions. On 23 February, the president of the Russian Federation, Vladimir V. Putin (*b.* 1952), declared that preparations had to be made to "return Crimea to Russia", in order to "give the inhabitants the opportunity to decide their own fate".[2] On 6 March, following violent clashes between Crimean Tatar and pro-Russian demonstrators in Simferopol' (Russian/ Ukrainian; Crimean Tatar: Aqmescit) and the growing presence of pro-Russian combatants without insignia, the Crimean parliament voted for "re-annexation" by Russia. Some ten days later, there followed a referendum (contravening Ukrainian law); it was reported that 96.77 per cent of the electorate had voted for Crimea's annexation by the Russian Federation – a most dubious figure. A day later, an application was made to Moscow; it was ratified on 21 March by Russia's Federation Council.

Those, then, were the real events of 2014, which the Soviet Russian writer Vasilii P. Aksënov (1932–2009) anticipated in *The Island of Crimea* published in the 1980s. A "clear-sighted Crimea novel", as the journalist Reinhard Veser quite correctly noted in 2015,[3] the work was based on the question as to

> What if Crimea really were an island? What if, as a result, the White Army had been able to defend Crimea from the Reds in 1920? What if Crimea had developed as a Russian, yet Western, democracy alongside the totalitarian mainland?[4]

In the novel, Crimea – not the real peninsula, but a fictional island – is a kind of hypermodern Slavic variant of Taiwan; it is not a pro-Soviet but a pro-Russian "Common Fate League" under the aegis of the journalist Andrei Luchnikov, who is stylized as a kind of James Bond figure. He harbours hopes of reunification with the mother country and the resulting democratization of the Soviet Union. He and his followers are deceived; instead of a peaceful merger, "the Committee for Physical Culture and Sports of the Soviet of Ministers of the USSR, together with the Ministry of Defense and the All-Union Voluntary Society for Assistance to the Army, Air Force, and Navy, have decided [. . .] to carry out a series of war games in the Black Sea area under the general name of Spring".[5] And this "Spring" was nothing other than the invasion of Crimea.

In the novel, the Soviet invasion puts an end to the development of a supranational Crimean identity. Its members of Slavic, Tatar and other origin call themselves "Yaki", a bastardized form of the Turkic *yahşi* (good). In this satirical work of science fiction, they ultimately represent a largely unsuccessful plan, since they are subjugated to those who advocate annexation by the Soviet Union and with it the primacy of the Russian language.

Today, in so-called reality, it is hard to say how satisfied Crimea's inhabitants are with the new "reunification of Crimea with Russia", as it is usually referred to. According to recent surveys, at least the vast majority of people do not clearly identify with the Russian Federation; some 63 per cent named "the place where I live" as their home – and that is Crimea, not

Russia.[6] For centuries, Crimea was home to many peoples: the peninsula on the northern shore of the Black Sea has always been the object of "almost sexual yearnings of possession",[7] as the British journalist Neal Ascherson (b. 1932) fittingly puts it – not just for the Russians in 2014. It was the classical Tauris, so closely interwoven with Hellenic mythology, as well as a Greek and Roman colony. It has always been traversed, conquered and settled by countless peoples: Cimmerians, Scythians, Greeks, Ostrogoths, Khazars, Genoese, Venetians, Turko-Tatars and inhabitants of Kyivan Rus' inhabited and ruled it before it came under the control of Russians and Ukrainians from the late eighteenth century onwards. They and many others all had a lasting impact on Crimea's culture and, in their respective times, its politics. Located between the Black Sea and the Sea of Azov, the peninsula remains a fascinating area to this day, not least due to its long-standing multiconfessional and multicultural character, captivating not only scholars but also travellers, culture enthusiasts and politicians.

Even today, Crimea still resists *every* national claim to ownership. Not even the waves of ethnic cleansing in the twentieth century could change that – neither the National Socialist genocide perpetrated against large sections of the Jewish population between 1941 and 1944 nor the deportation of the Crimean Germans ordered by Joseph Stalin (Ioseb Besarionis dze Jughashvili; 1878–1953) in 1941, nor the deportation of the Crimean Tatars, Bulgarians and Greeks following the Second World War.

Since the spring of 2014, Crimea has *de facto* been part of the Russian Federation, although by international law it still belongs to Ukraine. Irrespective of its shifts between various actors and empires throughout its history, it has always been nationally heterogeneous. This is not least due to the influx of Crimean Tatars returning from Central Asian exile in the 1990s, which goes some way to making the peninsula seem, from a northern (Russian and Western European) perspective, an exotic, oriental region.[8] However, since the second Russian annexation of 2014 – the first came under Catherine II (1729–96) in 1783 – many of them have once again had to leave the homeland they had only recently regained.

The perceived exoticism of Crimea is doubtlessly also due to a climate which is somewhat Mediterranean compared to the Central Russian and Central Ukrainian areas and which has made its mountains and particularly its southern coast a popular tourist destination since the nineteenth century. For Tsarina Catherine II (and subsequently the inhabitants of both the tsarist and the "Red" empires), the region's charming landscape made it the "pearl of the empire".[9]

With its diverse cultural strata, the odes several literary figures have written to it, and its turbulent history – always in connection with empires and forever a transit space – the peninsula has attracted special attention, and continues to do so. But it also remains the subject of a good deal of political controversy: its takeover by the Russian Federation in March 2014, considered by most legal experts to be in contravention of international law, turned it into an inner-European crisis region, even if Russia's takeover has, fortunately, cost fewer lives than the ongoing conflict in eastern Ukraine, which has resulted in over 12,000 deaths to date (i.e. in February 2019). Certainly, the relevance of "Crimea" is quite obvious,[10] particularly since, it is feared, an unsolved and presumably long-lasting frozen conflict has emerged in Eastern Europe that is also highly relevant in a global context; many actors in the field of global security/politics have to see the Russian Federation as an important but difficult partner. Hitherto, the increased interest in the Black Sea region in general and the Crimean peninsula in specific evident in recent years in the media, politics and the public sphere has not been able to draw on a literature that meets scholarly standards while remaining readable. This book aims to fill this gap. Despite valuable individual studies,[11] there has yet to be a synthesis of the history of Crimea from 'mythical times' to the present day.[12]

In the German-speaking world, from which the author emanates, it is easy to see the relevance of a survey of the "History of the Crimean Peninsula": it is not just East Germans who have enjoyed or at least heard of the famous *Krymskoe*, Crimea's sparkling wine.[13] Goethe's and Gluck's rendering of the "Iphigenia in Tauris" theme form part of the German-speaking canon and are hence familiar to many from their schooldays. Many are also familiar with the efforts to trace a medieval "German Crimea" popularized by several German-speaking travellers from the eighteenth century onwards in relation to Crimean Goths. More famously, this fed Adolf Hitler's (1889–1945) attempts to implement his bizarre "Gotenland" fantasies as part of his criminal Eastern Campaign during the Second World War.[14] After the breakup of the Soviet Union, the tourist industry collapsed in the former "All-Union sanatorium"– a term for Crimea said to go back to Lenin himself. However, in the new millennium, the stream of visitors began to increase. Tourists also came from the German-speaking countries, assisted by the one-way visas for EU citizens provided by Kyiv in 2005; incidentally, it wasn't until 2017, after long negotiations, that the European Union came to comparable arrangements with Ukraine. In the noughties, the peninsula was a destination for commercial travel agents and was no longer driven only by specialist promoters of educational trips. Both former East German citizens and the large number of former Soviet citizens of German descent have a special connection to Crimea; it was the dream destination for millions of people in the Eastern Bloc. For instance, many of them came to know and love the peninsula in the Artek international communist youth camp located in the little town of Hurzuf (Russian: Gurzuf) on the picturesque southern coast.

When discussing the fascination Crimea has held for German speakers, one name cannot be overlooked: Joseph Beuys (1921–86), a German artist of world renown. Beuys often related how, as a German soldier, he was shot down over the peninsula in his Stuka by enemy flak in 1944 and rescued by Crimean Tatars, who healed his wounds with felt, fat and honey, materials that would play an important role in his later works.¹⁵ The considerable success of Liudmila Ulitskaia's (*1943) novel *Medea and Her Children*, set in Crimea, or the Scythian exhibition in Berlin, Munich and Hamburg in 2007/08 are further indication of the great public interest in the history of the region. All these elements (and plenty of others) are ornamentation associated with the concept of Crimea but cannot be placed in a wider context. This monograph on the subject – expressly meeting scholarly standards and with extensive notes – seeks to fill this striking lacuna. There is now keen scholarly interest in the Black Sea region and with it Crimea, but mostly in connection with the specific historical space of the former.¹⁶ In analogy to Fernand Braudel's conception of the Mediterranean with its own peculiar combination of characteristics, in the future we can expect greater academic and scholarly examination of the region. It goes without saying, then, that Crimea cannot be understood and described independently of its relationship with the Black Sea and its hinterland.

Russia's occupation of Crimea following the Ukrainian Euromaidan of November 2013 and its subsequent annexation in March 2014 was not foreseen by experts (including the author). Even though making predictions is, happily, not part of the historian's professional remit, these events made it clear just how great a need there is for well-founded statements on the history of Crimea and the region.

This survey essays a wide arc. It considers matters generally, but not strictly, in chronological order, beginning with Crimea as a mythical space but not restricted to the world of classical mythology, for Crimea has always captured the imagination of its visitors, Josef Beuys being just one example; as a mythic locus, Crimea even plays a role in collective narratives of nationalities that one would not necessarily associate with the peninsula.

Notwithstanding its enormous mythic potential, from the perspective of the respective centres of power, Crimea has always been on the periphery: this was already the case in Antiquity, when Herodotus gave us one of the first descriptions of Tauris and the Scythians who lived there. The inhabitants of Greek colonies on the coast lived in sometimes peaceful, sometimes violent reciprocity with (semi)mobile large groups who drove into Crimea from the northern Eurasian areas. Contact between these and the Hellenic colonies or Rome/Byzantium promoted the longstanding, influential idea of Crimea as a marginal region, as a zone at the intersection of civilization (or ecumene, as the entire known inhabited world was termed in Graeco-Roman Antiquity) and barbarism – dichotomous terms that must, of course, be used with the appropriate distance but which have played a large role in discourses on Crimea at all times. Its peripheral location did not prevent world history from being decided in the peninsula well before the Crimean War (1853–6) or the Yalta Conference (1945): for instance, in the first century BC, Mithridates VI, the king of Pontus, came into conflict with Rome due to his ambitions to extend his sphere of influence to regions in Asia Minor. Rome did not want to give up power on the northern Black Sea, leading to what became known as the Mithridatic Wars (89–63 BC). Ultimately, it was due to Byzantine influences that Crimea later became a site of early Christianity. For Goths, Huns and many other peoples for whom scholarship has found only very imprecise names, if any at all, the peninsula was a transit region or (temporary) home. Finally, from the seventh century onwards, the Khazars became a regional power before a new actor repeatedly advanced to the shores of the Black Sea and Crimea in the tenth century, without becoming established, however: Kyivan Rus'. In the thirteenth century, the maritime republics of Venice and Genoa established trade colonies along the coast, and 200 years later the Muslim Crimean Khanate emerged, which was soon subjugated to the suzerainty of the Ottomans. Eventually – in 1783 – the peninsula became part of the Russian Empire; it is only since then that it has been a permanent factor in Russian and Ukrainian history. This very complex development is presented in individual chapters, as are the revolutions of 1917, the World Wars (including both German occupations), the Soviet era and the years when Crimea was part of the Ukrainian state, which it remains by international law. The time after 2014, for which we cannot make a final historical assessment, is also considered. Since Crimea has always inspired poets and artists too, attention will also be devoted to this aspect. However, "literary Crimea" will not receive its own chapter, since it is due a separate work that should be written not by a historian but by an expert in the field of comparative literary studies.

1

Crimea in Myth and Legend

When thee a deep mysterious destiny
Brought to this sacred fane, long years ago.
To greet thee, as a treasure sent from heaven,
With reverence and affection, Thoas came.
Benign and friendly was this shore to thee,
Which had before each stranger's heart appall'd,
For, till thy coming, none e'er trod our realm
But fell, according to an ancient rite,
A bloody victim at Diana's shrine.

[. . .]

And hast thou, since thy coming here, done nought?
Who cheer'd the gloomy temper of the king?
Who hath with gentle eloquence annull'd,
From year to year, the usage of our sires,
By which, a victim at Diana's shrine,
Each stranger perish'd, thus from certain death
Sending so oft the rescued captive home?
Hath not Diana, harbouring no revenge
For this suspension of her bloody rites,
In richest measure heard thy gentle prayer?[1]

These verses are probably familiar to lovers of German literature, even to those who generally only began to consider the Crimean Peninsula and its geographical location in the context of its annexation by the Russian Federation in the spring of 2014. They were written by the great German poet Johann Wolfgang von Goethe (1749–1832), who – like other artists of the eighteenth century – repeatedly returned to the then popular Iphigenia theme.[2] Goethe's work drew on the version by the Hellenic tragedian Euripides, *Iphigenia in Tauris* (written around 414/412 BC). In Classical mythology, Tauris, or Taurica, was where the goddess Artemis/Diana took Agamemnon's daughter after kidnapping her to save her from being sacrificed by her father, who as a military leader intended to offer her up to the gods after they had caused the winds to drop, thereby preventing him from crossing the sea to wage war on Troy. In exchange for her rescue, Iphigenia had to serve as a priestess sacrificing humans in the land of the barbarians, for every shipwrecked sailor washed up on the coast of Tauris was doomed to die. In Iphigenia's homeland, on the other hand, her mother Clytemnestra, thinking that her daughter had been killed, avenged her death by murdering her husband; in turn, Iphigenia's siblings, Orestes and Electra, killed their own mother – quite the stuff of tragedy. But it didn't end there: Orestes – descended from the house of Tantalus – was now cursed and asked the Oracle how he could escape the wrath of the gods and the eternal torment (of the Tantaluses). He was instructed to rescue a "sister" from Tauris. Believing Iphigenia to be dead, he thought the Oracle meant Apollo's twin sister, the goddess Artemis/Diana, and assumed his task was to steal her statue from the temple in the peninsula, and so he set out with his old friend Pylades.

Their destination, "Tauris", was Crimea, which ancient Greek authors had already called the "Tauric Peninsula" (*Chersónesos Tauriké*) or the "Land of the Tauri", and which they considered to be located on the edge of the inhabited world, the ecumene. They considered the periphery to be less civilized than Hellas; it was a barbaric world.[3] This evidently uninviting region was inhabited by the Tauri, who according to one interpretation gave the peninsula its Classical name and settled the southern coast and the mountainous region. Little is known about them, their origins or their language; we only encounter them in the narratives of Classical authors. For instance, Herodotus, who will also play a large role in the following chapter, relates:

> [T]hey sacrifice to the "Maiden" both ship-wrecked persons and also those Hellenes whom they can capture by putting out to sea against them; and their manner of sacrifice is this:—when they have made the first offering from the victim they strike his head with a club: and some say that they push the body down from the top of the cliff (for it is upon a cliff that the temple is placed) and set the head up on a stake; but others, while agreeing as to the heads, say nevertheless that the body is not pushed down from the top of the cliff, but buried in the earth. This divinity to whom they sacrifice, the Tauroi themselves say is Iphigeneia the daughter of Agamemnon.[4]

For both Euripides and Goethe, Iphigenia is not a goddess but rather someone acting against her own will at the behest of Artemis/Diana. In Goethe's play and even in Euripides' tragedy, the story eventually has a happy ending for the trio of Iphigenia, Orestes and Pylades: they are able to leave Tauris. There are crucial differences, however; separated by over 2,000 years, the two works reflect their authors' lifeworlds and worldviews, shaped by their respective times. Euripides's Tauri are ideal-typical barbarians, even if their Greek antithesis is not portrayed as wholly humane and civilized. Euripides's Iphigenia does not feel any connection with the autochthonous population, and she manages to escape from Tauris only due to a ruse – that is, without the Tauric King Thoas's permission. This is not the case in Goethe's work; here the king and Iphigenia have an affinity for each other which is able to soften the wild ways of the barbarians:

> Who cheer'd the gloomy temper of the king?
> Who hath with gentle eloquence annull'd,
> From year to year, the usage of our sires,
> By which, a victim at Diana's shrine,
> Each stranger perish'd, thus from certain death
> Sending so oft the rescued captive home?

Moreover, Goethe's Tauri are generally much less savage than those of Euripides.[5] Nevertheless, in both variants two poles collide – even though his fondness for Iphigenia tames him, King Thoas represents an archaic, mythic principle, while Iphigenia personifies civilization. In Tauris – that is, in Crimea – two systems meet: the centre and the periphery interact, but despite their partial rapprochement they cannot be united.

And this applies not only to this myth associated with Crimea, but also to other mythological narratives "surrounding a historical figure, a historical event, a historical fact or a historical development" whose central content is fixed while they are "otherwise non-complex narratives enjoying variable reception and reproduction".[6] It may be something to do with its peripheral location – at least as seen from a central perspective – that the peninsula was able to remain the site of myth and legend across epoch boundaries and different cultures; knowledge of remote regions is, of course, patchy, and where there is a paucity of facts, the imagination fills in the gaps. This is certainly the case in the context of the peninsula, where some of the events forming the foundations of the myths have been verified by historians while others remain highly controversial. Particularly the new myths constructed in the so-called Age of Nationalism were often "more convincing than historical research",[7] and Crimea was no exception here. This is clearly demonstrated by the "internal relatedness" between the nation, as the result of modernization, and myth. One can go so far as to say that the idea that "nations [are] ineluctable forms of societal organization or even form the goal of history itself has the character of a myth".[8] The Crimean Peninsula is a vivid example of this.

Not only is Crimea the presumptive setting of Classical myths, but it also occupies such a large place in the Russian national memory that one can speak of a Russian national myth of Crimea.[9] That might not be particularly surprising given Russia's rule over the peninsula from the late eighteenth century on, but what is perhaps more remarkable is that Crimea also occupies a firm place in Polish, German or even British legend.[10] As we will see, Crimea, termed exotic or even Asiatic, is a part of Europe, its collective memory and its past and present.

The Polish Sarmatian myth

The nomadic Sarmatians, whom we will describe in greater detail later, spoke an Iranian language and gradually spread from the Volga and Don regions towards the Black Sea and into Crimea in the late fourth century BC. From there, as Neal Ascherson vividly puts it, they "rode out of the Polish national imagination and were appointed Poland's ancestors".[11] The background to this statement, as remarkable as it initially appears, is the grave finds in today's southern Poland described more precisely by archaeologists, including Poland's Tadeusz Sulimirski (1898–1983). The finds indicate that Sarmatian tribes settled the area in the third century AD.[12] Further details would be beyond the scope of the present examination; most importantly, in the course of the seventeenth century, the Polish-Lithuanian Commonwealth's aristocracy, the *szlachta*, underwent a specific cultural transformation that today's cultural historians term Sarmartism and that – whether or not it was true – established a connection between East Central Europe and Crimea.[13] The multiethnic aristocracy of the Polish-Lithuanian Commonwealth thus constructed for itself a common, integrational identity drawing on its chosen Classical ancestors. It was based

> primarily [on the] external appearance of a conservative landowner, anti-urban and anti-intellectual, characterized by artificially excessive religiosity, with a tendency for luxurious profligacy and snobbery. In terms of representative culture, this attitude was manifested in expensive robes, jewels, at least silver-plated if not gilded weapons and saddles covered in precious stones and expensive horses.[14]

These 'Polish Sarmatians' considered themselves on the periphery, although not between civilization and barbarianism but between (Roman Catholic) Christianity and confessional and religious Others. In the early modern period, these Others were the Orthodox Muscovite state or the Muslim Ottoman Empire, then in competition with the Polish-Lithuanian great power. The Viennese historian Christoph Augustynowicz thus sees in the topos of the *Antemurale Christianitatis* – the idea of being the "barbican of Christendom" – the central cultural motif of Polish Sarmatism.[15]

One function of Sarmatism was the ideological battle with the external foe; Polishness – synonymous with the aristocratic elites, since the peasantry was expressly excluded from the nation – was identified with Roman Catholicism, which increasingly ostracized the Protestant (mostly Calvinist) and Orthodox aristocrats who also formed part of the Polish-Lithuanian Commonwealth. It might seem surprising that the Polish *szlachta* sought to secure its own superiority by drawing on the Sarmatians, a Eurasian people who from the perspective of the venerated Classical authors were barbarian nomads. It is not uncommon, however, to see positive assimilations of purportedly 'uncivilized' large groups, particularly in the East Central

European and Eastern European space. Between the World Wars, this form of self-orientalization can be seen in the Eurasians, a group of Russian intellectuals very active in exile between the wars for whom Russianness meant a combination of the European and the Asian worlds and was thus superior to being European.[16]

The Magyars and Crimea

The Hungarian founding myth is even closer to Polish Sarmatism and also connected to Crimea: the brothers Hunor and Magor are considered the original fathers of the tribes of the Huns and Magyars. A medieval chronicle claims their father was Nimrod, although it is unclear whether this is the same Nimrod as in the Bible. Other sources claim that Hunor and Magor were the sons of Magog and thus grandchildren of Noah, lending (alleged) Hungarian descent particular prestige. Magog, on the other hand, is considered the progenitor or king of the Scythians.[17] There are a number of interesting things here: one is the assumed relatedness of the Magyars and the Huns, who had a mixed reputation, being considered savage and cruel (cf. Chapter 5). Like the Scythians, as we will see in the next chapter, both groups also had a direct connection to Crimea: while the Magyars are said to have arrived in the peninsula during the Migration Period, the Huns settled there before the seventh century BC. But that is not all; Hunor and Magor married the daughters of Dula, prince of the Alans – the Alans themselves were considered a branch of the Sarmatians, also located in Crimea, and are supposed to have advanced west with the Huns to the territory of today's Hungary.[18] These, then, are the national myths it is impossible to verify.

According to the US anthropologists and myth researchers Littleton und Malcor, there is even a connection between the British legend of King Arthur and the northern Black Sea region. They assume there is a connection between the Arthurian legends and the Sarmatians, who arrived in the British Isles as Roman auxiliary troops in the second century. That would mean that the idealized, heroic King Arthur, his knights of the Round Table and the Holy Grail are not an original element of Celtic mythology but imports from the Black Sea region.[19]

A Germanic Crimea? From the Gothic myth to the National Socialist "Gotengau"

The German-speaking world also developed a special interest in the Black Sea peninsula, which became known throughout Europe following its annexation by the tsarist empire in 1783 and subsequently became a destination for German-speaking travellers. Later, Germans arrived with less friendly intentions during the First and Second World Wars (cf. Chapters 30 and 32). From the nineteenth century onwards, German visitors' interest in Crimea was piqued not only by the beauty of the landscape or the mild climate, as evidenced by the large number of travel reports by German-speaking authors both male and, in some cases, female;[20] they are characterized at least in equal measure by an eager search for traces of 'Gothic life' that had long since vanished.

The real Goths – or the peoples who were labelled as such and will be examined further in the following chapters – are said to have appeared in Crimea from the second century AD on. Their origins are the subject of a longstanding controversy: some researchers have rejected the notion, expressed as early as the sixth century, that the Goths were originally from Scandinavia, subscribing to the theory that they were an autochthonous group from the Vistula region who later migrated towards the Black Sea.[21] German Crimea enthusiasts, especially the National Socialists with their obsession with race, favoured the former version, preferring to refer to German rather than to Slavic heritage. While many nineteenth-century authors primarily had a historical interest in the Crimean Goths, National Socialist interest groups such as the Pan-German League (*Alldeutscher Verband*, ADV) took recourse to a formerly Teutonic Crimea – for which there is no historical basis – advancing clear claims to this and other regions in Eastern Europe.[22]

The idea of a 'German Crimea' had two main reference points: firstly, there was great enthusiasm for the notion that the mountainous Principality of Theodoro, which existed for a few centuries before the Ottomans entered the peninsula in the late 1600s, had been a Crimean Gothic state and hence in a way German. This view was also supported by the assumption that the Germans' forebears had been able to create a state on the Black Sea. In fact, Gothic inhabitants of Crimea withdrew to the inaccessible mountains for safety when the Huns invaded; hence the population of Theodoro was ethnically mixed, comprising not only Goths but also Greeks, Alans and others whose *lingua franca* was presumably Greek.[23]

However, a sixteenth-century source was often used as evidence suggesting that a Germanic dialect, Crimean Gothic, had long been prevalent there: the Ogian Ghislain de Busbecq (1522–92), who served Emperor Ferdinand I (1503–64) in Istanbul between 1555 and 1562, not only introduced the tulip bulb to Europe but also left what for a long time was the only small corpus of the Crimean Gothic language, consisting of just 101 characters.[24] In the Ottoman capital, it had been his wish, he wrote, to make the acquaintance of two inhabitants of Crimea, with whom he communicated via an interpreter, noting words such as "plut" (similar to German *Blut*, blood) or "thurn" (*Tür*, door) and hence identifying the language as Germanic. While his 'sources' – just two people – are somewhat problematic, linguists do not fundamentally dismiss the possibility that a language with Germanic roots existed in Crimea. However, that does not prove that the peninsula was formerly inhabited by Germans.[25] Nevertheless, in later times there was enthusiasm for the idea that there had been a 'German Crimea' from the Middle Ages well into the modern era. Incidentally, Busbecq's slim corpus of Gothic words has recently been added to by Russian scholars, who have managed to decipher stone fragments unearthed by an excavation in the 1930s: the authors date the artefacts to the ninth or tenth century and consider them a sensation allowing extensive findings on the history of Crimea, including the presence of viticulture and the status of a Crimean Gothic language in relation to Greek.[26]

Against this backdrop, the National Socialist "Gotenland Plans" are less surprising. The main actors were the Reich Ministry for the Occupied Eastern Territories (*Reichsministerium für die besetzten Ostgebiete*) headed by the leading Nazi ideologist Alfred Rosenberg (1892–1946) and the "Führer" himself. During the Second World War, Rosenberg considered various roles for Crimea in the context of the criminal policy of creating "Lebensraum" – that is, settling the occupied territories of Eastern Europe with Germans while enslaving and exterminating the local population.[27] Hitler allocated a special role to Crimea as part of the policies manifested in his so-called "Generalplan Ost" ("General Eastern Plan"). This is already evident in the fact that as early as 1941, months before the peninsula was captured, he was thinking about creating a so-called Gotengau (Gothic administrative region) whose territory would have stretched beyond Crimea to include other areas such as the Kherson region, located west of the peninsula and not to be confused with the ruins of Chersonesus in Crimea.[28] (As Stefan Albrecht and Andrei Vinogradov have demonstrated, under Byzantine rule the city of Chersonesus was known as Cherson from c. 550 onwards.[29] However, to maintain the clear distinction from Kherson, the text will continue to use the Classical form "Chersonesus".)

Hitler's "Gotenland" fantasies, including renaming Sevatopol' (Crimean Tatar: Aqyar) "Theoderichshafen" and Simferopol' "Gotenburg", became one of his "pet projects", relates the historian Norbert Kunz.[30] A core element of his plan was the territory's Germanization by settlers from the South Tyrol – an intention that was dependent on liquidating and/or disenfranchising the local population. Fortunately, this did not happen, but it shows that the National Socialist Crimea policy was influenced by more than just military and economic considerations; myth also played a role.

Slavic Russian myths of Crimea

The unshakable conviction shared by many Russians that Crimea is a constitutive part of Russia went (and still goes) hand in hand with a close collective emotional attachment to the scenic peninsula on the Black Sea. Consequently, it remains a leading mythic space in Russia, but also in

Ukraine and many other regions of the former Soviet Union. For this reason alone, it would be impossible to provide a comprehensive outline of all the legends associated with the place. Hence it must suffice to select particularly outstanding examples from the spheres of religion and literature – two fields that in their different ways have attempted to underpin the legitimacy of Russian rule in Crimea.[31]

In the collective Russian Slavic imagination, there is a widespread idea that Crimea is an important Orthodox Christian *lieu de mémoire*, a notion that was heavily popularized from the second half of the nineteenth century onwards.[32] A reason for this, besides defeat in the Crimean War, was the development of religiously-charged national sentiment. As in other parts of Europe, Russian elites increasingly debated the essence of their nation and tended to agree that Orthodoxy played an important part in it. In these debates, the Crimean War was stylized as a holy war the imagined Russian nation had lost to Islam (that is, the Ottoman Empire) and Anglican and Roman Catholic Christianity (Britain, France and Sardinia-Piedmont). That this battle was largely fought in Crimea lent extra weight to the combat, since it was already a place steeped in older myths and legends. As an early site of Christianity,[33] the peninsula was also of great symbolic value to the Russian Empire because it was possible to construct a centuries-old connection between the Holy Land, Crimea and what would later become a Russian state, even if most historians agree only in part. These legends are centred on today's ruins of Chersonesus/Korsun', the largest excavation site during the Soviet era[34] and a suburb of today's Sevastopol'. The three legends related here became particularly popular from the 1850s on,[35] but are actually much older; while two of these stories – like most myths – have a true core, in the sense of a real historical event, the third belongs entirely to the realm of the imagination. All three, however, helped underpin the idea of a special, unbreakable bond between Crimea and the Central Russian territories.

The oldest and least likely story concerns St Andrew the Apostle's journey from the Holy Land to Lake Ladoga near today's St Petersburg. He is said to have visited Crimea in 33 AD in order to preach to the Scythians. This story is presumed to have first been recorded by Eusebius of Caesarea (260/64–339/40), considered the father of Church history, before it eventually found its way into the Old Church Slavic *Primary Chronicle* (also known as *Nestor's Chronicle* or *Povest' vremmenych let* [The Tale of Bygone Years]), which remains to this day the most important source on the history of the Old East Slavic state of Kyivan Rus'.[36] The apostle's visit to Crimea before he headed north and marked the site where Kyiv, the so-called "mother of East Slavic cities", would later be built by erecting a crucifix (St Andrew's Cross), is dealt with in a single sentence: "When Andrew was teaching in Sinope and came to Kherson (as has been recounted elsewhere), he observed that the mouth of the Dnieper was near by."[37] This brief mention nevertheless sufficed for the construction of a special connection between the Holy Land, Crimea and Rus' or Russia.

An even more important narrative – based on a 'real' event – relates the visit to Crimea by the two apostles of the Slavs, Constantine (c. 826–69) and Methodius (c. 815–85), in 860, a time when much of the peninsula was under the rule of the Khazars, whom the two preachers sought to convert to Christianity.[38] Their mission was ultimately a failure, for the Khazar elites later adopted the Jewish faith. The visit by the two missionaries, who are said to have given the Eastern Slavs their alphabet and for this reason alone are venerated in Slavic Orthodoxy to this day, played an important role in the construction of a connection between the peninsula and Russia. The life of St Constantine in particular is full of stories marking Crimea as a holy site of Christianity that have entered the collective inventory of legends for many Orthodox believers – for instance, the miraculous rescue of the relics of the exiled and later canonized Clement of Rome, who was martyred in Crimea in 94 AD. The two apostles are said to have taken his relics to Rome years later.[39] The following tale seems to be of even greater significance, even if it is related to the decidedly shaky historical notion that Crimea was inhabited by a significant population of Slavic descent or at least speaking a Slavic dialect:

> And here [Crimea] he [Constantine] found a Bible and a psalter written in Old East Slavic letters [Russian *ruskimi pis'menami*; Old Church Slavic *rus'sky pismeny*],[40] and he found a man who spoke this language. And he spoke with him and understood the meaning of this language and connected the differences between the vowels and the consonants in his own language. And, praying to God, he soon began to read and to speak. Many were astounded and praised the Lord.[41]

Nineteenth-century Russian writers were greatly enthused that Constantine had discovered a Slavic language invented "here in Korsun'; after all, Korsun' was a city where the most manifold tribes and their different languages met".[42] The special connection between the peninsula and Russia, purportedly going back to well before the annexation of 1783, was narrated over and over in myriad versions. The voices of scholars, such as the historian Vasilii Kliuchevskii (1841–1911), who considered the "presence of Slavs [...] amidst these old peoples" in the later southern Russian region to be marginal,[43] were paid relatively little heed. But what are the *rus'sky pismeny* mentioned in the life of Constantine all about? Medievalists largely agree "that it is a scribe's error, and that it originally [said] 'surskie' and thus must have been a case of letters unfamiliar to the Greeks".[44]

However, the most influential of the religious myths concerns the baptism in Korsun' in 988 of Grand Prince Vladimir/Volodymyr (c. 958–1015), ruler of Kyivan Rus', who, the relevant sources suggest, had hitherto led a life that was anything but Christian. His baptism preceded the so-called mass baptism of Kyiv and with it the beginnings of the Christianizing of Old East Slavic Kyivan Rus', although processes of Christianization were widespread in Eastern Europe in the tenth century, as demonstrated by parallel developments in Poland, Bohemia or Hungary, for instance. Even if history has not provided us with more precise details of the circumstances surrounding Vladimir's baptism,[45] the siege of Chersonesus by Vladimir and his troops around 988 is undisputed and is also mentioned by other sources, including Arabic chronicles.[46] It is unclear whether Vladimir set out for Crimea to help the Byzantine emperors Constantine VIII (960–1028) and Basil II (958–1025) put down a rebellion in the city or for other reasons.[47] The *Primary Chronicle* relates: as thanks for their military assistance, the imperial brothers promised the heathen Vladimir the hand of their sister, Anna Porphyrogenita, on the condition that he was baptized, to which he agreed in advance. However, just before the wedding in Chersonesus, he refused, whereupon God punished him with blindness. Anna convinced him his sight would be returned to him if he were baptized – and verily, after the local bishop had performed the ceremony, Vladimir's sight returned. The chronicle continues: "[...] Vladimir glorified God, saying, 'I have now perceived the one true God.' When his followers beheld this miracle, many of them were also baptized."[48] After returning to Rus', he introduced Christianity. That this doubtlessly important step originated in the peninsula was repeatedly emphasized in the Russian debates on the subject and used to legitimize possession of Crimea, above all in the nineteenth century. A recent example is the speech by Vladimir Putin to the Federal Assembly some months after the annexation of Crimea. He stressed Crimea's sacral and civilizatory significance to Russia, which he claimed was comparable to that of Jersualem's Temple Mount to Jews and Muslims, for it was in Chersonesus/Korsun' that Vladimir had been baptized.[49]

Crimea: A centre of Russian culture?

In several of these myths, Crimea functions as a contact zone between what appear to be competing spheres: between the sacred and the heathen, between the civilized (= Christianity) and the uncivilized (cf. Chapter 2) or between Christianity and Islam. This image of a contact zone is also reflected in many literary works connected to Crimea, a locus of great important particularly in Russian,[50] but also in Ukrainian or Crimean Tatar literature.[51] What many Russians consider the non-negotiable Russian character of the peninsula was and still is often 'explained' by the fact that it possesses a relevance for Russian culture comparable only to that of St Petersburg or Moscow.[52] Indeed, the list of authors who sought and found artistic inspiration in Crimea is impressive: it was there that Leo (Russian: Lev) Tolstoi (1828–1910) wrote his famous *Sevastopol' Sketches*, vividly conveying the horrors of the Crimean War in a fashion that still speaks to readers today, and Anton Chekhov (1860–1904) created a literary monument to Yalta with his novella *The Lady with the Lapdog*. The house in Köktöbel (Crimean Tatar; Russian/Ukrainian: Koktebel') owned by the painter and poet Maximilian A. Voloshin (1877–1932), credited with the Silver Age movement, attracted many other greats of Russian literature, especially in summer, including Marina Tsvetaeva, Osip Mandel'shtam or Andrei Belyi.

FIGURE 1.1 Portrait of Alexander Pushkin, *painting by Orest Kiprenskii, 1827*.

But the author admired most in Russia to this day is Alexander Pushkin[53] – and it was he in particular who helped establish Crimea as an eternal site of Russian culture. Remarkably, this 'Russian' narrative centres on a Muslim man – a Crimean khan – and a Polish woman. It is perhaps even more surprising that the core of reality can be traced to a love affair between the khan Qırım Giray (often known as "Crimea Giray"; 1717[?]–69) and Dilâra Bikeç (Russian/Ukrainian: Diliara Bikech).[54] The fluidity and flexibility of the mythic repertoire beyond linguistic and cultural boundaries is clearly visible here; this myth can be considered Russian, Crimean Tatar or Polish.

In 1820, Pushkin was banished from the capital due to some poems ridiculing leading public figures. Instead of being forced into the much more unpleasant and more common exile to Siberia, he was allowed to travel south, arriving in Crimea via the Caucasus. Like many travellers before and since, he was inspired by the unusual, 'exotic' Crimea. Heavily influenced by Romanticism at the time, Pushkin had presumably already heard of the Tatar legend of a Crimean khan's unbridled love for a Christian captive;[55] the poet used it to develop the story of a southern Oriental love triangle entitled *Bakhchisaraiskii fontan* (The Fountain of Bağçasaray [Crimean Tatar; Russian/Ukrainian: Bakhchisarai]): a nameless khan falls hopelessly in love with a Polish captive by the name of Maria Potocka (Russian: Mariia Potoska). However, as a Christian, it is impossible for her to love a Muslim. In the harem, she seeks consolation in the effigy of the Virgin Mary. But this calm is deceitful, since the chaste Maria has a bitter enemy, the khan's former favourite concubine, a Georgian by the name of Zarema. Zarema has become almost Oriental (and hence – in the common European perspective of the time – 'savage') and can only vaguely remember her Christian origins: "Not here beheld I first the light, / Far hence my native land, but yet / Alas! I never can forget / Objects once precious to my sight."[56] She misses her undisturbed happiness with the khan and issues her rival with an unveiled death threat:

> But listen! the sad prey to scorn
> If I must live, Princess, have care,
> A dagger still doth Zarem wear,–
> I near the Caucasus was born![57]

The chaste Christian maiden does indeed meet her end, although it is unclear whether it is by her own hand or that of Zarema, or from a broken heart due to what is perceived as a harsh fate to be alone among Muslims.

> Days passed away; Maria slept
> Peaceful, no cares disturbed her, now,–
> From earth the orphan maid was swept.
> But who knew when, or where, or how?

If prey to grief or pain she fell,
If slain or heaven-struck, who can tell?[58]

The khan, himself unhappy due to Maria's death, has Zarema killed too and heads north (towards Russia or the Polish-Lithuanian Commonwealth) in order to rob and pillage there again. But the poem has him appear less savage following his love for a Christian and he erects a fountain in her memory. The real fountain on which it is based can still be seen in the Khan's Palace in what was the Khanate's capital, Bağçasaray: water droplets from a marble lotus blossom fall via a series of basins until they meet only briefly before flowing apart again to disappear in a stylized snail. For many observers, including even Pushkin himself, the "former fountain" from which the water dripped as if from "rusty iron pipes" was a disappointment.[59] Nevertheless, it is not least due to the national poet's text that the Khan's Palace still stands at all: when, following Crimea's recapture by the Soviet army in 1944, Stalin ordered the deportation of the Crimean Tatar population for alleged collaboration with the German occupiers, the palace survived the order to destroy Crimean Tatar cultural heritage, since Pushkin had created a literary monument to it and hence "virtually beatified" it.[60]

The historicity of a Maria Potocka in the khan's harem in Bakhchisarai cannot be verified. The renowned Austrian Orientalist Joseph Freiherr von Hammer-Purgstall (1774–1856) cautiously writes that "[T]he daughter of a Polish great (presumably Maria Potocka) stolen by the Tatars" is supposed to have existed and married a descendant of the Giray dynasty, which always provided the Crimean khan.[61] The lady on which the easily infatuated Pushkin based his Maria has been sought by generations of literary scholars. It is generally assumed that the poet met Sofia Potocka in St Petersburg in 1818 or 1819 – that is, before his southern exile – and that she related to him the unhappy fate of her namesake. Her later marriage to a high-ranking military officer is said to have inspired the deeply saddened Pushkin to write the poem.[62] During his short life, ended by a duell, he repeatedly returned to the subject of Crimea, which had made a profound impression on him and countless other writers and fed the idea that the peninsula was a place in which the barely determinable "Russian culture" was firmly rooted.

However, non-Russian writers too drew inspiration from the beauty of the peninsula; hence, if one wanted to, one could use it to justify other national claims to Crimea. Here we can point to Poland – it is not just via the abovementioned Sarmatism that it cultivated a special bond with the peninsula. Poland's national poet and contemporary of Pushkin's, Adam Mickiewicz (1798–1855), wrote his famous *Sonety krymskie* (Crimean Sonnets). Having been banished to the south by Tsar Alexander I (1777–1825) in 1824, he too wrote of the Fountain of Tears. He placed the emphasis elsewhere, however, and not on the alleged irreconcilability of Christianity

FIGURE 1.2 *The Fountain of Tears in the Khan's Palace, Bağçasaray.*

and Islam. Instead, he was more interested in the fate of his partitioned Polish homeland under Prussian, Austrian and indeed Russian rule, a fate personified by his supposed countrywoman Maria:

At Potocka's Grave

In the land of springtime, between splendid orchards,
You, young rose, faded! In the final moments,
Flying away from you like golden butterflies,
they threw insects into the depths of your heart.
There, in the north, towards Poland, stars glow,
Why do so many glow on this path?
Has the sight of you, aflame before expiring in the grave,
Forever flying, burned into bright traces?
Polish maiden! – I too will end my days in lonely mourning:
May a handful of earth be thrown to me here by a friendly hand.
Pilgrims often speak at your grave,
And then the sound of the homeland's Polish language wakes me:
And the bard who sings his lonely song of you
Sees your nearby grave, and sings for me.[63]

This hope was fulfilled – for Mickiewicz is to the Poles what Pushkin is to the Russians or Goethe to the Germans. The *Crimean Sonnets*, this expression of yearning for a lost love and a lost homeland – "the love lost in the lost fatherland makes the stay in Crimea a doubly painful experience", as the literary scholar Michel Cadot neatly puts it[64] – were, like Pushkin's "Fountain of Tears", a great commercial success, albeit less so with Russian readers, who could not overlook the anti-Russian undercurrent. They remain popular in Poland to this day; they have not resulted in political 'claims' to Crimea, however.[65]

The course taken by political history meant that it was not until the 1950s that Crimea became Ukrainian; in the nineteenth century the Ukrainian elites were too busy with their own nation-building project to be concerned with the issue of a Ukrainian Crimea. Nevertheless, the Potocka motif also resonated in Ukrainian literature as a mythic Crimea narrative. The historian Mykola (Russian: Nikolai) Kostomarov (1817–85), claimed by the Ukrainian national movement as one of their own, made the unhappy Polish prisoner a Ukrainian in his poem "To Maria Potots'ka":

Mocking faith in God –
Stands the cross below the moon!
You hapless Ukrainian,
It tells of you![66]

Of course, Crimea is of equal importance to the myths and legends of the Crimean Tatars, on which there is not sufficient space to elaborate here. An example of the significance of collective traumas, as a kind of negative myth, as it were, would be the deportation of the Crimean Tatar population by order of Stalin in May 1944, examined in detail in Chapter 33.

2

Greeks, Scythians and Others

Now the region of the Euxine [. . .] has, apart from the Scythian race, the most ignorant nations within it of all lands: for we can neither put forward any nation of those who dwell within the region of Pontus as eminent in ability, nor do we know of any man of learning having arisen there [. . .]. By the Scythian race one thing which is the most important of all human things has been found out more cleverly than by any other men of whom we know; but in other respects I have no great admiration for them: and that most important thing which they have discovered is such that none can escape again who has come to attack them, and if they do not desire to be found, it is not possible to catch them: for they who have neither cities founded nor walls built, but all carry their houses with them and are mounted archers, living not by the plough but by cattle, and whose dwellings are upon cars, these assuredly are invincible and impossible to approach.[1]

Herodotus's words strongly reflect the idea outlined in our introduction that the northern Black Sea region, and with it Crimea, represented a transition zone between civilization and barbarism. Unlike his fellow Greeks, whom the "father of history" does not mention here, the inhabitants of the Black Sea region or the Pontus Euxinus (Greek: "the welcoming sea") were not too concerned with scholarship. Only the nomadic Scythian people appeared to have developed successful tactics in the art of war or its avoidance, which Herodotus considered all the more praiseworthy in that they had been able to defeat the enemies of the Hellenes, the Persians. He expressed great respect for their ability to withstand and capture all their enemies. A little later, he writes soberly but with evident distaste about what he considered their barbarous customs, according to which every warrior drinks the blood of his first kill. As a rule, the Scythian fighters presented their king with the heads of each enemy they had managed to kill, since this determined their share of the booty. They also turned heads into vessels bound in cowhide, some of which were elaborately gilded inside.[2]

Herodotus's depiction implies that the foreigners inhabiting what was thought to be the edge of the world were not just different but also cruel.

Indeed, the notion that the so-called Other is brutal and lacking rationality is generally widespread across cultures and epochs.[3] The Scythians were no exception; Herodotus reported that they were superstitious; "they divine with a number of willow rods".[4]

More recent Herodotus research no longer considers the Greek author a prototypical representative of the view that one's own culture is superior to that of one's enemies.[5] Nevertheless, we can sense the discomfort he must have felt when he compared the familiar life of the sedentary Hellenes in the Greek Polis with that of the Scythians, "whose dwellings are upon cars".[6] Other authors, such as Ephorus of Cyme in the fourth century BC, saw the otherness and exoticism of the Scythians in a more positive light.[7]

But whom did the Greeks actually mean when they wrote about the "Scythians"? It should be noted that the term Herodotus and other authors of the age applied to the inhabitants of the northern Black Sea region including Crimea was not the latter's own name, but a general Greek expression used for all barbarians – that is, non-Greeks – in this region between the steppe and the coast.

The term "Scythians" passed down to us by Classical authors such as Herodotus can only be "defined chronologically and culturally [...] but not ethically", as the prehistorian Hermann Parzinger emphasizes.[8] Fundamentally, this holds for all premodern mobile collectives that cannot be termed a 'people' or a 'nation'.[9] It also applies to those who arrived in Crimea in pre-Scythian times, about whom we are told not only by Herodotus but also by other Greek authors. There are reports, for instance, of the Cimmerians,[10] in sources from the eighth century on; Parzinger believes both they and the Scythians actually originated from east of the Urals.[11] The general scholarly opinion is that the two Eurasian communities of warrior riders are related but not identical.[12]

The Scythians have left a rich material cultural legacy, not least due to their burial rituals, as also described at length by Herodotus.[13] Archaeological finds in Scythian burial mounds, known as kurgans, encountered in a region stretching from Eurasia far into Europe, include intricate gold jewellery worn on the body and on robes[14] ascribed to the Scythians. This runs counter to the view that they were uncultured barbarians. It is more difficult to make any pronouncement about the Tauri we have discussed in the context of the "mythic Crimea" (Chapter 1), who are also considered pre-Scythian and are assumed to have lived in southern Crimea and the mountainous region. Despite Bronze Age remains of ceramics that are attributed to them,[15] the only written sources are Classical authors. Herodotus, for instance, saw in them the only autochthonous people living in Crimea.[16] As is usually the case with inhabitants of the periphery, they are considered dangerous: "This people has its living by plunder and war."[17]

In the Black Sea region, Hellenes now encountered these barbarians described as comparatively backward and violent – be it Cimmerians, Tauri or Scythians and later the Sarmatians. They maintained relations with them not only in the economic sphere, but also in terms of their overall lifeworld, resulting in a gradual mutual assimilation between barbarians and Greeks. This was largely due to the influx of a large number of Greek colonizers to the region. The "Ionian Colonization" (eleventh/tenth century BC) and the "Great Colonization" (eighth to sixth century BC) had a large impact on the Black Sea region and with it Crimea. Consequently, many Greek *apoikiai* were established in the peninsula, such as Chersonesus, originally an Ionian and later a Dorian settlement before today's ruins became a suburb of Sevastopol'. Theodosia, today's Feodosiia (Russian/Ukrainian; Crimean Tatar: Kefe; also known as Caffa or Kaffa), was a Milesian settlement, and today Panticapaeum, presumably also a Milesian settlement, is Kerch (Crimean Tatar: Keriç; Russian: Kerch'), on the peninsula's eastern-most coast.

The Greek migrants in the Black Sea region, known as the Pontic Greeks, formed an important part of their contemporary authors' narrative of the Ancient Greek collective identity.[18] Migration to the regions beyond the core Hellenic land shaped this narrative into a complex settlement myth that helped cement their belief in their own superiority over the autochthonous population. All these stories about the foundation of Greek colonies, be it in the Iberian Peninsula, in the Mediterranean or in Crimea, have a very similar structure: a mother city sends a considerable number of colonists to a foreign

FIGURE 2.1 *Scythian archers, Panticapaeum, 475–450 BC.*

region, where they establish a settlement that is battled fiercely by the indigenous population. Of course, in the end, the superior Hellenes triumph over the barbarians.[19] The real emigration from the motherland was usually preceded by social and/or political tensions in the metropolis, which forms the historical backdrop to the Greek colonizing movement. In the narratives that became legends, however, the travellers usually consulted the Oracle of Delphi, who prophesized their emigration with the blessing of the gods.[20] This very linear narrative pattern is contradicted by archaeological findings that suggest they weren't smooth-running success stories. For instance, the ancient historian Hermann Bengtson describes the so-called Great Colonization from the sixth century BC onwards as "an inestimable sum of manifold uncontrollable individual events, of a colourful series of plans, attempts, successes and failures".[21] The same can be said for the Greeks along the coasts of the Black Sea, including the Crimean Peninsula. They nevertheless remained important actors in the region, until they fell victim to the Stalinist deportations in 1944 (cf. Chapter 33).[22]

How should we imagine relations between the Greek colonies on the Black Sea's northern coast? Initially, their ties were limited, while they maintained intensive political and economic contact with their respective mother cities; for instance, the Ionian *apoikiai* in the east of the peninsula, such as Theodosia or Panticapaeum, remained in close contact with Miletus, while Dorian colonists, who had established settlements in the southwest of Crimea such as Chersonesus, maintained relations with their mother city of Heraclea Pontica. In times of external and internal pressure, as well as for

FIGURE 2.2 *The ruins of Chersonesus.*

economic reasons – particularly to ensure tight organization of the grain trade – parallel local alliances were formed, at least when an individual polis was threatened by nomadic pressures, for instance.

The most important league of cities, and for a long time the most prosperous, was the Bosporan Kingdom, which emerged around 480 BC and existed until 362/375 AD.[23] On both sides of the Cimmerian Bosporus, today's Kerch Strait, it formed a league reaching beyond the peninsula itself, under the leadership of the city of Panticapaem. This commonwealth wasn't oriented around the tradition of Attic democracy; it was not a republic. While it was ruled by an archon who was officially elected, he functioned *de facto* as a monarch who in this particular case established a hereditary dynasty. After the Archaianactidae, a dynasty presumably originating in the mother city of Miletus, the Spartocid dynasty took power around 438 AD and remained the rulers until the second century AD, pursuing a firm policy of expansion.[24] It is possible that the Spartocids were of Hellenic origin, although this remains uncertain. The population of the Bosporan Kingdom was ethnically and cultural heterogeneous, as was generally the case in Crimea and along the northern Black Sea coast, with 'new settlers' such as the Greek colonists and more established groups. The important Soviet archaeologist Viktor F. Gaizukevich (1904–66) thus referred to the Bosporan Kingdom as "Greco-Scythian",[25] many excavations pointing to processes of cultural and ethnic syncretism. It can be assumed that at least the elites were of Hellenic descent, even if they were in constant cultural contact with Scythian sections of the population (or those who were labelled as such by Greek authors) and should perhaps be considered, more accurately, to have been partially Hellenic.[26]

Crimea as a polyethnic transit and settlement zone

Ethnic, cultural and religious diversity, accompanied by constant merger over the course of time, is a constitutive feature of the Black Sea region and Crimea. It was not until the twentieth century that its history was marked by a profound caesura; for millennia, this diversity was characteristic of the entire region, from the very earliest times.[27] Over the years, Asiatic groups (Cimmerians, Scythians, etc.) and Greek colonists formed "mixed civilizations", as the Russian Classicist Mikhail I. Rostovtsev (widely known in the English-speaking world as Michael Rostovzeff; 1870–1952) put it in the early 1920s.[28] He thereby rejected the idea of a distinction between civilized – that is, Greek – and barbarian populations propagated by Greek authors and at least hinted at by Herodotus, questioning the notion of the existence of 'pure' cultures that enjoyed great popularity in the first half of the twentieth century, although it was less common in the Russian humanities from the late nineteenth century on than in Western Europe, since several Russian intellectuals in the tsarist empire interpreted their 'Asiatic heritage' as a thoroughly positive trait.[29] This also explains Rostovtzeff's interest in describing the region he called, in the typical parlance of the day, "South Russia" (and not, for instance, "southern Ukraine"), the space between the steppe and the Black Sea, between nomadic and sedentary peoples, as highly developed and as the result of complex cultural symbioses, despite its peripheral location. This was also part of an attempt to secure for the Eastern Slavs 'their' share of the Classical world so revered by European intellectuals since the Enlightenment, the Black Sea being indisputably connected to Antiquity. Later Soviet Classical scholars also emphasized that "the heritage of the peoples of the northern Black Sea region became an essential element of the culture of the Eastern Slavs. Hence it is one of the sources of the culture of our homeland".[30]

Modern cultural studies shares this notion of difference and equality in examining these nomadic and sedentary cultures;[31] today, the field largely assumes that "in history", nomads and sedentary peoples form "a mesh of relations in which aspects of difference and lines of conflict intersect with integrative movements by both sides on almost all levels of social action".[32] Here is not the place to assess whether these were fundamentally "asymmetrical trade relations" based on "endemic conflict", as is sometimes claimed.[33] In the dominant national and/or racial(ist) discourses of the 1920s, however, ideas like Rostovtseff's were rather controversial. The fact is that in Crimea and throughout the northern Black Sea region, different economic groups came into contact with each other and found themselves in a complex relationship of mutual dependence characterized by phases of co-existence and conflict in equal measure. This is another reason why for a long time, a permanent, supraregional dominant centre did not develop. Located between the steppe and the coast, at the interface of empires and nomads, Crimea remained a peripheral space – albeit one in much demand, as emphatically demonstrated by the relentless movement of peoples who migrated to, passed through or remained in the peninsula.

Clearly, it is necessary to explain Ascherson's dictum, cited in our introduction, that Crimea has always sparked the desire to possess it. Why did the peninsula attract so many peoples despite its relatively peripheral location? Was the climate ideal and/or was the peninsula of particular strategic and economic value? Presently, researchers postulate that Crimea is a relatively young region in Earth's history[34] and that it was already settled in pre-Classical times due to its favourable position between the Black Sea and the steppe region, and especially due to the Mediterranean climate on its coast.[35] However, not all of its environmental features are as inviting as they are in the south; Crimea consists of three different topographical and climatic zones. There is the steppe landscape of the north, the central zone characterized by the Crimean Mountains, the highest peak, Roman-Kosh (Ukrainian/Russian; Crimean Tatar: Roman Qoş), reaching 1,545 metres, and the southern region, where as early as Antiquity the Mediterranean climate allowed the cultivation of grapevines and other important arable produce. The northern steppe was ultimately ambivalent insofar as it allowed both the transit of goods from the Eurasian regions and the advance of nomadic groups that engaged in violent or more peaceful interactions with the inhabitants of other zones. Many authors reporting their Crimean travels went beyond placing these three zones in sober geographical categories: for instance Ascherson, who considers Crimea a living organism whose coasts represent the "mind", its mountains its "spirit" and the steppe its "body".[36] This Scottish writer thereby drew on a metaphor widespread since Antiquity in describing a geographical entity as an animate body.[37] The "zone of the spirit", the Crimean Mountains, might represent a certain geographical obstacle and a meteorological and climatological divide between the northern steppe and the coast, but it was clearly not an impenetrable barrier to peoples advancing from the Eurasian regions, such as the Scythians, who became just as much part of the economy and lifeworlds of the Black Sea in Antiquity as the Pontic Greeks.

The time up to the fourth century BC is considered an age of prosperity:[38] Scythian tribes and the Greek cities that were often obliged to pay them tribute formed a close-knit production and trade network that was protected militarily by the Scythians; fundamentally, the relationship can be labelled pragmatic, although conflicts disrupting business relations did occur. Besides grain, of great importance to Athens,[39] and wax and honey, slaves became one of the most important exports. Crimea supplied a large part of the Classical world with these goods. Ascherson observes that "on the profits of the grain and the slaves [. . .] both the Greek merchants and the up-country Scythian princes grew very rich indeed".[40] For all partners, this was a 'win–win' situation, as one would say today. However, during the third/second century BC a decline set in, manifested *inter alia* in the significant decrease in grain yields. This was not least a result of the increasing pressure exerted on the coastal regions by inhabitants of the northern and eastern steppes.

One of the most important customers for grain up to that point, Athens, had been beset by an economic crisis following the wars with Macedonia, and the trade flows had shifted; for one thing, grain producers in the Black Sea region found themselves in competition with Egypt. Another factor was the advance of new nomadic and semi-nomadic groups. What was already a diverse collection of peoples in the peninsula was gradually changing.

3

New Actors:

Sarmatians and Others

Now the Amazons at midday used to scatter abroad either one by one or by two together, dispersing to a distance from one another to ease themselves; and the Scythians also having perceived this did the same thing: and one of the Scythians came near to one of those Amazons who were apart by themselves, and she did not repulse him but allowed him to lie with her: and she could not speak to him, for they did not understand one another's speech, but she made signs to him with her hand to come on the following day to the same place and to bring another with him, signifying to him that there should be two of them, and that she would bring another with her. The young man therefore, when he returned, reported this to the others; and on the next day he came himself to the place and also brought another, and he found the Amazon awaiting him with another in her company. Then hearing this the rest of the young men also in their turn tamed for themselves the remainder of the Amazons; and after this they joined their camps and lived together, each man having for his wife her with whom he had had dealings at first [. . .].[1]

These ties between Scythians and Amazons, at least as Herodotus relates, gave rise to the Sauromatians: "and from thenceforward the women of the Sauromatai practise their ancient way of living, going out regularly on horseback to the chase both in company with the men and apart from them, and going regularly to war, and wearing the same dress as the men."[2] This can be considered an indication that women, as is usually the case in (semi-) nomadic communities, were not limited to the areas of life commonly denoted as 'female' – the home, the garden, the family, etc. The question as to whether there is evidence of forms of matrilocal or matriarchal societies in the Black Sea region and Crimea has been discussed repeatedly, including against the background of the Amazon theme.[3] Whether it is a myth or not, one should always be careful about applying modern terms such as "equality" or "equal rights" to past eras, but there are certainly valid archaeological indications that women carried weapons and were probably also involved in combat. In kurgans, female remains have often been found buried with weapons,[4] feeding the image of the Amazons as armed fighting women. An epic attributed to Arctinus of Miletus (c. 750 BC), for instance, relates how the quasi-mythical Amazons rushed to the aid of the Trojans, in vain, during the Trojan War. Following the defeat, they managed to escape from Greek captivity and flee to "Scythia" – that is, to the northern Black Sea. The Amazons' 'noble descent' and their connection to one of the core 'events' in Greek mythology explains why the Sarmatians/Sauromatians have played such a large part in the mythology of so many nations (cf. Chapter 1).

The terms "Sarmatians" and "Sauromatians", mentioned in the same breath in many old texts, are perhaps a little confusing and may require some explanation: in some Classical sources they denote distinct peoples, while in others they are used synonymously.[5] Today, "Sarmatian" is usually considered an umbrella term for various nomadic tribes of Iranian descent, including the Aorsi, the Iazges, the Alans, the Roxolani, the Siraces and the Maiotians.[6] However, this interpretation is also contested, since the term 'Iranian peoples' also includes ethnic groups who spoke Indo-Iranian languages. Some scholars, such as Anca Dan, point out that it is not known which language(s) the so-called Sauromatians/Sarmatians actually spoke; Classical Greek texts have preserved only one doubtlessly Sarmatian word – "marha", a battle cry. On the other hand, further proof of the Sarmatians' Iranian descent is provided by the name itself; it is plausible that it originates from an Indo-Iranian language.[7] Even more confusingly, Classical authors often failed to distinguish between "Sarmatians" and "Scythians": "Many [...] authors of the Roman imperial era repeatedly mention in excurses Scythians, although this term actually refers to the Sarmatians."[8] And the Greek geographer Strabo (c. 63 BC–23 AD), whose famous *Geographica* was an important source on the Scythians and whose seventh book also remains an important source for the history of Crimea, often uses the two terms synonymously.[9]

It is difficult to say, then, exactly who these Sarmatians were. Dan has aptly summed up the 'Sarmatian problem': "[O]ur current image of the Sarmatian is the result of loose readings of texts and archaeological evidence, nourished by nationalistic convictions."[10] Ultimately, however, this applies not only to the Sauromatians/Sarmatians or the Scythians, but also to many other peoples who had permanent or temporary contact with Crimea. Although much remains unclear, most scholars nevertheless presume that new actors entered Crimea from the east from the third century BC, presumably belonging to the Indo-Iranian language family; in the interests of practicality, they will henceforth be referred to as Sarmatians in the present work. Until the fourth century AD, when they were forced out by or became acculturated with the Goths (which is, of course, another imprecise collective term for highly heterogeneous ethnic groups), they had a sustained influence on life in the peninsula.[11]

For one thing, this is evident in the fact that the Sarmatians gradually drove out the Scythians or acculturation took place between the two, which would suggest the Sarmatian groups were not "barbarian", especially as the Scythians' way of life had undergone considerable cultural transformations: the majority were no longer nomadic, had established various urban-like facilities and had built the capital Neapolis (located in today's Simferopol' region). According to the excavation site's official website, this is "the biggest and the best investigated barbarian settlement of the North Pontic region".[12] Founded by the Scythian ruler Skilurus, the city existed from the late third century BC to the second half of the third century AD, and long withheld the threats emanating from the steppe until it was destroyed by the Goths. The Scythian Empire extended north beyond the peninsula itself, to Olbia in the lower Dnepr (near today's Parutyne, Mykolaïvs'ka oblast'). In Crimea, their conquests included the Chora of Chersonesus, the Hellenic city's agricultural region The population was ethnically mixed, as was usually the case in Crimea. Archaeological finds demonstrate the syncretic cultural character of the city; for instance, the Greek architectural elements or coins with Greek inscriptions testify to the influence of Hellenism. Soon, however, the Sarmatians appeared, posing a genuine threat to both the Scythians and the Greek colonies in Crimea.

4

The Mithridatic Wars:

Crimea under Roman Rule

The geographer Strabo provided a sober account of the end of the independent Bosporan Kingdom with its long prosperity under "equitable rulers" and the Roman takeover of large swathes of Crimea:

> Panticapaeum is a hill inhabited on all sides in a circuit of twenty stadia. To the east it has a harbour, and docks for about thirty ships; and it also has an acropolis. It is a colony of the Milesians. For a long time it was ruled as a monarchy by the dynasty of Leuco, Satyrus, and Parisades, as were also all the neighbouring settlements near the mouth of Lake Maeotis on both sides, until Parisades gave over the sovereignty to Mithridates. They were called tyrants, although most of them, beginning with Parisades and Leuco, proved to be equitable rulers. And Parisades was actually held in honour as god. The last of these monarchs also bore the name Parisades, but he was unable to hold out against the barbarians, who kept exacting greater tribute than before, and he therefore gave over the sovereignty to Mithridates Eupator. But since the time of Mithridates the kingdom has been subject to the Romans. The greater part of it is situated in Europe, although a part of it is situated in Asia.[1]

This development was not necessarily predictable; during the reigns of the Spartocid Leukon I (389/8–349/8 BC) and Paerisades I (349/8–311/10 BC) considerable territorial gains had been made before Paerisades V (c. 150–108 BC) submitted to the Pontic king, Mithridates VI (c. 134–63 BC), in 108 BC. This was a decisive moment for Crimea as a whole, as we shall soon see. The severe crisis that set in from the fourth or third century BC onwards impacted not only on the Bosporan Kingdom in the eastern peninsula but also on the more western colonies, such as Chersones – then more closely associated with the local Scythians and the Pontic mother city of Heraclea – and even Theodosia. Allied to increasing economic problems was the mounting pressure of Sarmatian tribes at the borders, for which the initial remedy was to pay the Scythians for military service and build up fortifications. These measures did not offer lasting respite, however; as Strabo describes, not only the Bosporan Kingdom but also cities such as Chersonesus sought the assistance of the king of Pontus, Mithridates (VI) Eupator, another fixture in the abundant mythology of Crimea and the Black Sea region. Legend has it that following his father's murder, he spent seven years in the wilderness, took regular doses of antidotes in order to immunize himself to any attempts by his enemies to poison him, murdered his own mother and brother and – according to Pliny the Elder (*c.* 23–79 AD) – spoke some twenty-two languages. No wonder, then, that artists of many epochs (including Jean Racine [1639–99] and James Joyce [1882–1941]) have made reference to this figure.[2]

However, Mithridates was also considered an able military commander, one of whose achievements was to put down an uprising in the Bosporan Kingdom in 108/107 BC. As was then typical, slaves were part of the economy in this ethnically mixed commonwealth. These slaves and the Scythian underclasses, mostly free but socially disadvantaged, did not take kindly to their subjugation by the Pontic Kingdom. Led by the slave Saumakos (Savmak), they rebelled in 108–107 BC, initially with success, removing Paerisades V, and Saumakos was proclaimed the new ruler. He even had his own coins minted, as archaeological finds demonstrate. It took the Pontic commander Diophantes, sent by Mithridates, to defeat them, whereupon the Bosporan Kingdom became part of Pontus. It is hardly surprising that Saumakos's uprising, which occurred some years prior to the rebellion against the Roman Empire led by the Roman slave and gladiator Spartacus (in the seventies BC), enjoyed a "particularly colourful" depiction in Soviet historiography, as Helmut Neubauer writes in an essay of 1960 which remains essential reading to this day; for instance, he relates how an unnamed Soviet historian proclaimed in 1955: "The rebellion of the Bosporan Scythians is the first known movement of enslaved masses against their masters on the territory of the USSR." Mithridates thus received a corresponding reception by Soviet scholars as an exponent of a slave economy.[3]

Mithridates ruled over what was then the most powerful kingdom in Asia Minor, to which he was then able to add the areas of Crimea inhabited by Greeks seeking his protection. But his aspirations did not end there, for after getting a foothold on the Black Sea he attempted to extend his sphere of influence to other regions in Asia Minor, which brought him into conflict with Rome. The Hellenic cities thus became embroiled in the three Mithridatic Wars (89–63 BC), from which the kingdom of Pontus did not emerge victorious. Faced with defeat, the king – with another touch of drama – committed suicide.[4] After Rome's conclusive victory in 63 BC under Pompeius (106–48 BC), the western part of the kingdom was incorporated into the Roman province of Bithynia-Pontus,[5] while the east and the Bosporan Empire continued to exist as a client state dependent on Rome,

Panticapaeum gradually losing its Hellenic character.[6] In western Crimea, in Chersonesus, an oligarchic republic emerged, led by supporters of Rome; this republic formed the main basis of Roman rule in the peninsula without being organized as a Roman province.

This Roman 'administration' alone shows that from the perspective of the Roman Empire too, Crimea was a peripheral region; they were either unwilling or unable to integrate it into the imperial structures. This is also demonstrated by the Romans' policy towards stationing troops in the peninsula; as a rule, the Greek colonies had to defend themselves against bellicose incursions by nomadic invaders. This included repeated military campaigns to pacify Scythian groups in order to secure the borders, for instance in the sixties BC, although this didn't really banish the barbarian threat from the north, even if cities such as Chersonesus were usually able to defend themselves due to their effective fortifications. Archaeological finds unearthed in the nineteenth century[7] indicated that Roman troops were stationed in the peninsula for a long time, for instance in the second century AD; more recent excavations have confirmed this interpretation.[8] In principle, the intensity of the Roman presence in Crimea in the first half of the first century and in the early second century depended on the general situation in the east of the Roman Empire – that is, even when considering these early times, we must examine Crimea in the broader context of the northern Black Sea region. For instance, when the Dacian Wars[9] – named after the Dacians inhabiting the Carpathian region and the lower Danube – began in the late first century AD, Rome's clients felt the consequences whenever the empire withdrew or reduced its troops in Crimea. Not all of these consequences were negative; a client state like the Bosporan Kingdom had more room for manoeuvre, for instance in the age of Emperor Domitian (81–96): the Bosporan rulers Rhesuporis I (68/9–93/4) and Sauromates I (93/4–123/4) had coins with their own faces on them minted, which was not only symbolic but also indicated that Rome had less influence.[10]

It is important to bear in mind that Roman rule, be it nominal or *de facto*, did not extend to all of Crimea, for in the north of the peninsula lay the Scythian Empire and its capital Neapolis with its shifting ties with Rome. As in earlier centuries, relations between the barbarians (Scythians) and the civilized (Rome and the Bosporan Kingdom) oscillated between pragmatic cooperation, which was particularly necessary when Sarmatian tribes invaded from the north, phases of peace and open military conflicts. For instance, in the late second century AD, under Sauromates II (174/175–210/211) the Bosporan Kingdom inflicted a heavy defeat on the Scythian Empire from which late Scythian culture did not recover. A barbarian invasion in the third century AD dealt another severe blow, culminating in the destruction of Neapolis. The groups still called Scythians, who had already undergone transformations due to relations with several other cultures, finally began to disappear for good as actors in Crimea.[11] This was due to new migratory movements.

5

Goths, Huns, the "Great Migration" and Its Impact on Crimea

Their wild tribe, as the historian Priscus relates to us, inhabited the banks beyond the Maeotic swamp, having no other occupation except for hunting; finally, having grown as large as a nation, they disturbed the peace of the neighbouring peoples through their thefts and raids. Some hunters from among them, searching for prey on the banks beyond the Maeotic swamp, as was their wont, suddenly saw a doe appear before them, entering the swamp, and, advancing and stopping, she offered to guide their way. The hunters followed her and crossed the Maeotic swamp by foot, which they previously considered to be unsurpassable, like a sea. When the Scythian land revealed itself before them, the doe disappeared. I believe that the evil spirits from whom the Huns descended did this out of envy of the Scythians. The Huns, however, who were not aware of any other land beyond the Maeotic swamp, and were overwhelmed with admiration for the Scythian land, and since they were sharp people, believed that a deity disclosed that road previously unknown to man; they returned to their home, exposed what happened to their people and praised Scythia until they persuaded the people to hurry to leave for it on the path shown by the doe.[1]

These lines were written by Jordanes, a sixth-century historiographer (who died after 552), whose Latin *Getica* is one of the most important sources on Gothic history.[2] We learn that Crimea remained multiethnic during the early centuries AD, since various Gothic and other tribes settled there. He also writes of new invaders – who arrived in the eastern peninsula via the Kerch Strait, attracted by a mysterious doe. Incidentally, the usual interpretation of this passage is that in a harsh winter the invaders, identified as Huns, crossed the frozen strait, which is almost twenty kilometres wide.[3] Ultimately, confusion seems to prevail with respect to the labelling of the various tribes; besides the Scythians, diverse Gothic groups are named, as are Vandals, who are also considered Germanic but whose mention in the Crimean context is something of a surprise. This brief passage thus combines essential elements of the history of Crimea that have survived the passage of time: its polyculturality, its character as a migration and transit region, its propensity for being treated as a mythic space, here in the form of a mysterious cloven-hoofed creature that attracted the "Huns" to the peninsula, and the rather fluid use of ethnonyms applied to various groups or featuring as unspecific umbrella terms.

Nor is it possible to provide a simple, linear and easily narrated history of Crimea for the time of the Great (Germanic) Migration either, which is usually considered to have lasted between the fourth and the eighth century AD. In the lead-up to this mass migratory movement, some of the Goths,[4] whom we have already discussed in greater detail in the context of mythology, not only posed a considerable threat to the Roman Empire but also entered the peninsula in the third century AD – an advance usually dated to 257. Spilling in from the north, they were the final nail in the coffin for the Scythian Sarmatian settlements. On their passage from the north to the Black Sea, they are thought to have joined forces with other groups that are usually labelled Sarmatian too,[5] or at least this is the interpretation if one doesn't subscribe to notion that the Crimean Goths were of autochthonous ethnogenesis, as some recent scholars believe.[6]

The Gothic groups were also able to extend their sphere of influence along the rest of the Black Sea coast (for instance in Olbia, further to the west), gaining a permanent foothold in the region. This development was furthered by processes of reciprocal exchange and adaptation, particularly with the Scythian Sarmatian groups, but also with Rome. The Goths were thus able to expand their rule to large swathes of Crimea, including the Bosporan Kingdom – with the exception of eastern Panticapaeum and Chersonesus, which remained Roman, in the southwest of the peninsula. The gentile Gothic Empire reached the full extent of its power under the ruler Ermanaric, who reigned from 350 to 375. This peak was short-lived, however; Crimea once again became a transit region for mobile groups, this time the Huns, as Jordanes relates. The term 'Huns' is also an umbrella term for a polyethnic Central Asian community of horse riders who were initially nomadic and whose origins cannot be established. However, it is also an example of "how much strength can be inherent to a single name", as the Classical scholar Timo Stickler puts it.[7] Under this pressure, the Gothic gens under Ermanaric collapsed. Particularly the Goths in the peninsula's eastern steppe now joined the groups of Huns and advanced to the west, where they remained established for almost a century. However, the Gothic population in the mountains and in southern Crimea largely remained safe from Huns, who were used to steppe terrain, and the settlement Dory or Doros (today's

Mangup-Kale) soon developed on one of the high plateaus of the Crimean Mountains.⁸ With the help of a new actor from the southern shore of the Black Sea – the Eastern Roman Empire – this principality became a bulwark against nomadic groups, whose invasion attempts remained a constant threat to Crimea.

6

Crimea as a Site of Early Christianity

In the *Life of Constantine the Philosopher* (cf. Chapter 1), who stayed in Crimea in the ninth century, discovering the relics of Clement Romanus or Clement of Rome (around 50–97 or 101) and salvaging them from the waters, we read:

> When he heard that the relics of Saint Clement still lay in the sea, he prayed and said, "I believe in the Lord and I hope for Saint Clement that I can find his bones and rescue them from the sea.' And he persuaded the archbishop and the priests and the pious people to take a ship, and they sailed to the place where the sea became calm. Upon arriving there, they began to dig, and while they dug they prayed. And a strong fragrance spread, as if from a large amount of incense. And then the bones showed themselves, and they took them with great honour and glory. And all the priests and citizens took them into the city.[1]

Considered the second or third successor to St Peter the Apostle, the bishop of Rome was martyred in Crimea, at least according to the *Life*, an important work, not least for the role it played in popularizing the legend: with an anchor round his neck, he was sent to a watery grave, whereupon a temple rose from this very spot in the sea holding his remains, until they were saved centuries later by the Apostle of the Slavs Constantine. He and his brother and fellow apostle Methodius later passed them on as relics to Pope Hadrian II (792–872). Today, the relics can be found in the Basilica di San Clemente al Laterno – or at least some of them can, since the Kyiv Monastery of the Caves also claims to be in possession of some relics of St Clement, including his head.[2] If we consider the story of St Andrew the Apostle in the peninsula (cf. Chapter 1) to be merely a legend, Clement of Rome's martyrdom in Crimea in the first century AD would be the first indication of Crimea's contact with Christianity. However, that would be to overlook the fact that some pre-Constantinian sources assume St Peter's successor died of natural causes.

What is beyond dispute is that Crimea was a site of early Christianity, the archaeological traces of which can be dated back to the early fourth century.[3] Its beginnings presumably developed within the Jewish communities that also existed in this region on the Black Sea, for instance in the Bosporan Kingdom. Firstly, there were Christians in Crimea and, secondly, a Church structure and nomenklatura developed: there is firm evidence that bishops from Crimea participated in the immensely important Council of Nicaea in 325, although it is not clear how many. Scholars debate whether besides a Bishop Kadios/Kadmos of Bosporus (Kerch) a Theophilus of Gothia and an ecclesiastical representative of Chersonesus by the name of Kapiton were also in attendance, which would indicate that there were already other episcopal sees under Constantine I ("the Great", between 270 and 288–337).[4] It has not yet been fully established whether a Chersonesus didn't exist until 381, when a bishop of Chersonesus attended the Council of Constantinople.[5] For a long time, there was also debate as to whether the Theophilus of Gothia described as a participant at the Council of Nicaea was not actually a representative from Crimean Gothia (Doros) or whether this figure didn't preach to the Terwingi settlements north of the lower Danube. And even if there were Christians among the inhabitants of Doros in the late third century, it is rather unlikely there was a Crimean Gothic episcopal see in the first half of the fourth century.[6]

Scholars agree that Crimea and above all Chersonesus, then under Eastern Roman rule, was a prominent place of exile, especially for high-ranking Christian clerics. As the story of Clement shows, the peninsula has a remarkably high proportion of martyrs; in the 1920s, this moved the important Byzantine scholar Vasil'ev to wonder whether the population of Chersonesus might have simply fabricated the stories in order to lend the city special significance.[7] Certainly, two things are clear from these assessments: firstly, that Chersonesus's peripheral location within the Eastern Roman Empire made the city a preferred place of exile, and secondly, that there was considerable tension between Constantinople and the upper echelons of the clergy.

One of the most notable figures among the genuine or purported martyrs who met or are supposed to have met their fate in Crimea is Pope Martin I (c. 600–55). Pontiff from 649 to 653, he came into conflict with the emperor in Constantinople. In 653, the emperor had him forcibly taken by ship from Rome to Constantinople, tortured and banished to Crimea, where he died a few weeks after his arrival. A Martin cult soon developed in Chersonesus.[8] The backdrop to this exile was the Byzantine Papacy of 537–752. The popes needed imperial approval for their episcopal consecration, which gave the emperor in Constantinople considerable power.

During the Church's Iconoclast Crisis in the eighth and ninth centuries, Chersonesus and the southern coast of the peninsula ultimately became a preferred place of refuge or exile for both iconoclast and, later, iconodule clerics.[9] The long-held conviction that it was the iconodule exiles who gave us what remains to this day a large and impressive network of cave monasteries in the peninsula's mountainous region[10] is not supported by the archaeological excavations of recent decades; there is "no evidence of intensive building activity" for this period,[11] and hence they must have emerged in a different era.

In a political, cultural and religious sense, then, southwestern Crimea was considerably influenced by the Eastern Roman Empire and Orthodoxy, while the steppe landscapes of the hinterland saw further invasions and pragmatic cooperation with nomadic peoples from Eurasia.

7

Crimea between the Eastern Roman Empire, Crimean Gothia and the Khazar Empire

In 965, Svyatolslav I (c. 942–72), grand prince of the first Old East Slavic realm of Kyivan Rus', and his warriors defeated the Khazars in battle. Their victory was depicted in the *Primary Chronicle*:

> When Prince Svyatoslav had grown up and matured, he began to collect a numerous and valiant army. Stepping light as a leopard, he undertook many campaigns. Upon his expeditions he carried with him neither wagons nor kettles, and boiled no meat, but cut off small strips of horseflesh, game, or beef, and ate it after roasting it on the coals. Nor did he have a tent, but he spread out a horse-blanket under him, and set his saddle under his head; (65) and all his retinue did likewise. He sent messengers to the other lands announcing his intention to attack them. He went to the Oka and the Volga, and on coming in contact with the Vyatichians, he inquired of them to whom they paid tribute. They made answer that they paid a silver-piece per ploughshare to the Khazars. 6473 (965). Svyatoslav sallied forth against the Khazars. When they heard of his approach, they went out to meet him with their Prince, the Kagan, and the armies came to blows. When the battle thus took place, Svyatoslav defeated the Khazars and took their city of Bela Vezha.[1]

The prince is portrayed as frugal, leading the ascetic, 'soldierly' life of a classical fighter. Hence it is not really surprising that he inflicted a defeat on the Khazars that would prove to be the beginning of the end of their reign over large stretches of the northern and eastern Black Sea coast, which had emerged in the late seventh century. The Turkic Khazars were thus a major power determining the order in the region for almost 300 years, along with the Eastern Roman Empire in southern Crimea (including Chersonesus).[2] Smaller territories such as Crimean Gothia paid them tribute, and another important source of income emerged with their control of most long-distance trade – including the sale of slaves – between the Black Sea and Asia.³

Relations between the Khazars and Constantinople – another important centre of power in the region – fluctuated: alliances were made against invading nomadic groups such as the Pechenegs or the Persian Sassanid Empire and dissolved when it suited.⁴ Scholars differ in their assessment of the relative strength of these two players, particularly in the context of their interactions in the peninsula. Presently, the prevailing view is that there were at least some phases of joint Byzantine–Khazar rule over Crimea.⁵ The Khazar Empire stretched far beyond the peninsula itself, over the steppes of today's southern Ukraine and southern Russia between the Dnipro and the Volga and into the Caucasus. The Khazar Khaganate has repeatedly attracted the attention of researchers, since it is probably an exceptional case: the upper strata and other social groups predominantly practised Judaism, possibly a "syncretically distorted" form of it.⁶ One reason for the adoption of the Jewish faith, at least according to the Soviet historian Mikhail I. Artamonov (1889–1972) in 1962, was to create a binding religious ideology that gave this political entity a unique character – setting it apart from Christian Byzantium and the Muslim Arabs who were advancing into the Caucasus.⁷ The failed mission to convert the Khazar elites embarked upon by the "apostles of the Slavs", Constantine and Methodius (cf. Chapter 1), has received attention from Russian (and Soviet) scholars in particular, since it offered another opportunity for a linear historical interpretation of the connection between the Black Sea region and Orthodoxy.⁸ Regarding the internal structure of the Khazar Empire, all that can be said here is that one can speak of a "sacral kingdom": according to P. B. Golden, the khagan (roughly the great khan) reigned over the Khazar Empire, but didn't rule it. This responsibility fell to a member of a certain clan, named in the sources as the beg, yilig or shad, which can be translated as "king". This king stood below the khagan in the hierarchy, the latter having a largely spiritual function: "The Qağan is a heavenly mandate intermediary between the divine and this state." A kagan's reign was limited to forty years, since it was believed that his spiritual powers were then exhausted and he had to be replaced.⁹

Crimea's role as a cultural contact zone (cf. Chapter 2) and as a place of exile on the periphery of empires and kingdoms is further illustrated by the example of the Byzantine emperor Justinian II (668/669–711). To this day, he is most renowned for having his enemies' noses cut off, although he did not introduce the practice himself. Later, the same fate befell him, and hence he became known by the epithet "Rhinometos" ("the one with his nose cut off"). While his foreign policy concerning the Arabs advancing from the Mediterranean was initially successful, he was unable to realize his plans for rapprochement between the eastern and western Churches.¹⁰ His domestic policy saw both the underclasses and the elites turn against him, leading to his fall in 695, the public removal of his nose and his exile to Crimea, to the

Byzantine outpost of Chersonesus. He still sought to regain the imperial throne, however, and continued to pursue this aim in exile. The "openly highly treasonous speeches he gave there"[11] appear to have unsettled the Chersonites, who informed Constantinople about his actions. Fearing capture or worse, in 698 or 704 the dethroned emperor fled to the peninsula's mountains, to Crimean Gothia (Doros), which was extremely difficult for armies to access. It is not entirely clear what status Doros enjoyed at this time: was it already under direct or at least indirect rule by the Khazars, as some scholars assume,[12] or was it neither Byzantine nor part of the Khaganate but a neutral territory, as Vasil'ev insisted?[13] Thomas S. Noonan (1938–2001), indisputably one of the most prominent historians of the Khazars in the Black Sea region, wrote that Byzantine sources assumed that large parts of Crimea, including Chersonesus, were under the control of the Khaganate during the seventh century, although it is not possible to make any definitive statements concerning the ninth and tenth centuries. On the other hand, some scholars assume that Byzantium again dominated Crimea during this period,[14] while others consider it likely that large parts of the peninsula were part of a Byzantine–Khazar condominium. The latter idea is supported by the fact that this practice was certainly part of the Byzantine repertoire of the time; Cyprus, for instance, was ruled jointly by Constantinople and the Arabs.[15]

Whatever the case may have been, Justinian II certainly quite intentionally took refuge in Doros as a place that was clearly beyond the reach of Byzantium. In Doros, he managed to forge an alliance with the khagan, Busir Glavan (late seventh/early eighth century; Russian/Ukrainian Ibuzir Gliavan), who underscored the arrangement by giving him his sister's hand in marriage. Emperor Tiberius II (?–706, Byzantine emperor from 698–705) then pressured the Khazars to kill or extradite Justinian, who fled once again, this time to Phanagoria (on the Taman Peninsula), where he made a pact against Constantinople with the Bulgar khan, Tervel (700–21). He was thus able to take Constantinople in 705, after laying siege to the city for several days. Justinian became emperor for a second time and – legend has it – took revenge on his enemies, among them Chersonesus, which had secured the protection of Justinian's brother-in-law Busir Glavan. However, Justinian could not relax, for a rebellion took place in 711 under the aegis of an exiled Byzantine military man of Armenian descent by the name of Vardanis. With the assistance of the Chersonites and the Khazars, Vardanis was crowned emperor (as Philippucus Bardanes, 711–13), sailed to Constantinople – and had Justinian II and his son, still a child, killed.[16] It was neither the first nor the last time the fate of empires and their rulers would be decided in Crimea – and hence, from the metropolitan perspective, in a peripheral region of the world.

Justinian II and his fight for the throne exemplify the important role Chersonesus in southwestern Crimea played in the context of the Byzantine imperial structure. Overall, what from Constantinople's perspective was a peripheral outpost of the empire from Antiquity to the fifteenth century was of great importance for the history of Crimea and the Black Sea region as a whole.[17] This is largely due to the city's strategically and economically significant location and its associated function as a mediator between the steppe and the metropolis and between settled and nomadic cultures. Not only did it have great relevance in the context of Crimea itself (including its role in mythology transcending various cultures – cf. Chapter 1), but it is also undoubtedly one of the "best-researched Byzantine cities". Chersonesus is "the prime example of a Byzantine city of the 'dark centuries'", writes Wolfram Brandes, who nevertheless also urges caution regarding this very assessment. He emphasizes the city's special status "on the edge of Byzantine culture and in close proximity to various barbarian peoples – mostly nomadic horsemen" and that great energy was put into archaeological research at the site from the late eighteenth century on[18] – although it would be more accurate to say the early nineteenth century.[19] We thus have more knowledge of this city's various historical layers than of other comparable conglomerates.

Crimea's significance as a contact zone between the religions is also apparent throughout its history and has already been repeatedly examined in the present study. Throughout the ages, religious actors sought to forge a common lifeworld without the use of violence, both as a matter of principle and for pragmatic reasons. Nevertheless, in Crimea too consensus between the various religious and confessional groups has sometimes been disrupted. In this context, the literature repeatedly mentions a rebellion against Khazar rule in 786/787 that also gives some indication of the "ups and downs of the Byzantine–Khazar relationship in southwestern Crimea".[20] John of Gothia (?–791), the first bishop of Crimean Gotha – according to Vasil'ev[21] – is said to have led the revolt. This Crimean-born cleric returned to the peninsula after many years in the Caucasus, probably around 758; the usual explanation is that he was a representative of the then dominant iconoclast movement within the Church – a position he would reinforce in Crimea.[22] John, later St John, and his followers clearly sought to bring Doros under Byzantine rule.[23] They did not receive support from Constantinople, since the "emperor clearly didn't want to disturb the status quo" in Crimea.[24] The rebels nevertheless succeeded in the short term in shaking off Khazar supremacy and chasing away the tudun (a kind of governor). A few months later, however, the Khazars returned, and the ringleaders were punished or banished from Crimea, although some managed to flee. Or at least we are told as much by the Life of Saint John,[25] which usually forms the basis of descriptions of this rebellion, although some questions remain.[26]

Khazar power in Crimea had been challenged by John and his supporters, but this did not reduce its influence in the long term. However, in the course of the tenth century, the Khaganate found itself increasingly vulnerable to invaders from the Eurasian steppe, such as Alans and Pechenegs. Further threats came from the northwest – in the form of Kyivan Rus', for, as we have seen in the *Primary Chronicle*, Grand Prince Svyatosláv "sallied forth against the Khazars. When they heard of his approach, they went out to meet him with their Prince, the Kagan, and the armies came to blows. When the battle thus took place, Svyatoslav defeated the Khazars and took their city of Bela Vezha".[27] The increasing weakness of the Khaganate – including in the military context – was certainly noted by contemporaries. For instance, in the famous didactic treatise *De Administrando Imperio*, which appears to have been written in the first half of the tenth century and is usually ascribed to the Byzantine emperor Constantine VII Porphyrogenitus (905–59), the decline in Khazar power becomes clear: the Alans "may do them [the Khazars] great hurt by ambushing their routes and setting upon them when they are off their guard". But the Alans were not the only enemies; other potential foes are mentioned, including descendants of "Black Bulgaria" (the Turkic Bulgars).[28] Nevertheless, judging from the degree to which administrative structures prevailed in the peninsula, Khaganate rule must be considered to have been particularly successful, creating a certain stability in the region for around three centuries.

8

Crimea between Kyivan Rus', Byzantium and Eurasian Semi-Nomadic Groups

The didactic treatise *De Administrando Imperio* mentions a number of goods (spices, fabrics, etc.) that played a role in the economy of the Black Sea region and for which Chersonesus was a major hub:

> Yet another folk of these Pechenegs lies over against the district of Cherson; they trade with the Chersonites, and perform services for them and for the emperor in Russia and Chazaria and Zichia and all the parts beyond: that is to say, they receive from the Chersonites a prearranged remuneration in respect of this service proportionate to their labour and trouble, in the form of pieces of purple cloth, ribbons, loosely woven cloths, gold brocade, pepper, scarlet *or* "Parthian" leather, and other commodities which they require, according to a contract which each Chersonite may make or agree to with an individual Pecheneg. For these Pechenegs are free men and, so to say, independent, and never perform any service without remuneration.[1]

The passage also provides information about the economic intertwinement and dependences between the Byzantine outpost of Chersonesus, the Pechenegs and Rus', or "Russia" in the anachronistic translation from the Greek. The Pechenegs, who in the ninth and tenth centuries controlled large expanses of the steppe in today's Russia and Ukraine, including northern Crimea, were another polyethnic, multilingual collection of (mainly Turkic-speaking) individuals, or a "non-territorial professional community", to cite the medievalist Omeljan Pritsak.[2] Having advanced from Asia, they were of great relevance for the economy and the political balance of power in the Black Sea region; it is for good reason that Constantine advised his successor that "it is always greatly to the advantage of the emperor of the Romans to be minded to keep the peace with the nation of the Pechenegs and to conclude conventions and treaties of friendship with them and to send every year to them from our side a diplomatic agent with presents befitting and suitable to that nation [...]".³ The inhabitants of Rus' were also interested in reaching an understanding with them, since "they buy of them horned cattle and horses and sheep, whereby they live more easily and comfortably, since none of the aforesaid animals is found in Russia".⁴ The Pechenegs themselves also sought to reach pragmatic arrangements with their neighbours and pursued a flexible policy of alliances – as indeed had been common in the region in earlier times. They concluded pacts with Byzantium (e.g. 914, 968, 972), Rus' (944) and other neighbours.⁵ However, this flexibility also included invading them, for instance in 968, as the *Primary Chronicle* relates: "The nomads [i.e. the Pechenegs] besieged the city with a great force. They surrounded it with an innumerable multitude, so that it was impossible to escape or send messages from the city, and the inhabitants were weak from hunger and thirst."⁶ In 972, Rus' finally suffered a devastating defeat at the hands of the Pechenegs: "Svyatoslav approached the cataracts, where Kurya, Prince of the Pechenegs, attacked him; and Svyatoslav was killed. The nomads took his head, and made a cup out of his skull, overlaying it with gold, and they drank from it."⁷

Although this conflict and others took place north of the peninsula, in the steppe or in the centre of Rus'– such as the siege of Kyiv in 968 or the Battle of Kyiv in 1036 – they nevertheless had an impact on Crimea. Between the late ninth and well into the eleventh century, Pechenegs (sometimes in league with other groups of Eurasian descent) repeatedly invaded the peninsula. In the early tenth century, particularly northern Crimea and its neighbouring mainland regions again became a transit zone; no central power could establish itself there. In contrast, the south or the southwest (Chersonesus and its environs and Crimean Gothia) remained under Byzantine influence. Pecheneg rule would also prove temporary. In 1036, the grand prince of Rus', Iaroslav I ("Mudryi" [the Wise], *c.* 978–1054) registered a decisive victory over them, which in retrospect must be seen as an indication that their zenith had passed. While they still attempted individual offensives towards Constantinople to the south, they suffered heavy defeats. And in the east, new mobile groups threatened these peoples, who ultimately withdrew westwards to the Danube region or became acculturated. The Pechenegs are last mentioned in Russian chronicles with reference to the year 1169.⁸

The advance of Rus' towards the Black Sea was not a linear process; rather, it occurred in phases. As far as the sources relate, from the mid-ninth century on there was contact with the Khaganate and Byzantium (some of it peaceful, some of it military), and this contact later became "systematic".⁹ An event with a large impact that can still be felt today – at least on the level of discourse – was the episode around 988 (cf. Chapter 1), when the grand prince of Kyiv from the Rurik dynasty, Vladimir/Volodymyr, initially laid siege to Chersonesus under circumstances that are not entirely clear before being baptized in the city (presumably) and marrying Anna Porphyrogenita, the sister of the emperors of Constantinople; certainly, his baptism and marriage to a princess born in the purple significantly increased the prestige of the hitherto heathen Rus'. The mere fact that Byzantium entertained this demonstrates the importance ascribed to Rus'. In contrast to most landlocked players hitherto, Rus' had "permanent access to maritime resources and made use of them too".[10] Especially from the tenth century onwards, relations between Rus' and Byzantium were characterized by peaceful trade alternating with sporadic looting raids on Constantinople by Kyiv.

In this context, it should be noted that in the Taman Peninsula, opposite Panticapaeum/Kerch, the Greek settlement of Hermonassa developed into a Slavic principality/Hermonassa. Known as Tmutarakan', it came under the

FIGURE 8.1 The Baptism of Rus', *painting by Viktor Vasnetsov, 1890.*

rule of a branch of the Rurik dynasty in the late tenth or early eleventh century. According to the *Primary Chronicle*, one of Vladimir's sons, Mstislav (*c.* 988–1034/36), took the city after winning a wrestling match with the previous ruler, Prince Rededia. Rededia had proposed that the two of them fight rather than pitting their armies against one another: "If you win, you shall receive my property, my wife, and my children, and my land. But if I win, I shall take all your possessions." When Mstislav looked like losing the fight, he called on the "Virgin Mother of God" and "stabbed Rededya".[11]

This divinely ordained dominion over Tmutarakan' did not last long, however; the advance of the Kumans in the twelfth century (cf. Chapter 9) spelt the end of the principality. It is last mentioned by Russian chronicles in 1094. Subsequently, it fell under the rules of various powers.[12] Russian historiography during the nineteenth century and beyond repeatedly interpreted the constellation of sporadic expansion south by Rus' – with periods of sustained success – and the existence of Tmutarakan' on the Kerch Strait as evidence that the northern Black Sea region and above all Crimea were exposed to permanent Slavic influence from the ninth/tenth century on. Not least, this interpretation suited the apologists for Russian rule over the region from the late eighteenth century onwards; it was believed that the annexation of Crimea in 1783 could thus be interpreted as regaining old Slav territory.[13] In Vasil'ev, even an undisputed authority on the medieval history of Crimea claimed that while the peninsula didn't have a relevant proportion of Slavic inhabitants, Rus' established a short-lived protectorate of Crimean Gothia from 962–72.[14] Another authority, the important Russian historian Vasilii O. Kliuchevskii (1841–1911), rejected such views, however.[15]

9

Kumans, Polovtsians and Kipchaks

Then Prince Igor stepped into his golden stirrup, and set out in the open field. The sun barred his way with darkness, night groaned to him; and roused the birds with terror; the shrill tones of beasts aroused him; Div arose crying calls on the tree-top; he commands a hearing from the Unknown Land, the Volga, the sea-border, and the Suki country on the Sea of Azov, Korsun, and thee, thou idol of Tmutarokan.

But the Polovtsy on trackless roads ran to the mighty Don. The carts creak at midnight, like swans released.[1]

The Song of Prince Igor (*Slovo o polku Igoreve*), here in Leonard A. Magnus's prose translation, is a monumental but controversial work of literature. Its authenticity has repeatedly been doubted by historians and linguists,[2] although the majority of them consider the tale of the unsuccessful campaign against the Polovzes launched by Prince Igor Sviatoslavich of Novgorod (1151–1201) in 1185 and his lament on the discord among the princes of Kyivan Rus' to be genuine and to have been written shortly after the events. This view is held, for instance, by the great Soviet medievalist Dmitrii S. Likhachëv (1906–99)[3] or the linguist A. A. Zalizniak (1935–2017). The latter's linguistic analysis led him to conclude that a forgery could not be discounted entirely, but only if it had been undertaken "by an utter genius".[4] Whatever the case may be, the important aspect for our context is the mention of Tmutarakan' and the cities of Sudak (Russian/Ukrainian; Crimean Tatar: Sudaq)[5] and Korsun'/Chersonesus on Crimea's south coast, which again demonstrates the existence of a connection between the peninsula and Rus'. However, a third player had positioned itself between them, as the epos relates: the Polovtsians (as they are known in the Slavic tradition),[6] Kumans (as they are called in the Turkic sources) or Kipchaks/Qipčak (in Islamic texts).[7] Once again, another – Turkic-speaking – collection of horsemen had advanced from Eurasia into today's Russian/Ukrainian steppe region. From here, they shaped Crimea's fate by beginning to control the trade routes in the course of the eleventh century. They too had an advantage over their foes due to their mobility: "The Polovtsians have fled/By untrod paths to the mighty Don", the *Song of Prince Igor* relates. This ruling collective was also flexible politically; for instance, they established trade relations with Byzantium in which Sudak played an immensely important role as an economic hub. Relations with Rus' also improved from the thirteenth century on (that is, in the centuries after Igor's campaign), with several marriages and military alliances.

The latter would prove particularly important: a Mongol incursion into Crimea in 1223 is considered a precursor to the so-called Mongol Storm[8] so firmly rooted in the Russian collective conscious. Both invasions laid waste to Sudak and other settlements. In the long term, the Mongol threat reinforced the alliance between the Polovtsians and Rus': in the Battle of the Kalka River (in today's southeastern Ukraine) in May 1223, the now united rulers of the regional principalities of Kyivan Rus' and their allies set out to defeat the invaders. They failed miserably, but the victors initially left.[9] When the Mongol Tatar victors once again advanced westwards one-and-a-half decades later and remained, the Polovtsian dominance in northern Crimea and the bordering steppe regions finally came to an end. Some of them became acculturated to the culture, economy and lifeworlds of the new rulers, or the two groups assimilated to one another, while others headed west, thereby following an established pattern in Crimean history. The Mongol invaders showed great potential: while driving westwards, Batu Khan (1205–55), grandson of Činggis Qaɣan (Genghis Khan; *c*. 1155, 1162 or 1167–1227), who had managed to unite the thitherto separate Mongolian tribes, had pursued an ambitious plan: "to conquer the divided land of quarreling Rus' [...] princes, the lands of Turkish Bulgars and Kipchaks and the Christian lands of Eastern Europe", as the Orientalist Brian G. Williams summarizes.[10] Indeed, Batu Khan was able to further expand Mongol Tatar rule on the Black Sea and in large swathes of Rus' (apart from the northwest), administering his empire from the city of Sarai founded on the lower Volga. Incidentally, some scholars have departed from the long dominant notion of the proverbial "Mongol yolk" that was thought to have weighed so heavily on the Eastern Slavic regions, although they do not overlook the violent aspects. For instance, religious tolerance prevailed within the Golden Horde, or, more precisely, "the Khan was indifferent to the religion of the subjugated peoples". Moreover, no attempt was made to "unify the linguistic, legal, economic, social or cultural situation".[11]

The Horde's centre in Crimea was Eski Qırım (Crimean Tatar; Old Fortress) – Solcati, as it was called by the Italians who arrived in the peninsula, to whom we will return later. Before the invaders from the east took the town, it was ethnically and culturally diverse, as was usually the case in Crimea; along with the Romance and Turkic-speaking inhabitants, there were descendants of the Greek colonists or Armenians, who had a wide network of traders. Staryi Krym (Ukrainian/Russian; Old Fortress or Old Crimea), as the settlement is known today, occupies a favourable strategic position between the southern foothills of the Crimean Mountains and the northern steppe region, allowing extensive control over large parts of the peninsula.

In the coastal region, on the other hand, the balance of power had fundamentally changed in the early thirteenth century, since Constantinople lost outposts such as Chersonesus. What had happened? The southern Crimean cities had long been able to resist the surge of nomadic collectives or found compromises with them. This was one of the reasons Christianity had become established so early, particularly in Chersonesus. The supremacy of Christian Byzantium had not faced serious challenges from the Polovtsians, whose religions were probably originally shamanic,[12] from the Jewish Khazars or from the Muslim inhabitants from the north. It was followers of their own faith that brought an end to Byzantine Crimea.

10

The Fourth Crusade (1202–04) and Its Consequences for Crimea

Wilhelm von Rubruk (German; Dutch Willem van Ruysbroek, usually Anglicanized as William of Rubruck; between 1215 and 1220–70), a Franciscan monk whose scholarly and diplomatic destinations included the empire of the Golden Horde,[1] described Matriga in the Taman Peninsula (the former Classical Phanagoria) and especially Soldaia (today's Sudak) in Crimea as prosperous trade cities and hubs for all kinds of goods:

> In the middle on the south side – at the apex, as it were – lies a city called Soldaia, which looks across towards Sinopolis, and there land all the merchants who come from Turkia and wish to visit the northern regions, as also those who come from the opposite direction, from Russia and the north and wish to cross over to Turkia. These latter carry squirrel and miniver [*varium et grisium*] and other valuable furs; the others bring lengths of cotton or *gambasium*, silk cloth and fragrant spices. And on the eastern side of this territory lies a city called Matrica, where the river Tanais flows down into the Sea of Pontus through an estuary twelve miles wide.
>
> Before this river enters the Sea of Pontus, it has formed to the north a sea which is seven hundred miles in length and breadth and nowhere reaches a depth of more than six paces. For this reason large vessels do not enter it, the merchants from Constantinople landing at the aforesaid city of Matrica and sending their boats as far as the river Tanais in order to buy dried fish, namely sturgeon, shad, eel-pout and other fish in vast quantities.[2]

Merchants, not only from Rus' (not "Russia", as the above translation falsely states) and 'Turks' (meaning Turkic-speaking traders from the Horde's lands[3]) clearly did good business there, since they wore "miniver and other valuable furs". Once again, Crimea's overall significance for the exchange of goods between the north, south and east of the Black Sea region and the Caucasus becomes clear in Rubruck's description. Soldaia in particular enjoyed great economic prosperity in the period between the eleventh and the fourteenth centuries, especially as it gained an important position in the silk trade. Ibn Baṭūṭah, an important Muslim traveller in the fourteenth century (1304–68 or 1369), went so far as to compare its port with that of Alexandria.[4] Doubtlessly, with Soldaia (or later "Kaffa", today's Feodosiia), whose rise was principally due to the Italian city states of Genoa and Venice, Crimea played a large role in the economic 'world system' that was already emerging in the thirteenth century, to which we will return in connection with the Pax Mongolica.[5] As in the previous centuries, Crimea's role as an economic hub peaked whenever there was peace in the northern steppe and forest regions and the maritime straits between the Dardanelles and the Bosporus were open to the various economic actors, such as the Republics of Venice and Genoa, which were "impatient to break through the Narrows into the markets of the Black Sea". Much to the chagrin of these ambitious maritime states, at times their plans were scuppered by the later Byzantine emperors.[6] In the course of the thirteenth century, however, they managed to establish themselves in the region.

This was preceded by the extensive erosion of Byzantine power in Crimea, beginning with the sack of Constantinople in 1204 during the Fourth Crusade, which led to a "considerable power-political vacuum" while also serving as a "catalyst for processes that were already developing".[7] Of course, Innocent III's (late 1160/early 1161–1216) papal bull "Post miserabile" of 1198 calling for the Holy Land to be retaken from the Muslim Ayybubid dynasty did not have the outcome he had anticipated: the Crusaders were to travel by sea instead of over land, and hence assistance was sought from the experts, the mighty Serenissima Repubblica di San Marco (the Most Serene Republic of St Mark) – that is, the Republic of Venice.[8] It was agreed that fifty new ships would be built in addition to pre-existing boats; together, they would carry a total of 4,500 knights, 9,000 squires and around 20,000 foot soldiers. In return, the Crusaders promised Venice rich rewards, including in the form of land in the conquered territories.[9] The undertaking was at risk of failing, however, since far fewer potential Crusaders had responded to the pope's appeal than expected, which threatened the outcome and Venice's reward. As compensation, it was agreed that they would loot the Dalmatian (Christian) city of Zadar. It soon became evident that this wasn't the only element of this crusade that didn't target so-called infidels (i.e. non-Christians); while the Crusader army was still wintering in Zadar, the decision was made to sack Constantinople. Innocent III's attempt to prevent this by threat of excommunication did not dissuade the Crusaders. They considered the Byzantines schismatics undeserving of mercy. Above all, however, they were tempted by the idea of finding unimaginable riches in Constantinople. Additionally, Alexios Angelos (1182–1204), the son of Emperor Isaac II (c. 1155–1204), who had been dethroned by his own brother, promised the Crusaders led by Boniface of Montferrat (c. 1150– 1207) Byzantine soldiers and rich booty if they helped him oust his uncle and install him as emperor.[10] The extremely complex events that followed cannot be reproduced here in detail; suffice it to say that the Crusaders arrived at Constantinople on 24 June 1203. Following a period of negotiations, mutual threats and demonstrations of military power, the invaders stormed the city; contemporary sources report a huge bloodbath within its walls in the early summer of 1204.[11] It is beyond dispute that it was not only the theological and ritual alienation expressed in the Oriental Schism of 1054 that obstructed rapprochement between Orthodoxy and Roman Catholicism; the memory of the atrocities of Constantinople did sustained damage to relations between the faiths.[12]

However, other consequences were of greater relevance for the history of the Crimean Peninsula: granted trade privileges by Byzantium as early as the late tenth century, the Venetians had long possessed a base in Constantinople in the form of Pera on the Golden Horn – and were able to further strengthen their position in the northern Black Sea region in the course of the thirteenth century. It was to their advantage that in 1204, before taking Byzantium, they had signed the *Partitio terrarum imperii Romaniae* with the Crusaders: Venice would receive three-eighths of the conquered Byzantine lands, although it was a "matter of course for the sea-oriented Venetians" that they amounted to "an entire web of coastal and island territories".[13] Since the once so mighty Byzantine Empire was now merely reduced to its rump in the form of the Latin Empire, Venice's influence, financial and otherwise, temporarily increased. However, in 1261 Venetian ambitions on the Black Sea suffered something of a setback in the form of the reconquest of Constantinople and the re-installation of the Byzantine Empire. Although it would never return to its old strength, for some time Byzantium blocked the Venetians' passage through the straits. This benefited their archenemies, the Genoese, whom the reconquerer of Constantinople and presumptive emperor, Michael VIII Palaiologos (1224 or 1225–82), had agreed to reward with trade privileges hitherto the preserve of the Venetians in return for supporting his fleet.[14]

The arrival of the Genoese transformed the Black Sea; as the important Romanian politician, historian and later victim of the Securitate Gheorghe I. Brătianu (1898–1953) put it in his *Les Génois et les Vénitiens dans la mer Noire aux XIIIe–XIVe siècles*, still considered a standard work, it was transformed into a "lac génois".[15] Paying greater attention to the Venetian share of Italian dominance over the region, Charles King, on the other hand, calls the Black Sea a "Mare Maggiore" ("Great Sea").[16] Indeed, these city states established important trade centres in Crimea and the rest of the region, frequently competing but sometimes cooperating with each other.[17] Venice initially developed its business via the flourishing Soldaia, for which William of Rubruck had expressed his admiration. However, the Serenissima Repubblica di San Marco soon fell behind the Genoese, who established important trading posts in Crimea in the form of Cembalo (today: Russian/Ukrainian Balaklava; Crimean Tatar Balıqlava) and Lupico (today's Alupka), but especially Caffa, which along with Pera would become the most important colony on the Black Sea.[18] Soon all posts in the Black Sea would be subjugated to Caffa.[19] When exactly the Genoese were able to install their regime in the settlement is not entirely clear,[20] but it was certainly 1261 at the latest. Caffa, but also other trading centres under Italian rule, should not be thought of as ethnically and cultural coherent Italian/Italian-speaking outposts; as economic hubs and lifeworlds reflecting old realities in the peninsula, these colonies were multiethnic, multicultural and multireligious.[21]

In the course of the thirteenth century, the situation in Crimea was, then, typical of the story we have told hitherto: there was still no central power that ruled over the entire peninsula; instead there were several different ethnic, religious and cultural actors in a process of exchange oscillating between coexistence and confrontation. Specifically, this meant that the following conglomerates existed alongside the so-called Italian colonies: Chersonesus, Crimean Gothia and the neighbouring areas settled by, among others, Christian Alans[22] entered into ill-defined power relations with the Empire of Trebizond, while other areas – such as Soldaia/Sudak, in theory promised to the Venetians but in practice ruled by the Polovtsians– could barely be subjugated. The Empire of Trebizond had freed itself from Byzantium in the late twelfth century – before the Fourth Crusade, then – and subsequently became one of the three successor states to the Byzantine Empire.[23] Unlike the Nikaia Empire or the Despotate of Epirus, under the Grand Komnenos dynasty the Empire of Trebizond enjoyed free access to the Black Sea. Hence, according to the interpretation offered by the Soviet medievalist G. G. Litavrin (1925–2009), Trebizond could become, as it were, the heir to the Byzantine overseas territories on the northern shore of the Black Sea. Litavrin states that although it is impossible to establish how and when exactly the transition took place, it is beyond doubt that the Crimean colonies regularly paid taxes and that their archons were directly subordinate to the Grand Komnenos.[24] In the first decades of the thirteenth century, the remaining Crimean territories were dominated by the Polovtsians/Kumans/Kipchaks (cf. Chapter 9); there then followed a phase that would last until the mid-thirteenth century in which the Oghusik Seljuks, originating in Asia, ruled over Sudak and some other places for two periods. Despite the relatively short duration of their rule, there was considerable immigration and partial acculturation between the old and the new inhabitants – again, a very common phenomenon in Crimea, where a contact zone developed between Byzantium, the Eastern Church and Islam.[25] Ultimately, the Golden Horde was able to establish Eski Qırım as its centre in Crimea.

11

The Pax Mongolica, Trade, Slavery and the "Black Death"

Important historians have discovered that besides 'autochthonous' peoples, i.e. peoples born locally, there were also 'autothalassic' peoples, i.e. peoples shaped by the sea who were never land treaders and had no interest in terra firma other than as the boundary to their purely maritime existence.[1]

Many authors have taken up the distinction between so-called "land treaders" and "sea rovers" – in the words of the above-cited Carl Schmitt (1888–1985), an important German scholar of state law and political philosopher, albeit one whose stance on National Socialism made him a highly controversial figure. If we examine the period between 1280 and 1360 in Crimea (and beyond), especially the example of the interactions between the Golden Horde and the Italian protagonists, Schmitt's description of the difference between land and maritime peoples is ostensibly rather apt. Indeed, in his work *Land und Meer* (*Land and Sea*) he wrote of Venice, praising not only its wealth but also "the diplomatic superiority with which the maritime power was able to exploit the land powers' differences".[2] He made no mention of the mighty Mongol Empire, however. This was certainly not without good reason; in comparative research on the role of imperia in history, it is repeatedly noted that historians long considered great maritime empires more developed and more modern than their continental counterparts (not always convincingly). More recently, imperial research has abandoned this strict dictum and acknowledges the innovative potential of "land treaders".[3] As we shall see, the question of interactions between Italians, Mongols and Tatars and their consequences for the Crimean Peninsula is also extremely interesting if we consider categories such as 'backwardness' or 'success'.

The fact is that both the supposedly modern Italian city states and the allegedly backward Golden Horde expanded their territories over a certain period of time but developed and maintained very different dominions in terms of the way they worked and were structured. Furthermore, it would be ahistorical to assess these state systems that emerged in the premodern era by our contemporary standards.[4] Nevertheless, there were some phenomena which even appear progressive or effective today and which were established by the 'more backward' continental imperium, including, for instance, the system of taxation and conscription and the road and postal system introduced by the Horde.[5] The Mongols were responsible for other modern phenomena too: from the late thirteenth to the mid-fourteenth century, the Black Sea region and with it Crimea became an intensive contact zone between the Mongols, who controlled the Eurasian areas, and the Italian city states, who dominated maritime trade. This era has subsequently become known as the Pax Mongolica, roughly spanning the period from 1280 to 1360. During this phase, traders could largely go about their business in safety – and thus had an immense radius of activity that ultimately stretched from China to Europe and Africa. This security was generated by the Mongolian state or (probably more accurately) federation, which, incidentally, was not a despotic regime as we would understand the term today,[6] since the khan was rather a *primus inter pares*.[7] One side effect of the Pax Mongolica was the spread of elaborate (cultural) technologies in the fields of medicine, mathematics and astronomy – from East to West.[8]

The Pax Mongolica came to an end following the gradual disintegration of the Mongol Empire and its collapse into individual khanates – one of them being the Crimean Khanate. Another factor in its decline, however, was the outbreak of bubonic plague, which spread quickly due to the heavy exchange of people and goods. Yet this did not mean the end of the Italian colonies in Crimea; it was a good century before Caffa was incorporated into the Ottoman Empire in 1475 and the majority of Italian and Armenian merchants migrated to Pera (cf. Chapter 14) or ended up in slavery.[9]

Power relations between the metropolitan centres – Sarai or Venice and Genoa – and the outposts/colonies, not only in Crimea, did not correspond to the early modern pattern of colonialism that Jürgen Osterhammel has described as a relationship "between collectives in which the fundamental decisions about how the colonized live their lives are made and pushed through by a minority of colonial overlords who are culturally different and barely willing to adapt, consideration being given to external interests".[10] The Italian city states oversaw more of an "emporium" – that is, a network of trading posts – than an imperium, and paid little attention to the way the local population went about their lives in the so-called colonies, or at least as long as their main interests, which were primarily of an economic nature, remained unaffected.[11] Cities like Caffa enjoyed a certain independence, then, sometimes even being able to mint their own coins. Indeed, emphasis must generally be placed on the number of private, local entrepreneurs involved in Black Sea trade in this period.[12]

On the other hand, one characteristic of Mongol rule was the rapid acculturation to the autochthonous populations of the conquered regions and an elaborate system of collecting tribute and taxes,[13] which also involved the Italian traders.[14] Both the Mongolian and the Italian actors certainly threatened and in some cases exercised violence as a means of asserting their interests, but in the case of the Horde, too, it was a last resort rather than the method of choice. Nevertheless, during the Pax Mongolica there were also conflicts between the colonies of the maritime powers in Crimea and the Horde, some of them escalating into violence; for instance, from 1307 on, when Khan Toqta (Toktu; c. 1270–1312/13) had the Italian traders in Sarai arrested before sending them back to Soldaia/Sudak and confiscating their wares. The khan then sent troops to Caffa; they laid siege to the city for eight months before its inhabitants sailed to safety on their ships after setting fire to it. It was not rebuilt until 1316.[15] The Italian maritime cities also fought wars against each other, such as the Second Venetian–Genoese War (1294–9), which was fought not least over supremacy on the Black Sea; the Genoese would win this conflict in the medium term.[16]

The goods traded during the Pax Mongolica and in the period that followed it had remained more or less the same since Antiquity: grain, furs, wax, honey, silk, salt, spices and slaves.[17] The Horde and the Italian city states worked together – including when it came to human cargo.[18] The Horde procured the people, while the Italians then sold them on from Caffa, Tana and other colonies on the Black Sea. The Christian merchants' role in the human trafficking on the Black Sea, its consequences and the discourses on their involvement are now well researched.[19] It is unclear whether the turnover ever reached the same levels as the transatlantic slave trade,[20] but it was certainly a significant economic factor. After the treaty between Michael VIII Palaiologos and the Egyptian sultan Baybars (c. 1223–77), in which the latter recognized the former's right to annually import two shipments[21] of slaves from the Black Sea region, the 'sector' took on a particularly dynamic development. Genoese and Venetians established flourishing slave markets in Caffa, Tana and Alexandria. Even after the end of the Pax Mongolica, business was healthy: in Caffa alone, some 10,000 imported slaves are said to have been sold to Venice between 1414 and 1423.[22] Since Antiquity, the Black Sea slave trade had been a most international affair, involving many ethnic, cultural and religious groups, such as the 'Ancient' Greeks so revered by members of the educated European elites from the Renaissance on, or Slavic traders from Kyivan Rus'.[23] In Western discourses, however, emphasis has mostly been placed on Muslim involvement in this global trade – something to which we will return in the context of the Crimean Khanate.[24] It should be noted, however, that the Venetians – and also the Genoese – were "a nation of slave traders" from the very outset.[25]

We have already emphasized the positive consequences of the Pax Mongolica, which in the words of Brătianu made the Black Sea an "international trade hub";[26] it was not only goods that circulated, but also knowledge. But there were just as many negative consequences – including the spread of the Great Plague,[27] which devastated and depopulated entire swathes of Europe[28] and has left traumatic traces in the continent's collective memory.[29] Neal Ascherson succinctly summarized this dialectic: "The Silk Routes brought wealth, but then death."[30] For centuries, scholars have associated Caffa with the plague's spread to Europe, a view held even by epidemiologists in our current era. At the centre of this interpretation is a story that is repeatedly told with slight variations, the authenticity of which must be severely doubted. It certainly says a lot about the European image of Muslims: during the conflicts that flared up between the Horde and the Genoese, in 1347 the Mongolians laid siege to Caffa and catapulted the bodies of plague victims in the army into the largely Christian city in order to weaken the citizens' resistance. Western research has now long presumed that this story, which goes back to the legal scholar Gabriel de Mussis (*c.* 1280–*c.* 1356), from Piacenza, cannot be true. The current consensus is that de Mussis could not have witnessed events in Caffa – and indeed never visited the place, as he was long assumed to have done. Presumably the plague was "transmitted to the besieged city [...] in other ways", for instance via infected rats or fleas, which must have come into direct contact with its inhabitants.[31] Recently, a medical journal established that the path of infection described in the legend is unrealistic for *Yersinia pestis*, to give the disease its Latin name, since infected fleas leave dead bodies, which can thus no longer be contagious in and of themselves.[32] However, the trebuchet story was often interpreted as an early form of bacteriological warfare invented and executed by the sinister members of the Asian Horde.[33] However it came about, the epidemic spread from Crimea with great speed and, as we know, with terrible humanitarian consequences. The economic impact of the plague on settlements such as Tana or Caffa was mixed, however: initially, the situation deteriorated due to the conflicts between the Golden Horde under the rule of Khan Ǧani Beg (Jani Beg; ?–1357; khan from 1342–52) and the depopulation of several cities in the Black Sea region as a result of the pandemic;[34] but since the Black Death caused a huge shortage of workers throughout Europe, the price of human cargo rose – and the Italian colonies profited as hubs for the slave trade.

Albrecht and Herdick note that it was only then, in the second half of the fourteenth century, that Genoa began to "develop from an essentially economic into an important political factor in Crimea".[35] In 1365, for instance, Genoa defeated Soldaia/Sudak, previously under Venetian rule, dealing a considerable blow to its longstanding competitor. The Peace of Turin (1381), which ended the Fourth Genoese–Venetian War, even forbade Venetian vessels from docking in Tana for two years. Hence it proved that "Genoa, however, was mightier"[36] – than Venice.

In a parallel development, things also changed for another actor, since after the death of the khan Ǧani Beg, the Golden Horde gradually slid into decline as the particular interests of local emirs grew stronger. While Emir Mamāi (1335–80), who had built up a power base for himself on the lower Don and in Crimea, attempted to reunite the secessionist territories, he was unsuccessful: his attempt to reassert Mongolian dominance over Kyivan Rus', almost all of whose territories had been obliged to pay tribute since the thirteenth century, culminated in the Battle of Kulikovo Pole (Snipes' Field) in 1380, an event that remains famous in the Russian collective memory to this day. The defeat of Mamāi's troops was retrospectively interpreted as the beginning of the end of Mongolian rule over Rus'. Some interpretations go even further: Lev N. Gumilëv (1912–92), the son of the great Russian poet Anna Akhmatova and a historian with so-called Eurasian tendencies, declared this battle the birth of the Russian nation: "People from Suzdal', Vladimir, Rostov, Pskov took to the field of Kulikovo to fight as representatives of the principalities, but they returned from there as Russians."[37] He thus ascribed to the battle world-historical significance. For the history of Crimea, the most relevant aspect is that leading up to the military engagement with Rus' there had been improvements in Mongolian–Genoese relations following the tensions in the first half of the century. Consequently, after the defeat, Mamāi sought – and found – refuge behind the walls of Caffa, where he fell victim to poisoning, however.[38]

Although he rejected many of Mamāi's particular approaches, the khan of the Golden Horde, Toktamış (Tokhtamy/Toqtamis/Tohtamysh; ?–1406/1407; khan from 1380–95) continued the policy of cooperation with the Genoese that Mamāi had revived, to the disadvantage of the Venetians, who were already losing influence on the Black Sea. Thenceforth, Genoa ultimately dominated the entire southern Crimean coast, including the Sea of Azov and the Taman Peninsula. However, many territories in the region became embroiled in the intensifying conflicts between the Golden Horde and the Timurid Empire under Timur (Lenk, the Lame; 1336–1405).[39] His military successes and talents, but also his propensity for violence are frequently compared to those of the great Mongol khan Činggis Qayan.[40] During their advance westwards in 1395, Timur's troops laid waste to Tana and parts of Crimea.

12

The Principality of Theodoro and a Lithuanian Intermezzo

In the hieromonk Exarch Matthew's tale of his journey to Crimea, presumably in the spring or summer of 1396, originally written in a mixture of Ancient and the vernacular Greek of his day, the author makes use of an extremely interesting narrative composition:

> I see extraordinary churches and splendid palaces, wonderful colourful chiselling underground, up above columns, dusty graves. And why do you stand abandoned, without a crowd of people? For even if the land of Khazaria were unsettled, you, most charming one, should be settled, alone even. Weeping, from the depths of her soul, her wailing and lamenting, she [the city] told unto me the following from her sad heart: [...] When I tell you of my frequent losses, of wars and the horrors [...] of the tribes of people that surrounded me a whole seven years [...] and the massacre and swinging of lances by those within and those without, [...] I will fill with many sighs and laments but sate you with wailing and tears.[1]

The narrator Matthaios/Matthew, introducing himself as an "inferior and paltry priest",[2] has the reader experience Crimea through the eyes of a "foreigner". This foreigner is probably Matthew himself, given how his words reveal knowledge of the region.[3] He or the foreigner share with the reader the clearly intensive experience of beauty he felt when viewing his surroundings. The aspect significant for Crimea is remarkable for the late fourteenth century, however:

> As soon as I had suddenly seen and caught a glimpse of her [the city] from afar, I was enraptured, stood completely still in wonder.
> After a short walk, I found an old path; supremely calm water, irrigated gardens, fountains bubbling before my eyes, the place having a good climate.[4]

As he draws closer to the city, however, he sees its destruction and enters into a dialogue with it; it seems empty and almost uninhabited to him, but he still perceives its former beauty ("splendid palaces, wonderful colourful chiselling underground"). The city tells him of its seven years under siege, the "massacre and swinging of lances" and how it was subsequently surrendered by its inhabitants. Recent research identifies the city as Theodoro in the mountainous southwest of the peninsula, the former Doros in Crimean Gothia and today's Mangup-Kale, which with its picturesque location on a high plateau and its cave settlement dug into the rock attracts many visitors to this day. The city evidently 'tells' the foreigner about Mamāi's siege of Theodoro, which began in 1373, and its conquest by Toktamış in 1381. With his troops, the latter was able to hold the city until 1395, when Timur's army succeeded in advancing into the peninsula's mountain region. The Byzantinist Hans-Veit Beyer insists that a strict distinction must be made between the two occupations: "Under Tohtamyš, life in the city went on; under Timur it was extinguished for some time."[5]

If on the basis of Matthew's narrative we turn to subsequent events in Crimea in the late fourteenth century, it becomes clear that Toktamış, faced with his defeat by Timur, recalled an ally of his former opponent Mamāi – the Grand Duchy of Lithuania, which had entered into a personal union with the Kingdom of Poland in 1386. This union had extended its geographical reach; its sphere of influence now stretched to the Black Sea[6] – and for a brief period as far as the Crimean Peninsula. For a long time, Lithuania had been the only regional power able to resist the Golden Horde militarily. Toktamış, seeking support following his failures against the Timurids and having since been dethroned by Emir Edigü (Idiqu; 1352–1419) and Timur Kuthlug (Timer Qotlığ; 1370–99),[7] now turned to Grand Duke Vytautas (Witold; 1354 or 1355–1430) in order to return to power within the Horde. In 1398, this alliance was indeed able to retake the Horde's centre in Crimea, Eski Qırım, and probably Theodoro, from the Timurids; according to Albrecht and Herdick, one reason for this success was that Timur's former supporter, Edigü, "the new leader of the Golden Horde, was concurrently in conflict with the Genoese".[8] It could have been the beginning of a more or less permanent presence of Lithuanian power in Crimea, but the defeat of the Lithuanians and Toktamış in 1399 at the Battle of the Vorskla (a tributary of the Dnipro), one of the largest battles of the Middle Ages,[9] put paid to this. Lithuanian influence was only felt in Crimea in the short term, in connection with these conflicts for dominance within the territories of the Golden Horde. The Horde itself continued to disintegrate rapidly, particularly after Edigüs's death in 1419. Even if the Golden Horde formally existed until the early sixteenth century, the secession of the Khanate of Kazan' (1438) and especially Crimea (around 1441/1443) were a clear sign of the erosion of Mongol power.

The Principality of Theodoro (Crimean Gothia) in Crimea's mountainous southwest has already been mentioned in the context of the Gothic fantasies in German-language discourses (cf. Chapter 1) and as a successor state to the Byzantine Empire within the Empire of Trebizond. No part of the Byzantine Empire was able to retain its independence for longer; it was not until 1475 that it was conquered by the Ottomans. Its population was diverse (as usual in Crimea): in addition to the descendants of the Crimean Goths, Greeks, Armenians, Alans or Crimean Karaites (to whom we will return later) there were Turkic-speaking inhabitants – and an Orthodox majority. Crimean Gothia played a considerable role in the extremely significant multireligiosity or multiconfessionality that characterized Crimea for most of its history; along with Chersonesus, it represented Orthodoxy while Roman Catholicism had been introduced to the peninsula by the Italian territories and Islam by the Horde. As already mentioned, Jews had lived in Crimea before Khazar rule; there is evidence of their existence in the peninsula since the first century AD.[10]

It is not easy to establish the principality's political status and role within the extremely complex power relations between the Horde and the Italian colonies (foremost Genoa): firstly, little is known about the situation inland in the fourteenth and fifteenth centuries,[11] and secondly, there is a significant discrepancy between Genoa's claims to Theodoro and its ability to assert them: in the course of the fourteenth century, the prevailing stance within the Genoese administration in Caffa was that the principality was a vassal, but in practice Caffa lacked the real power to enforce such relations. For their part, the princes of Theodoro had been able to liberate themselves from their former dependence on the Empire of Trebizond in circumstances that remain "veiled in obscurity", as Vasil'ev put it.[12] And Caffa evidently sought to fill this 'gap'. The principality itself was certainly independent in the years prior to the fall of Constantinople; for instance, it maintained very intensive foreign relations with "other small and medium-sized powers in the Black Sea region" such as Bulgaria, Serbia, Moldavia or Walachia.[13] These alliances were reinforced not least by an active and successful marriage policy.[14] Certainly, in the first half of the fifteenth century, Theodoro developed into a third power centre in the peninsula – along with Genoa and the emergent Crimean Khanate, to which we will return later.[15] The rise of the principality, which is all the more remarkable given the vast depopulation only a few decades earlier (and which Exarch Matthew depicted so vividly), was largely associated with Prince Alexios I (presumably 1403–44, 1445 or 1447', who is assumed to be a member of the Gabrades (Gabras) aristocratic dynasty originating from the Empire of Trebizond. Conflicts with the Genoese were thus more frequent than those with the Muslim actors in the peninsula. A constant point of conflict was Cembalo, today's Balaklava, which had belonged to Theodoro until 1345 and which Alexios now sought to retake from Caffa – along with the other coastal stretches that had formerly been part of the principality.[16] Although Genoa paid Theodoro considerable sums in compensation, it was not enough to satisfy Alexios. In the periods 1422–4 and 1433–41 there was armed conflict between the two parties. The Genoese feared what they saw as an exceptionally persistent, "insolent Alexis", as Vasil'ev cites sources from Caffa.[17] Success in these conflicts essentially swung back and forth, both sides gaining and losing the upper hand. Alexios's policy was certainly to gain a share of the lucrative Black Sea trade. In 1427, he made considerable progress towards this goal: he had a new fortress built in the Chersonesus Peninsula, on the territory of today's Inkerman, using the foundation walls of a strategically well-located but razed Byzantine fortress from the eighth/ninth century. He named it Kalamita. Henceforth, it shielded the nearby port of Avlita, which would be the only one in the principality. The decision-makers in Caffa must have considered it serious competition; they repeatedly launched attacks on Avlita and its inhabitants.

Despite the existence of Avlita, taking Caffa itself – the undisputed centre of trade in Crimea – remained Theodoro's top priority.[18] Alexios used Genoa's conflicts with other powers (including the Principality of Moldavia and Trebizond),[19] foremost with its number-one enemy, Venice, to enter into an alliance with the latter.[20] The conflict that had raged since 1433 ended in 1441, having been fought out by the two Italian antagonists in two theatres, at home and on the Black Sea. Yet there was no real victor, at least not in Crimea: although the Principality of Theodoro lost Cembalo, for instance, it was able to hold out on other sections of the coastline, including in Avlita, which had become an essential post. Genoa's economic situation deteriorated, however, even though it continued to assert itself in the region for several decades.[21] Nevertheless, both Theodoro's and the Genoese colonies' days were numbered; new players appeared on the scene.

13

The Crimean Khanate:

The Beginnings

The lineage of the Tatar Khans and princes from the ancient dynasty of Genghis is indisputable; the other Khans are descended from the first Khan Lokhgon [...]. In the peninsula he found Greek princes living in Mankop and Ingermen, and Genoise ones in Iamboli and Capha, as well as other tribes inhabiting these places, with whom the Khan's successors continuously and persistently maintained peace treaties and friendship, and even had a joint mint, which I have seen, before they were all conquered by the weapon of the Turk. The Turkish Sultan Selim, having conquered this people, and having occupied fortresses and almost all the cities in the peninsula, subdued Khan Mehmet-Girey to his power. [...] Ever since the Khans have recognized the Turk's suzerainty.[1]

This brief passage is from one of the first surviving extensive travel reports on Crimea from the age of Humanism. It was written in 1579 by Marcin Broniewski (sometimes spelt Broniowski), a diplomat in the service of the Polish king Stephan Bátory (Hungarian: Báthory István; Lithuanian: Steponas Batoras; 1533–86). Broniewski is thought to have died in 1593. Written in Latin, the report is based on his ambassadorial missions representing Bátory to the Crimean Khanate in 1578 and 1579. The work first appeared in Cologne in 1595, under the author's Latin name: Martinus Bronovius de Biezdzfedea.[2] True to the Humanist didactic ideals then widespread among the European elites, the author intended to demonstrate to the king his scholarliness and eloquence; for Albrecht, whose German translation of 2011 remains the only scholarly rendering, he did not succeed in the latter aim, "[for] despite the linguistic zeal he displayed in his 'Descriptio', it cannot be claimed that he [Broniewski] wrote beautiful Latin".[3] Nevertheless, his report is of great importance to historians and archaeologists working on Crimea, since it provides one of the few descriptions of the Khanate in the sixteenth century, its topography and above all the manners, customs and faith of its inhabitants and the military tactics they employed in armed conflicts.[4] Indeed, it is no exaggeration to regard this report as an attempt to gain a better understanding of an enemy that over time repeatedly proved dangerous to the Polish-Lithuanian Commonwealth; in today's terms, one may certainly speak of 'intelligence' or 'espionage'.

The cited passage contains a host of highly relevant information – including on the origin and legitimation of the Crimean khans, power relations prior to the establishment of the Khanate and the subsequent transition to a dependence on the Ottoman Empire, to which we will later return in greater detail: as Broniewski puts it fittingly, all the khans, including those long after Broniewski was writing, legitimized their rule via their (at least proclaimed) descent from Činggis Qaγan, the first grand khan of the Mongols. This legitimizing 'ruse' was ultimately impossible to prove, but it emphasized the pretenders' desire. The Crimean khans were by no means the only ones to justify their claims to power via recourse to old, famous and/or particularly glorious forebears.[5] The Polish emissary certainly mentioned other dominions and peoples living in Crimea at the same time as the "Khan Lokhtonus": the Principality of Theodoro, which included "Mancopia" – that is, Mangup/Theodoro/Doros – and "Ingermen" (Inkerman/Kalamita); the Italians living in "Capha" (i.e. Caffa) and elsewhere "and, further, the other peoples in the peninsula". According to Albrecht, Broniewski's "Khan Lochtonus" was Toktamış,[6] described in detail in our previous chapter. Broniewski also mentions the Crimean khans' recognition of "the Turks' suzerainty" (= that of the Ottomans), which took place in 1478. All in all, he thus succeeded in providing a very precise depiction of the political events in Crimea between the late fourteenth and the late fifteenth centuries. The only detail that does not correspond to today's knowledge of the situation is his claim that Lokhtonus/Toktamış was "the first ruler in Tauris, or of Chersonesus in Tauris, or the peninsula".[7]

The first 'real' ruler of a Khanate that was independent from the Golden Horde is considered to be Hacı I Giray (*c.* 1397–1466), whose origins are as unknown as those of the Crimean Tatar ethnos as a whole.[8] It is assumed that he was born in Lida, then part of the Grand Duchy of Lithuania.[9] There has been some controversy about whether he was actually the grandson of Taş Timur – the dates for whose life cannot be established but who was certainly khan of the Golden Horde between 1395 and 1396 and laid decisive foundations for the later development of a Crimean entity independent from the Horde[10] – or whether he was even related to Toktamış. This was discussed extensively, for instance by important nineteenth-century Orientalists such as Vasilii D. Smirnov (1846–1922).[11] Hacı was certainly a member of the group known as the Lipka Tatars, between 10,000 and 15,000 of whom still live in the former territories of Poland-Lithuania. The first Tatars arrived in the Grand Duchy as religious refugees in the late thirteenth and early fourteenth century, refusing to accept Islam over their shamanic beliefs. Later, in the late fourteenth century, during the reign of

Grand Prince Vytautas, an ally of Khan Toktamış, Tatars settled in Lithuania for various reasons:[12] they went there voluntarily, by invitation of the grand prince, or were taken north as prisoners in the course of the Crimean campaign against Emir Edigü and Timur (cf. Chapter 3). There were also some, however, who voluntarily went into exile in Lithuania as a result of the upheavals in Crimea resulting from the fighting.

The obvious question as to how a Tatar (presumably) born in the Grand Duchy of Lithuania could become the founder of what would prove to be the longest-existing successor state to the Golden Horde is, like so much of the early history of the Khanate, unclear. Most scholars subscribe to the version put forward by Smirnov in the late nineteenth century.[13] Using a variety of sources, some of which are no longer available today, the Orientalist writes that in 1443 "the Tatars of Perekop, Barin and Shirin, whose tsar ['tsar'] had died without an heir, expressed to Casimir, the grand duke of Lithuania, the wish that he give them as ruler Hadzhi-Gerai who, having escaped the Horde, was now living in Lithuania".[14] And this wish was fulfilled, if we accept the Crimean Tatar version of this calling, a topos that is widespread in history in general.[15] This time, Hacı was able to establish a khanate that was independent from Sarai, unlike some years earlier: he had first held power in Eski Qırım and played a considerable role in the conflict between the Principality of Theodoro and Genoa (cf. Chapter 12), presumably between 1428 and 1434. According to Vasil'ev, he is supposed to have encouraged the prince of Theodoro, Alexios I, also an ally, to join the fight against Genoa for the coast around Balaklava/Cembalo.[16]

Although this first attempt failed, in the 1440s Hacı was evidently able to develop an effective strategy that would sustain his rule for almost forty years. According to Williams, he established a state "based on Mongol steppe traditions".[17] There were several levels to these "traditions": it was partly symbolic, but it also tied in with domestic and foreign policy. On the symbolic level, adopting the title the Horde had introduced for rulers of the Mongolian nomadic riders of Central and Middle Asia – Khan – was a claim not only to power but also to the direct lineage of Činggis Qayan. His own coin with his own crest, known as a tangha and based on that of the khans of the Golden Horde,[18] also underlined continuity and legitimacy. While the act of transferring the capital from Eski Qırım to Qırq Yer (today's Čufut-Kale) in southwestern Crimea might appear to contradict this policy, this was not the case: it was there that the Palace of Bağçasaray was later built, establishing the Khanate's symbolic and administrative centre, where even during the Russian era the peninsula's 'Muslim heart' continued to beat. What motivated Hacı to move the old power centre was his desire to at least partially evade the influence of the established local elites so that he could do as he pleased.[19] At the same time, it was part of the logic of old steppe traditions that every khan had to secure the loyalty of these elites, which the new ruler evidently managed to do. As Alan Fisher describes Hacı's strategy, "[his] first step was to see as many allies as he could".[20]

On the domestic front, he and his successors had to strike a compromise with the representatives of the influential clans – that is, members of the nobility, or *mirza*s (to use the Crimean Tatar term, derived from Persian). These four families or, as Mária Ivanics, for instance, calls them,[21] tribes, who had only recently installed Hacı as khan, were the Barın und Şirin, whom we have already encountered in Smirnov, and the Argın and Kıpçak.[22] Besides maintaining good relations with these *karaçı bey*s, every khan also had to pursue a skilful foreign policy – and, as was usually the case in the northern Black Sea region, this primarily meant a flexible one. As long as the Golden Horde still existed and the young Crimean Khanate had yet to be recognized as its actual successor,[23] Muscovy had been a welcome partner for the rulers in the peninsula. Later, there had been phases when the khans sided with Poland-Lithuania, particularly whenever the East Central European conglomerate state came into conflict with Moscow. Broniewski's visit to Bağçasaray served to forge an alliance between the Khanate and the Rzeczpospolita (Poland-Lithuania).

In the course of the fifteenth century, the Golden Horde had collapsed into several independent khanates; the Crimean Khanate established in the south by Hacı Giray was just one of them. There were also the Khanates of Kazan' and Astrakhan' on the Volga, the Khanate of Sibir' in the east, the White Horde in today's Kazakhstan and the Nogai Horde. It can be stated that the Crimean Khanate was indeed the successor to the Golden Horde, particularly given that it existed for over 300 years, well into the eighteenth century, although this claim cannot be made without some qualification. There is no disputing that it was not until 1502, with the final defeat of the Golden Horde by Hacı's successor Mengli I Giray (1445–1515) and the murder of its last ruler, Shaykh Ahmad, three years later[24] that the rise of the Crimean Khanate was really secured. The Orientialist István Vásáry stresses that it was only then that it was possible "to absorb [. . .] and maintain [. . .] all the Genghisid claims and the heritage of the Golden and the Great Hordes for more than three hundred years".[25] This proved attainable in the long term because other serious contenders, such as the Khanates of Astrakhan' or Kazan' (1556 or 1552), lost their independence much earlier[26] – to Muscovy, which was collecting the Horde's lands and to a certain extent can also be termed its successor. During Hacı I Giray's reign, however, the Khanate's existence as an independent entity had yet to be secured. Incidentally, its territory stretched beyond the peninsula, encompassing the southern steppe regions of today's Ukraine, the northern shore of the Sea of Azov and Kuban.

But the khan was not the only ruler in the peninsula; other powers remained: the Principality of Theodoro, with which the Crimean Khanate had cooperated in the past (cf. Chapter 12), and the Genoese colonies, foremost Caffa, where a significant number of the population were now Muslims, however.[27] The khan had no power in these areas, and in large parts of the north his influence was only limited or his power repeatedly questioned; this region was inhabited by (semi-)nomadic groups who were reluctant to be part of administrative and subaltern structures. These groups included the Nogai Tatars, who had been moving westward since the fifteenth century and would repeatedly challenge the khans over the centuries that followed. In 1454, Khan Hacı found an ally that was particularly interested in helping him gain hold of the lucrative Black Sea trade centred in Caffa: the Ottoman Empire, which had taken Constantinople the previous year after several failed attempts since 1349.[28] This marked the start of a special relationship between the Khanate and the Sublime Porte. Broniewski claims that as a result of this, in 1478 "the Turkish emperor [. . .] [subjugated] the Khan [. . .] to his rule"; whether this was really the case will be examined in the next chapter.

14

The Establishment of the Crimean Khanate

Krim (the Crimea)

This territory is governed by a Khan, who has the privilege of coining, and of having the Khotba read in the mosques, his name being mentioned immediately after that of the Osmanli Emperor, who has the right of appointing and changing the Khans. The residence of the Khan is at Baghcheserai, and that of the Sultan at Ak-mesjid. The subordinate officers are styled Shirin-begs and Masur-begs.[1]

Evliyâ Çelebi (Mehmed Zilli; 1611–82 or 1683), an Ottoman "Quran reciter and prayer leader, musician, poet and prince's companion, courtier, administrative official and envoy",[2] visited the Crimean Khanate in 1641 and 1665/1666. As with his many other journeys, he wrote a report or "travel book" (Ottoman Turkish: *Seyâhatnâme*). This report still awaits complete translation into a Western language,[3] despite the fact that it was included in UNESCO's Memory of the World Register in 2013.[4] When Evliyâ Çelebi visited and wrote about Crimea, the peninsula had already had a peculiar relationship with the Ottoman Empire for over 150 years. In the literature, this relationship is frequently referred to as "vassalage".[5] Even if we assume that this subordination underwent changes during the 300 years it existed and may not have been static by any means,[6] Evliyâ's lines suggest that the khan enjoyed a privileged relationship with the sultan: he writes that the khan ruling in Crimea had the right to mint his own coins. Additionally, in the Friday prayer (*Khotba, Khutbah, khuṭbah*), an especially important element of Islam, the khan's name was mentioned immediately after the sultan's. However, the latter had "the right of appointing and changing the Khans". Moreover, we also learn from Evliyâ that there were both Crimean Tatar and Ottoman royal seats in Crimea (Bağçasaray and "Ak-mesjid" respectively, the latter being Crimean Tatar Aqmescit, today's Simferopol'). This would suggest that while the Sublime Porte had a heavy presence as a factor of power in Crimea, there was also a Crimean Tatar capital. Finally, the abovementioned Şirin and Mansur dynasties are mentioned; according to Evliyâ, they provided the subordinate military men.

Overall, Evliyâ paints a very accurate picture of the power relations between the khan and the sultan in Crimea: both the khan's right to mint his own coin and his being mentioned immediately after the sultan in prayer clearly indicate that this was no normal vassal status. It is beyond doubt that the sultan in Istanbul had the right to appoint and remove the Crimean khan, who was always from the Giray dynasty, and that he increasingly made use of this right from the seventeenth century on[7] – demonstrating that although there were phases that gave the impression of greater independence from the Sublime Porte, the Crimean Khanate found itself in a relationship of suzerainty. The only thing Evliyâ got wrong was his assessment of the subordinate role played by the Şirin and Mansur clans, since they certainly had great influence over the fate of the Khanate. But before we examine the undoubtedly special Ottoman–Crimean Tatar relationship that existed over the years and its various aspects, we must first consider the circumstances in which it was initially established; it is only fair to ask why "the Khanate, only liberated from the Golden Horde for a few years", gave up the "freedom it had achieved for a new relationship of dependence".[8]

Once again, the Genoese outpost of Caffa played a key role in trade on the Black Sea: during his first reign, Hacı had received tribute from the city, which he considered merely a first step towards taking possession of it, however. Caffa was already under pressure for a number of reasons, which limited its room for manoeuvre against the khan: its position as an intermediary between Asia and North Africa, which had hitherto been so lucrative, had been in decline since the 1420s. As a result, it was no longer possible to satisfy the Mamluk Empire's increased demands for slaves from the Black Sea region. To an extent, the shortage of slaves was a problem of the Genoese's own making, partly because new rules for human 'cargo' comprising these 'goods' had been introduced in Genoa itself following controversial debates on the slave trade. For instance, from 1448 on a law in Caffa demanded that slaves that had run away from Muslim owners had to be freed and not simply sold on. Those who had fled from Christian masters and sought sanctuary in the territories of the bishop of Caffa could not be returned to the 'market'; they now had to be baptized and their freedom had to be bought.[9]

A further problem besetting Caffa was that the conflicts with the Horde or the Khanate, the Principality of Theodoro and the Venetians dragged on.[10] Ultimately, the fall of Constantinople, where, incidentally, the Genoese and Venetian inhabitants of the Christian Pera district had been some of the staunchest defenders of Byzantium,[11] fundamentally changed not only the situation on the southern shore of the Black Sea but also, indirectly, in the peninsula itself. New alliances were formed in Crimea: Caffa was able to extricate itself from a first joint military assault and siege by the Ottomans and the Crimean Tatars – the former from the sea, the latter with their already notorious cavalry[12] – by agreeing to pay a higher tribute to the khan. Formally, Caffa's administration, spooked by the events in Constantinople, had sold the city in November 1453 – to a private company, the Banco di S. Giorgio, which had been something of "a veritable State within a State" inside its walls for decades.[13] As it would prove, the days of the once so mighty Genoese Caffa were numbered.

Originally, the Crimean khan Hacı I Giray had certainly not intended the Khanate's joint venture with the Ottoman Empire under Sultan Mehmed II ("the Conqueror"; 1432–81). However, following Hacı's death (presumably by poisoning) in 1466, the alliance was reinforced under his successors. The Ottoman Empire, having risen "from the status of a regional player to the rank of a great power",[14] was beginning to make its presence felt in the region. It soon developed economic, strategic and religious-ideological ambitions to gain influence not only in Crimea but along the entire northern coast of the Black Sea.

It is possible that the Ottomans also felt the Muslim Khanate would be a particularly reliable supporter in the so-called Turkish Wars against their Christian enemies, the first of which was the campaign against Venice from 1463 to 1479; the Khanate's geographical location alone made it a kind of buffer between the Ottomans' opponents: the Polish-Lithuanian Commonwealth and Muscovy. After the death of Hacı, the fight to succeed him also played into Istanbul's hands; the Sublime Porte was able to exploit the conflict for the throne between his first-born son, Nur Devlet (?–1503), and his sixth, Mengli (1445–1515). A few months after their father's death, Mengli drove out the reigning Nur Devlet, only to be deposed himself, repeatedly, by his older brother. Mengli's khanships (1466, 1469–75, 1478–1515) showed clear signs of the clans' influence that would be so important in later periods too: in 1468, Mengli was able to gain control over parts of the peninsula with the assistance of the Şirin and the governor Mamak and with the additional help of the Genoese city of Caffa. A few years later, however, the Şirin, under their new leader Eminek (Russian also: Imenek; from 1473 on *karaçı bey*/leader of the Şirin) successfully rebelled against him, contributing to the end of his second reign in 1475; he sought and was soon granted exile by his allies in Caffa. Alan Fisher assumes that the reason for the Şirin's change of heart was Mengli's attempts to reduce the clans' influence in the long term.[15] But nor were the Şirin happy with the policies of the new-old khan Nur Devlet, whom they repeatedly reinstalled; he cooperated closely with the Genoese. They soon curried favour with Sultan Mehmed II in Istanbul, requesting his military intervention in Caffa, just to rob Nur Devlet of an ally.[16] Since the Sublime Porte's was already aiming to take control of the northern Black Sea coast, they attacked Caffa in May 1475. After a siege lasting many days, the once so mighty Genoese colony capitulated.

Mengli, still in exile in Caffa, was taken to Istanbul, where he was long held captive. It appears it was there that he decided to regain power over Crimea by pursuing a flexible policy of alliances and involving a strong partner. He thus promised the Ottomans he would transfer to them suzerainty over the Khanate, suzerainty "whose character and legality was not easily determined, however"[17] – an aspect to which we shall return. Mengli's strategy certainly proved a success: in early 1478, the Ottomans installed him as the Crimean khan. He was unable to rule over the entire peninsula, however; the Sublime Porte had mainly secured for itself the coastal areas of strategic and economic importance, above all Caffa, which they thenceforth called Kefe.

The sustained ties between the Ottomans and the Crimean Tatars cannot be attributed solely to Mengli's desire to be reinstalled as khan – this time permanently – with the help of the former. Rather, there were several reasons for this alliance: geopolitical and strategic circumstances favoured collaboration between Istanbul and Bağçasaray, and there were also financial motives for the khans and the upper strata of Crimean Tatar society. There was also common ground when it came to political and religious ideologies "based on historical and legendary traditions", as Alan Fisher observes.[18] The fact that the Ottomans fundamentally derived their legitimacy from the fact that they were (Sunni) Muslims[19] certainly facilitated an alliance with the Crimean Tatars, who were Sunni themselves. Particularly under Süleyman I ("the Magnificent" or "the Lawgiver"; 1494, 1495 or 1496–1566) religion became more significant as an element legitimizing Ottoman rule: a newly formed law school was dedicated primarily to the relationship between the sultan, the Ottoman dynasty and Sunni Islam, also serving to establish its legislation.[20] Even if not all Ottoman sultans placed equal emphasis on their function as caliphs[21] – that is, as defenders of Islam and the *ummah*,[22] the Muslim community – the religious proximity between Crimea and the Porte strengthened their ties in the long term. This went along with cultural similarities such as their related language and ethnicity.[23] The title "Ruler of the Kipchak Steppe" (*Padişah-ı Deşt-i Kıpçak*), also held by the sultan, was further used to create a connection with the Mongols and Činggis Qayan,[24] which was a source of legitimacy for the Girays themselves.

In this phase of the power struggle between the two Giray brothers Nur Devlet and Mengli, which is difficult to describe with historiographical precision, the familiar actors were joined by new ones who would also have a sustained impact on relations in the region in the early modern period. As we have seen, the rise of the Ottoman Empire was highly significant. However, the Golden Horde could not be entirely written off; in 1476, for instance, it attempted to regain control of the peninsula via military intervention. But its zenith had passed, which in turn aided the rise of Muscovy. While the Grand Duchy was formally obliged to pay tribute to the Horde, it had distinguished itself in several conflicts with the Mongols. It should be noted that in their opposition to the Horde, Moscow and the

Khanate had shared common interests, which explains their cooperation in the subsequent decades.²⁵ It was not so much a case of "the enemy of my enemy is my friend" as of "the enemy of my friend is my enemy"; the Crimean Khanate remained opposed to the Polish-Lithuanian state: with the rise of Muscovy, competition with the Grand Duchy of Lithuania had developed for primacy in the lands of Kyivan Rus', which had long since fragmented into appanage principalities.²⁶ The Union of Krewo of 1385, which established the Polish-Lithuanian Union and marked the beginnings of the Christianization of the hitherto pagan Lithuanian population, only tempered the conflicts between Lithuania and Moscow in the short term. Overall, Poland-Lithuania's power grew – as did its engagement in Crimea. As we have already seen (cf. Chapter 12), Lithuania had already exerted its influence on the fate of the peninsula in the fourteenth century; for instance, an alliance between the Grand Duchy and the Golden Horde in 1398 had been able to retake parts of Crimea from the hands of the Timurids. At any rate, relations between the Crimean Khanate and the Polish-Lithuanian state would not improve until the sixteenth century; Broniewski's visit to Crimea (cf. the introduction to Chapter 13) can be interpreted as a measure intended to build trust.

A good century before the Polish diplomat's journey to the peninsula, a further player had made itself felt: the Principality of Moldova, which itself had been under the suzerainty of the Polish crown since 1387.²⁷ The principality also bordered the Black Sea until 1484, when it lost important trading cities such as Kiliia (Ukrainian/Russian; Romanian: Chilia [Nouă]) and Akkerman and with them its access to the waves. Ştefan III cel Mare ("Stephen the Great"; *c.* 1433–1504), probably Moldavia's most important prince, also formulated his political agendas independent of Poland or the Ottoman Empire,²⁸ to which Moldavia paid tribute from the early 1450s on,²⁹ and these strategies also related to Crimea, or, more specifically, the still existent Crimean Gothia/Mangup, where he was able to influence politics via his dynastically motivated marriage to Maria, the daughter of the prince of Theodoro.³⁰ With his help, one of Maria's brothers, Alexander, was able to dethrone the rightful heir, Isaac. Alexander became the last ruler of Crimean Gothia, since Ştefan III was unable to realize his plan to prevent Ottoman dominance on the Black Sea via the formation of a kind of Christian alliance.³¹

Fear of the Ottomans – or the Turks, as they were often referred to inaccurately³² – played a central role in the history of the so-called Occident.³³ "Fear of the Turk", as a potent cultural-historical and political topos was repeatedly portrayed from a variety of perspectives.³⁴ For instance, the fall of Constantinople in 1453 received enormous attention from the 'European public' (to use another term that is not quite apt for the fifteenth century). Several contemporary authors have considered this event too, and here too they tend to exaggerate the cruelty of the (religious and cultural) 'Other' – in this case the Muslim 'Turks'.³⁵ The fall of Crimean Gothia in late 1475 after it was besieged by Ottoman troops for six months has also found resonance in contemporary studies of various provenance,[36] albeit not to the same extent as the events of 1453. Nineteenth-century German authors obsessed with the Goths also wrote about the demise of Mangup, although some of them subjected the sources to critical examination: the linguist and independent scholar Richard Löwe (1863–after 1931) was one of them.[37] In his work *Die Reste der Germanen am Schwarzen Meer* (The Remains of the Germanic Peoples on the Black Sea), he produced a nuanced assessment of the report of a "German contemporary who had spent three years living in Turkey [sic]": the gunsmith Jörg von Nürnbergk.[38] Nürnbergk had written a *Geschichte von der Türkey* (History of Turkey), which was published in Memmingen in 1496. The gunsmith depicted the siege by the Ottomans and the events following the city's capture thus:

> Thereafter he [the 'Turk'] set out for a city by the name of Sandtodero [Theodoro], where there were three kings and XV thousand people young and old, he was unable to win and had to leave with losses. Thereafter, after three months they surrendered voluntarily. He [the 'Turk'] killed the kings and all the people.[39]

Above all, Löwe considered the author's claim that Theodoro had a population of 15,000 to be a gross exaggeration. We can only speculate as to why Jörg von Nürnbergk assumed Mangup to have been so populous: perhaps it was a stylistic device to enhance the drama, for his readership may have found the case of a city of 15,000, then a relatively large population, and the murder of its ruler and every single inhabitant particularly disturbing.[40] Researchers disagree on the fate of the ruling family, incidentally; it is not entirely clear whether they died in Mangup, as Jörg von Nürnbergk reported, or whether they were killed only once they had been taken to Istanbul. What is certainly less plausible is the assumption that the entire population of Mangup was wiped out by the Ottoman troops. It was both more pragmatic and more common for the latter to enslave their captives; slaves were, after all, in great demand in the region. Another reason to doubt the claim is that inscriptions from the time of the city's fall point to the continued existence of Christian institutions – and hence the existence of a Christian population – in Crimean Gothia. Experts are also unanimous in their assumption that after taking over the former principality of Theodoro in 1475, the Ottoman Empire did not suppress Christianity.[41] Rather, the Sublime Porte practised a form of pragmatic tolerance of the religions of the book – Judaism and Christianity – that was based on the millet system with its roots in Islamic law and made a fundamental distinction between the religious "Other" and Muslim or Jewish communities in Western and Central Europe at the time.[42]

Generally speaking, however, non-Muslim monotheistic religions experienced fluctuating privileges and restrictions that changed with the times in both the Ottoman Empire and the Crimean Khanate: according to the Orientalist Matuz, Jews and Christians lived "in favourable circumstances, although [...] additional, but not particularly onerous taxes had to be paid".[43] Ultimately, we do not know what the plan was, in contrast, incidentally, to our knowledge of the Russian Orthodox Church in bordering Muscovy, which pursued a very rigid policy of forcibly Christianizing the Muslim population after the conquest of the Khanates of Kazan' and Astrakhan' in the mid-sixteenth century and in subsequent phases.[44]

Nineteenth-century Russian-speaking authors nevertheless frequently attempted to justify the annexation of Crimea by the tsarist empire in 1783 by arguing that the Christian population had been fundamentally oppressed under the Crimean khans and hence it had virtually been the tsarist empire's duty to 'retake' old Christian soil and 'save' the remaining Christians.[45] But here too, the exception proves the rule: for instance, the scholar Feoktist Khartakhai (1836–80), descended from an old Crimean Greek – that is, Orthodox – family disputed this view in a study published in 1867, emphasizing the close ties between Muslims and Christians. He argued that Hacı I Giray, the first khan, had maintained friendly relations with the Christians in Crimea and that his son Mengli had even been raised by the Christian inhabitants of Caffa for eight years, and hence there could be no talk of the persecution or oppression of Christians in the Crimean Khanate. Khartakhai accused his Russian compatriots of conflating the free Christian inhabitants of Crimea with the Christian slaves that had also existed in the peninsula.[46] Here, he was probably alluding primarily to the temporary alliances between Christian and Muslim actors in Crimea from the fifteenth century on. The development of common Christian and Muslim lifeworlds was only of secondary interest to him. Khartakhai's positive assessment of the first Crimean khans may have been influenced by the fact that they had maintained very good relations with Muscovy. Nevertheless, as demonstrated time and again in the peninsula from Antiquity onwards, it was possible to overcome religious and cultural differences whenever it was of practical or strategic benefit to the parties involved.

15

The Crimean Khanate:

Ottoman Suzerainty and the Balance of Power in Eastern Europe

I now wish to tell you a little bit about the Khan's power and way of governing [. . .]. According to treaties into which the Khans entered with the Porte long ago, the latter has the prerogative to appoint the former, and grants the honour of confirming him to the Tartar [sic] nobility, who then seldom object to their new Khan out of fear of displeasing [the sultan]. But if the Turkish court wants extraordinary assistance from the Tartar nation during a war, the latter occasionally grants to the nobility the honour of electing their prince, and confirms him.[1]

These lines were written by the Habsburg subject Nikolaus Ernst Kleemann (1736–presumably after 1800).[2] According to this merchant's travel report, first published in Vienna in 1771, he travelled to the Black Sea between 1768 and 1770, also visiting Crimea. He was even granted an audience with one of the last of the Crimean khans, Qırım Giray, who reigned from 1758 to 1764 and from 1768 to 1769. And he clearly made an impression on the mercantile traveller, since Kleemann wrote, "This land is said to have never had a leader greater, cleverer or more loved by his nation than the Crimean Gerey Khan, with whom I spoke myself." He praised his "intellect, his mind, his skill and experience in war".[3]

We have already referred to the complex relationship between Istanbul and Bağçasaray, which the Hungarian early modern historian Sándor Papp quite rightly calls one "of the big themes of research on the Crimean Khanate".[4] In the following, we will take a closer look at the specific form taken by ties between the Ottomans and the Crimean Tatars. According to Kleemann, there was a kind of triangular relationship between the sultan, who had the right to appoint the khan, the khan himself and the *mirza*s, the Tatar nobility. The khan, we are told, granted unto the nobility the right to confirm him. The nobility clearly appreciated this arrangement, at least in the Habsburg subject's assessment, and sought to maintain good relations with Bağçasaray. A renowned central element of the relationship between Istanbul and the Khanate was the latter's duty to lend support in the case of war or campaigns to conquer territories, also mentioned by Kleemann.[5] Occasionally, it would seem there were situations ("if the Turkish court wants extraordinary assistance from the Tartar [sic] nation during a war") in which the sultan would forego his right to appoint the khan in order to secure the support of the *mirza*s. In such cases, he usually left it to the nobility to choose the new khan. Unlike Broniewski around 150 years earlier, Kleeman apparently didn't know that every khan was necessarily a Giray and descended from Činggis Qaγan. He nevertheless noted that relations between the Sublime Porte, the khans and the *mirza*s were not always free of tension.

In multiethnic empires such as that of the Ottomans, there were usually a number of different legal relations between the metropolises,[6] in this case Istanbul, and the so-called peripheries.[7] The Crimean Khanate enjoyed "a privileged position in comparison with other parts of the empire".[8] While there were no significant changes over the years on the symbolic level outlined above, there were certainly some on the level of actual politics: over a century after the Khanate had become dependent on the Sublime Porte in 1478, as a rule the sultan approved the khan proposed by the *mirza*s, although he retained a veto. However, according to Papp, who has studied the Crimean khans' inauguration process, there was a caesura between 1608 and 1628.[9] During this period, the Ottoman rulers' influence grew, and they were able to appoint or remove the presumptive khan directly. Every candidate now had to collect his certificate of appointment from the Sublime Porte in person – that is, he had to travel to Istanbul and appear before the sultan. On the one hand, this procedure was supposed to have underpinned a special loyalty,[10] but on the other hand it can also be interpreted as a gesture of subordination; the lower-ranking partner had to request his inauguration from the higher-ranking sultan. However we choose to see it, in the course of the seventeenth century Istanbul's influence grew to the extent that it had a considerable say in the Khanate's internal affairs,[11] as noted by the Ottoman observer Evliyâ Çelebi (cf. Chapter 14) during his journey to Crimea.[12]

The very first Crimean khans – Hacı I, Nur Devlet and Mengli I Giray – had not been able to rule without interruption, although this was not due to interference by the Sublime Porte but was a result of conflicts within Crimea itself. However, from the seventeenth century on, the sultans regularly used their right to install or remove a khan in order to "keep their own but not always obedient vassal in check".[13] Occasionally, however, the sultan's word was not enough to secure Istanbul's interests, and military intervention had to be used against the Crimean rulers.¹⁴ As Kleemann alluded to in his description of the power constellation in the peninsula, Istanbul also made use of the power held by the *mirza*s. In particular, clans such as the Barın and Şirin were able to help depose a ruler in Bağçasaray who had fallen out of favour due to stubbornness or for other reasons. Sometimes the Sublime Porte even offered financial rewards to secure acceptance for a ruler's removal.¹⁵ Matuz reports that a hostage policy was another measure employed to shape political developments in Crimea: relatives of the Girays were held captive in Istanbul's Topkapı Palace to lend weight to Ottoman demands; if necessary, there also the option of threatening to kill or maltreat these 'guests'.¹⁶ A side effect of this practice was that presumptive Crimean khans were educated along Ottoman lines during their stay in Istanbul.¹⁷

The particular regard in which the Khanate was held by the Ottomans – and later by the tsarist empire too (cf. Chapters 21 and 22) – was due in no small part to its military strength. The resulting obligation for Crimean Tatars to fight for the Ottomans had a whole series of side effects. One such side effect, which we shall examine in detail, is the image of the Crimean Tatars in a collective European memory oscillating between fear and admiration. Another side effect was of a financial nature; the khans and their warriors enjoyed specific economic advantages: not only were they exempt from paying tribute to the Ottoman Empire, but the rulers in Bağçasaray evidently received rather generous payments and rewards from Istanbul, not merely due to their esteemed descent from Činggis Qaγan but also due to the widely renowned skill of Crimean Tatar soldiers on the battlefield. No sultan wanted to or indeed could afford to do without such good fighters. Other rewards reinforcing ties between the peninsula and Istanbul were the transfer of extensive lands in other parts of the Ottoman Empires to the Crimean khans, a kind of annual pension or a form of bodyguard (the *sekban*).⁸ The provision of the *sekban* for the khan's protection proved to be a particularly well-thought-out measure, since it meant that Istanbul possessed armed forces in close proximity to the khan who were financially dependent on the sultan and hence would be loyal to him in the event of conflict or doubt. On the whole, compared with other parts of the Empire, the Crimean khans received generous funding from Istanbul.¹⁹ The Sublime Porte also considered the Khanate to be the true heir to the Golden Horde, for the khan could continue to raise the annual tributes (Polish: *upomniki*; Russian: *pominki*) that Muscovy and Poland-Lithuania had had to pay since the days of the Mongol Empire.

The deployment of Tatar auxiliary troops in alliance with the Sublime Porte vastly extended the Crimean Khanate's military range.²⁰ They were involved in Ottoman campaigns against Hungary or Persia, for instance, or in the First (1529) and Second Siege of Vienna (1683).²¹ For example, in a study of 1976 which meets scholarly standards while nevertheless using language marked by stereotypes of a cruelty peculiar to the 'Orientals', we read that the Crimean Tatar horsemen before Vienna adopted the practices of their ancestors from the European steppe: they are reported to have left a trail of devastation the likes of which Europeans had not witnessed since Batu Khan's invasion of Central Europe in the mid-thirteenth century.[22] What is beyond dispute is that during the Siege of Vienna in 1683, Crimean Tatars were among the perpetrators of acts of violence, here too against civilians.[23] Yet violence is inherent to military conflicts and cannot be seen as a quasi-primordial characteristic of certain cultures or groups of people. On the whole, it can be said that "Crimean Tatar involvement in the Turkish War of 1683–1699 [. . .] remains insufficiently researched".[24]

As a matter of principle, the Sublime Porte expected the Khanate to adapt its foreign policy to Istanbul's, or at least consult with it.[25] However, the khans frequently resisted, pursuing their own interests. For instance, the Khanate maintained more or less independent ties within the Ottoman Empire itself, such as with the Danubian Principalities of Moldavia and Walachia, which were virtually vassals of the sultan themselves, although they too had favoured autonomous status.[26] But the Crimean Khanate also repeatedly featured as an independent actor beyond the context of the Ottoman Empire, at times maintaining diplomatic relations with the kingdoms of Denmark and Sweden.[27] As a rule, the Khanate sent emissaries to the large European courts such as Vienna[28] and Moscow[29] or, from the late sixteenth century on, to rising powers such as Brandenburg-Prussia.[30] Apart from the above-mentioned interventions by the sultans and their resulting influence on the Khanate's domestic policy (see below), differences also emerged in the field of foreign policy – whenever the Crimean Tatars' range was to be restricted by Ottoman policy. This was mainly the case whenever the Ottomans advanced into the northern Black Sea region, which the Crimean Tatars saw as their very own sphere of influence; these were territories that had formerly belonged either directly or indirectly to the Horde. There was particularly frequent conflict whenever the Ottoman Empire set its sights on the Khanate's northern neighbours – that is, against Poland-Lithuania and Muscovy. For instance, after most of Polish-Lithuanian Podolia fell to the Ottomans during the Ottoman–Polish War of 1672–6, relations with the vassal in the peninsula deteriorated quickly: the Khanate no longer had access to an economically important region; it had long supplied Podolia with something for which there was heavy demand: slaves.[31] In the seventeenth and early eighteenth centuries, then, the Khanate made several attempts to break away from the Sublime Porte with the aim of freeing itself from the Ottoman Empire. These attempts remained unsuccessful, however.[32]

As early as the nineteenth century, the Russian Orientalist Smirnov recognized the 'rule' by which the rulers in Bağçasaray operated in the field of foreign policy concerning Poland-Lithuania and Muscovy: they preferred to support whoever was the weakest;[33] today we would call it a balance of power policy. That is, when Bağçasaray's considered the balance of power to be under threat, the result was sometimes disobedience towards the Sublime Porte. In 1569, under Devlet Giray (1512–77), the Khanate undertook what would prove an unsuccessful joint campaign with the Ottomans against the former Khanate of Astrakhan', which Muscovy had conquered in 1556. Since Devlet Giray, like his predecessors in the Palace of Bağçasaray, considered himself the sole legitimate heir to the Mongols, he had dedicated himself to the task of collecting the lands of the Golden Horde; his aim was to drive the Muscovite Tsardom out of the region, something he hoped to achieve with the Ottomans by his side. However, when the Ottomans began to build a canal in the steppe that would connect the Don and the Volga, which would have strengthened the sultan's influence over the areas to which the Crimean Tatars laid claim, the situation changed. Istanbul's medium-term plan was to transfer the Ottoman Black Sea Fleet to the Caspian Sea in the anticipation that building the canal would secure huge economic benefits.[34] When Devlet became aware of this, he withdrew with his troops "in the midst" of the military campaign against Astrakhan', somewhere on the Volga, writes Fisher.[35] This act of stubbornness alone would have earned him his place in the Crimean Tatar culture of remembrance, but it also immortalized him in the Russian collective memory, where he plays a negative role, however; he was responsible for the devastating looting of Moscow, in the wake of which the city was burnt down in May 1571. Nikolai M. Karamzin (1766–1826), the important Russian writer, linguistic reformer and official imperial historiographer at the tsar's court, described this event in his influential *Istoriia gosudarstva Rossiiskogo* (History of the Russian State; 1816–29) as follows:

> Devlet-Girey performed a great deed [*podvig*]: he did not wish to besiege the Kremlin, and from the Sparrow Hills he looked upon his triumph, heaps of smoking ash with a circumference of thirty versts, [and] he immediately decided to withdraw out of fear [. . .] of the inaccurate rumour that the Prince or the Great King was approaching with a great army. Ioann [= Ivan IV, "the Terrible"] in Rostov had received the news of the enemy's retreat and ordered Prince Vorotynskii to follow the Khan, who succeeded, however, in destroying the majority of Moscow's southeastern regions and taking more than 100,000 prisoners to Tauris. Not having the generosity to be his subjects' consoler in the moment of the terrible catastrophe, [and] afraid of having to see the scene of the terror and the tears, the Tsar did not wish to go to the burnt-down capital. [. . .] There was no one who could bury the dead. He [Ivan] ordered that Moscow be freed of the rotting corpses. [. . .] Only aristocrats and the rich were buried with the Christian rites. The bodies of the others filled the Moskva with the effect that the river could no longer flow. They lay in piles, poisoned the water and the air with their putrification; and the wells were dried out and without water. The remaining inhabitants perished of thirst. In the end, they sent for the people from the surrounding

cities; they pulled the corpses from the river and buried them. Thus the endless wrath of Heaven poured over Russia.[36]

Along with the criticism typical of Karamzin's work when it comes to Ivan IV (1530–84),[37] who lacked the grace to act as "his subjects' consoler in the moment of the terrible catastrophe",[38] these lines convey destruction of almost apocalyptic proportions: a city largely devastated by the Crimean Tatars in which only the Kremlin remained unscathed, everywhere corpses with no one to bury them. And those who survived had to enter into slavery in Tauris – that is, Crimea. All this Karamzin interpreted as divine punishment of the Russian lands.

The Crimean Tatar invasion of Muscovy in 1571 was neither the first nor the last of its kind, but it was probably the most devastating. Particularly in the sixteenth century and in the context of the fight for the legacy of the Golden Horde, Crimean Tatar troops repeatedly pushed north; exactly fifty years earlier, in the summer of 1521, there had been an unexpected campaign in which troops from Crimea had almost reached Moscow before retreating. Incidentally, this was connected to the Crimean Tatar attempts to prevent a permanent Muscovite presence on the Volga. Since 1521, the Crimean Khanate had repeatedly succeeded in placing Girays on the khan's throne in Kazan'. This had temporarily prevented Ivan III (1440–1505) from taking the Crimean Khanate, something the Crimean Tatars had achieved in alliance with the Khanate of Astrakhan' and the Nogai.[39] But their delight did not last long, since Ivan IV took Kazan' in 1552 – and this time he was able to secure it for his empire.

The above examples demonstrate that the Crimean Khanate was certainly able to assert itself against the Ottomans as an independent actor – and did just that. Finally, how, then, are the Crimean Khanate's position in the northern Black Sea region in the early modern period and its influence extending as far as Eastern and East Central Europe to be assessed? There is some disagreement among scholars; the Russian historian Ilya Zaytsev, for instance, considers the khans' power to have always been "a reflection of the power of the Ottoman padişah [sultan]".[40] This is correct insofar as a powerful sultan, as we have seen, found it easier than a weak one to hand power to individual pretenders to the throne from the Giray dynasty and to withdraw it. However, due to their proclaimed descent from Činggis Qaɣan and their shared faith, in the eyes of the Istanbul court the khans certainly also enjoyed a privileged position over other vassals.[41] One indication of this status is the fact that more than a few Girays occupied high positions of office there. That the Ottoman Empire saw other Crimean Tatars as primitive and backward, as Islamized barbarians "whose task", according to Zaystev, "was to protect the northern border of the Empire",[42] speaks at least for the esteem in which they were held in the field of warfare if not in the sphere of non-military culture. Further studies on the Ottoman elites' view of the Crimean Tatar lower strata would certainly be desirable.

For a long time, the relationship between the Crimean Khanate and the Ottoman Empire was rather one between allies than between vassal and feudal lord; the elites were obstinate and willing to implement both domestic (see below) and foreign policies independent from the Porte. Even if their room for manoeuvre decreased over time, Fisher's assessment of the Khanate is compelling: "The Crimean Tatar Khanate was one of the most important states in eastern Europe from the early sixteenth century until the end of the seventeenth century."[43]

16

Slavery and the Topos of the Crimean Tatar Warrior

> The Tatars usually wage war against the Poles, the inhabitants of Rus', Moscow, the Circassians, Moldavia and Hungary. Many of the prisoners they take from these people they turn into slaves. They know no other activity besides waging war.[1]

This description of the Crimean Tatars by a Dominican monk by the name of Jean de Luc was written in 1625. It is characterized by a certain timelessness, in that the idea that the Crimean Tatars "know no other activity besides waging war" and that the Crimean Khanate was a parasitic state living at the expense of its neighbours continued well into the twentieth century: "The principal activity of the Crimean Tatars was war and looting raids with the aim of plunder and profit",[2] explains the *Great Soviet Encyclopaedia* (*Bol'shaia Sovetskaia Ėntsiklopediia*, BSĖ) of 1953, for instance. It may be somewhat surprising to read this negative assessment of a nationality that had, after all, been granted limited special rights as an Autonomous Soviet Socialist Republic (ASSR) in the 1920s, but it can be explained by events during the Second World War. The Crimean Tatar population had been deported to Central Asia in May 1944 and the ASSR had been dissolved in 1945 because Stalin had placed them under collective suspicion of having collaborated with the National Socialist occupiers. Decisively, the Crimean Tatars found themselves without a lobby in the post-war USSR (cf. Chapter 34).

Another thing that becomes apparent from these quotations is that neither the monk de Luc nor the unnamed author of the *Great Soviet Encyclopaedia* entry on the Crimean Tatars were thinking of the Crimean Tatar women when they considered the nature of this group of people. A common thread in these and other descriptions is that "The ideal-typical Crimean Tatar was [...] male, had long been concerned more or less exclusively with war [and] was not fond of order and cleanliness."[3] Most authors from the north perceived the Crimean Tatars as warriors who owned at least one horse, of which every Tatar took greater care "than of himself", to cite de Luc once more.⁴ The Polish diplomat Broniewski went so far as to dedicate an entire section to the subject of the Tatars and horses, in which he expressed his admiration for the quality of these animals: "All [Crimean Tatars] use as they require Tatar horses, which are very good, strong, fast, of medium height and very comfortable and withstand all strain."⁵

There was a simple reason why non-Muslim authors long focused more on Crimean Tatar warriors than on Crimean Tatar peasants, for instance: for almost 300 years, contact between the Crimean Khanate (either in alliance with the Ottoman Empire or on its own) and their northern neighbours was largely of a warring nature, and this 'experience' had a sustained impact on the collective conscious of Poles, Russians and Ukrainians. Generally, and not only in connection with the Crimean Tatars, centuries of shifting Eastern Slavic–Muslim relations gave rise to a specific Russian image of the Muslim as a warrior.⁶ Since the Crimean Tatar army essentially consisted of cavalrymen, the topos of the mounted Crimean Tatars firmly took root. Broniewski vividly described this phenomenon with its inherent element of deception and cunning:

> Very many in the Tatar army are thoroughly un-warlike and unarmed, and due to the large army they take an almost endless number of horses into battle with them – for even a Tatar of the lowest [social] standing is not satisfied with one or two, indeed not three or four or more horses he can lead with one hand. Hence the Tatar army appears to be so large, giant and indeed fearsome, which – seen from afar – is considered by our people to be a fairly mighty and large and significant army.⁷

Not all contacts between the Crimean Khanate and Moscow or Poland-Lithuania were of a martial nature, however. Often, the khans also functioned as mediators between the Kremlin and the Sublime Porte: for instance, when Russian merchants sought to intensify trade with the coastal cities in the Black Sea region and required good relations with the Ottomans, they ran into concrete problems. The road to Istanbul was long and the Ottoman court ceremonial was complex, which made the exchange of embassies difficult. For this reason alone, as early as the sixteenth century the Russian merchants doing trade with the Ottoman Empire turned to Bağçasaray to request their mediation in mercantile affairs.⁸

Due to their geographical location, the Black Sea and the Crimean Peninsula had an important mediating function: situated between the periphery and the metropolis or between the steppe and the coast, the region had been the site of important trade hubs for all manner of goods since Antiquity – and human trafficking, typical of its time and across cultures, was an important branch of the economy.⁹ From a cursory reading of contemporary or even current accounts such as those by de Luc or the BSĖ, one nevertheless gains the impression that the slave trade was the exclusive profession of the Crimean Tatars, occasionally in alliance with the Ottoman Empire. The victims of this business are thus reported without exception to be the Slav peasant population in the steppe belt bordering the peninsula, known as the Wild Fields (Russian: Dikoe Pole; Polish: Dzikie Pole; Ukrainian: Dike Pole), which is thus said to have become an insecure border region unfit for permanent settlement and farming. This assessment is not to be dismissed, since it is beyond dispute that the Crimean Tatar horseback armies headed north to raid almost annually.[10] Economically speaking, the fertile regions were thus of limited use to both Poland-Lithuania and Muscovy, also requiring extensive border fortifications. While in the latter case, a limitless tsarist army could go about securing the area without resistance (albeit by no means always successfully), for Poland-Lithuania this was not such a simple task. The Polish-Lithuanian king was faced with very confident noblemen who "in asserting their particular interests largely [resisted] the demands" for their financial support.[11] And after the Union of Lublin in 1569, securing the southern region was the sole obligation of the rulers, who thenceforth imposed special taxes on the Polish Jews, which were not sufficient to cover the costs of fortifying the border, however.[12] Furthermore, the incursions by the armed riders from the south exacerbated a problem besetting all European states in the early modern period – a population shortage which was already acute enough due to a low excess of births over deaths, natural catastrophes, epidemics and wars, quite without slave raids. The number of people from Eastern Europe who permanently or temporarily ended up in slavery has long been controversially discussed: for instance, in 2002, Michael Khodarkovsky thought it likely that between 150,000 and 200,000 subjects were enslaved in the first half of the seventeenth century alone.[13] The price to buy back every individual – in Muscovy under Ivan IV, buying slaves' freedom was considered a Christian duty, and a special tax was introduced for the purpose[14] – stood at around five roubles, and hence for said period a sum of between 750,000 to one million roubles would have been payable. That was quite a sum in addition to the tribute, "gifts" and taxes that already had to be paid to the Khanate.[15] In Poland-Lithuania, incidentally, there was no organized buying back of subjects who had been taken captive.[16] In either case, the human loss was immense; new estimates propose around two million people in the period between 1500 and 1700.[17] It also unclear whether in the early modern period the Black Sea slave trade surpassed its transatlantic counterpart.[18]

Undoubtedly, the fate of many slaves was a harsh one. Broniewski, who otherwise painted a picture of the Crimean Tatars that was not entirely negative,[19] was quite clear in this regard: "The fate of the captives with the Tatars is quite pitiful, for the more common ones are oppressed by hunger, nakedness and beating, with the effect that they would rather die than live."[20] Alan Fisher too recently came to a similar assessment on the basis of contemporary reports: "[O]ften in chains and always on foot",[21] many of them died on the way to the most important slave hub on the northern Black

Sea – Kefe, formerly Caffa, in Crimea.[22] There the people who did not have to spend their days as slaves in the peninsula itself were sold; a certain percentage of captives were distributed on site. For instance, the Crimean khan and his military leaders were entitled to a share of the 'goods', and evidently laid claim to them regularly. Broniewski described the distribution as follows:

> As soon as he has arrived at the border [of the Khanate], the Khan receives from the entire army the tenth part of the [socially] high-ranking captives. The leaders of the troops, however, receive [slaves] from the individual departments, and those that bring a larger number of captives receive [slaves] from the remaining high-ranking captives. The remaining Tatars from the common people share the captives within their troop units.[23]

At least if our Polish diplomat is to be believed, the khan thus took less than the obligatory fifth to which Allah had entitled him, according to the Quran.

After the middlemen in Kefe had bought up the remaining slaves, the latter were taken to Istanbul on ships. The ships of the age required ten days for the crossing, with a stop-off, usually in Sinop on the northern coast of the Black Sea. There they were sold on unless an envoy of the sultan said they were required: attractive women were frequently taken for the palace harem; strong men became messengers – and were often castrated on site. Many male slaves from Eastern Europe also ended up in the sultans' galleys, where a very high death rate typically prevailed.[24]

As demonstrated, the fate of many people from Eastern Europe captured by the Crimean Tatar horsemen was indisputably extremely tough. However, human trafficking via the Black Sea and Crimea was by no means a Tatar or – if we consider Istanbul's role in their onward sale – an Ottoman, or indeed an exclusively Muslim affair. Rather, it was international.[25] In that era too, institutionalized slavery transcended the borders of empires, religions and cultures.[26] When examining the slave trade, we should thus not forget that the Hellenic culture so revered by the European elites since the Renaissance was based on a slave-owner economy. And as late as 2003, an unnamed Russian author, taking a clear sideswipe at the Western, purportedly developed, Europe shaped by Roman Catholicism, complained about the city states of Venice, Genoa, Pisa and Florence, which held great sway over the Black Sea for so long and without whose contributions the slave trade would not have been possible; as he quite rightly remarked, the European Renaissance and the slave trade developed "hand in hand".[27]

If the phenomenon was a global one, its assessment was uneven, as Mikhail Kizilov has shown on the basis of sources from Christian, Muslim and Jewish authors: without fundamentally questioning slavery – which was then a normal trading activity – an implicit and explicit distinction was frequently made between who was a victim and who was a perpetrator, between what was acceptable and what was unacceptable human trafficking.

Christians were particularly disturbed by the capture of their countrymen by Muslims, since they would then be exposed to what they considered the harmful influence of Islam. They also assumed that Muslims were particularly cruel. At the same time, however, they did not criticize the bonded work performed by their own serfs.[28] On the other hand, there are fewer complaints from Muslim authors about the fate of their brethren in captivity, particularly since "the Quran, and later Islamic tradition, admitted that slavery was a common human institution".[29] The biggest differences in the Jewish, Muslim and Christian discourses on slavery probably concerned the subject of potential conversions: while most Jewish authors strictly rejected the conversion of their brethren who had fallen captive, both Christians and Muslims occasionally considered it a legitimate option for improving one's personal fate.[30]

Nevertheless, procuring the 'goods' – that is, the slaves – in the Black Sea region was not usually the task of the inhabitants of the Italian colonies, who were more commonly involved in their sale. Before the Genoese were driven out by the Ottomans in 1475, procurement was in the hands of the Tatars – and emissaries of Eastern Slav noblemen from Muscovy also delivered the desired wares from the ranks of their own countrymen to the slave markets in Caffa or Tana.[31] Even after Caffa had become Ottoman Kefe, only a small proportion of the trade was the responsibility of Muslims. For the most part, it was conducted by Greeks, Armenians, Italians or Jews.[32] Poland-Lithuania and Muscovy also took their own prisoners during the Ottoman and Crimean Tatar raids – either keeping them for themselves or selling them to Western Europe.[33] Hence there were also slave markets in Moscow, where people from the Baltic or German-speaking territories were sold too – and until the mid-seventeenth century, the buyers included Muslim traders.[34] When it comes to the slave trade or the buying back of captives in the Black Sea region, it is too simplistic to distinguish between state actors (in the broadest sense, for instance the Crimean Khanate or Muscovy) and private ones (Greek or Armenian traders, etc.). Rather, there were other groups of actors who were fundamentally loyal to a ruler – or, more accurately, were supposed to be – and who were involved in this business. These included, in particular, the clans that frequently acted independently within the Khanate:[35] the Nogai, the Zaporog Cossacks and the Don Cossacks.[36] While we have already considered the *mirza*s as a factor in the history of the Crimean Khanate, the Zaporog Cossacks and the Don Cossacks require further examination, not only in the context of slave raids.

17

The Nogai as a Factor in Early Modern Crimean History

[T]heir obedience is very privileged. They follow him [the khan – S.K.J.] to war, giving him part of their booty, and paying him from one rixdaler [= Reichstaler – S.K.J.] to three ducats for each prisoner [...]. They eat horse flesh, drink mare's milk, in a word having as little taste for cleanliness as their ancestors, they have flat, blackish-brown and wrinkled faces, small and sunken eyes, hooked noses and a little facial hair. They are inclined to plunder, and when they can find an opportunity to rob some traveller, they do not pass it up; but they are not murderers, and when they think themselves safe, they prefer to sell their prisoners.[1]

These lines, first published in 1784 (and thus posthumously) were written by the Swedish scholar Hans Erich Johann Thunmann (1746–78). Specializing in Scandinavian, Balkan and Romance studies in Halle an der Saale in the Electorate of Saxony, he held the somewhat grandly titled "Professorship of Worldly Wisdom and Eloquence".[2] He dedicated himself to the study of Eastern Europe including the Black Sea region not only in his small treatise on the "krimschen Staat" (Crimean State), as the German original was entitled, but also in his extensive work *Untersuchungen über die Geschichte der östlichen europäischen Völker* (Studies On the History of the Eastern European Peoples).[3] As in the description of the Crimean Tatars by the Dominican monk de Luc, here too we read of warriors who clearly had a symbiotic relationship with their horses, ate horse meat and drank mare's milk – and thus, like their forebears, had little taste. They too took prisoners, via raids or – and here the Swedish scholars' report begins to diverge from de Luc's – by ambushing travellers, who were occasionally robbed but not murdered, for "they are not murderers" and it was better to sell them. Thunmann then reports extensively on the appearance of the people he describes; they clearly did not correspond to the 'European type' with which he was familiar, but they did not look like the typical Crimean Tatars of the south coast or the mountain regions either, it can be assumed. Rather, the professor of "Worldly Wisdom and Eloquence" depicted people (again, men) who looked very different with their flat, dark and wrinkled faces and hooked noses: the Nogai. De Luc had already made a phenotypical distinction between the Tatars of the steppe and the south, thereby providing a catalogue of characteristics that would prove rather stable over subsequent centuries:[4] he wrote that the Nogai had flat and full faces, large heads, small eyes and flat noses. He did mention that there were also female Nogai, who in his assessment were only pretty in their youth, however; in old age they were ugly.[5]

Indisputably, the ethnogenesis of the Nogai was linguistically, culturally and anthropologically different to that of the Tatars in the mountain regions and the coast and was much more similar to that of the inhabitants of the Kasakh steppe.[6] This also applies for their way of life; the Nogai settled in the northern Crimean steppes and the bordering mainland remained at least partially nomadic well into the nineteenth century, unlike the other Tatars in Crimea, who had entered into a process of mutual acculturation with the descendants of the Greek, Goth, Alan, Italian or other inhabitants much earlier, spent the whole year living in towns or villages and mainly engaged in trade, crafts or the cultivation of wine,[7] tobacco or fruit. The two groups nevertheless entered into close exchange, including in the economic sphere, since 'the south' was dependent on 'the north' in terms of the goods produced on the pastures of the steppe. Conversely, 'the north' needed 'the south' as a sales market and in its function as an intermediary. Economic aspects and lifeworlds also influenced religious practices; sedentary Tatars tended to follow the Ottoman expression of Islam, which on the whole was much more institutionalized than that of the nomadic groups.[8] Non-Muslim authors often took this to mean that the Nogai were less religious and less 'fanatical'.[9] Another interesting aspect in this context is that due to the Nogai's appearance, perceived as foreign, and their largely nomadic way of life, the sedentary European authors thought that the rest of the Tatar population in Crimea were more civilized and hence more attractive. For instance, a Russian traveller in the second half of the nineteenth century was enthused with the mountain Tatar women, who had fair skin, looked European and were thus "sometimes even beautiful". The same held, he wrote, for the little Tatars, who were similar to Russian children, since there was no Mongolian blood flowing through their veins. The author concluded:

> If you recall the many customs of the Tatars of the southern shore, the freedom of their women, the observance of some Christian holidays and monuments, their love of sedentariness, and compare these findings with their external appearance, then at first glance you will be convinced that the so-called Tatars are just as close to the Caucasian root as we ourselves.[10]

Many European authors developed comparable hierarchies between 'us' and the 'Other' in its constructed gradations. One such author was Harry

Willes Darell de Windt (1856–1933), in his time an extremely popular explorer and travel writer. He considered the coastal Tatars "more refined in appearance and manner" than the Nogai and traced this back to their connections to the Greeks and the Genoese. At the same time, however, they were "more indolent", which he put down to the mild southern climate.[11]

The Nogai Horde was one of the ruling conglomerates that succeeded the Golden Horde and traced its name back to the emir and successful Mongolian commander Nogai (?–1299). Like many other hordes, the Nogia were ethnically heterogeneous and organized in clans. From the fifteenth century on, they advanced from the East well into the Pontic–Caspian steppe, proved very flexible in their alliance policy – and after Muscovy's impressive victories over the Khanates of Kazan' and Astrakhan' in the sixteenth century, they sought protection by entering into an informal relationship of suzerainty with the Crimean Khanate.[12] Just like the Crimean Khanate in its relations with the Ottoman Empire, the Nogai showed themselves to be strong-willed vassals, regularly resisting Bağcasaray's policies towards the steppe. This included pursuing their own campaigns to the north, manifested in their independent procurement of slaves (cf. Chapter 16). Their raids were also one of the factors behind Slavic settlers' inhabiting Crimea's northern steppe regions only temporarily and only in small numbers. Right up to the Crimean Khanate's departure from the Ottoman sphere of influence in the second half of the eighteenth century, the Nogai remained a rebellious element within the Khanate, at times allowing themselves to be instrumentalized by its enemies.[13]

18

Cossacks as a Factor in Early Modern Crimean History

Unlike in contemporary reports of raids, looting and enslaving cited hitherto, in another account the 'perpetrators' were not the "Turks" or the Crimean Tatars, but the "Zaporoizhian Cossacks":

> Nevertheless, from this region have come these valiant people who now bear the name of Zaporizhian Cossacks, and who have been dispersed for so many years in many places along the Borysthenes and in surrounding areas. Their number now approaches some 120,000 men, all trained for war, and ready to answer in less than a week the slightest command to serve the [Polish] king. It is these people who often, [indeed] almost every year, go raiding on the Black Sea, to the great detriment of the Turks. Many times they have plundered Crimea, which belongs to Tatary, ravaged Anatolia, sacked Trebizond, and even ventured as far as the mouth of the Black Sea, three leagues from Constantinople, where they have laid waste to everything with fire and sword, returning home with much booty and a number of slaves, usually young children, whom they keep for their own service or give as gifts to the lords of their homeland.[1]

This description was written by Guillaume le Vasseur de Beauplan (c. 1600–73), a French fortress architect and cartographer. His much-read and oft-cited *Description d'Ukraine* contains one of the first lengthier descriptions of Ukraine as a region distinct from the Polish-Lithuanian Commonwealth and of its inhabitants, who included the "valiant" Cossacks.

These multiethnic (later largely Slavic and Orthodox) egalitarian communities of what were known as Free Warriors (= Cossacks; Tatar *qazaq*) that formed in steppe borderlands between the Dnipro, the Don and the Terek from the fifteenth century on, at the latest, must also be regarded as actors in Crimean history, as suggested not least by de Beauplan.[2] The mixture of serfs who had fled the Slav territories, displaced warriors, including those of Tatar origin, and many other men[3] who had good reason to leave the centres of power (in some cases as religious refugees) had become established in the spaces between Poland-Lithuania, Muscovy and the Crimean Khanate, spaces over which it was difficult to assert dominion. They formed, to cite Andreas Kappeler, "small groups of people who organized hunting, trapping, fishing, border service and raids".[4] The Zaporog Cossacks, for instance, operated from military camps they had set up on the islands in the Dnipro, which were hard for most potential opponents to access due to the strong rapids. It did not take them long to become embroiled in conflicts with the Khanate and its Ottoman suzerain, and from the mid-sixteenth century on they were increasingly entrusted with defence and keeping watch over Poland-Lithuania's border fortresses. This applied at least to those who were directly subordinate to the Polish crown and were known as Service or Register Cossacks.[5] There were nevertheless free Cossack groups on Polish-Lithuanian territory, in the Don region and further to the east as well as mercenary Cossacks, the latter earning their keep with looting raids. Particularly between 1550 and 1650, both they and the Cossacks on the rulers' pay role rarely recognized either (Polish) kings or (Russian) tsars as their leaders, although they did on occasion. The Cossacks became distinct actors and were frequently a thorn in the side of Poland-Lithuania or Muscovy, often opposing them.[6] This may be a characteristic typical of the population of a complex borderland zone that can be defined as follows: "No clear assignment to the neighbouring and competing dominions, an ambivalent loyalty on the part of the ethnically and religiously heterogeneous population, socially fluctuating structures and constant skirmishes" with other actors.[7] Like the Nogai, the Cossacks undertook their own raids into neighbouring territories – but in the opposite direction, to the south.

Today, when one thinks of Cossacks one usually pictures them – like the Tatars – on horseback. But this was not until later; initially, their "primary habitat [was . . .] not the steppe, the impassable 'wild field', but the river. [. . .] They were skilled boatmen not only on the rivers but soon also on the Black and the Caspian Seas", writes Kappeler.[8] Their destructive forays into Ottoman and Crimean Tatar territories on land and water, also described by de Beauplan, repeatedly led to profound upheavals in foreign policy, both the Sublime Porte and the Khanate complaining that the Cossacks made their own.[9] In the early seventeenth century, they repeatedly attacked Kefe, justifying themselves to the Polish crown, and others, by claiming they had intended to free Orthodox slaves who were being sold there. That they used the opportunity to make a rich bounty was certainly not an unwelcome side effect, however. Incidentally, the image of the marauding Cossack is not compatible with the concept put forward by today's Ukrainian nationalist circles, for whom the Zaporog 'Free Warriors' are a central element of their national mythology.[10] Historiographers in neighbouring countries, on the other hand, take a critical view of them: as early as the nineteenth century, the above-cited tsarist Orientalist Smirnov remarked that it was not only the Crimean Tatars who took prisoners and demanded ransoms, but also the

Cossacks.[11] For the Polish historian Skorupa too, many Cossack assaults on Crimean Tatar and Ottoman territory were more raiding than defensive in nature.[12] A particularly harsh assessment of Cossack communities is voiced by Neal Ascherson: "Compared to the Indo-Iranian peoples of antiquity, and to some of the Turkic peoples who followed them, the Cossacks were primitive. Force, race and maleness are seldom the values of a stable and traditional society, but rather of bandits."[13] Undoubtedly, today's post-Soviet neo-Cossackhood is characterized by chauvinism, machismo and xenophobia,[14] but the Cossacks of the early modern period should also be read in the context of the specific political and economic conditions of the Eastern European borderland culture.

And one aspect of this culture was, as we have already seen in several instances, an alliance policy adapted to the respective circumstances and needs of a community. A particularly consequential example of the flexibility of the actors in the northern Black Sea region was the alliance between the Zaporog Cossacks and the Crimean Khanate during the Khmel'nyts'kyi Uprising of 1648,[15] a rebellion against the Polish aristocratic republic. The background to the insurrection was social (the reduction of Cossack privileges by the Polish king) and confessional (discrimination against Orthodoxy). An alliance Het'man Khmel'nyts'kyi (1595–1657) originally sought with the tsarist empire had not come to fruition at this point, but he had succeeded in allying himself with the Khanate, promising land and slaves in return for its support. In various battles (Zbaraż [Polish; Ukrainian Zbarazh] 1649, Zborów [Polish; Ukrainian Zboriv] 1649, Beresteczko [Polish; Ukranian Berestechko] 1651), Cossack and Crimean Tatar units led by Islam III Giray (1604–54) fought side by side. Islam's foreign policy, like that of his predecessors, also sought to prevent any of his neighbours from becoming too strong. Hence when he considered Poland-Lithuania to have become sufficiently weak, he gradually withdrew his support for the Cossacks. Khmel'nyts'kyi was repeatedly forced to turn to Muscovy – and in early 1654 the Pereiaslav Agreement was forged under Tsar Aleksei/Alexis Mikhailovich (1629–76). In the Russian interpretation, under this agreement the Cossacks subordinated themselves to the tsar, while to this day the Ukrainian side prefers to speak of a treaty between equals.[16] The Crimean Khanate thus also had a hand in this highly significant event in Russo-Ukrainian relations. In the Russo-Polish War of 1654–67, the Khanate changed sides for good – fighting alongside Poland-Lithuania against Muscovy. Following the Truce of Andrusovo negotiated by the Rzeczpospolita and Muscovy in 1667, Russia finally began its efforts to draw the Crimean Khanate away from the influence of the Ottoman Empire.

19

Inside the Crimean Khanate

> Although their soil is very fertile, few are engaged in agriculture and grain farming; the majority do not work the field and do not sow grain; they eat horse, camel, ox, beef and mutton, of which they have plenty. The noblest and richest consume bread, beef, brandy and mead [...]. Tatars serve the Khan and the nobles not for pay, but for being clothed and fed; the others are mostly idle.

This passage from the description of Crimea by the Polish ambassador Broniewski in 1579 conveys an image of the 'foreign' Crimean Tatar population that has remained timeless: from the perspective of a Christian European, most Crimean Tatars (again, just the men) are described as not particularly industrious, indeed even as lazy, irrespective of their social standing. Broniewski's more or less implicit criticism is that although nature has evidently blessed Crimea with fertile fields and abundant fauna, the inhabitants do not make use of this capital. Only a few work for payment in kind (as subservient "hirelings") out of sheer necessity, but most are "always idle". Incidentally, his depiction of Crimea contains contradictions; elsewhere he reports of "[s]plendid orchards, vineyards, vegetable gardens" – indeed, they are "innumerous"[2] – and someone must have taken care of them, since fruits, vegetables and grapes do not grow without careful tending. Broniewski or the travel writer de Winct (cf. Chapter 17), who would visit Crimea over 300 years later and didn't exactly think the Crimean Tatars of the south coast were particularly industrious either – blaming it on the pleasant climate – are just two of many critical authors from the so-called Christian Occident. Broniewski's claim of 'lazy' Muslims conveys a common stereotype of 'the Oriental' as such;[3] the only surprising thing in the cited passage is the reference to the Muslims' consumption of alcohol in the form of brandy and mead, although, as we have already seen, the Muslim population of Crimea not only produced alcohol but also drank it. Even highly educated travellers who were committed to objective scholarship, such as Peter Simon Pallas (1741–1811), a Prussian-born researcher in the service of Russia and a member of its Academy of Sciences, complained that the Crimean Tatars did not know what to do with the peninsula's rich natural resources.[4] When he visited in 1793 and 1794 on behalf of Tsarina Catherine II in order to survey the economic situation and make proposals for St Petersburg's future policy,[5] he lamented:

> It is, however, to be regretted, that all the fine, warm dales of the southern coast are inhabited partly by useless, inactive, and, in certain cafes, dangerous Tartars [sic – K.S.J.], who understand the art of destroying better than that of rearing; and, on the other hand, that the crown-lands have been granted to such proprietors, as possess neither the ability nor the good-will of establishing colonies for the public good, in situations thus favoured by nature.[6]

In the interests of both economic and security strategy, he recommended that the Russian administration expropriate the Tatar landowners' property and deport them to the interior, since they were "unprofitable and unworthy inhabitants of those paradisiacal vallies [sic], in which they have always shown themselves the first and most ready to revolt against the Russian government". He suggested that "industrious settlers" be sent in their stead.[7] This was a policy the Russian rulers would follow in subsequent decades (cf. Chapter 24). From a Western perspective, the Crimean Tatar population was, then, universally considered to be of little use and dangerous – the latter with reference to the historical perception that every Crimean Tatar was also a warrior. The deep-rooted European discourse that since the early modern period had held the Crimean Khanate to be a parasitic state based solely on raiding, looting and the slave trade thus proved extremely influential. However, the Khanate's internal constitution, the composition of its population and its economic and military structures were much more complex than this image would suggest.

We have already stressed several times that diverse processes of acculturation had always existed in Crimea and gave rise to a particular blend of cultures and religions; it is something of a common thread throughout the peninsula's history. The period under the Crimean Khanate is no exception, and hence early modern Crimea is particularly well suited to observations and research on the "hybrid cultures" that have enjoyed so much discussion in recent scholarship.[8] For a long time, largely nomadic groups such as the Nogai became partially sedentary, while other ethnic and religious groups – the descendants of the Italian colonists, Armenians, Jews, Karaites, Greeks, etc. – became partially Tatarized, in terms of language and dress, for instance. The religious situation also underwent transformations: in the sixteenth century in particular, the coastal regions, cities and mountain regions saw an increasing number of conversions to Islam. And unlike during the period under the Russian Empire, when exogenous marriage practices (that is, marriages between members of different religions) were very much the exception,[9] this phenomenon was much more common in early modern times. It is well known that changing faith secured former non-Muslims economic advantages, since it meant they no longer had to pay the special taxes levied in the Ottoman Empire and the Khanate. Occasionally, the large number of conversions even became a problem for the Muslims, since it meant less tax revenue.[10] Certainly, until shortly before the Khanate's annexation by Russia, as a rule the non-Muslim groups lived in peaceful co-existence with their Muslim neighbours; it was only later that larger interreligious conflicts arose.

Throughout the peninsula's history, diversity and consequently a remarkable cultural melting pot have prevailed, without preventing the development of protonationalist cultures, however. And this also holds for the specific Crimean Tatar culture for which even nineteenth-century Russian authors expressed their admiration, despite their reservations concerning everything they considered Tatar.[11] And despite the destruction of mosques, archives or parts of today's much smaller Palace of Bağçasaray over the years – and most decisively in the late Stalinist era after the Second World War – the remnants of Crimean Tatar culture remain impressive. The centrepiece is still the Khan's Palace, on which construction began under Khan Sahib I Giray (1501–51).[12] A few decades before work began on it, in the late sixteenth century, Broniewski could not but praise the palace complex and the settlement: the city, he wrote, was not insignificant, and the building itself was made from "exquisite stones" and decorated "in opulent and grand fashion with buildings, temples, mausoleums and baths".[13] Travellers from the Ottoman Empire, who were familiar with the splendorous architecture of the Topkapı Palace in Istanbul, which had provided orientation for the Persian, Ottoman and Italian architects in Crimea, also expressed their admiration: Evliyâ Çelebi, who toured Crimea a good three-quarters of a century after Broniewski, also praised the palace's architecture and acknowledged the infrastructure, the villages and the cities in the peninsula.[14]

The elaborate Crimean Tatar culture itself clearly resisted the label "barbaric", even from critical authors who rather rejected the Khanate; much of what they saw in the peninsula was simply too impressive. Due to their specific experience of the Crimean Khanate (in war), it was easier, at least for Christian authors, to reduce the source of this prosperity to raids and the collection of tribute. Even the most profound scholar of Crimean Tatar history, Alan Fisher, remarked at one point in his important book that the Khanate's economy was primarily based on looting and tribute as well as financial support from the Sublime Porte.[15] Even if these income streams were undoubtedly of great relevance, the agrarian capacity of Crimeans, including the Muslim population, should not be underestimated: as outlined above, the inhabitants of the northern steppe practised animal husbandry and some of them also grew grain. In the mountainous region in particular, small-scale arable farming was an important factor, as Broniewski noted, as was beekeeping.[16] The great Soviet archaeologist and art historian of the northern Black Sea region Anatolii L. Iakobson (1906–84) recognized the

FIGURE 19.1 *The Khan's Palace of Bağçasaray.*

sedentary Tatars' successes in the field of orcharding and viticulture, crafts and architecture. However, he claimed that their abilities were due to early assimilation to the descendants of the Greek colonists – they had learnt from them, as it were.[17]

Undoubtedly, military activity was of central importance to the Khanate. For instance, from the sixteenth century onwards, every male Tatar was obliged to heed the call of the Crimean khan when he wished to "mount his horse" – that is, ride into battle.[18] Resistance, failure to appear for roll call or cowardice in the face of the enemy were punishable, including by death, as was commonplace in those times – not only in Muslim cultures.[19] The Khanate did not maintain a standing army, then – and it was not alone in this; the practice was only gradually emerging in the nascent territorial states of the early modern period. Standing armies were a response to mercenaries, who frequently proved unreliable and who ultimately included the Register Cossacks in Poland-Lithuania, as described above. It was also common practice to employ militia.[20] The extremely powerful and feared army of the Crimean Tatars primarily consisted of militia; only a comparatively small number of Tatars were exclusively warriors – in the context of the age, they were more of an older-type army. But a more effective mobilization policy made it possible to gather tens of thousands of warriors – in rare cases as many as 80,000, it is assumed – within a very short time, which represented a great advantage over enemy armies.[21]

The majority of Crimean Tatar men were thus not exclusively devoted to warfare, contrary to the opinion widely held by Christian authors. Only a small percentage of Crimean Tatars could afford to dedicate their lives to the military; the others were dependent on additional sources of income. Due to their close contact with horses that began in childhood, at least for the (semi-)nomadic Tatars, and their important weapon, the reflex bow, the use of which was also honed from an early age, the khan's armies nevertheless perfected the art of warfare, plundering and taking captives.[22] However, when the khan did not call on them to do battle, most male Crimean Tatars tended their livestock and land or worked as craftsmen.

Fields were usually worked collectively, incidentally, and taxes were also paid collectively to the respective landowner, usually a member of the influential clans.[23] A crucial difference to the neighbouring regions of Poland-Lithuania and Muscovy was that the Crimean Tatar peasants were not serfs; that is, they enjoyed personal freedoms and mobility – the latter at least *de jure*. There were also the slaves, however, who were considered 'speaking property'. Incidentally, even after Crimea's annexation by the Russian Empire in 1783, the Crimean Tatar population was not forced into serfdom. Besides Bağçasaray and Kefe, which belonged to the Ottoman Empire, there was a nuanced urban life that predated the Tatar period and in which the Tatar population played a large role, indeed often representing the majority; important cities included Gözleve (Turkish; Crimean Tatar: Kezlev; today's Ievpatoriia/Evpatoriia [Ukrainian/Russian]) in the western peninsula, an important trading centre for the Khanate, Aqmescit (Crimean Tatar; today's Simferopol' [Ukrainian/Russian]) in the interior, or Qarasuvbazar (Crimean Tatar; today's Bilohirs'k/Belogorsk [Ukrainian/Russian]). The Armenians, Georgians, Greeks or Karaites (the latter primarily in Qarasuvbazar), largely Tatarized both in terms of language and customs, had a large influence on trade and finance.[24] Incidentally, in the coastal cities in particular, not all Tatar inhabitants were subjects of the Crimean khan; rather, they were often subjects of the sultan. In the course of the early modern period, the Crimean Tatar population as a whole – that is, the groups in the coastal and mountain regions, whom ethnologists usually refer to as "Tat" or "Yalyboyu" respectively,[25] and the Nogai in the north – came to constitute the majority in Crimea. Magocsi estimates that in the sixteenth century, half a million people lived on the territory of the Crimean Khanate, which of course extended beyond the peninsula.[26]

We have already mentioned the limits to the khans' power not only due to the Ottoman sultan but also because of the clans. The prominent position enjoyed by these families was a common phenomenon in the successor states to the Golden Horde, but unheard of in the Ottoman Empire. The clan leaders were part of what was known as the Divan, the khan's advisory body. Besides this Divan, there was the Kurultay, the assembly of clans consisting of large landowners and warlords which functioned *inter alia* as a mouthpiece to the sultan and wielded enormous influence over affairs of state.[27] Throughout the Khanate's history, none of the Giray khans were able to restrict the clans' influence and strengthen their own central power.

It remains to be considered how the Crimean Khanate differed in its structures from other early modern European states, where in the Central European context at least, nuanced legal concepts and forms of organization emerged in the cities and the territorial state headed by a sovereign gradually took shape. These tendencies were absent in the Crimean Khanate. Nor is the Khanate comparable with the East (Central) European context of the age. Instead, it must be seen as an exception; Alan Fisher observes: "Unlike its neighbors [i.e. Poland-Lithuania, Moscow, and the Ottoman Empire] the Khanate was not a feudal monarchy, an absolute monarchy, a patrimonial state, or an oriental despotism. It was something quite different, perhaps without European or eastern European parallel."[28] In this regard, then, the Khanate resists clear assessment, particularly since we cannot ignore the complex relations with the Ottoman Empire we have outlined above. It can certainly be established, however, that the Khanate was not the barbaric, despotic parasite state as which it is often depicted.

20

The Lead-Up to Annexation:

The Strengthening of the Russian Empire, the "Greek Plan" and the Treaty of Küçük Kaynarca of 1774

Do you not see the crescent moon sinking
Dimly in weather-laden clouds
With the silver's twinkling
Down into the black sea?

When it once with storm-sped
Gait rose from the desert,
The Dardenelles darkened
And the birds' song fell silent.

[...]

And there raged about the walls
Of Byzantium thunderstorms,
Until the moon with bloody brightness
Stood still on Sophie's tower.

[...][1]

The author of this poem, presumably written at the time of the Crimean War (1853–6), is a German writer and Classical scholar largely forgotten beyond his native Waldsassen in the Upper Palatinate by the name of Franz Binhack (1836–1915).[2] His work, running to a total of twenty-six strophes, is entitled

"Die orientalische Frage" (The Oriental Question) and adopts a Christian European perspective in describing the question's beginnings – the Ottoman conquest of Constantinople in 1453 – as a catastrophe to which even nature reacted in horror, for the "birds' song fell silent". The terror awaiting Constantinople's Christians is described in drastic terms; the invading Muslims are merciless in destroying signs of Byzantine culture (the "Greek crown" is "smelted to lumps", the imperial throne is "blood-stained") – and, worse still, they damage objects sacred to Christians:

> Knocked over on the altar
> Bright in pieces under rubble
> Lay the chalice, and spilt
> The ash drank Christ's blood.
>
> And the storms furiously chased away
> Over land and sea
> On besmirched, tattered,
> Loose leaves Christ's word.[3]

Then, the poet continues, there sank over Constantinople a "long night" lasting "[t]hrice a hundred years" before the nightingales stirred to "greet the morn" and fruits once again grew "on the Golden Horn" – that is, in the bay of the Bosporus in Istanbul, which divides the European part of the city into southern and northern areas and where new life tentatively returned.[4] Three hundred years after the conquest of Constantinople – in the mid-eighteenth century – power relations in the Black Sea region and on its northern shore had indeed shifted to the detriment of the Sublime Porte and hence indirectly to that of the Crimean Khanate too. There were a variety of reasons for this: for instance, the long-feared Ottoman and Tatar mounted troops were becoming less of a match for the technically and strategically superior tsarist army. The Muscovite tsars' forces increasingly relied on artillery, modern firearms and wagon forts as defensive formations against the mobile cavalry from the south. Additionally, they employed highly disciplined Kalmyk mercenaries, who often emerged victorious from battle with the Crimean Tatars.[5] Meanwhile, the Polish-Lithuanian state had modernized its own cavalry tactics; mounted troops now advanced together with the infantry and artillery and were thus better able to withstand the enemy's charge, which primarily posed a problem for the Nogai.[6]

The Crimean Khanate and the Ottoman Empire had failed to keep up with these innovations in military technology. But there were also economic problems on the domestic front: in the Ottoman Empire, taxes and duties levied on the population had risen drastically since the end of the sixteenth century, and there was a food shortage due to the strong population growth in the Mediterranean and Black Sea regions. The risk of rebellion was increasing, which in turn preoccupied the armed forces.[7] Given what remained, despite all peculiarities, close ties between Istanbul and Bağçasaray, this situation was not without consequences for the latter. Further, both failed to put in place new economic structures that could have replaced the slave trade, which, like any business, was subject to fluctuation, as the traders in the Italian colonies had discovered (cf. Chapter 11), be it due to demand or shortages resulting from external factors leading to a rise in prices. For instance, at times it became more difficult to procure large numbers of captives as the Cossacks grew in strength from the late sixteenth century on (cf. Chapter 18); they frequently put a stop to the Tatar raids.[8] On the other hand, during the alliance between the Khanate and the Cossacks under Het'man Bohdan Khmel'nyts'kyi, from 1648 onwards the Tatars had few problems collecting tribute and "harvesting the steppe for slaves", as Brian L. Davies puts it.[9]

Following the Cossack–Russian Pereiaslav Agreement of 1654, however, the Crimean Tatar cavalries again faced more restricted access to the steppe, and the number of captives sank. Another factor was global developments; during this period the trade routes and streams of goods were undergoing transformation the world over; ultimately, the transatlantic trade would eclipse the Black Sea trade.

Moreover, the accumulation of capital and with it the development of a functioning system of money lending was not pursued decisively enough in either Istanbul or Bağçasaray. One consequence was the relatively small number of manufactories, which of course were an element of the nascent early capitalism.[10] And finally, in the first decades after what is known as the Time of Troubles (Russian: *smuta*) around 1613 and the inclusion of the Cossacks in the fabric of the empire, Muscovy was able to become stabilized and gain power.[11]

Hence it was no coincidence that it was during this period that we encounter the first plans[12] by the Crimean Khanate's northern neighbours to make short work of their southern opponents. Interestingly, specific ideas were developed not by Polish-Lithuanians or Russians, but by a Catholic Croat: Juraj Križanić (1618–83) was a theologian, writer and politician who rose to fame partly due to having served as military chaplain to the Polish king Jan Sobieski (1629–96) during the Second Great Turkish Siege and the relief of Vienna. In this capacity, he died from his wounds a day after the battle on the Kahlenberg hill.[13] Residing in Muscovy between 1659 and 1676, Križanić spent some time working in the Kremlin as an archivist before he fell out of favour with the tsar and was banished to Siberia. Whether Catholic missionizing or his engagement as a kind of proto-Slavophile played a role in the decision is not entirely clear. What is certain is that he advocated the unification of all Slavs under the leadership of the tsar and the pope (!). The leading role Križanić envisaged for Moscow was contingent on the conversion of the Orthodox Eastern Slavs to the Roman Church, something Tsar Alexis Mikhailovich (1629–76) did not agree with; despite his epithet "Tishaishii" ("the Quiet", "the Most Gentle" or "the Most Peaceful"), the ruler promptly ordered the Croat's exile. In two chapters of his principal work, *Politika ili razgovory ob vladatel'stvu* (Politics or Conversations on Rule), written between 1663 and 1666, Križanić outlined how a common army consisting of Eastern, Western and South Slavs would be able to defeat the Khanate.[14] While these plans were not realized, the idea was nevertheless out there, the balance of power began to shift, and a caesura in relations between the tsars and the Ottoman Empire, and, indirectly, the Khanate, became manifest, at least retrospectively.

An important precondition for this development was the Truce of Andrusovo negotiated by the Rzeczpospolita and Muscovy in 1667, which put an end to a long-standing military conflict between the two parties and had a large impact on the balance of power in this part of Europe; the tsarist empire began to gain the ascendancy over Poland-Lithuania: the Rzeczpospolita had to accept losses both in the north (Smolensk Voivodeship) and further south, giving up Left-bank Ukraine (the part east of the Dnipro) as well as Kyiv and its environs. Originally, this city that was of great importance, also symbolically, was supposed to be ruled by Muscovy for just two years, but the latter would hold it for centuries. The Cossack Het'manate was supposed to be treated as a sphere under the joint rule of the two empires, insofar as they were supposed to fight together against the Ottomans and Crimean Tatars. In fact – and this proved relevant in the following two decades – the Cossack territories were relegated to a political football between the two powers or, as the historian Orest Subtelny puts it, "an object".[15] In the long term, this treaty meant the Het'manate was divided between the two conglomerate states.[16] In Andrusovo, Poland-Lithuania and the tsarist empire also agreed to join forces to defend themselves against the Ottoman Empire and the Crimean Khanate. For the Russian historian Vozgrin, this agreement also marks a turn in the communication of Russian foreign policy; it was the first time it consciously produced decidedly anti-Muslim propaganda.[17]

During the first Russo-Ottoman War of 1676–81 – there would be a total of ten up to 1877/78 – the entire complexity of the northern Black Sea region with all its different actors once again became clear:[18] together with the Crimean Tatars the Ottoman Empire fought the tsarist empire for the territories that form part of today's southern Ukraine. At the same time, various Cossack leaders fought on both sides and against each other. The most renowned was Petro Doroshenko (1627–98), het'man of Right-bank Ukraine on the right bank of the Dnipro. He struck up an alliance with the 'infidel' Crimean Tatars and Ottomans against Muscovy and the Cossacks of Left-bank Ukraine – and lost.[19] Hostilities finally ended in 1681 with the Treaty of Bağçasaray, which was intended to form the basis of a twenty-year truce (which did not last, as it turned out) and established the Ottoman–Russian border along the Dnipro. Further, all participants were forbidden from settling between the Southern Buh (Polish: Boh; Ukrainian: Pivdennyi Buh; Russian: Iuzhnyi Bug) and the Dnipro, creating a kind of buffer zone.[20] For the history of Crimea, which is of course our focus, the most relevant aspects of the peace are firstly that despite the restrictions on settlement, the Nogai retained the right to traverse these areas, which would secure the basis of their existence. Secondly, Khan Murad Giray (1627–96) led the negotiations in Bağçasaray in the sultan's stead, which again indicates the important position the Khanate occupied in the structure of the Ottoman Empire. However, the khans thenceforth lost this role, at least according to the Habsburg Orientalist Hammer-Purgstall:

> Until then, there had been direct communication by envoys between Russian and Crimea. However, because Murad Geraj mistreated the Russian envoys, from then on Russian envoys were no longer sent to Crimea and Russia's diplomatic communication remained limited to Constantinople.[21]

It is not clear how Murad Giray, known foremost for his participation and reservations towards the Great Turkish Siege of 1683, had the Russian envoys mistreated, but the decline in the Khanate's importance certainly became evident.[22]

These events had no impact on the territorial integrity of the Khanate – if we can speak of such a thing given the open, fluid northern border.[23] Initial concrete attempts by the tsarist empire to end the existence of this commonwealth followed only a few years later, however, with the Russian campaigns of 1687 and 1689 under the command of Vasilii V. Golitsyn (1643–1714). A year earlier, Muscovy had joined the anti-Ottoman Holy League (originally an alliance of the Holy Roman Empire, the Vatican, Poland-Lithuania and Venice); Moscow now had ideological justification for advancing on the Khanate as a vassal of the Sublime Porte. For the time being, they were unsuccessful; in both 1687 and 1689, the Tatar troops under the command of Khan Selim I Giray (1631–1704) were able to prevent the sustained conquest of the peninsula and a Russian presence on the northern Black Sea coast. For a foreign contemporary, Golitsyn's failure was due not so much to the Crimean Tatars' performance on the battlefield as to their skill at the negotiating table: he claimed that the Crimean Tatar emissaries had drawn out the discussions with the military leaders for so long that the Russian army ran out of supplies and was thus forced to retreat. He wrote that the campaigns against the Khanate were generally a failure for the "Muscovites".[24]

It was not until the reign of Peter I (1672–1725) that this would change – in Azov Fortress, the former Italian Tana, he was able to take territory from the Ottoman Empire, at least temporarily. Previously, both the Dnipro Cossacks (1559) and the Don Cossacks (1637) had made attempts to conquer it; the latter had been able to take the fortress, but Tsar Mikhail I (1596–1645) soon returned it to the Ottomans in 1642 in order to avoid armed conflict. In 1696, Peter I finally conquered Azov after a first attempt had failed a year earlier.[25] Even if he had to return the town a few years later – after the Treaty of the Pruth, which ended the fourth "Russo-Turkish War" of 1711 – Russia had succeeded in its aim of gaining access to the Black Sea. For the plan to succeed, the Crimean Khanate, which had the function of a buffer zone between Russia and the Ottoman Empire, had to be taken out of the game, something Russia would achieve in the medium term.

Parallel to these international developments, the domestic political situation within the Khanate became increasingly unstable. One indication was the frequent change of rulers from the late seventeenth century on, a whole series of khans being installed and deposed.[26] This would suggest that either the influential *mirza*s or the Ottoman sultan were dissatisfied with the respective khans – and that the latter was unable to resist particular interests. Among the clan leaders, there were various camps, some that fundamentally questioned Ottoman supremacy and demanded that the khans reorder relations with the Sublime Porte to achieve greater independence. Separatist tendencies led by the Şirin and Barın clans dominated from the 1760s on; they even sought to achieve full independence from the Ottoman Empire. But there were also *mirza*s who were quite satisfied with the sultan and his power to install or remove khans; it gave them leverage to rid themselves of unwelcome rulers who proved too independent in their dealings with these clans.[27] The Sublime Porte demanded Crimean Tatar troops with increasing frequency in order to pursue its interests in the Caucasus or in Persia, for instance – sometimes against the express wishes of the clan leaders. Moreover, the "Crimean khan's uncertain cantonists",[28] the Nogai, were again a source of unrest, repeatedly being instrumentalized by the clans to install or depose the khans.[29]

One of these Nogai rebellions was a consequence of the Peace of Karlowitz of 1699, which the Ottoman Empire signed with its adversaries the Holy Roman Empire, Poland-Lithuania, Venice, the Vatican and Russia – the twice-reigning Khan Devlet II Giray (1648–1718; khan from 1699–1702 and 1709–13) proving a decisive ruler for the first time.[30] In 1701, he succeeded in putting down the insurrection by the Nogai, who were rebelling against the ban on entering and raiding the Khanate's northern neighbours. Devlet II Giray further enhanced his reputation during the Great Northern War (1701–21). Tsar Peter I, who was fundamentally more interested in securing his empire's position in the Baltic region, also had to deal with the Khanate and Devlet II Giray: after the tsar's victory over Sweden and some of the allied Cossacks at Poltava in 1709, the turning point in this war, Devlet II, then in his second reign, pursued a policy that did not go down well with Istanbul:[31] in order to prevent the tsarist empire from advancing south, he supported the Cossack bands allied with Sweden and led by Ivan Mazepa (1639–1709)[32] and the defeated Swedish troops under King Carl XII (1682–1718), granting them refuge in the Khanate. At the same time, he warned the Sublime Porte, which was considering compromise with the tsar, of further Russian ambitions on the Ottoman Empire and the Khanate. Opposing these designs, in 1711 Devlet marched north independently with an army of over 80,000 Tatars in addition to Mazepa's Cossacks and Swedish soldiers. Having initially ignored the khan's warnings, fearing another war with the tsarist empire, the Porte now began another war with Russia for better or for worse, until the Treaty of the Pruth was signed in the summer of the same year. In 1713, Sultan Ahmed III (1673–1736) found a pretext for removing Devlet II for a second time and exiling him on Rhodos: he was accused of having acted improperly towards Carl XII. Russian historian Vozgrin considers this a turning point in the history of the Khanate: "From now on, the khans could only wait and see which of their mighty neighbours would first stretch out their hand towards this ripe fruit – Turkey [sic], Russia or Poland."[33] Ultimately, it was the Russian Empire that succeeded in plucking Crimea, but it would be some decades before it did so.

Under Tsarina Anna Ivanovna (1693–1740), St Petersburg once again turned its focus more strongly towards the Ottoman Empire and hence the Crimean Khanate, particularly since the situation to the north had tilted towards the tsarist empire or Peter I as a result of victory in the Great Northern War. However, the next Russo-Ottoman War of 1735–9 was not a great success for the tsarist empire; its territorial gains were marginal, although it did finally get a sustained hold of Azov. The economic impact was immense, since Istanbul restricted the trading rights of Russian traders on the Black Sea in the years that followed. All the same, the Russian military under Count Burkhard Christoph von Münnich (1683–1767) managed to advance into the peninsula for the first time, taking Bağçasaray and with it the power centre of its long-standing adversary. The Russian emissaries' glee was short-lived, however, for again supply shortages[34] and this time epidemics (presumably bubonic plague) prevented a sustained conquest of Crimea.[35] The Russian invasion nevertheless had a profound effect on the economy and infrastructure of the Khanate, since the invaders left a trail of destruction: "Münnich's campaign through the beautiful Crimea laid waste to fields and towns", wrote Hammer-Purgstall – but tsarist historians such as Vasilii Kliuchevskii also criticized the brutality of the Russian military in the peninsula.[36] The invaders' act of partially burning down the Khan's Palace can certainly be seen as deliberate political symbolism, the destruction of an enemy's cultural insignia being a core element of warfare. The fire in the Khanate's capital also meant the destruction of most of Crimean Tatar written culture,[37] which was held in the palace. Scholars consider it an irreplaceable loss.[38] After the Russian army withdrew, the palace was swiftly rebuilt, but only partially, and it never returned to its original dimensions.[39] The decline of the once so powerful Khanate was now manifested in material terms too.

Although at this point it had proved impossible to either permanently conquer or destroy the Crimean Khanate, the balance of power had shifted towards the Russian Empire. At the same time, a new ideological quality was manifesting itself: securing the open, volatile borders and preventing the loss of people had long been the most urgent and, given the situation, predominant task for Muscovy or the tsarist empire; and since incursions by Crimean Tatar troops continued into the second half of the eighteenth century – the last raid took place in 1769, under Qırım Giray (1717–69) – this is quite understandable. As already observed, the religious motif took on greater importance in the second half of the seventeenth century, especially as Muscovy joined the anti-Ottoman coalition, which also understood its mission as Christianity's fight against Islam. Ultimately, however, the Crimean question became much more complex – and this became even clearer in the course of the nineteenth century, culminating in the Crimean War from 1853 to 1856.[40] Scholars interpret the issue of Crimea as part of the so-called Oriental Question, which has been examined in such great detail.[41] Hence it is impossible to reduce the subject merely to religious differences.

Competition among the European Great Powers for influence over the Ottoman Empire began during the eighteenth century and is usually considered to be due to the growing technological, military and economic deficits of the once so mighty Sublime Porte, which the Great Powers sought to exploit. They instrumentalized national movements within the Ottoman Empire, such as that of the Greeks – to which the poet Binhack also alluded – as well as the religious differences between Islam and Christianity. The Russo-Ottoman competition was, then, an important, albeit not the only, element of the nascent Oriental Question. France, which had usually been a significant supporter of the Sublime Porte during the eighteenth century but sought to enrich itself at Istanbul's cost following the Revolution of 1789 and Napoleon Bonaparte's Egyptian expedition of 1798/99, Britain and the Habsburg Empire all did their bit to make the Oriental Question a permanent fixture in European diplomacy. Ultimately, the "seas question" – and hence the Black Sea region – posed a considerable problem.[42]

What role did the peninsula play in this international context? Clearly, not a small one: for the author of a history of the Black Sea, Charles King, the Crimean question was its "true heart"; it was connected to the issue of the straits, but also, and principally, to the Crimean War and its consequences.[43] The German historian Edgar Hösch came to a similar conclusion over fifty years ago in an essay that remains a standard work, arguing that for Russian diplomacy, for a long time the Oriental Question was solely a matter of relations with the Crimean Khanate,[44] which is only natural given the repressions to which the Eastern (and Western) Slavic territories were subjected by the Crimean state for so many years. While they still had to deal with raids by Crimean Tatar horsemen until 1769, their loot had diminished due to better defence measures and a successful Russian offensive strategy. Russia soon had further motives, however, aiming to eliminate the Crimean Khanate as a buffer state: the trade restrictions the Ottomans repeatedly imposed on Russian merchants (see above) angered St Petersburg. The tsars often protested to the Sublime Porte, particularly Catherine II: "In her repeated complaints to the Porte, she most emphatically supported and secured free merchant shipping on the Black Sea with particular emphasis and announced her growing interest in economic exploitation of the south",[45] observes Hösch. However, she was not the first to do so; towards the end of the reign of Elisabeth Petrovna (1741–62), private individuals in the tsarist empire expressed greater interest in Black Sea trade. As a result, in 1759 the Chamber of Commerce and the Senate commissioned a study of new trade routes between the Het'manate and Istanbul. The study concluded that these routes would run through the Khanate and hence require special military – and thus also state-supported – protection. A report on the economic potential of the Black Sea trade written by Privy Counsellor Dmitrii Ladygin in 1762, just a few months after Catherine II ascended to the throne, piqued the interest of the new tsarina. The prospect of playing a larger role in the lucrative Black sea trade may certainly have been a factor behind the Russo-Ottoman War of 1768–74,[46] which had such far-reaching consequences for Crimea, as we shall see.

A constitutive element of the Oriental Question in the eighteenth century is considered to be the "Greek Project"; for Hösch, it was Russia's attempt to solve the former problem.[47] From Catherine II's ascension in 1762 onwards, there crystallized a plan to carve up the European part of the Ottoman Empire between Russia, which had set its sights on the Black Sea coast, the Habsburgs, who were interested in the Danubian Principalities of Moldavia and Walachia, and the Republic of Venice. According to this "Greek Plan", the region around Tsar'grad, as Istanbul was known in Russia, would become a secundogeniture of the Romanovs. The literature sometimes sees the decision to name Catherine's second-born grandson Constantine in 1779 in connection with this plan; moreover, he was weaned by a "Greek wet nurse specially summoned to Moscow" and grew up with Greek playmates, which some consider proof that Constantine was chosen for this task.[48] It is beyond the scope of this study to examine whether Constantine's upbringing was motivated by Russia's designs on the Ottoman Empire. However, it is beyond dispute that a Greek Plan predates this: there is evidence that a kind of Greek Project relying on the elimination of the Crimean Khanate was hatched during the reigns of Alexis Mikhailovich and Tsarina Anna Ivanovna (see above).

In the course of the 1770s, the Russian plans to knock out the strategically important Crimean Khanate became much firmer, but the form the campaign would take was debated controversially at the tsar's court. Nikita I. Panin (1718–83), who shaped Russian foreign policy until 1781,[49] advocated exerting indirect politico-military influence on the Khanate. However, Chancellor Mikhail I. Vorontsov (1714– 67), soon to be echoed by others, was in favour of direct Russian rule over Crimea. Upon her ascension, Vorontsov handed Catherine II a memorandum tellingly entitled "Report to Empress Catherine II After Her Accession to the Throne, Depicting the System of the Crimean Tatars, Their Dangerousness for Russia and the Demands of Them. On Small Tataria". The report examined the Khanate in the context of Russo-Ottoman relations, portraying its Tatar inhabitants as dangerous and as a significant obstacle to the tsarist empire's dominance over the Black Sea.[50] As long as Crimea "remains under Turkish subjugation, it will always be dangerous to Russia", Vorontsov wrote in his memoir – to his mind, everything in the south was generally in a state of chaos and needed Russian power to create order, partly because of the autonomous Cossacks.[51]

In 1771, in the course of the Fifth Russo-Ottoman War, the tsarist troops under the command of Vasilii M. Dolgorukov (1722–82) succeeded in taking large parts of Crimea. However, unlike during the first occupation under von Münnich a few decades earlier, this time greater caution was exercised in dealing with the civilian population.[52] Catherine II even exploited the dispute among the clans concerning relations between the Khanate and Istanbul – about which the St Petersburg court was evidently informed: she had a manifesto published promising the Crimean Tatars the restoration of their lost independence; they had been innocent slaves of the Porte, but had now been liberated by Russia.[53] While power relations had been reversed, Catherine, who preferred Panin's model to that of Vorontsov, was not at all interested in genuinely incorporating the Khanate into the tsarist empire – not yet.

In the Peace of Küçük Kaynarca concluded by St Petersburg and the Sublime Porte in July 1774, the tsarist empire's gains included the Dnipro Estuary (and with it access to the Black Sea) and parts of the North Caucasus. It was also granted unrestricted trade in waters previously controlled by the Porte. The fortresses of Kerch, Yeñi Qale (Crimean Tatar; Russian: Enikale; Ukrainian: Ienikale) and Kinburn (Russian/Ukrainian; Turkish: Kılburun), previously held by the Ottomans, were handed over to Russia.[54] While the Crimean Khanate was referred to as an independent state by both Russia and the Ottoman Empire, in fact it was under considerable Russian influence. However, as caliph, the sultan retained a say in religious affairs in the Crimean state, and hence the treaty of 1774 was neither a total defeat for the Porte nor a complete triumph for Russia.[55]

For the Crimean Khanate, which had been closely connected to the Ottoman Empire since 1478, the peace of 1774 heralded a new and, it would prove, solitary phase of formal independence.

21

The 'Independent' Crimean Khanate and Russian Annexation (1774–83)

> Therefore, here are the two issues, the solution to which was bound to become the primary concern of the government. It is the Turkish and the Polish question. The essence of both questions was very simple. The Crimean Tatars, themselves not using the fertile soil of Southern Russia, did not allow the Russian population to use it either, tearing these vast and fertile lands from the European agricultural circuit. It was necessary to snatch them from them and safeguard these steppes. But the Crimean Tatars found support in Constantinople; hence, the economic acquisition of South Russian steppes could only be achieved through struggle with Turkey. This is what the Turkish question consisted of for the government of the XVIIIth century; and then it consisted of nothing else. [. . .] The solution to the first question involved bringing the South Russian border to its natural limit, i.e., to the coastline of the Black Sea; this question had to be resolved for the success of the Russian national economy. [. . .] The second question – the Polish one – consisted in the reunion of Western Russia with the core Russian lands; it had to be resolved [. . .] to ensure national security and for the satisfaction of the religious sentiment.[1]

In the late nineteenth century, the Russian historian Kliuchevskii presented a withering assessment of tsarist foreign policy between the death of Peter I (1725) and the accession of Catherine II (1762). He considered it to have been rather aimless and a failure even. It wasn't until Peter III (1728–62) was ousted in a coup initiated by his wife, Catherine, and she ruled alone that Kliuchevskii saw the turn to an active policy that solved the "two principal questions" he identified. There is no question that the Russian Empire was given considerable imperial impetus under the aegis of the empress later dubbed "the Great". This would also solve the two problems Kliuchevskii recognized: Poland was removed from the map of Europe for over a century – albeit not by Russia alone, but in partnership with the

Habsburg Empire and Prussia – via successive partitions in 1772, 1793 and 1795,[2] and in 1783 Crimea was annexed by a Russian state for the first – and not the last – time in its history.

Prior to that, in a phase in which the Khanate was merely ostensibly independent, beginning in 1774, the tsarina attempted to "test a model for exercising indirect rule [...]. Even then, the peninsula [was] something of a laboratory"; it became a testing ground for modes of 'modern' colonial policy.[3] The tsarina was wholly unimpressed with the advice of her counsellors, some of whom had already advocated the formal annexation of the Khanate around the time of the Peace of Küçük Kaynarca in 1774. Catherine even resisted the intervention of the philosopher Voltaire (= François-Marie Arouet, 1694–1778), whom she held in high esteem and who repeatedly wrote to her advocating the swift implementation of the so-called Greek Plan (cf. Chapter 20) and the elimination of the Khanate, on which said plan depended. For instance, in a letter of February 1773 – before the peace of 1774, then, which postulated the peninsula's 'independence' from the Sublime Porte – he wrote:

> [Y]our Imperial Majesty was not made to govern fools. It is this which has always convinced me that nature destined you to rule over Greece. I keep harping on my favourite topic; this will come to pass. In ten years' time, Mustapha will fall out with you; he will quibble with you over the Crimea, and you will take Byzantium from him. You are well used to partitions; the Turkish Empire will be partitioned, and you will have Sophocles' *Oedipus* performed at Athens.[4]

Voltaire would be proved wrong insofar as the tsarina was unable to "take Byzantium" from "Mustapha" – Sultan Mustafa III (1717–74) – and Greece would not achieve independence from the Ottoman Empire during their lifetimes. He was right about one thing, however: the peace between St Petersburg and Istanbul, of which there were early signs in 1773, would not last – not even the ten years he predicted. For in 1787 there was another Russo-Ottoman War. And one of the causes of this armed conflict was the Crimean Question.[5]

The establishment of a Khanate formally independent from both powers in 1774 had briefly been in the balance; Khan Sahib II Giray (1726–1807), who reigned from 1771 to 1775, arrested the Russian envoy P. G. Veselitskii, who had been sent to negotiate the treaty, along with his wife, who was pregnant at the time. Russian troops were able to free them both, however,[6] and after the negotiations the couple remained in Crimea, which somewhat revealed the merely ostensible nature of this "state" from the outset and was a bone of contention in the Khanate. The Khanate's political elites fundamentally disagreed on whether this new status was advantageous. The khan was faced with the problem that his responsibilities were not precisely defined by the Treaty of Küçük Kaynarca, and hence he had difficulty legitimizing his policies both at home and abroad. A considerable number of the *mirza*s soon wished to return to the old position of Ottoman suzerainty.[7] Devlet IV Giray (1730–81), however, who had first been khan from 1769 to 1770, could not come to terms with the influence of 'infidels' (i.e. Russians) over the peninsula. In 1775, he and his supporters set out from the Taman Peninsula to Kerch, occupied Kefe, drove out Sahib II Giray and took on the khanship once again.[8]

Fisher divides the history of the Khanate between 1774 and 1783 into three phases: during the first phase (1774–6), members of the elite in the Khanate gauged the room for manoeuvre they hoped to gain between the two great powers; for instance, Devlet Giray's relatively unproblematic installation as khan was accepted by the Russians without intervention, which would indicate a certain degree of autonomy on the part of the Crimean Tatars. In a second phase (1776–8), however, they installed a second khan, Şahin Giray (1745–87), with the help of the Nogai Tatars, who were notoriously dissatisfied with Bağçasaray: "[U]nder Catherine's tutelage he tried to modernize the Crimean government along Western lines", writes Fisher. In the third phase, from 1778 to the annexation of 1783, Khan Şahin finally attempted to break with the traditional Muslim Tatar institutions, without succeeding in establishing new ones, Fisher continues. As a result, Catherine II ultimately "lost patience" and annexed Crimea.[9]

What, then, was the domestic situation in Crimea, and how did the Ottoman and Russian Empires respond during this period? One might assume that Catherine supported the project of a formally independent Crimean state as long as Russian interests remained unaffected. The fact is, however, that developments in the Khanate were complicated and thus difficult for the tsarist empire to predict, and hence from the tsarina's perspective, annexation ultimately seemed the last resort. Many had already considered Sahib II Giray a Russian puppet, and the Tatars had finally had "enough of the Russophile Sahib and ousted him in the spring of 1775 in favour of an energetic and clever member of the khan's family – Devlet IV Giray III", as Valerii Vozgrin puts it succinctly.[10] The tsarina had not objected to Sahib's ouster and Devlet's takeover (phase 1), since on the domestic front she was preoccupied with the aftershocks of the Pugachev rebellion of 1773/1774 and her forces were required there. Additionally, at this point in time, St Petersburg's and Istanbul's interests converged insofar as both, like the *mirza*s, did not wish to see a consolidated, genuinely independent Khanate. This was one of their reasons for rejecting Devlet's desire to establish a hereditary khanate.[11] When in 1776 it became clear that the khan had lost all his domestic backing and the Ottoman Empire was, moreover, embroiled in a war with Persia, Catherine II saw the opportunity to kill two birds with one stone, as it were: firstly, she could formally maintain a Crimean state by installing a pro-Russian pretender to the throne from the Giray dynasty, which would lend the affair the necessary legitimacy, without – secondly – formally violating the terms of the treaty of 1774 (phase 2). A suitable candidate was quickly found, since he had been known in St Petersburg since the early 1770s and had even had dealings with the tsarina herself: Şahin Giray (see above), who would become the last Crimean khan. He had been a member of a pro-Russian delegation of Crimean Tatar noblemen in St Petersburg that concluded the Treaty of Qarasuvbazar (Crimean Tatar; Russian: Belogorsk; Ukrainian: Bilohirs'k) in 1772, a treaty that has largely been ignored by historiography, since it was ultimately inconsequential, establishing an alliance and "eternal friendship" between the tsarist empire and the Khanate.[12] Şahin Giray spent over a year in St Petersburg, and the tsarina was impressed with him. She told Voltaire he was mild-mannered, intelligent and wrote Arabic verses. As a theatre enthusiast, she was particularly impressed that he was not one to miss a performance.[13]

Female rulers, particularly those with as much power as Tsarina Catherine, have piqued the interest of both historians and a curious public, especially since politically influential women have been something of an exception in history (and continue to be in the twenty-first century). And while the many and often influential lovers of male potentates have often enhanced the latter's reputations, power and virility seemingly being inseparable, when female rulers live out their sexuality, it is often viewed with a combination of suspicion, disgust and fascination – all the more so in the case of Catherine II. Her relationships with men and her sexual activities have been the subject of many discourses and have often been exaggerated.[14] In this context, it is interesting that Catherine's Crimea policy of the 1770s and 1780s is frequently explained in terms of her having had a 'soft spot' for Şahin Giray, or even sexual relations with him.[15] This is not entirely fanciful, given that personal fondness or antipathy are of course a factor in politics (and by no means the preserve of women), and in the case of the tsarina a parallel would exist in her installing her former favourite, Stanisław Poniatowski (1732–98), as king of Poland. Perhaps the emphasis on this (assumed) private factor is merely due to the fact that scholarship has yet to find a final explanation for why the tsarina acquiesced to the experiment of an 'independent' Khanate. Edward L. Lazzerini suggests that since she considered herself to be an enlightened ruler, faced with the prospect of a violent solution to the question of the southern border she may have sought to draw attention to a – less violent – alternative.[16] This might not seem surprising if we consider the first partition of Poland only a few years earlier, which had been criticized by the European public as a demonstration of power politics without historical precedent. Scholars also point to the tsarina's ultimately respectful attitude towards non-Christian religions, manifested in the ban on Orthodox missions converting the Crimean Tatar population after 1783, for instance.[17] Ultimately, her motives for deciding in favour of annexation cannot be fully explained. The fact is, however, that within a few years Şahin Khan would become a burden to the tsarist empire.

Şahin, initially confident he had the tsarina's support, attempted to restructure the political, military and economic situation as well as foreign policy (phase 3). Like many khans before him, he too sought to establish a hereditary khanate, which would have limited the power of the clans. One of his measures was to abolish what had been the independent state council, the Divan, which was composed of the clans' representatives; he replaced it with forces well-disposed to him. Moreover, he also demanded that Istanbul return territories the Khanate had lost in the peace of 1774, including in Kuban. He also questioned the religious supremacy of the caliph – that is, the Ottoman sultan – which also alienated Islam dignitaries in the Khanate. On the whole, possessing a Western education, the khan did not grasp the religious and cultural sensitivities of the *mirza*s or, probably, many of his subjects. Measures such as dressing his soldiers in European uniforms, opening up the army to Christians and relieving them of their obligation to pay higher taxes didn't win him any friends either. While the early Russian efforts to colonize the Khanate with Slavic and Greek settlers – usually termed "Albantsy" – increased the proportion of Christian and presumably pro-Russian inhabitants, it made the local Muslim population deeply suspicious. With good reason too – most of these settlers were not normal subjects but pro-Russian military men[18] prepared to intervene on St Petersburg's behalf in the event of a crisis. Şahin's aims were, then, partial westernization after the Russian model, detraditionalization and autocratization – and all this went too far for influential Crimean Tatars, with the result that half a year after the change of ruler, a revolt was led by the formerly twice-incumbent khan Selim III Giray (1713–86). However, it was quickly and brutally put down by Russian troops and the Albantsy.[19]

The experiment continued, for the tsarina continued to lend Şahin her support, and he recommenced his restructuring. Resistance repeatedly flared up, and a khan dependent on Russian weapons and financing was repeatedly kept on the throne. Retrospectively, it seems incomprehensible that the tsarina withdrew the larger part of the Crimean Christian population from the peninsula in 1778, thereby removing the element that had to support Şahin's project in their own interests, as Fisher observes.[20] Catherine II had entrusted pursuing Russian interests in the south to her close confidant Prince Grigorii A. Potemkin (1739–91). Resettling Christians had been his plan. According to his biographer, Detlef Jena, the aim was to weaken the Tatar state to the extent that it would be amenable to 'voluntary' annexation to Russia without the need to send in vast numbers of troops. He was also aiming for an influx of 'useful' subjects to the notoriously underpopulated Russian Empire. However, poor planning meant that the undertaking was "downright chaotic".[21] Correspondence between the tsarina and Potemkin reveals that St Petersburg's impatience with the khan and the situation in the Khanate had been growing since 1781/1782; particularly for Catherine, who had been hesitant for so long, suddenly the formal appropriation of Crimea could not be completed quickly enough. Potemkin had long tried to persuade the tsarina to formally annex the peninsula, his main argument being its geographical location: he wrote that especially in connection with policy concerning the Ottoman Empire, the Khanate was a hindrance – whatever they decided to do, "we must take the Crimea into account"; it was "a wart on our nose" that had to be removed – then "the situation of our borders suddenly becomes excellent".[22] When revolts again broke out in the peninsula in the summer of 1782, Russian troops led by Potemkin intervened to prop up Şahin Giray one last time. Speaking to Crimean Tatar dignitaries, Potemkin made sure that there were also advocates of direct rule by the Russian Empire. On 8 April 1783, Tsarina Catherine II's "Manifesto on the Annexation of the Crimea" was published.[23] With Russian annexation, a formally independent Crimean state ceased to exist.

22

The First Decades of Russian Rule in Crimea

In 1787, Tsarina Catherine II wrote a poem thanking Prince Potemkin for the peninsula's incorporation into the Russian Empire four years earlier and the elimination of the Crimean Khanate as an independent player on the Empire's southern border:[1]

> I lay at eve in the summer-house of the Khan,
> Amidst the infidel and the faith Mohammedan.
> 'Cross from the house there stood a mosque most tall,
> Whither five times a day an imam the people did call.
> I thought to sleep, my eyes barely shut for the night,
> When, with ears stopped, he did roar with all his might . . .
> Oh, miracles of God! Who amongst my kin of yore
> Slept calmly, free from the Khans and their hordes?
> And disturbed from my sleep amidst Bakhchisarai
> By tobacco smoke and cries. . . . Is this place not paradise?
> Praise to you, my friend! This land you did seize,
> Secure it now with your vigilance, as you please.[2]

She wrote these verses during her Tauric Journey, when she travelled to the new acquisition in the south with imperial and royal entourages (of Joseph II and King Stanisław Poniatowski of Poland respectively) – in the very former centre of Tatar power, the Palace of Bağçasaray, where she resided. European contemporary readers followed this media event with great interest, since it mobilized an unprecedented amount of people and materials: between January and July 1787, the journey covered over 6,000 kilometres, some of them by boat on the Dnipro. The illustrious group travelled to Crimea and back from St Petersburg via Smolensk, Kyiv and Ekaterinoslav – accompanied by around 3,000 servants and military men. The preparations were correspondingly elaborate and state of the art: travelling by river guaranteed speed and was extremely popular with travelling rulers at the time.[3] The ships were designed in the Classical style as Roman galleys; the food, courses and drinks were, like the accommodation, refined and befitting the calibre of the passengers.[4] Even nature was assigned a role in the journey's staging; the tsarina was to set eyes on her new jewel, Crimea, just as spring was awakening.[5] Potemkin, soon made "Prince of Taurida", had feared that the tsarina might be dissatisfied,[6] but his concerns were not justified; Catherine, like most of her fellow passengers, was delighted with her freshly conquered province and Potemkin's work. This rather contradicts the negative myth of the Potemkin villages that sprang up in connection with the Tauric Journey and has become synonymous with 'typical' – stereotypical – Russian deception and incompetence: sections of the European public were convinced that Potemkin had merely presented his illustrious travellers with an illusion of southern landscapes in bloom with the use of dummies, papier-mâché buildings and people brought in specially for the role. Scholars have since taken a more nuanced view of this unbending allegation; there were "neither fake villages nor plaster palaces".[7] It is also worth remembering that to a certain extent, steps to hide reality have always been part and parcel of the preparations for all visits by rulers or politicians, and not only in Eastern Europe.

Shortly after the conquest, the tsarina had expressed the wish to take a look at Crimea for herself, but the journey was repeatedly postponed – one reason being security concerns. The twenty-fifth anniversary of her accession finally offered the external excuse to undertake the journey, although the real reason was war with the Ottoman Empire, which had long been looming and which would break out a few months later. During her journey, the tsarina discussed joint efforts against the Ottoman Empire, principally with Emperor Joseph II (1741–90). The Ottomans would declare war on the Russian and Austrian powers shortly after the Tauric Journey had ended.

Istanbul was not willing to take the loss of large parts of the northern Black Sea coast lying down. But its belligerence was in vain: the Russo-Austrian war against the Sublime Porte ending with the Treaty of Jassy (Russian/German; Romanian: Iași) brought the Russian Empire further gains on the Black Sea, and the Sublime Porte was forced to finally recognize Catherine's acquisition of Crimea. However, contrary to Russian hopes, the war did not lead to the destruction of the Ottoman Empire and realization of the "Greek Plan". The Tauric Journey in the lead-up to the war was certainly of imminent political significance and was intended to convince potential allies of Russian strength, military and otherwise. In this respect, Russia was successful; for instance, Joseph II effusively praised the natural harbour of Sevastopol' as "the most beautiful port I have seen in my life",[8] adding that while only a little over twenty ships were anchored there at the time, over 150 would have fitted comfortably in the bay, which was well protected by three batteries. Joseph, a critical character and not easily impressed, pronounced that the developing city and its harbour had a great future: he observed that there were already many houses, storehouses and barracks, and if the Russians continued as they were, Sevastopol' would certainly flourish.[9]

The Holy Roman emperor was not remotely interested in the peninsula's exotic beauty that would enchant so many travellers in the late eighteenth century. But while the rather sober ruler was not captivated, his fellow passengers were: it was not least the texts written during the Tauric Journey that popularized the idea that Crimea was part of 'Asia' – due to its mild coastal climate and its Muslim inhabitants. At the time, the European elites were famously preoccupied with 'Asia' as an artistic subject, which would have a sustained influence on the idea that Crimea was an Oriental place. Here we see the ambivalence towards the so-called Orient that developed as part of the intellectual paradigm of "Orientalism": while the European elites mostly considered the real, contemporary Orient backward, dangerous or uncivilized, the Orient of their imagination was a burgeoning, sexualized and sultry land full of eastern promise.

A year before the tsarina's journey to the southern provinces, there had been a kind of dress rehearsal when the English aristocrat Lady Elizabeth Craven (1750–1828) toured the peninsula under the auspices of the Russian administration – and presumably in close consultation with Potemkin himself. Her travel report, published as a collection of letters almost two years after the Tauric Journey, became a European bestseller, not least because of the author's lifestyle. Quite spectacularly for the time, she had separated from her husband in order to marry another aristocrat, Margrave Karl Alexander of Ansbach and Bayreuth, prince of Say (1736–1806).[10] Her immensely successful description of Crimea certainly helped convince a significant portion of the European public that Russian rule over the former Khanate was a success. At the same time, she popularized images of the exotic or Classical Crimea. This was no mean feat, given that immediately prior to embarking in St Petersburg in 1786 her plan to travel south had been met with sheer incomprehension: the high-ranking members of courtly society feared the Englishwoman would die, the air in Crimea being unhealthy and the water poisoned.[11] In the 1780s, it was not foreseeable, then, that in the following decades the peninsula would become a favourite summer retreat of the Russian nobility. Lady Craven, however, had great foresight when she described Crimea as a "delicious country" and "an acquisition to Russia which she should never relinquish".[12] It is also quite remarkable that she followed the tsarina's express wish that Tatar place names be replaced by Hellenized alternatives: Craven thus visited "Tauride", not Crimea, and sailed on the "Boristhenes" instead of the Dnipro. This was at once both an expression of the eighteenth-century reverence for Antiquity and the Russian ruler's attempt to remove all traces of Crimean Tatar culture.[13]

The international group of crowned heads and diplomats that visited the peninsula in 1787, conversing with each other in French, ultimately succeeded in disseminating the image of the 'magical Crimea'. As is often the case in travel reports of the time, the authors consciously blurred the lines between fact and fiction in order to create excitement and interest;

occasionally they depicted not so much the real Crimea as a metaphorical paradise. Particularly influential reports on the Tauric Journey were presented by diplomats: France's Louis Philippe de Ségur (1753–1830);[14] the Habsburg Empire's Charles-Joseph François de Ligne (1735–1814)[15] and Saxony's Georg Adolf von Helbig (1757–1813).[16] De Ségur and de Ligne produced positive, at times enthusiastic, depictions, praising the Russian successes; Helbig, on the other hand, is held responsible, not unfairly, for the Tauric Journey's negative reception and is even considered to have invented the rumour about Potemkin villages.[17]

For de Ségur and de Ligne, Crimea was evidently a place where the stories of the *Arabian Nights*, immensely popular during the eighteenth century, could have played out[18] and where the Crimean Tatars, who for so long had spread fear and terror throughout vast swathes of Europe, had been domesticated by the Russian power. De Ligne writes, for instance, that the Crimean Muslims lay around idly on the rooftop, from which they only "dignifiedly [. . .] climbed down to lock up their sheep instead of their wives, whom they always keep hidden during the day".[19] However, despite its unproductive inhabitants, he described the peninsula as the "most splendid region in the world [. . .]. Fig trees, palms, olive trees, cherries, apricots, peaches blossom, permeate the air with their scent and protect [one] [. . .] from the hot sun. The sea's waves wash diamond stones at [. . .] [one's] feet".[20] The participants in the Tauric Journey such as de Ligne or the tsarina herself went searching mentally and physically for a magical land in Crimea where elements of Classical mythology like those of the Iphigenia story merged with a construct of the Orient the European elites extrapolated from the *Arabian Nights*. This perspective was fostered by the peninsula's location on the border between Europe and Asia and its then mostly Muslim population.[21] But what did this stylized magical world imagined by members of the European elites have in common with the real Crimea? How did the situation there develop? To what extent was tsarist rule over the former Khanate accepted by the local population and the former suzerain, the Ottoman Empire?

One indication that there were at least reservations towards the new ruler may be seen in a report written during the preparations for the imperial journey of 1787. It demonstrates that the triumphal entry of the high-ranking visitors via a guard of lavishly outfitted Crimean Tatar horsemen was by no means a spontaneous display of honour; rather, it was a staged event involving administrative coordination. The homage paid by Tatar dignitaries that so pleased the empress had been carefully planned by the Russian vanguard.[22]

As it would prove, however, the actors in St Petersburg and in the peninsula certainly didn't give as much thought to all aspects of their future Crimean policy as they did to the journey of 1787; on the contrary, many measures in the period that followed were erratic and the kind of ad-hoc decisions often encountered in imperial contexts rather than a result of thorough planning. The only thing that was certain was that St Petersburg's incorporation of the peninsula was intended as a long-term measure and not as an intermezzo. The tsarina's manifesto of April 1783 had already claimed that Crimea was henceforth "forever" part of the Russian Empire.[23] The significance accorded the region in the context of the "Greek Plan" (cf. Chapter 20) necessitated political and economic measures and a restructuring of the population in order to make it a stable part of the empire. The business of strategically securing the new acquisition was at least tackled "[m]ore firmly than the rather woolly vision of a Romanov on the throne of Byzantium".[24] Troops from the northern regions were transferred to the peninsula and in 1784 Potemkin inaugurated three Tatar regiments, which were even deployed in the Russo-Ottoman War of 1787–92.[25] Although the tsarist administration's distrust of the Crimean Tatar population as a whole, but mainly its soldiers, would not dissipate until the end of the Russian Empire due to historical experiences,[26] the regime did not wish to do without their legendary fighting skills. Even if Crimean Tatar warriors would prove themselves in battle with their Muslim brethren, Russian doubts about their loyalty remained. Until universal conscription was introduced in 1874, they served only as volunteers.[27]

The acquisition's military significance was at the heart of Russia's Crimean policy, then, irrespective of the ideological-religious aspect emphasized in the course of the nineteenth century that we have seen in the context of Crimean mythology (cf. Chapter 1). This was manifested by the establishment of the military port of Sevastopol' on the site of the small Crimean Tatar settlement of Akhtiar or Ak-Jar immediately after the annexation. At the time, it wasn't foreseeable that it would occupy a special place in the collective Russian memory due to its 'heroic' defence in the Crimean War and the Second World War, as a result of which it is considered an inalienable part of Russia.[28] The imposing natural harbour moved a captain 2nd rank (the Russian system's equivalent to a commander) by the name of Ivan Bersenev to recommend it to Catherine II as the base for the future imperial Black Sea Fleet,[29] and development of the port facilities and military infrastructure was begun in earnest. However, this drive soon waned and Odesa (as a trade port) and the Baltic Sea (as a naval base) received more backing from St Petersburg than the garrison town in southwestern Crimea. On the whole, its capacity both as a military and a trading post did not live up to the collective emotional aura ascribed to it in the tsarist empire and its successor states (and hasn't to this day).[30]

For the Muslim population, still the overwhelming majority, there were more important measures: the former Khanate was to be incorporated into the Empire administratively and without special status. Furthermore, reflecting the typical outlook of the age, it was to serve the Empire's interests. In practice, however, it soon became clear that for the imperial administration, Crimea was largely *terra incognita*, which was an obstacle to effective policy. Tatar society's plural and religious system of loyalty oriented around clans irritated the new rulers. The new administrators were even unsure how to classify the geography and the climate, and there weren't any valid figures on the new acquisition's economic capacity either. Immediately after the annexation, Potemkin thus commissioned an extensive survey of Crimea, with reports on the topography, the state of agriculture, information on expected tax revenue, conflicts within Tatar society or the number and state of Christian and Muslim villages and places of worship. To this end, the Russian administration drew on the local and linguistic knowledge of the autochthonous population by also entrusting Tatar personnel with the task of data collection. The information was printed and made available for use in imperial service;[31] it was intended to assist with the effective and 'useful' administration of the new colonial acquisition.

Ultimately, the Russian Empire in Crimea made use of effective hegemonial tools; while it was a transcontinental empire, it was also a modern one. Earlier scholarship on the Empire partly denies this, but this reading is not supported by more recent studies.[32] In the Crimean context, it is striking that the Russian imperial elites only seldom referred to it as a colony, although it indisputably was one, despite all attempts at historical legitimization. The loss of its independence is not the only factor here: the conquest exposed local society to far-reaching transformations via (proto-)industrialization and detraditionalization measures. In the minds of Russian elites, who did not question the 'imperiality' of the tsarist empire, the peninsula and its autochthonous population oscillated between something that was their own and the Other. There were no shortage of racist remarks, but they were less prominent than in the British Empire, for instance, which is frequently used as a yardstick.

Initially, the tsarist regime sought to secure the former Khanate by building trust and gave the impression that "the old Muslim elites still had a certain say"; "for a short transitional phase, essential tasks of the polity (such as tax collection) [remained] in Tatar hands".[33] When, in early 1784, the former Khanate received "a special order" to form a "Local Administration of Crimea" (*Krymskoe zemskoe pravitel'stvo*) involving several of the *mirza*s who had been influential under the last khan, this was only a transitional measure.[34] The formation of the administrative entities Tavricheskaia oblast' (Taurida Province) in 1784 or, later, the Tavricheskaia guberniia (Taurida Governorate) underlined the will for integration into the imperial structure.[35] Parallel to this, there was a military administration that was led by Count Osip A. Igel'strom (Otto Heinrich Igelström, 1737–1823), from the Baltic region,[36] and directly subordinate to Governor Potemkin. Although he had only been in office for a few months, Igel'strom pursued a pragmatic and integrative policy concerning the Muslim subjects, in line with what the tsarina considered her commitment to the Enlightenment and religious tolerance.[37] This also particularly benefited the Tatar *mirza*s, whose integration was considered important; as is often the case in colonial contexts, the strategy in Crimea was to co-opt the elites.[38] For instance, the leadership under Potemkin thought about the content and staging of the oath to the tsarina the representatives of the Crimean Tatar *mirza*s had to swear in the spring of 1783. They ensured that local customs – for example, kissing the Quran as a sign of solemnity or sacrality – were part of the ceremony.[39] Co-opting the elites, expressed *inter alia* in their integration into the tsarist empire's Table of Ranks (*Tabel' o rangakh*),[40] was a successful integrative measure. One of the reasons it worked was probably that it applied to a rather small group of around 500. Soon, however, Crimean Tatars would barely play a role in the administration of the peninsula; the reason given was that their Russian wasn't good enough.[41] On the whole, it can be established that "according to this, on the legal level, the *mirza*s had the same privileges as Russian aristocrats in Moscow or Saratov" – when the authorities recognized them as their equivalent, which was certainly not always the case.[42]

Overall, the new administration had a difficult task, since Crimea wasn't a pretty picture after annexation: invaders from the tsarist empire and civil-war-like battles had largely laid waste to the peninsula. Another problem was a vastly depleted population due to regular victims of the war and the exodus of Christian inhabitants in the 1770s.[43] Additionally, after 1783 Tatar and Ottoman subjects left the region now ruled by 'infidels' (= Orthodox Christians) for the Sublime Porte; scholars speak of several tens of thousands of people up to the Ottoman–Russian Peace of Jassy at the turn of 1791/1792,[44] the Tatar exodus reaching its zenith in the years after the Crimean War (cf. Chapter 27). It was only in the early twentieth century that this stream appreciably ended.[45] The Russian response to the loss of a considerable section of the Muslim population was ambivalent: on the one hand, the tsarist empire pursued an active settlement policy typical of the age in an empire dramatically underpopulated for the size of its territory,[46] while on the other hand, from the annexation to this day the Russian Crimea discourse has been permeated by the attitude that a Crimea without Crimean Tatars would be "better still", as Prince Potemkin put it in a letter to his tsarina in 1783.[47] In 1944, under Stalin, the peninsula was almost entirely bereft of its Crimean population. It would remain so for decades (cf. Chapter 33).

Further administrative problems were keeping the troops supplied and equipped and preventing disease.[48] The latter remained an issue throughout the Black Sea region well into the nineteenth century and repeatedly necessitated extensive quarantines.[49] The problems were compounded by the new regime's lack of local knowledge – or, one might say, its excessive ignorance: for instance, the destruction of the Tatar freshwater system by foreign troops, lamented by contemporaries such as Peter Simon Pallas, massively increased the risk of disease; the Russian soldiers had smelted the pipes for munitions or sold them.[50] The Empire had primarily set its sights on Crimea in the interests of power politics and strategy, but it also had high economic hopes, as demonstrated not least by the question of the straits: "[t]hey would never be fulfilled to the degree anticipated, however".[51] For one thing, agricultural production suffered a labour shortage due to the Crimean Tatar emigration that was only partly compensated for, and with considerable delay, by settlers from other parts of the Empire (chiefly of Russian or Ukrainian origin), the southwestern German-speaking areas, Switzerland and Scandinavia. Up to 1819 and again after the Crimean War, a somewhat consistent settlement programme was implemented in the northern Black Sea region, including the peninsula.[52]

Despite these and other difficulties, the imperial elites in the tsarist empire – that is, those that engaged with the reality of the Empire intellectually or artistically – were most taken with the acquisition of Crimea, after initially displaying scepticism. Men of letters close to the crown such as Gavrila R. Derzhavin (1743–1816) wrote enthusiastic odes such as "Na priobretenie Kryma" (To the Acquisition of Crimea).[53] In western Europe too, there was mostly joy that the tsarist empire had wrested ancient 'Taurida' from 'the Muslims'. Works such as "An das Bild der Selbstherrscherin aller Reussen auf der Medaille von der Unterwerfung der Krimm im Jahre 1783. Gesungen von C.L. v. Klenke, zu Berlin 1789" (To the Picture of the Autocrat of all Russians on the Medal of the Subjugation of Crimea in the Year 1783. Sung by C.L. v. Klenke, Berlin 1789) were published – and apparently read too.[54]

This generally positive assessment of Russian rule over the former Crimean Khanate was influenced not only by a Europe-wide 'fear of the Turk' but also by the Tauric Journey, which as a piece of propaganda had ultimately proved an "epic open-air performance", as Larry Wolff aptly puts it.[55] Despite the anti-Russian myth of Potemkin villages surrounding the journey, the man associated with them seized the moment, using annexation, the ruler's tour and victory in the Russo-Ottoman War of 1787–92 not only to drive the Ottomans from the northern Black Sea coast, but also to dispel from the minds of some members of the European elites the negative image of the Russian Empire as a comparatively backward realm.[56]

23

Multiethnic and Multireligious Crimea under Tsarist Rule:

The Tatar Population – Gender Relations

I now proceed to give some account separately of other colonists [...]. The Nogay Tatars, if not the original inhabitants of the country, at least wandered over the immense steppes of New Russia, with their tents, flocks, and herds, at the time of the Russian Conquest, and the ages before [...]. The government has at length conquered the inveterate prejudices of this wandering horde, and induced them to lay aside their roving habits, settling them in villages, and inciting them to cultivate the ground. They are, however, of all the colonists, far the worst cultivators.[1]

This description of the Noğai was written by the Englishwoman Mary Holderness, who made her mark primarily with an account of her stay in Crimea (presumably) from 1816 to 1820, which enjoyed several print runs. Together with her husband and children, she spent some years there as an agricultural colonist. The family had followed the call of the Anglican clergyman Arthur Young (1769–1827), who had conducted many agricultural studies in Russia by invitation of the Russian government and had acquired a large estate near the former Kefe (Feodosiia) in 1810; this was the only reason he was worth studying, in the harsh assessment of his own biographer[2] – unlike his more famous father with the same name (1741–1820), a renowned agronomist and publicist. Nevertheless, it is due to Young's engagement that we have a report on Crimea that is interesting for several reasons: it was written by a woman, which in itself is not exceptional for a travel journal about the peninsula, if we recall the renowned description by Lady Craven prior to the Tauric Journey (cf. Chapter 22).[3] What is noteworthy, however, is Holderness's comparatively long stay, which enabled her to examine the location and its inhabitants more closely than her countrywoman Craven had been able to. Holderness herself stressed in her preface that despite "numberless deficiencies", her longer stay and being a woman had benefited the work: "I am induced to think that, as a resident and a female, I possessed advantages for acquiring information, superior to those of the passing traveller."[4] However, as in countless other European travel reports of the age – not only on Crimea, but on purportedly exotic regions in general – the assessment of foreign cultures and nationalities by members of a nation that considered itself civilized were characterized by a superiority complex: despite the fact they were representatives of the new ruling power, all the Russian inhabitants of Crimea are portrayed as uneducated unless they are members of the upper nobility.[5] The Nogai – as in earlier reports – fare even worse; they are depicted as miserable farmers but nevertheless such good horse thieves that even the Cossacks are no match for them, as she remarks ironically. Her overall assessment of the non-sedentary inhabitants of northern Crimea was withering: "The moral character of the Nogays is of the worst description, and there is hardly any kind of mischief which they will not perpetrate."[6] Once again, we see the disdain for nomadic communities that has been the hallmark of many reports on Crimea since Antiquity (cf. Chapter 2); perhaps this stark distinction between civilized and uncivilized also took into consideration the tastes anticipated of the readership, since it is contradicted somewhat by the descriptions of Muslims produced in an administrative context: until the Crimean War, the tsarist administration reported more pragmatically or analytically on its new subjects, usually refraining from making normative comments despite fundamentally mistrusting them.[7] Of course, a readership expecting entertainment and excitement sought a less sober depiction of the Other on the European peripheries – and writers often pandered to such expectations.

The advantage of being female addressed by Holderness herself mainly applied when she wrote about a sphere which was indeed inaccessible to men: the Tatar women, for the extensive segregation of female and male worlds prevailed in Crimean Tatar centres such as Bağçasaray or Qarasuvbazar into the first decades of the twentieth century. Hence firsthand (male) accounts about Muslim women are rare or, rather, products of the imagination.[8] While Holderness's assessment of the male Tatars of the southern coast is more or less as stereotypical as her portrayal of the Nogai, she produced interesting descriptions of relationships between mother and child or Tatar weaning practices.[9] She took a rather different view of gender relations in Muslim society in general: for most Western European authors, the Orient of their imaginations was a place of female slavery and often a sphere where it was assumed unbridled passions were lived out, the topos of the harem or polygamy (a less common practice in Crimea, for economic reasons) being cited as evidence. But enormous prudery was also considered typically Oriental.[10] Holderness's assessment was no exception:

A Tatar wife is most completely the slave of her husband, and that the men consider her such, I had from the mouth of one of the most respectable of them. Thus she is only desirable as she serves to gratify his passions, or to connect him with some Tatar of better family or greater riches than himself.[11]

It was only in peasant families that she thought she recognized an emotional closeness in couples amounting to true love.[12] Parallel to the gender relations in her own culture and society, for instance with respect to the widespread economically and politically motivated marriages (among the upper strata), she observed that women had room for manoeuvre in both the Christian and the Muslim cultures.

Current scholarship cannot assess the extent to which tsarist rule over Crimea influenced the gender relations within the Muslim communities. What is beyond dispute, however, is that not all Muslim women in Crimea practised veiling.[13] Marriages between Muslims and Christians of any confession were the exception in the tsarist period,[14] but the Russian administration certainly wished for them to take place. Compared to Western European colonial empires, there was less racism, and Russian actors hoped that ties between Muslims and Christians would acculturate the Muslim cultures to the Slavic Orthodox majority population.[15]

On the whole, the annexation of 1783 had a huge impact on the former titular nation, irrespective of gender. The loss of the (limited) independence of the early modern Khanate and involuntary incorporation into a nation of 'infidels' were in themselves profound caesurae. But it was the consequences for the development of the population, the economy, culture and general participation that had a particularly sustained effect.[16]

As already mentioned, St Petersburg's colonial policy towards the former Khanate aimed at the new subjects' inclusion, one reason being to prevent the risk of a strong pro-Ottoman opposition that would strive to re-establish ties with the Sublime Porte.[17] To this end, a corresponding system of incentives was devised: along with the co-option of Tatar *mirzas* (see above), the Muslim clergy (*ulema*) were among those that profited from Russian rule, and hence they remained loyal to the Romanovs too until the demise of the tsarist empire. The clergy's traditional rights in the peninsula were largely recognized. For the state, the advantage of this policy of 'divide and rule' was that Islamic scholars and the nobility, mostly excluded from local politics in the course of the first decades after Russian annexation (except in Bağçasaray and Qarasuvbazar), developed different interests – and didn't form a common front against the new power.[18] The *ulema* were 'granted' a large degree of self-coordination: a mufti selected by the tsarina or the tsar headed a Muslim "Clerical Assembly" formed in 1794. As was common practice in the tsarist empire, this mufti received an aristocratic title and was responsible for religious affairs in Crimea or the Taurida Governorate.[19]

The mufti and the other Muslim clerics were paid by the state, which ensured that they remained loyal to Russian rule. The Muslim community's property – mainly, but exclusively, land – was exempt from state taxes.[20] The Muslim community was also granted control of the *vakıf* (foundation) assets.[21] The religious and ritual affairs and administrative tasks such as keeping registers of births and deaths also remained a domain of the *ulema*.[22]

This older order and administrative structure was supplemented with new ones introduced from the metropolis: it is quite common in imperial contexts for traditional and newly implemented legal and other systems to exist in parallel, at least for a transitional period.[23] In the case of Crimea, however, St Petersburg's mid- to long-term aim was – as outlined above – to adapt the structures as much as possible to those of the Central Russian territories. The Empire also desired the acculturation of Crimea's non-Slavic, non-Christian population, which was encouraged by legislative and administrative measures and ideally culminated in Orthodox baptism. This aim was never achieved; there were no significant waves of voluntary conversions in either Crimea or other areas of the Empire. In one respect, however, the situation in the peninsula was different to other territories with a large Muslim influence, such as on the Volga: while there had been phases of mass Orthodox missions in the conquered former Khanates of Kazan' and Astrakhan' in the mid-sixteenth century, often culminating in violent coerced conversions, such practices were already forbidden in Crimea by Catherine II.[24] Nevertheless, from the 1840s onwards, representatives of the Orthodox Church made ever greater efforts to reinforce Orthodox Christianity in the still predominantly Muslim peninsula and to create an Orthodox infrastructure by (re-)building churches and monasteries. To this end, they drew on the myth of Crimea as the site of the baptism of Rus' (cf. Chapter 1). Ecclesiastical circles also sought to use archaeological excavations to prove that Crimea had been a place continuously shaped by Christianity *and* Slavs from the third century on. However, the results were rather modest: missions to convert the non-Orthodox population were subject to tight restrictions imposed by St Petersburg and in some cases by the local administration too. Missionizing without limitations was only permitted if aimed at Christian groups outside the Orthodox Church, such as the Old Believers, Catholics (e.g. landowners of Polish descent) or Protestants (e.g. from among the German colonists). Even after the Crimean War, when the peninsula was collectively reinterpreted by the Russian-speaking public as a sacred 'Russian' space (cf. Chapter 25), this rule introduced by Catherine II remained *in situ*. Nevertheless, Crimea's own Orthodox diocese was established in 1860.[25]

We have already discussed the cooption of the upper strata of Crimean Tatar secular society into the Russian Table of Ranks. This indirectly promoted the acculturation of the *mirza*s, some of whom discovered the lifestyle of the Russian aristocracy and the Russian language, a few even being baptized Orthodox.[26] They included members of the Şirin clan, who had been so influential under the Khanate and had recognized that adopting Orthodox Christianity was a prerequisite for gaining political/social relevance. Individual members of the family, which now went under the Russified name of Shirinskii (= Şirin) and had princely status conferred on it in 1836, obtained great esteem and important positions in the Russian Empire. Platon A. Shirinskii-Shikhmatov (1790–1853), for instance, had a particularly spectacular career as a graduate of the imperial naval academy he fought *inter alia* against France in the Patriotic War of 1812–14. After holding various positions in the Ministry of National Enlightenment (*Ministerstvo narodnogo prosveshcheniia*), he was made its minister in 1850. He was also a member of the Academy of Sciences, where one of his achievements was helping to compile dictionaries of Old Church Slavic and the Russian language. He was also a literary writer.[27] It was possible, then, for non-Slavic, 'alien' subjects to climb the hierarchy of the Empire if the state conferred on them (social) equality and they adopted the language, religion and habitus of the metropolitan culture. Such 'success stories' were much more common in the Russian than in the British Empire.[28]

For the Muslim peasantry, incorporation into the Empire represented a caesura with sustained impact, although this was not necessarily obvious at first glance: they retained their personal liberties, since serfdom, which prevailed in the Central Russian territories until 1861, was not introduced to the newly conquered areas on the northern Black Sea. For instance, in 1857, over 60 per cent of peasants in Kyiv Governorate were serfs, compared to only 6 per cent in Crimea. The latter were not Muslim subjects, but mainly Slavs (in today's terms, primarily Russians and Ukrainians) who had followed their landowners from the northern territories.[29] This situation notwithstanding, the Crimean Tatar peasantry's situation deteriorated appreciably, partly because large Russian, but also Tatar landowners constantly attempted to limit traditional peasants' rights (e.g. the use of water or meadows) and sought to heavily increase the number of serfs in Crimea. The landowners, irrespective of where they were from, argued that the local peasants had insufficient capacity for work or, interestingly, that it was necessary to achieve uniformity across the Empire and hence the peasantry in the peninsula had to be organized as in the Central Russian territories, which would have practically meant subjecting Tatar peasants to serfdom. However, the tsarist administration would not entertain these aristocrats' wishes, particularly under Governor General of Novorossiia (1823–44) Mikhail S. Vorontsov (1782–1856).[30]

Within the Empire, the Crimean Tatar population did not have unequal rights *de jure*, particularly as they retained their personal liberties, unlike the inhabitants of the Central Russian territories. Regarding the other Muslims in the Empire, it should be noted that overall, Catherine II's reign represented a caesura, since it brought an end to the previous policy of repression towards the Muslims, for instance in the Volga-Ural region. Islamic institutions were reinstalled following a period of forced integration policy in the first half of the eighteenth century; Islam saw a cultural renaissance and mullahs could be appointed to low-ranking positions of office. A relevant difference to Crimea was that in the Volga-Ural region, there were rarely institutionalized foundation administrations, and in the mid-nineteenth century only relicts of a state-recognized nobility remained.[31] Hence the Crimean Muslims appear to have enjoyed a privileged position. Nevertheless, tsarist policy towards the peninsula's Muslim inhabitants – like the later Soviet policy, incidentally (cf. Chapter 31) – was characterized by a "discrepancy between (legal) norms and (lived) practices". These could be "situationally to the benefit or disadvantage of the Crimean Tatar population".[32]

In the tsarist era, it was not only members of the elites such as the Shirinskii-Shikhmatov dynasty that were able to profit from the new circumstances; less socially prominent actors were also able to rise in standing. This does not apply to the majority of the Crimean Tatar peasants, however, despite their status as free men. This is most obvious in the Crimean Tatar exodus to the Ottoman Empire, which has been extensively studied by Brian G. Williams and is one of the most significant phenomena of this first 'Russian phase' in Crimea's history. Analytically, this wave of migration must be seen separately from the *sürgün* – the deportation of May 1944 (cf. Chapter 33) – both in terms of its implementation and with respect to the motivations of the different actors. This is not obvious at first glance, however: fundamentally, population shifts between Christian and Muslim empires were not uncommon between the late eighteenth and the early twentieth century. For instance, there was comparable migration in the Caucasus, the Balkan Peninsula under Habsburg rule, in northern Africa, whose territories had fallen to France, or within the lands ruled by the sultan. What were the reasons? Islamic studies frequently points to the commandment stating that it is every Muslim's duty to emigrate from territory ruled by non-Muslims. This was intended to protect the Muslim community – the *ummah*. This religiously motivated emigration (*hijra; hiğra*) may have played a role in many migration waves during this era, but for many Islamic scholars it is an exaggeration to speak of an actual duty to emigrate from the land of the infidels.[33] In the case of the peninsula, there were a number of motives that indirectly caused the exodus: besides religious reasons, on which it would be impossible to elaborate in detail here, profound economic transformations, including the introduction of capitalist conditions of production, plunged Crimean Tatar agrarian society into a crisis that encouraged emigration.[34]

In the eighteenth century, around 90 per cent of the peninsula's population were still employed in arable and livestock farming. This is by no means an unusual number for the time, but clearly problems in this area had an impact on the economy as a whole. The plight of the peasantry was compounded by conflicts with landowners, the cultivation of products unsuited to the climate by farmers who had immigrated or the water shortage that was in part caused by the Russian occupiers.³⁵ Other factors were the political situation in general and the attitude of imperial actors towards the Muslims: Potemkin's opinion that a Crimea without the Tatars would be a better Crimea, expressed in direct connection with the annexation of 1783, was shared by a considerable number of the elites in later decades too. After the Crimean War in particular, distrust of the religious Other was so palpable that rumours – as "information in the medium of hearsay without an identifiable author"³⁶ – moved many Crimean Tatar families to emigrate. As Edward Lazzerini summarizes: "[E]ndless rumormongering [...] fed the anxieties of many Tatars, thereby contributing significantly to the episodic, and sometimes frenzied, flight abroad."³⁷ Marc Bloch's observation that rumours have always moved the masses can certainly be seen in the case of the Crimean Tatars, with drastic consequences.³⁸

24

Multiethnic and Multireligious Crimea under Tsarist Rule:

'Old' and 'New' Inhabitants – Economic Development

> The character of the Greeks is exceedingly litigious; they are jealous of each other's prosperity, and anxiously engage in the pursuit of gain. They live in the most parsimonious manner, and I have seen them, though employed in day labour, subsisting on onions, or garlic and bread.[1]

Mary Holderness, who lived in Crimea between 1816 and 1820, described the Greek inhabitants of the peninsula as "litigious", "parsimonious" and out for profit – but they were also "respectable merchants" and characterized by their strict adherence to the rules of their faith.[2] Overall, the English colonist arrived at an ambivalent assessment of the Crimean Greek population, the descendants of the Hellenic colonists (cf. Chapter 2) who had settled on the northern shore of the Black Sea in pre-Christian times and had entered into a process of reciprocal exchange with the many peoples who came into contact with Crimea over the millennia.

If we consider the European context of the age, Holderness was cautiously countering the opinion held by the majority of the European elites, who had a particular affection, and in some cases enthusiasm, for Greeks: the Greek war of independence from the Ottoman Empire fought from 1821 and into the 1830s[3] had triggered a veritable love affair with Greece among intellectuals, expressed not only politically and intellectually but also aesthetically in art and literature.[4] Many also looked to Crimea, to cite Goethe's *Iphigenia in Tauris* (cf. Chapter 1), "[m]y soul still seeking for the land of Greece".[5] Philhellenism was not solely fuelled by enthusiasm for the 'Ancient Greeks' and their cultural achievements; there was also a contemporary, anti-Ottoman element to it. This is evident even today in the

Russian *Wikipedia* entry on the lemma "Philhellenism", which is described as sympathy or assistance for the Greek fight "for liberation from the Turkish yoke" ("za osvobozhdenie ot turetskogo iga").⁶ The implication is that Ottoman rule was as oppressive as Mongol hegemony over the territories of Kyivan Rus', to which Russian refers as the Mongol yoke (*mongol'skoe igo*) (cf. Chapter 11). Certainly, even decades after the failure of Catherine II's "Greek Plan", many Russian intellectuals remained fervent supporters of Greek attempts to gain independence – and this was reflected in their opinion of the Crimean Greeks. For instance, the alleged business acumen of which Holderness writes was often praised by Russians. Moreover, as 'Hellenes' and Orthodox Christians they seemed 'similar' to Russians, who considered them religious brethren, especially in comparison with the 'foreign' Muslim population. An additional advantage of this anticipated similarity was that it countered the view held by some members of the European elites that the Russian upper strata were not of equal social or cultural standing; they were now 'related' to the Greeks and laid claim to the assumed dignity of their ancient civilization.⁷ However, this construct had to (and did) overlook the fact that many Crimean Greeks had become largely Tatarized by the long acculturation processes during the era of the Crimean Khanate (mostly in terms of language and habitus, seldom in terms of religion).

But which Greeks was Holderness describing? The question arises since both the Albantsy of Greek descent settled after 1774 by order of the tsarina during the years of the 'independent' Crimean Khanate and the Pontic Greeks (and Armenians) with roots in Crimea had left the peninsula in the summer of 1778.⁸ The exodus of around 30,000 people had not only destabilized the rule of the last Crimean khan, who lost many of his supporters, but was also the result of a long-standing conflict between Muslims and Christians fought out primarily in the coastal regions, probably mostly for economic reasons.⁹ However, the 'new homeland' the tsarist authorities granted the migrants on the northern shore of the Sea of Azov and the Don Estuary, with their centres Mariupol', Taganrog (Russian; Ukrainian: Tahanroh/Tahanrih) and Rostov, was not without its problems. Despite being granted privileges (including land, tax exemptions for the first decade and exemption from military service, guaranteed forever but in fact lifted in the second half of the nineteenth century[10]), many of the former Christian inhabitants of Crimea were drawn back to the peninsula following its annexation. In Russian reports of the age, this was interpreted as an expression of a special connection to their old homeland and great loyalty to the Romanov dynasty. Hardly any writers doubted that the Greek population of Crimea had "earned the right to membership of the Russian state".[11] And indeed, up to the revolutions of 1917, the tsar's Greek subjects in the northern Black Sea region enjoyed a privileged status. On the other hand, it was not until the late nineteenth century that a small number of Russian Greeks began to identify with the Kingdom of Greece, despite the fact that it had existed since 1832.[12] Jumping forward somewhat: in the

USSR of the 1920s, the policy of promoting nationalities – known as *korenizatsiia* (Russian; rooting) – favoured Greeks too. After the Second World War, however, Russo-Greek ties were history: "[L]ike the notoriously 'disloyal' Crimean Tatars, the Germans, who didn't adapt to the Russians (1941), or the Bulgarians, allegedly so closely related to the Russians", the Crimean Greek population – over 15,000 inhabitants – was deported.[13] When they were forced to leave the peninsula under the threat of violence by the Soviet secret service troops in 1944,[14] the five-thousand-year history of Greek settlement in Crimea was over. The peninsula's Bulgarians, also favourites of the tsars, shared their fate, as did its Armenians.

> The Bulgarians, though ranking low in point of numbers amongst the other colonists of New Russia, are perhaps deserving the first notice, from the high character they bear, as a sober, industrious, and meritorious class. These people have migrated from the arbitrary subjection of the Turkish government, to the mild one of the Crimea, which, in affording a refuge from the despotic tyranny, possesses a sufficiently strong inducement to the peasant, who lives there in ease and independence, such as he can scarcely find equalled in any other part of the world.[15]

Like the Russian administration, Holderness was also enthusiastic about the few Bulgarians, as she was, incidentally, about Armenians:[16] the Englishwoman praised their upright character, their industriousness and their sobriety. Fleeing the "arbitrary subjection of the Turkish government", they had sought refuge under benevolent Russian rule, where peasants could live a pleasant and independent life. She had express praise, then, for the Russian administration, which had increasingly sought to settle Bulgarian subjects of the sultan from the Edirne (Turkish; Greek: Adrianopolis; Bulgarian: Odrin) region since the early nineteenth century. Like the Greeks, the new inhabitants of Crimea were considered 'similar' by the Russians, since they shared their Orthodox faith and they too were Slavs. Between 1801 and 1810, tsarist recruiters were successful in attracting many Greeks, Bulgarians and Gagauz from the Ottoman Empire due to the precarious situation in their home regions.[17] They settled in parts of the northern Black Sea region (which was now known as Novorossiia, "New Russia"), some of which were thinly populated or had been depopulated by war and the Crimean Tatar exodus, including Crimea,[18] where they established three villages and were, as was usually the case, under the authority of the "Guardianship Committee for Foreign Settlers in Southern Russia", which was responsible for foreign colonists until 1871. This was the year in which the Empire lifted all the privileges it had previously granted colonists, which was more about standardizing the structure of the Empire than Russification. On the whole, there were very consistent attempts to populate the newly acquired territories up to 1819, when the programme was shelved due to growing doubts in political circles in St Petersburg, and above all due to increasing fears that the colonists from the German-speaking areas in particular would import revolutionary ideas into Russia. This did not mean that immigration dried up, however; in the years that followed, several thousand people migrated to Russia, but they were no longer allocated free land.[19]

On the one hand, the Germans were highly desired colonists in the Black Sea region, while on the other hand they were the subject of intense debate in Russian-speaking circles, particularly from the late nineteenth century onwards: a decree of 1785 had moved Mennonites from the Danzig region to the southern regions of the Empire, including Crimea, where they were promised, among other things, religious freedom and the exemption from military service that went with it, things they had not been granted by the Prussian state. In subsequent decades, they were followed by Lutherans, Reformists and Catholics from the southern and western German-speaking territories, but also from Switzerland, Scandinavia and finally from regions of today's Estonia. Economically, these acts of settlement were a great success, with high earnings and birth rates, leading to a wide network of subsidiary colonies. In Crimea, Germans constituted over 22 per cent of the population in the Perekop region, as Dietmar Neutatz has shown using the census of 1897.[20] Nevertheless, the German settlers only partly lived up to the Russian leadership's expectations: unlike their conationals in the cities, who quickly acculturated to the majority society, most German colonists segregated themselves from their Slavic environment. Their marriages were strictly endogenous and hence they failed to fulfil the role the Russians had envisaged for them (and established by law in 1804), namely 'improving' the Slav peasantry by setting a good example. Many attempted to maintain the elements of their lifeworld that "seemed important to them for preserving their identity" and didn't adapt to their new environment any more than was strictly necessary.[21] There was no extensive acculturation, including knowledge of Russian, since it was usually only Germans responsible for 'foreign relations' that learnt the language.[22] Perhaps this is behind Holderness's disparaging assessment of the German colonists as slow and stupid; presumably, she was unable to converse with them: "[T]hey are low, and brutal in their manners, more especially the men, who appear the least civilized inhabitants of the Crimea".[23] Towards the end of the nineteenth century, wider (foreign) policy also played a role in the Russian state's relations with 'inorodtsy' colonists: the strong Russian nationalist tendency in tsarist politics that coincided with the imperial succession in 1881 fuelled distrust of groups declared non-Slavic, including German subjects. Moreover, the latter were also instrumentalized by chauvinist circles within the German Empire, largely without their own knowledge, consent or participation.

Relations between the new settlers and the populations with 'roots' in the peninsula were less affected by these developments: coexistence between Germans and Nogai in the northern regions of Crimea and the neighbouring territories was mostly free of conflict. The situation was evidently "determined by everyday interests beneficial to both parties", argues Dmytro

Myeshkov.²⁴ That such contact would largely pass without violence and take on a certain vitality had certainly not been predictable, given the conflicts that had arisen in the first decades of the nineteenth century when the Russian administration gave the new settlers land, some of which was claimed by the Nogai and their families. On the whole, contemporary reports indicate that the old and new inhabitants of Crimea coexisted peacefully and pragmatically, irrespective of nationalities and religions. In many communities, Crimean Tatar even served as a *lingua franca*, while fewer people had a command of Russian. Marriage remained unaffected, however; beyond the Russian-speaking – that is, Russian-Ukrainian²⁵ – groups, interethnic or interreligious marriages were something of a rarity.

The authorities' preference for confessional and linguistic similarity, already encountered in the case of Bulgarian settlers, was most evident with respect to the Russian or Ukrainian (then usually termed "Little Russian") peasantry. It was for this reason that they were the main group to be resettled to the southern territories of the tsarist empire, including Crimea; given their feudal bonds, their masters could do with them as they pleased anyway. Soon after the Crimean War, this group constituted around three-quarters of the population of Novorossia, a statistic which was considerably boosted by the Tatar exodus.²⁶ While they had fewer privileges than foreign colonists, they fulfilled an important function for the Russian state; their presence 'secured' the regions for the Empire. As mentioned above, it was hoped that their backwardness, which was even lamented by actors within the administration, especially with respect to their agricultural abilities, would be overcome by the good example set by foreign model colonies. That this wish was not fulfilled was due not only to the insularity of the colonists, especially the German-speaking groups, but also to the low level of education of the Slavic peasants. It was not until the second half of the nineteenth century that the heavily neglected Russian school system would be improved by the introduction of a system of local administration (*zemstvo/zemstva*). Holderness, who, incidentally, did not distinguish between the Russian and the Ukrainian population, considered the completely neglected education system the reason for the low level of civilization she observed on the part of the Eastern Slav peasants in Crimea; while she didn't suffer from any uncertainty concerning her own superiority and that of her countrymen, it cannot be said that the Englishwoman thought the "Russian" peasants were entirely beyond redemption: "That civilization will not raise the Russian boor to a more respectable rank in the scale of human existence, who can doubt?"²⁷

The Jewish population, some of whom had arrived in Crimea in Antiquity in connection with the Khazar influences, also contributed to the multiethnic and multireligious character of the peninsula during the tsarist era: Rabbinic Jews of Eastern European Jewish provenance, the Krymchaks (Krymchak: *Qrımçah*), themselves Rabbinic, and the Karaites (cf. Chapter 19) gathered in various places, including larger cities such as Feodosiia and Ievpatoriia. After successive sections of the northern Black Sea coast had fallen under Russian rule in the course of the eighteenth century, the region's Jewish inhabitants found themselves subjects of Catherine II. This could have meant much worse conditions in comparison with the tolerance towards Jews shown under the Ottomans and the Crimean Khanate. It may have been down to the tsarina's pragmatic tolerance or her fear of losing further swathes of the population, but whatever the reason, the authorities did not implement any coercive measures towards the new Jewish subjects or obstruct the establishment of new communities in Novorossiia. This policy stood in stark contrast to the usual treatment of Jews in the core Russian territories. Before the Polish Partitions of 1772, 1793 and 1795, Jews were rare exceptions in the Russian Empire, since they had been forbidden from settling there. In Crimea, the situation was traditionally different, and the English colonist Holderness thought there were a good many Jews in Crimea. Apparently not entirely familiar with basic division, she estimated that they constituted "in all the colonies from one-fifth to one-tenth of the whole population".[28] Her description is largely free of the anti-Semitic stereotypes of the age; she thought it worth mentioning that they were merchants and that the Russian government in the Novorossiian territories was attempting to employ them in agriculture. She didn't mention the relevant distinction between Jews and Krymchaks within Rabbinic Jewry, perhaps because she didn't notice it. The Krymchak Jews are thought to have arrived in Crimea in the first centuries AD and had become heavily Tatarized. Around seven thousand lived in the peninsula before the First World War. Scholars consider them a separate group within Jewry.[29]

Holderness was most impressed with the Karaite Jews; they were wealthy and "most respectable".[30] In this assessment too, she was entirely in line with the Russian state, and one might ask why they were distinguished from other Jews and enjoyed such a good reputation. The origins of the Crimean Karaites, a small number of whom can still be found outside Crimea in parts of Lithuania and Belarus, are ultimately unclear and a source of sustained controversy among scholars. The debate cannot be examined here; suffice it to say that some consider them descendants of the Khazars.[31] Like the Krymchaks, they spoke (and still speak) a Turkic dialect closely related to Crimean Tatar. Their main distinction from Rabbinic and other Jews is that Karaites recognize only the Tanakh and not the Talmud as the basis of their faith. The latter does not contain biblical commandments; instead, it presents their interpretation and application by rabbis. As is usually the case in confessional disputes, Karaites too claim to practise the original form of their religion, considering the 'others' to be dissenters. Hence they display similarities with Christian Protestantism insofar as believers do not need their faith to be mediated by learned figures (rabbis, pastors and so on), arguing that they can gain a full understanding of their religion's doctrine by reading the Torah for themselves. Karaite identity was retained in a lifeworld marked by separation from the Rabbinic Jews as well as members of other religions; up to the 1850s, the Karaite community primarily settled in the mountains, in Mangup-Kale and Çufut Qale (Crimean Tatar; Russian/ Ukrainian: Chufut-Kale). They forged good relations with the new rulers, the Russian Empire; one reason they were so successful in doing so was that they presented themselves as distinct from other Jews. As Neal Ascherson sums up this paradoxical yet successful strategy: "by attempting to be more intensely and primordially Judaic than other Jews, the Karaim ensured that Gentiles would consider them not to be truly Jewish at all."[32] In the medium term, they were able to gain exemptions from the many rules in the Russian Empire that discriminated against Jews, including living outside what was known as the Pale of Settlement, and in 1863 they were granted legal equality with Christians and Muslims. Not only Holderness but also many other contemporary European authors of travel reports – including Russians – included positive portrayals of these heavily Tatarized, religiously independent Jews. Karaites appear as a counterpart to the Crimean Muslims and the 'normal' Jews exposed to rapidly growing anti-Semitism. Russians in particular pointed to their (assumed) loyalty to the Tsardom – the unspoken implication being that they were unlike the allegedly disloyal Crimean Tatars. During the Crimean War, for instance, a most delighted Russian author travelled through a Karaite settlement and met the highly esteemed Sholem-Beim, who, he wrote, had portraits of Tsar Nicholas I, the empress and the then governor general, Vorontsov, hanging up in his house, and also had a good command of Russian.[33] In summary, the Crimean Karaites thus had ascribed to them a "remarkably positive role" in "the debates about the various peoples in the peninsula – as members of a Jewish sect, as an Oriental entity living a traditional way of life and at the same time as a 'good' and loyal group in the religious and ethnic sense".[34] The Karaites even 'escaped' the National Socialist race fanatics' genocide of the peninsula's Jewish population during the Second World War (cf. Chapter 32).

After the Crimean War, the peninsula lost almost 40 per cent of its population, mainly due to another Tatar exodus.[35] This was another blow to its agricultural and economic capacity, which was already weakened – despite the favourable climate. It did not help that the attempts to recruit 'useful' and 'loyal' (= Slavic and Orthodox) colonists were not as successful as had been hoped: in 1858, the Ministry of State Domains (*Ministerstvo gosudarstvennykh imushchestv*) began to resettle Slavic state peasants from the Central Russian regions to the deserted southern Russian territories.[36] From 1860 onwards, there was another influx of Bulgarian Gagauz from the Ottoman Empire and the regions of Bessarabia that Russia lost as part of the Treaty of Paris in 1856, in exchange for Crimean Tatar emigrants. While the new arrivals were considered reliable by the imperial authorities, they found it difficult to adjust to Crimea and the farmsteads the Tatars had abandoned, and a considerable number of them returned to their old homeland as early as 1862.[37]

Contemporaries were reserved in their assessment of the administrative attempts to (re)populate the peninsula after the Crimean War and the development of an efficient economic structure: for instance, a somewhat stereotyping observation written five years after the Crimean War had ended noted that replacing the "apathetic Crimean Tatars" with other ethnic groups was not considered a success, nor had there been any breakthroughs in other spheres such as infrastructure.[38] Progress in the fields of resettlement and the economy was modest in Crimea in the course of the nineteenth century, and the expectation that under Russian rule Crimea would develop into a horde of prosperity would be only partially realized.[39] While there were some achievements in the field of viticulture or tourism based around Yalta, the rest of the peninsula was slow to develop.[40] The authorities only recognized the drastic extent of the shortcomings and the erratic shifts in strategy in migration and economic policy in the course of Russia's failed campaign during the Crimean War: the infrastructure in the peninsula itself and its connection to the imperial centres in the north had not been sufficiently developed following an initial euphoric phase shortly after annexation. The lack of a link to the All-Russian railway network would have particularly dramatic consequences. While connection to the Russian network had been approved and planned since 1851, by the time the Crimean War broke out in 1853, work on the project had not been started, let alone finished, which presented the tsarist troops with immense problems as far as supplies were concerned.[41] Nor did the development of Sevastopol', as a trade hub as opposed to a naval port, proceed as desired. This too was due to an insufficiently consistent 'strategy': while a commercial port was first opened there in 1802, it was opened and closed four times before 1820 alone. The trade restrictions imposed on the Russian Empire by the Treaty of Paris of 1856 meant that international transit of goods did not recommence until 1867, before Feodosiia became the principal trading port in 1890.[42]

How should we assess the population policy, which is of course an important economic factor? By the turn of the twentieth century, the population had risen to over half a million – that is, there was not just consolidation but indeed an increase.[43] The multiculturalism and religious diversity so strongly characteristic of Crimean history was preserved under Russian aegis; it was not until after the Second World War that the peninsula was sustainedly homogenized by Stalin's regime (cf. Chapter 33). But the composition of the population had been transformed, with longlasting effect: the Muslim population, for several centuries the majority, had become a minority, constituting a mere third of the population. The peninsula had become 'more Russian'.

25

The Crimean War:

A 'Modern' War?

> The principal and cheering conviction which you have brought away is the conviction of the impossibility of the Russian people wavering anywhere whatever – and this impossibility you have discerned not in the multitude of traverses, breastworks, artfully interlaced trenches, mines, and ordnance, piled one upon the other, of which you have comprehended nothing; but you have discerned it in the eyes, the speech, the manners, in what is called the spirit of the defenders of Sevastopol. [...] Men will not accept these frightful conditions for the sake of a cross or a title, nor because of threats; there must be another lofty incentive as a cause [...] – love for his country. [...] This epos of Sevastopol, whose hero was the Russian people, will leave mighty traces in Russia for a long time to come.[1]

The great Russian writer Leo Tolstoi, who was stationed in the peninsula as an officer in the tsarist army during the Allied troops' 349-day siege of Sevastopol', rendered his experiences in the Crimean War (1853–6) into an immediate literary portrayal in *The Sebastopol Sketches*. First published while the battles still raged, they appeared in the journal *Sovremennik* (The Contemporary), founded by his no less famous literary colleague, the late Alexander Pushkin. There he described, with a vividness unusual for the age, the terrors of war with the dead and the disfigured, the blood and the torn limbs. At the same time, he praised the heroism of the soldiers and sailors and women and children defending the city, irrespective of their social status. Tolstoi depicted his "Russian people" as a national family. With remarkable prescience, he prophesized the collective emotional significance Sevastopol' and Crimea would thenceforth hold for the Russian population – a significance most recently seen in the annexation of Crimea in the spring of 2014.

The Crimean War also made a profound impact on the national memory of Russia's enemies in the conflict:

Half a league, half a league,
Half a league onward,
All in the valley of Death
Rode the six hundred.
"Forward, the Light Brigade!
Charge for the guns!" he said:
Into the valley of Death
Rode the six hundred.

[. . .]

When can their glory fade?
O the wild charge they made!
All the world wonder'd.
Honour the charge they made!
Honour the Light Brigade,
Noble six hundred![2]

Like Tolstoi's *Sebastopol Sketches*, the British poet Alfred Lord Tennyson's (1809–92) "The Charge of the Light Brigade" was written during the war (in December 1854) and remains immensely popular in the English-speaking world,[3] as evidenced not least by several artistic reworkings of the subject matter, such as Michael Curtiz's film of 1936 with Errol Flynn and Olivia de Havilland in the lead roles, or Iron Maiden's song "The Trooper" (1983).[4] The historical background to these and numerous other works of art and popular culture is the Battle of Balaklava, which took place on 25 October 1854. The site in the southwest of the peninsula was the British forces' military base during the war, hence the name of the knitted winter headwear. Probably due to a communication problem within the leadership, an assault by British cavalrymen on the Russian positions led to enormous losses for the former, and hence the term "Charge of the Light Brigade" has entered everyday speech as a synonym for a highly ambitious undertaking doomed to failure.

The Crimean War (1853–6), fought between the Russian Empire and the Allies (Britain, France, the Ottoman Empire, and towards the end Sardinia-Piedmont), has recently been labelled one of the most important but largely forgotten conflicts of the nineteenth century by the historian Hans-Christof Kraus.[5] This assessment is clearly due to his German-speaking perspective; Prussia and the Habsburg Empire were not among the warring parties, although this applies to Prussia more than to Austria, since while the latter officially declared its neutrality, it keenly pursued its interests behind the scenes, for instance in the Danubian Principalities, and played a decisive role in the lead-up to the peace negotiations in Paris. However – and this is a crucial difference to the tsarist empire and the Allies – in the German-speaking world, the Crimean War is certainly not part of the collective memory, since there were no dead to mourn and hence no monuments. Thus this conflict is not present in the German-speaking public sphere, unlike in the Russian or English context or that of the other actors.[6]

The Crimean War formed part of the "Oriental Question"; the European powers were ultimately concerned with (in)direct political and economic influence over the Ottoman Empire.[7] Since the late eighteenth century, however, they preferred to play the religion card, claiming to protect the non-Muslim subjects of the Ottoman Empire, who constituted around a third of the population (excluding Egypt).[8] The cause – but not the underlying reason – for the war was a real 'religious conflict', however: the "quarrel of the monks", in which Orthodox and Catholic monks fought over the right to use the holy places in Jerusalem, then under Ottoman rule. The tsarist empire then demanded the establishment of an official protectorate over the sultan's Orthodox subjects, which the Sublime Porte rejected. In July 1853, Russian troops invaded the Danubian Principalities of Moldavia and Walachia, tributaries of the Ottoman Empire. On 4 October 1853, Istanbul declared war on St Petersburg. France and Britain initially remained neutral, until an event that occupies a prominent place in the Russian culture of remembrance and in that of its enemies – for different reasons: the Battle of Sinop, which took place in the night between 30 November and 1 December 1853 (or 18–19 November, according to the Julian calendar). This was the first time the peninsula after which the war is named became indirectly involved; the tsarist sailing fleet departed from the military port of Sevastopol' before almost entirely wiping out the Ottoman warships that had dropped anchor before Sinop. Under the command of the highly regarded Admiral Pavel Nakhimov (1802–55), who died in battle, it was the first time that a naval battle had seen the use of explosive grenades fired from onboard a vessel, setting the Ottomans' wooden fleet alight. After Russian bombardment, the flames even spread to the city.[9] This represented an impressive victory for the tsarist navy, which was not exactly used to success, but the consequences of Sinop would prove severe: the British press, already anti-Russian, lambasted the Russian actions as dishonourable, since the victory had been achieved not in a regular fleet-to-fleet, man-to-man battle but in a night-time assault on an armada that had dropped anchor. Hence the Western European media wrote "of a massacre instead of a regular act of naval warfare".[10] This contributed to Britain's and France's entering the war on the side of the Ottomans.

The Crimean War was by no means fought exclusively in Crimea or on the Black Sea and in the Danube region; rather, it had many theatres: for instance, on the Baltic Sea the Grand Duchy of Finland, in personal union with the tsarist empire, was bombarded by the British navy, which also laid siege to Petropavlovsk in the Kamchatka Peninsula in Russia's Far East. The war was also fought in the South Caucasus and northeastern Anatolia. Nevertheless, the conflict that stretched beyond the geographical borders of Europe became known as the "Crimean War". How did this come about? A plausible explanation might be provided by a less military aspect: in comparison to previous wars, this one was "eminently readable and viewable" – and this readability and viewability was due to events closely connected to the peninsula.[11] Fundamentally, the Crimean War is unanimously termed the first war in which a large role was played by the public – who perhaps even helped decide its outcome – especially, but not only, in the British Isles. The war became "readable and viewable" due to technological progress in the form of the telegraph and photography. War reporters and photographers popularized the battles far away from home much more quickly than had previously been possible – and this also made

FIGURE 25.1 *The Battle of Sinop on 18 November 1853 (*The Night After the Battle*), painting by Ivan Aivazovskii, 1853.*

FIGURE 25.2 The Defence of Sevastopol' 1854–1855, *panoramic painting by Franz Rubo, 1904.*

the war more 'tangible' for non-participants. Pioneers were the London *Times* and figures such as William Howard Russell (1820–1907),[12] Roger Fenton (1819–69)[13] or James Robertson (1813–88). Their work went some way to ensuring that the conflict became inseparably associated with one of its theatres, Crimea, whence they sent so many reports. Photographs from the peninsula quickly found their way to the rest of Europe. The war and home fronts were thus more easily thought of as one, particularly in the case of the Allies' 349-day siege of Sevastopol', where men, women and even children became actors in the conflict.

In addition to the media aspect, many scholars also label it the first modern war due to the contrast with the previously "limited" or "cabinet" wars.[14] It is considered the first instance of static battle, and also involved the use of modern weapons systems by all sides.[15] At the same time, as remarkable as it may seem, for long periods the Crimean War was fought very badly by all parties in terms of basic strategy and sundry preparations (for instance victualing and supplies in general).[16] Britain and France's emphasis on the ideological dimension – the fight against the autocratic Russian Empire – as the cause of the war, and not as a subsequent explanation, is less convincing, however. This interpretation ignores the economic and power-political interests of the allies of the Sublime Porte. The Great Powers – and St Petersburg – considered the Ottoman Empire a kind of supplementary colonial sphere over which they sought influence. The notion that the Crimean War was above all a conflict between two poles of civilization (West versus East, i.e. Russia) simply doesn't stand up.[17]

The Crimean War was the first to involve women in the armament industry[18] and military nursing: while the war made Florence Nightingale (1820–1910) widely renowned as the founder or reformer of medical care, beyond the Russian-speaking world scant attention is paid to her counterparts in the tsarist empire, the Benevolent Sisters of the Order of the Raising of the Cross (Russian: *Sestry miloserdiia Krestovozdvizhenskoi obshchiny*). Members of the high nobility such as Grand Duchess Elena Pavlovna (1806–73) or aristocratic ladies such as Ekaterina M. Bakunina (1810 or

1811–94), who was related to the anarchist Mikhail Bakunin (1814–76), incidentally, funded this order of nurses or served in the war as nurses themselves.[19] They are held in great esteem to this day.[20] This also holds for so-called common women such as the sailor's daughter Dasha Aleksandrova "Sevastopol'skaia" (Dar'ia L. Mikhailova, 1836–92), whose father had fallen during the Battle of Sinop. She was immortalized by Franz A. Rubo (1856–1928) in his famous panorama of Sevastopol': opened in 1905 to mark the fiftieth anniversary of the defence of the city, the colossal painting depicts a day during the siege. A significant feature of the painting is that it not only portrays the 'common soldier' but also composes an "iconographed" view underlining a "mythic", transcendent quality in the "life of the 'Russian nation'".[21]

With respect to scholarly studies of the Crimean War, it is noteworthy that its diplomatic backstory is dealt with just as intensively as its consequences for the European Concert of Powers. There has been much examination of the principal outcomes of the new order created by the Treaty of Paris in 1856 (some of which were revised by the Congress of Berlin in 1878, however). It guaranteed the Ottoman Empire's existence and embedded it in a new European security architecture. By establishing rules concerning neutral merchant shipping, the treaty also represented progress in maritime law. But in terms of the basic patterns of peace-making it introduced, it was only a partial caesura, scholars have argued.[22] The war as such has been solidly examined in relation to factors such as technology, the media, military hospitals and strategy (see above). The same holds for the consequences of the warring parties' domestic policies; the conflict mainly forced the Ottoman and Russian Empires to implement far-reaching domestic reforms, since it revealed internal shortcomings: the Sublime Porte recognized a need for thorough revision of its policies towards its non-Muslim subjects, which resulted in the Imperial Reform Edict of 1856.[23] Ultimately, the "Great Reforms" under "Liberator Tsar" Alexander II (1818–81) must also be seen in the context of 'reform via defeat'.[24] While there has been much study of the conflict's different facets, the events in the main theatre of war – Crimea – remain curiously under-researched, with the exception of the 'heroic' defence of Sevastopol'. Both aspects will be examined more closely in the next chapter.

26

The Crimean War:

The Events in the Peninsula

> Ruined Pompeii is in good condition compared to Sebastopol. Here, you may look in whatsoever direction you please, and your eye encounters scarcely anything but ruin, ruin, ruin! – fragments of houses, crumbled walls, torn and ragged hills, devastation everywhere! It is as if a mighty earthquake had spent all its terrible forces upon this one little spot. For eighteen long months the storms of war beat upon the helpless town, and left it at last the saddest wreck that ever the sun has looked upon.[1]

Before attaining world renown as the creator of Tom Sawyer and Huckleberry Finn, the American writer Mark Twain (1835–1910) recorded his impression of Sevastopol' after setting eyes on the city in August 1867, over a decade after the siege had ended. As a reporter for the *San Francisco California Alta* newspaper, he embarked on a pleasure cruise on the Quaker City and published his impressions in 1869 in the book *The Innocents Abroad – Or the New Pilgrims' Progress*.[2]

The traces of the "storms of war", it would seem, had yet to be removed over a decade after the conflict had ended. The "helpless town" had been besieged by the Allies not for eighteenth months, as Twain wrote, but for 349 days – from 13 September (26 September) 1854 to 27 August (9 September) 1855. The resistance shown by the city's men, women and children, first termed heroic by Tolstoi (cf. Chapter 25), is probably the point in Crimea's post-1783 history that has done most to feed Russians' emotional appropriation not only of Sevastopol' itself but also of Crimea as a whole. Due to targeted remembrance policies and complex processes of collective memory, the peninsula became an indispensible homeland not only for the Russian population of Crimea but also for 'the' Russian people in many other parts of the country – with recourse to the '349 days'. Besieged Sevastopol' became a cipher for the glory and suffering of an entire nation – in both the tsarist and the Soviet eras. And it remains one to this day, as the widespread enthusiasm in the Russian Federation for the annexation of Crimea in 2014 demonstrates.³

Even if according to Twain (and other authors) the reconstruction of Sevastopol' was far from complete, immediately after the war, work began in earnest creating a tangible heroic military infrastructure with monuments and commemorative plaques, initially upon private – not state – initiative.⁴ Later, the city received several honours: in 1954 it was decorated with the Order of the Red Banner, and in 1965 it was awarded the title *gorod-geroi* (Hero City), commemorating the events of the so-called Great Patriotic War (cf. Chapter 32) as well as those of the Crimean War. The Soviet military historian E.V. Tarle (1874–1955) was thus quite right to entitle his book of 1954 *Gorod russkoi slavy* (City of Russian Glory).⁵ After the Second World War, Sevastopol' also took on a special administrative role: such was its military importance, from 1948 until well into the 1990s even Soviet citizens required special permission to visit. The city had its own budget, something quite unusual in the heavily centralized USSR.⁶ Its status as a "city of federal rank" was comparable only with that of Moscow and Leningrad.⁷

Incidentally, following the Russian annexation of 2014 it again enjoys a privileged position among the eighty-five union subjects of the Russian Federation.

It was the 'heroic defence' of the city during the Crimean War that lent Sevastopol' its particular nimbus. Originally built for military purposes,⁸ as Detlef Jena observes, the "Sublime City" (as the name translates) founded under Potemkin was entirely tailored to military requirements, with several barracks, storehouses, arsenals, shipyards and wide straight roads. In contrast to the structure of the population in other parts of the peninsula, Sevastopol' was mainly Slavic (i.e. Russian-Ukrainian), firstly because as a garrison city it was primarily inhabited by soldiers, and many male subjects of so-called foreign extraction (including the Crimean Tatars) served in the army only voluntarily prior to the introduction of universal conscription in 1874, and secondly because the number of non-Slavs was restricted for security reasons. Before 1853, Sevastopol' had a population of almost 40,000, with a disproportionate number of female inhabitants, which was the rule in military towns, where the only settlers were usually members of soldiers' families.⁹ Before the Crimean War, domestic and foreign visitors were impressed with the city's location and architecture, and after 1855/56 many also praised 'Russian heroism' – that is, the stoicism shown during the siege.¹⁰ Russian-speaking authors often compared the '349 days' to biblical or Classical events. It was not just Twain who referred to that cross-cultural synonym for catastrophes, the destruction of Pompey by the eruption of Vesuvius in 79 AD. In the 1880s, a Russian author compared the reactions of the inhabitants of both cities to the horror. While the Roman city's population fled in panic and passively surrendered to the incontrovertible forces of nature, in the besieged Sevastopol' the people resisted "the hostile power and even let loose the forces of nature in the proud wish to ultimately destroy everything that was impossible to defend".[11] Foreigners who visited the city in great numbers after 1855 as battlefield travellers, as they were known, also frequently paid tribute to the stoicism of its inhabitants with transcendental allusions: one German author wrote that Sevastopol' had quite rightly become "the Russian sanctuary of the Russian army, the Russian nation".[12]

While the siege of Sevastopol' during the Crimean War is thus very present for both contemporaries and scholars, far less attention has been paid to events in the rest of the peninsula. There has barely been any study of life and the situation beyond the battle. With the exception of Arsenii Markevich's (1855–1942) description of the Taurida Governorate, written in 1905, until recently there were no serious examinations of the history of the peninsula during the Crimean War.[13] Such studies are important if we are to understand the waves of Crimean Tatar migration in the years that followed: in September 1854, the peninsula became a theatre of war. This was the start of the phase contemporaries called "the chaos", which was not least a result of infelicitous military decisions made by the then supreme commander of the Crimean troops, Prince Aleksandr S. Menshikov (1787–1869). The long-serving Menshikov, who had fought during the Napoleonic Wars, decided to amass the Russian troops in Sevastopol' and leave the peninsula's expansive coastline defenceless against potential enemy assaults – a decision which in retrospect proved catastrophic.[14] His name is thus associated with two poor decisions in the Crimean War: in early 1853, he was famously sent to Istanbul by Tsar Nicholas I (1796–1855) to convey the Russian demands concerning the resolution to the "quarrel of the monks". The sultan's rejection of these demands, with which Menshikov had reckoned, gave St Petersburg its pretext for triggering the conflict.

Certainly, both his strategy of protecting solely the port city and his decision to evacuate civilian authorities and all state institutions as far north to the mainland as possible frightened the population. Defenceless, they fled in panic, irrespective of their nationality. The situation was compounded by orders to destroy the food stores so that they did not fall into the hands of the enemy, which led to supply shortages. Those who didn't have sufficient funds to head north under their own steam (which was the case with many Crimean Tatar inhabitants), found themselves in a risky situation. The result was looting and violence.[15] The authorities' attempts to de-escalate the situation by deploying Don Cossacks had the opposite effect, since they took part in the looting themselves and often used unreasonable force in dealing with suspected and proven looters. Many innocent people were arrested and local women were raped.[16]

Another seemingly 'modern' aspect was that the Allies considered inviting the tsar's Muslim subjects to collaborate in order to erode tsarist capacity for combat 'from the inside'. For instance, the French supreme commander Armand Jacques Leroy de Saint-Arnaud (1798–1854) issued a proclamation promising the Muslims abandoned by the Russian authorities protection and food. Not surprisingly, some Crimean Tatars took up this offer, especially in Ievpatoriia, where upon landing the Allies did not find any members of the tsarist army apart from a few wounded Russian soldiers. Instead, they were confronted with "a real humanitarian crisis"; almost 40,000 Tatar peasants who had fled to the town were languishing without provisions.[17] Against this background, the fact that there was some – but by no means mass – collaboration with the occupiers on the part of the Muslim inhabitants did not come as a surprise to contemporaries either. The exiled writer and critic of the tsar Alexander Herzen (= Gertsen; 1812–70) was just one of those who defended the Crimean population against the accusation of collaboration with the enemy.[18] However, the accusation of Tatar disloyalty that had been made since the annexation of 1783 was merely reinforced, with disastrous consequences in the medium term. When war broke out, Tatar representatives repeatedly declared their close bond with the ruling dynasty and reminded their brethren – and sisters – of the oath of allegiance to the Romanovs, but Russian circles were increasingly unconvinced.[19] Even the so-called Liberator Tsar Alexander II, who ascended to the throne after his father's death, is believed to have been ill disposed to the Crimean Tatar population and to have expressly approved their later emigration. It is claimed that it was not least their distrust of the tsar and rumours of planned resettlement – which in some cases did occur – and forced baptisms – entirely fabricated – that moved many Tatars to leave for the Ottoman Empire.[20] The deportations of the Crimean Tatar population in May 1944 were preceded by a long pre-history of mistrust (cf. Chapter 33).

Wars often involve not only fighting between combatants but also violence between combatants and the local civilian population, and even violence between various groups among the latter. Civilian or military authorities often take action against their 'own people', out of fear of betrayal and collaboration. The Crimean War was no exception. In contemporary debates it was pointed out, for instance, that the Tatar peasants in the Ievpatoriia region had rebelled against representatives of the tsarist regime as soon as they became aware of the approaching Allied ships, thereby abetting the foreign invasion. It was also claimed that they had attacked or even murdered fleeing Russians.[21] After the Russians had retaken Ievpatoriia under General Korf, there were drastic reprisals and forced resettlement of Crimean Tatars – there are claims of up to 20,000 – without examination of individual cases of collaboration.[22] The Allies themselves also perpetrated violence beyond the battlefield; for instance after the Russian army had surrendered Sevastopol', when the French leadership gave its soldiers permission to loot or only belatedly put a stop to it. There were excesses in the east of the peninsula too: the Allies had originally advanced on the Sea of Azov and taken Kerch in an attempt to cut off supplies to Sevastopol', but they were unsuccessful. However, the troops went on a "drunken rampage", devastating the city and harassing its inhabitants, according to Orlando Figes, who writes that Ottoman soldiers, together with Tatars, looted and destroyed Russian shops and raped Russian women.²³ British and French soldiers were also accused of rape – but they are said to have indiscriminately violated Russian *and* Tatar women.²⁴ Details of the events cannot be verified, but it can be stated firstly that military/ideological enemies are often accused of rape and secondly that sexual violence against women and men (the latter not as frequent) is a common practice in military conflicts, where it is not solely a matter of sexual satisfaction but also a demonstration of power.²⁵ Other 'capital' of symbolic importance to the enemy is destroyed or stolen; it was not just in the Second World War that looted art was an issue – the Crimean War was also thoroughly 'modern' in this respect: for instance, the French military took possession of various cultural monuments it found in the peninsula, including two sphinxes and several bas-reliefs, shipping them home, where they were exhibited in the orangery at the Tuileries Palace in the summer of 1856. Parisians could thus enjoy the booty and their troops' tangible victory.²⁶

First, however, the war had to be brought to an end. In Crimea, it gradually came to a stop in the autumn of 1855; Sevastopol' was evacuated in the September after three days of heavy bombardment. Before surrendering, the Russian defenders first blew up the fortifications; it was only then that French troops were able to take the city, most of which had been destroyed. Despite the fall of Sevastopol', the tsarist empire had yet to be defeated strategically,²⁷ since it remained on Ottoman territory in the Caucasus, for instance. An important operation was the siege of Kars led by General N. Murav'ëv-Karskii (1794–1866), which continued after Sevastopol' was evacuated and would be of consequence for the peace negotiations that began in Paris a few months later. In November 1855, the Ottoman and British defenders capitulated due to a cholera epidemic and food shortages. Tsar Alexander II, who had only recently ascended to the throne, nevertheless decided to accept the Allied peace offer. One reason for this was the advance of Austria into the Danubian Principalities; the Habsburg Empire was 'neutral' but openly threatened to wage war on Russia; another (and perhaps even more important) reason was fear of "inevitable bankruptcy" if fighting continued, as Winfried Baumgart argues.²⁸ As is so often the case, then, it was pragmatic considerations that led to the end of the war; Russia could simply no longer afford to keep fighting it.²⁹ An additional factor was fear of peasant rioting, the first incidences of which occurred with the conscription of the rural estates in parts of the empire far from the front.³⁰ There was also immense distrust of the non-Russian nationalities – not only the Crimean Tatars, since the Poles were also considered candidates for uprisings, as were the peoples of the northern Caucasus, where the tsarist empire had been fighting a 'small' hybrid war since the 1820s against the *Gortsy* (mountain dwellers) led by Imam Shamil (1797–1871). This war would last well into the 1860s. Despite the great distrust shown towards the non-Slavic groups of different faith or confession in the Russian Empire, the Crimean War actually demonstrated the stability of the multinational empire, since extensive rebellion did not take place; as the Russian historian Gorizontov puts it, it was "an evaluation of the robustness of the imperial structure".[31]

The Treaty of Paris, which was typical of the age and rather conventional, put an end to the first 'modern' war, but the peace did not last; its most significant achievements – at least until the Russo-Ottoman War of 1877–78 or the Congress of Berlin – were the neutralization of the Black Sea, the agreement not to rebuild fortifications, arsenals, etc., in Crimea and on the Baltic Sea the withdrawal from conquered territories and the exchange of prisoners.[32] Orlando Figes notes that "[t]o many at the time, the outcome did not appear worthy of a war in which so many people died". Russia had lost over 400,000 men, more to disease than to direct combat.[33]

Article V of the Treaty of Paris established that the signatories "grant a full and entire Amnesty to those of their subjects who may have been compromised by any participation whatsoever in the events of the War in favour of the cause of the enemy".[34] This was not fulfilled, however, as the Crimean Tatar exodus after the war demonstrates. Neither the Ottoman Empire nor the Russian Empire granted their subjects a "full and entire amnesty" for alleged or actual collaboration with the enemy; it was not just in the peninsula that there were massive demographic shifts as the treaty became forgotten. At the same time as approximately 200,000 Muslim Crimean Tatar inhabitants of Crimea, an estimated one million other people left the northern Caucasus for the Ottoman Empire, while Bulgarian, Gagauz and Greek subjects of the sultan headed in the opposite direction. This migration occurred for economic and religious reasons, to escape the climate of distrust and/or out of fear of repressions. Both empires thus used specific, structural mechanisms of violence against their own subjects – measures Mark Pinson fittingly labelled "demographic warfare".[35]

27

After the War:

Crimea between 1856 and 1905

Esther Kinsky (*1956) and Martin Chalmers (1948–2014) wrote a travel narrative based on a journey to the peninsula in October 2013 – before the annexation of 2014, then. Their work does not depict a mythologized magical world of beauty; rather, their destination is far from glorified, as implied by the subtitle *Aufzeichnungen von der kalten Krim* (Notes From Cold Crimea):

> At night I read Chekov in the spartan guesthouse, and when I looked westwards from the balcony in the morning, I could only think of Chekov with the giant rock on his shoulders, gasping words about plains onto paper under its weight. I had come here with a sketchy map in my head marked with, besides Chekov, the ineluctable Pushkin, and Mickiewicz's Crimean Sonnets, Marina Tsvetaeva in Feodossiia, Mandelshtam in Koktebel, always preoccupied with the arc of the White Nights of the cold North in this blue, warm land that held untearable threads of Antiquity. It was on these threads that Russia was bound to the cradle of culture, tied to Hellas, that the peasant in the northern snow was tamed. More light![1]

The passage cited contains some elements typical of perceptions of Crimea after 1856. As a Slavonic studies scholar and translator, Kinsky is well aware of these images of Crimea, but she will certainly have gone there with more than a "sketchy map in my head". The peninsula is aptly described as a place that inspired Russian and non-Russian authors of the nineteenth and twentieth centuries (such as the Pole Mickiewicz). This is followed by reference to the pride members of the Russian elites took in owning 'their' share of Hellenic high culture (cf. Chapter 22), a pride that extended well into the second half of the nineteenth century. In the decades leading up to the First World War, Crimea had become a yearned-for counterpoint to the

"White Nights of the cold North". This holds not only for artists who contributed to the emergence of the "Crimean text", as literary scholars call it, and the mythologizing of the peninsula as a site of Russian culture (cf. Chapter 1). It is not surprising that the upper echelons of Russian society also developed an emotional attachment to Crimea in their summer houses and rented retreats on its picturesque Mediterranean south coast. But how was Kinsky's and Chalmers's "peasant in the northern snow" tamed by Russia's possession of Crimea – that is, how were an allegedly savage bunch transformed into a cultivated people? And are there other 'true statements' about the peninsula behind authors' literary-artistic form?

By citing the famous words attributed (probably apocryphally) to Johann Wolfgang von Goethe: "More light", which of course generally stands for Enlightenment and progress, Kinsky and Chalmers lend expression to the idea that the link with Crimea provided the impetus for the modernization of a Russian Empire many Western European writers labelled "backward".[2] This may allude to the ambitious reform programme introduced by Alexander II (cf. Chapter 25) and begun after the Crimean War. Its centrepiece was the abolishment of serfdom in 1861.[3] However, given that Crimea had relatively few bonded peasants, this measure did not amount to a great caesura in the peninsula. On the other hand, the educational (1863 and 1871) and legal (1864) reforms and the introduction of local self-governing departments (1864 and 1870) had a sustained impact on Crimea, expanding opportunities for participation for many inhabitants irrespective of their ethnicity or religion.[4] Although there was a delay in repairing the damage caused by the war and the occupation of the peninsula, fundamental improvements were made in the medium term,[5] particularly with respect to long-overdue infrastructural measures: the road network in Crimea itself and the connections to the north had not been sufficiently developed following an initial phase immediately after the annexation of 1783. The lack of a connection to the All-Russian railway network had had drastic consequences for Russian supplies in the Crimean war; the situation was finally rectified in 1875. The tardiness of the authorities is well illustrated by the fact that a rail link had actually been approved in 1851;[6] it had simply not been implemented.

Connection to the railway network not only vitalized the flow of goods such as fruit, vegetables, wine or tobacco to the north. It also assisted the development of tourism; now more people could travel to Crimea faster than before – and see its beauty and historicity for themselves. In turn, this strengthened many tsarist subjects' collective bond with the peninsula, just as much as the memory of the 'heroic' but futile battle with the British, the French and the Ottomans. Incidentally, this is not a Russian phenomenon; scholars have demonstrated that modern tourism promotes the collective appropriation of spaces and territories. Previously unknown regions are felt to be part of one's own state and are emotionally appropriated.[7] Nor is it always necessary to see distant tourist destinations in person for this to happen – and in the case of Crimea, most people couldn't afford to anyway.

Knowledge of its special value to the Empire was widely popularized via channels such as travel reports,⁸ stories or postcards from acquaintances who had been there or by the media, which underwent particularly dynamic development in the tsarist empire during the late nineteenth century.⁹ The "peasant in the northern snow" could thus gain knowledge of Crimea's special status without ever setting foot in the peninsula, although whether that "tamed" him is another question.

Crimea had already become a preferred tourist destination during the tsarist era, with the southern coastal resort of Yalta as its capital.¹⁰ The metamorphosis of what was once a small Tatar village was impressive: in the late nineteenth century, Yalta had as many visitors as the Bohemian spa of Karlsbad.¹¹ Crimea as a whole failed to live up to the economic expectations placed on it, however.¹² This was felt particularly keenly in the agricultural sector, which fell into crisis following the mass exodus of the Tatar population as a result of the Crimean War. For it would prove that there were disadvantages to the 'better Crimea without Crimean Tatars' that had been envisaged since the days of Potemkin. The new Bulgarian or German settlers brought in to replace the Muslim peasants in the areas the Tatars had abandoned experienced difficulties farming the land.¹³ Viticulture, on the other hand, flourished in the second half of the nineteenth century, as did tourism, especially in Yalta, where it contributed to modernization and the development of a consumer society in this part of the Russian Empire – with both the positive and the negative consequences that come with it.¹⁴ The travel boom placed local government in Yalta and other coastal areas under great pressure, since the entire infrastructure – roads, water and energy supplies, etc. – had to be improved.

The peninsula had begun to develop into a sought-after destination after Catherine II's Tauric Journey in 1787 (cf. Chapter 22). It was followed by learned tourists such as Peter Simon Pallas, who in turn was followed by men and woman from all over Europe.¹⁵ They found an eager readership as the travel writing genre boomed in the first half of the nineteenth century. Accounts of Crimea proved particularly popular, since the peninsula had been of great significance in Antiquity in addition to possessing beautiful landscapes. In connection with the so-called Oriental Question and Crimea's military relevance, the region ultimately attracted travellers such as the Englishman Laurence Oliphant (1829–88). His account of his Crimean journey in the autumn of 1852, published the following year, was immensely popular and extremely well timed, being read both as entertainment and as a work of espionage providing information about the military capacity of the tsarist army and navy stationed there.¹⁶ After the Crimean War, all sorts of battlefield tourists were attracted to the peninsula. They too had a considerable hand in popularizing the destination. An even larger role was played by the Romanovs themselves, however.

In 1825, the tsarist dynasty had acquired their first property near Yalta in the form of the Oreanda Palace, although initially they used it only sporadically. It was not until the reign of Alexander II that the Romanovs regularly holidayed in the peninsula. Hence the once sleepy coastal town was a site of politics long before the famous Yalta Conference of February 1945 (cf. Chapter 34): after the Crimean War, many representative buildings sprang up along with the necessary 'capital' infrastructure as Yalta and its environs became the temporary seat of imperial government during the summer months. The rapid development of the telegraph and road networks, for instance, was not least due to the Romanovs' enthusiasm for the peninsula.[17] And this enthusiasm infected the nobility and wealthy members of the upper classes. In the late nineteenth century, the middle classes – which did exist in the Russian Empire, to a certain extent – also 'discovered' Crimea.

When in December 1920 Lenin (Vladimir I. Ul'ianov, 1870–1924) gave his famous decree "On the Use of Crimea for the Medical Treatment of the Workers" ("ob ispol'zovanii Kryma dlia lecheniia trudiashchikhsia"),[18] defining the role of the peninsula the Bolsheviks had just taken, this time for the long term, as an important spa for Soviet Russia or the Soviet Union (after 1922), he was drawing on foundations that had been laid well before the Revolution. Thenceforth, proletarians exhausted from building socialism would recuperate in the expropriated villas and palaces of the aristocracy and the bourgeoisie; new sanatoria soon followed.

Although mass tourism as we know it today did not begin until during the Soviet era, when Crimea became the 'bathtub of the USSR', the south coast was transformed irreversibly during the tsarist age. Modernism with all its contradictions came to the peninsula: on the one hand, tourism and the spa culture had a positive effect: besides better roads, there was a greater selection of goods, for instance, and medical care in Yalta and its environs was much improved.[19] The architecture changed, and the grand villas and other buildings that sprang up still attract and delight visitors to this day. On the other hand, a considerable number of locals and foreigners alike were already lamenting the high cost of living and the loss of the exotic flair in the nineteenth century.[20] However, many locals profited from this new branch of the economy and were happy to do business with the visitors: with the introduction of the self-governing bodies – the abovementioned *zemstva* – the spa and tourism sector became a matter for local actors from 1871 onwards. For instance, a pioneer and exponent of the fusion of private and political interests so common in capitalism was Yalta's first elected mayor, Sergei P. Galakhov (1806–73), who also owned the best hotel in town.[21] It was not only Slav inhabitants of Crimea who did business with the travellers; they were joined by other national groups: Tatars worked as coachmen, ice sellers or mountain guides, for example.[22] Tourism and the spas thus transformed the lives of the Crimean population, irrespective of their nationality.

Scholarship has provided many examples of how in the nineteenth century the spa became a "national mission".[23] This holds not only for

Russia and Crimea; some nineteenth-century Russian authors branded rich Russians' preference for foreign spas such as Baden-Baden or Bad Ems unpatriotic and recommended that they visit the spas at home instead – in the Caucasus, in the Baltic region or in the "Russian Italy" – that is, Crimea.[24] Increasingly, the last was no longer perceived as a foreign, Muslim region or as a colony; rather it was seen as an integral part of the Russian fatherland. The travel writer and ethnographer Evgenii Markov (1835–1903) was speaking for many of his countrymen when he wrote: "Everything you seek you will find in your own country, on the south coast of Crimea."[25]

28

The Crimean Tatar Population after the Crimean War

Not one of the high-ranking Crimean Tatars has sent his children to the [Crimean Tatar] school department, although it existed for 28 years. Many officials and election workers had and [still] have difficulty writing their fore- and surnames in Russian; they have always avoided, on some pretext or other, having their children learn Russian thoroughly. The result was that earlier, when the Crimean population mostly consisted of Tatars, the Tatar school department was of no use, that it was hardly necessary to keep it [running] for the Tatars. [...] Nobody has ever prevented the Tatar nobility from sending their children to joint [i.e. mixed nationality] educational establishments. On the contrary, all local powers have encouraged them to do so whenever they could, but to no avail, since they apparently refuse to raise their children together with other nationalities, apparently they are afraid that their children will stop being Muslims if they receive an education [...]. That is not libel, but the unadulterated truth.[1]

This was the dim view of the interest the Crimean Tatar elites took in their children's education expressed by an unnamed author writing in *Vesti*, the "Magazine of the Ministry for Public Education", in 1863. Like the Crimean Karaites, he continued, they kept "their children in profound stupidity", while the Rabbinic Jews took education seriously.[2] The author provided a detailed description of the state of the education system in Simferopol', the centre of the Taurida Governorate, in the early years after the Crimean War. In it, he was also critical of the state authorities, which he claimed were particularly neglectful of girls' education. He also touched on the great wave of Tatar emigration that began in the late 1850s: until their "resettlement" ("do vyseleniia"), they had constituted a third of the population, compared to only an eleventh in 1863; it is not clear whether or not he considered this a great loss.[3]

After the Crimean War, the Crimean Tatar community faced a fundamental crisis: the mistrust shown in them by sections of the tsarist administration and Slav subjects paired with the precarious economic situation had moved many of them to migrate. Culturally and socially, their situation was also characterized by passivity in the intellectual and artistic sphere, at least according to the expert on Crimean Tatar history Edward Lazzerini, a view that is supported by the refusal to send their children to state schools reported in *Vesti*.[4] However, it was by no means the case that the Crimean Muslims rejected schooling *per se*; there was a comprehensive network of Tatar educational institutions, which were also attended. These educational establishments were under the aegis of the Muslim clerics, however. The clerics were also responsible for registering births and deaths and held jurisdiction in legal matters concerning the Muslim community[5] – and had no interest in this changing. In the primary and upper schools – *mekteb* and *medrese* respectively – religious study, Arabic and the Quran remained predominant in the nineteenth century. These schools did not teach Crimean Tatar, either spoken or written, and the attempts of the imperial administration between the 1840s and the 1860s to introduce basic Russian lessons had been lacklustre and hence largely unsuccessful.[6] An additional factor was the unconvincing state of the Russian education system as a whole, which didn't really offer an alternative to the Muslim institutions. It wasn't until the reform era that it received a decisive boost, which also led to an increase in the number of Crimean Tatar pupils. The so-called Russian–Tatar educational establishments were largely funded by the education ministry; as one of its directives stated, they were intended to "promote the Russification and merger [*sliianie*] of all native aliens [*inorodtsy*] living within the borders of our homeland with the Russians", as a ministerial directive stated.[7] The assumption expressed in *Vesti* that the Muslim elite refused to send their children to these schools out of fear of alienation from the rules hitherto observed in their religion and in their lifeworlds were not without foundation, since this 'alienation' was a declared aim of the tsarist authorities. Given how their numbers had been decimated since the 1860s, Crimean Tatar actors felt it important that they retain their Muslim Tatar identity in an increasingly Slav Orthodox environment; many thus chose the path of segregation from the Slav majority society. Emigration too was an attempt to stabilize the construction of Muslim identity endangered by the pressures of modernization. This is underlined by a further wave of emigration after 1874 following the introduction of universal conscription throughout the tsarist empire; many Crimean Tatars feared that they would not be able to observe their religious obligations in the tsarist army.[8] At the same time, the Crimean Tatar soldiers were held in high regard.[9] Even after the Crimean War, during which the Tatar population were generally considered to have collaborated with Russia's enemies, Alexander II was impressed with their military achievements: in recognition of their merits, in 1863 he had a special cavalry unit formed and placed under his personal command.[10]

Crimean Tatar–Russian contact was characterized by a complex interplay between integration and self-isolation, between trust and distrust. Hence it should be mentioned that there were also manifestations of acculturation and reciprocal exchange between old and new inhabitants of Crimea – even if there were few marriages across religious boundaries.[11]

Russian authors were convinced that the 'backward' Crimean Tatars could be civilized solely by education in imperial institutions and in the Russian language; only then would they be full-fledged subjects of the Empire. However, as a rule, voluntariness was preferred to coercive measures and there was criticism of the failure of the tsarist authorities to provide sufficient incentive for attending Russian-speaking schools.[12] It is also interesting that the traditional Crimean Tatar educational institutions were sometimes rated rather highly: in the early 1880s, an analysis of the Crimean Tatar population in the post-emigration phase noted that some 70 per cent of both sexes (!) were able to read and write Crimean Tatar, but not Russian.[13] Even if this statistic says nothing about the quality of this ability, it seems high compared to other parts of the Empire, including the Russian-speaking areas.[14] There was no denying, however, that in Crimea's schools run by clerics, religious instruction was the top priority.

Some Crimean Tatars criticized this just as much as the generally pessimistic underlying mood among the Muslim population in the decades after the Crimean War. Finally, in the early 1880s, a movement emerged in Crimea itself (similar to an earlier one led by Tatars in the Volga region)[15] that would prove fundamentally important both for the peninsula and for the development of a specific Muslim Russian identity: Jadidism (which roughly translates as "new method"; Arabic: *al-usul al gadida*; Persian: *törki usul-i gadid*). İsmail Gaspıralı (Crimean Tatar; Russian: Ismail Gasprinskii; 1851–1914) is considered "the architect of modernism among Muslim Turkic subjects of the Russian Empire".[16] He was one of the first generation of "trans-imperial people" (James H. Meyer) among Russia's Muslims, including the Volga Tatars Yosıf Aqçura (Tatar; Russian: Iusuf Akchurin; 1876–1935) or the Azeri Əli bəy Hüseynzadə (Azeri; Russian: Ali-bek Guseinzade; 1864–1940), who maintained ties with intellectuals in the Ottoman Empire.[17] Like Aqçura or Əli bəy Hüseynzadə, Gaspıralı was educated in the tsarist empire itself (in Moscow), in Western Europe (Paris) and in Istanbul.[18] Scholars have repeatedly emphasized his role in creating a space of Muslim communication within the Russian Empire.[19] At the same time, as Ulrich Hofmeister has recently noted, as a Muslim from the Crimean Peninsula he evidently saw himself in a "mediatory position" between European Russia and its Muslim territories in Central Asia. As part of his vision, he identified education as a crucial factor for the so-called civilizing of the Muslim subjects and, unlike many of his Russian contemporaries, he did not fundamentally consider Islam as such an obstacle to modernization.[20] His treatise *Russkoe Musul'manstvo* (Russian Islam)[21] was published in

1881, and after 1883 the magazine *Terciman/Perevodchik* (The Translator) popularized his ideas far beyond a Crimean Tatar readership.[22] His core demand was the modernization of Islam in the tsarist empire via the adoption of the Western – specifically the Russian – model of education. The clerics' religious monopoly was to be abolished, and Russia's Muslims were to communicate using a standardized Turkic language he had developed, which was (to simplify the issue somewhat) a variant of spoken Tatar without Arab and Persian words. He also used this language in the Turkic-language section of the bilingual *Terciman*, which also carried articles in Russian.[23]

In order to spread this language, he developed a new, effective teaching method. In 1884, a reform school was founded upon his initiative in Bakhchisarai, where he had previously been the mayor for some years. This school taught reading and writing, secular subjects and Russian. Initially, Muslims in other parts of the Empire were not particularly impressed with Gaspıralı's efforts, but eventually his model was adopted by the Volga Tatars, for instance.[24] Gaspıralı and his followers – who included women, their equal participation in society being a key demand of the Jadidists[25] – were convinced that only a modern, secular Muslim society could avoid Russification in the long term.

Ultimately, a 'modern' group identity spread from Crimea, based on the 'common experience' of Turkic descent, a common linguistic and cultural community including religion, and recourse to a 'common history' (that of the Golden Horde). In Christian Noack's assessment, the "Jadidist [...] discourse thus created [...] a community of Muslim elites from all parts of Russia as a communication group".[26] Gaspıralı and his generation may have interpreted and planned Jadidism as a cultural movement, but their activities were ultimately political.[27] Nevertheless: what was the significance of a 'secular Islam' for the imagined community of all Muslims, the *ummah*, and for the role of the Ottoman Empire? Was Jadidism a kind of national movement of the Crimean Tatars or Russia's Muslims as a whole? How was the relationship with the ethnic Turkish population in the Ottoman Empire interpreted? What were the consequences for St Petersburg or Istanbul? Although Gaspıralı himself repeatedly stressed Russia's Muslims' attachment to the Empire – while firmly rejecting a Russification policy – he was repeatedly given the cold shoulder by nationalist and Orthodox Russian elites, who considered every Muslim a religious fanatic.[28] After the Russian Revolution of 1905, Jadidism would also receive criticism within the Muslim community: it was opposed by the Young Tatar Movement, which increasingly defined itself as Tatar or ethnic Turkish,[29] and by the traditional Muslim clerics, who were still granted privileges by the Russian authorities. The example of the movement Gaspıralı shaped demonstrates two things: firstly, it shows that the allegedly so backward Crimean Tatar population was in the early stages of a process of nation building roughly in parallel to other nationalities, a process that involved large sections of the intellectual elites in the years prior to the First World War at the latest.[30] This was the

FIGURE 28.1 İsmail Gaspıralı (Ismail Gasprinskii).

start of a development in which an increasing number of Crimean Tatars found an intellectual and emotional reference point in the peninsula instead of the Ottoman Empire or the abstract *ummah*.[31] Secondly, the room for manoeuvre enjoyed by the Crimean Tatar population or its elites becomes evident. It was not until the reforms throughout the Empire as a whole that this room for manoeuvre could be used in local self-government, for instance – and it certainly was used, as demonstrated *inter alia* by the installation of Gaspıralı's reform schools. Nonetheless: "[T]he Crimean Tatar elites [had] indisputably lost the primacy of independent political action and their ability to shape society for themselves [had] at least been restricted, as is usually the case in colonial contexts."[32] And the fact that the former Crimean Khanate was a colony and its titular nation was a subjugated nationality[33] is beyond doubt.

There are different forms and variants of colonialism, however. Unlike some of the Russian Empire's Central Asian conquests, for instance, Crimea was, as we have seen, firmly part of the Empire; most of the legal norms introduced to the Central Russian territories also applied there. Nor was the Crimean Tatar population subject to the "Statute On the Administration of the *inorodtsy* [native aliens]" ("Ustav ob upravlenii inorodtsev") introduced in 1822, which subsumed a large number of non-Slavic inhabitants of the tsarist empire under a special legal category and hence was not part of the legal code of the Central Russian territories. Nevertheless, Crimean Tatars were often referred to disparagingly as "inorodtsy", even if this term was not originally pejorative.[34] And these tensions, which also existed in the Soviet era, incidentally (cf. Chapter 31), were and are characteristic of relations between Tatars and the Russian regime in the peninsula: in the tsarist era too, there was no discrimination *de jure*. Rights were not restricted on the basis of nationality, although they were on the basis of social standing, and there was certainly plenty of structural and practised discrimination too. As the example of the Jadidists shows, however, actors were able to make use of the opportunities for participation, especially after the revolution of 1905.

29

The Revolution of 1905 and its Impact in Crimea

Lieutenant Petr P. Shmidt (1867–1906), who devised a number of revolutionary activities against the tsarist government during the Russian Revolution of 1905, wrote shortly before his execution:

> After the execution I ask emphatically and with all means that my body lie in state before Sevastopol's workers so that they are lord and master of my burial. I am their representative, I am proud of this title, for they gave my life more happiness than all the people I have ever met. [. . .] If the city should erect a monument at some point, then they should engrave the stone with my oath. [. . .] I raised the banner of the revolution of the Russian Fleet, which stayed true to the people, and let this flag of freedom flutter on my grave.[1]

After being arrested several times for clashing with the ruling powers, in the autumn of 1905 Shmidt had taken over command of the rebelling sailors on the cruiser *Ochakov* lying at anchor in Sevastopol'. They were able to raise the Red Flag but did not manage to realize their plans to take strategically important points in the city and arrest the officers loyal to the tsar. A telegram signed by Shmidt demanded that Tsar Nicholas II (1868–1918) immediately call a constituent assembly, to no avail, however. Units loyal to the government rapidly put down the revolt. The self-declared independent socialist Shmidt was the best-known, but not the only one to be arrested in Sevastopol', which was the tsarist navy's main Black Sea port during the First Russian Revolution. Following a short trial in camera, he and his comrades were sentenced to death and executed on the small island of Berezan', which today is uninhabited, near the Dnipro–Buh Estuary. The farewell letter by a figure who in the USSR's successor states remains a popular hero of the "revolutionary struggle of the masses", as he was dubbed by Soviet publications,[2] not only expressed the wish to receive a public funeral but also requested that his body be buried in Sevastopol' beside other victims of the revolutionary events of 1905. Not surprisingly,

FIGURE 29.1 *The battleship* Panteleimon *(formerly* Kniaz' Potemkin-Tavricheskii*), in a photograph from 1906.*

St Petersburg did not fulfil these wishes. It was only after the February Revolution of 1917 that Shmidt's remains were returned to the site of his revolutionary efforts. This took place under the then commander of the Black Sea Fleet and later protagonist of the White Movement, Admiral Aleksandr V. Kolchak (1874–1920), who was not remotely well disposed towards socialist elements. In order to calm the rebellious mood among the soldiers and sailors, he had some of the bodies of the victims of 1905 exhumed and reburied in Pokrovskii Cathedral in Sevastopol' in May 1917. The gesture did indeed help reduce tensions in the short term. In 1923, Shmidt's bones found their final resting place in the city's municipal cemetery.[3] The Bolsheviks demonstrated their keen sense of symbolism by having Shmidt's gravestone made from the memorial slab to Evgenii N. Golikov (1854–1905), who as captain of the battleship *Potemkin* had been killed during the mutiny of 1905 and was an emblematic figure for supporters of the tsarist order.[4]

The battleship *Potemkin* also became a revolutionary symbol: due to Sergei Ėizenshtein's (1898–1948) 1925 film of the same name (Russian: *Bronenosets Potëmkin*) – one of the most frequently cited works in the history of cinema, not least thanks to its famous "steps scene"[5] – the non-Russian-speaking world mainly associates the revolution of 1905 with the events on the *Potemkin* in Odesa. However, the revolution was by no means restricted to St Petersburg, Moscow or the southern port city.[6] There was revolutionary violence both in the countryside and in the peripheral regions of the Empire no longer inhabited by Russians, such as the Baltic region, the Caucasus or Poland.[7] Crimea was no exception. The events of 1905 helped inscribe Sevastopol' into the Russian culture of remembrance as a military-revolutionary site,[8] even if the Crimean War or the war of 1939/41–1945 undoubtedly loom more heavily in the collective memory. The Soviet politics of memory used Lieutenant Shmidt and his comrades to lend emphasis to the idea of Sevastopol' as a prolific revolutionary hotspot. Soviet historiography also sought to construct a revolutionary tradition claimed to pre-date 1905: for instance, the *zhenskii* or *chumnoi bunt* (the Women's Uprising or Plague Uprising) of 1830, caused by food shortages, was repeatedly interpreted as the beginning of the city's revolutionary history.[9] Although he wasn't a Bolshevik, Lieutenant Shmidt was ultimately part of the revolutionary-heroic material and non-material culture of monuments and remembrance that pervaded the entire Soviet Union, from Tver' in the west to Vladivostok in the east:[10] bridges were named after him, such as the first solid structure over the Neva in Leningrad (St Petersburg), known as the Blagoveshchenskii Bridge since 2007, and many writers wrote about him, including Boris L. Pasternak (1890–1960), the author of *Doktor Zhivago*, who dedicated a poem to him. At least two operas were also named after him – one by Nikolai I. Platonov (1894–1967) in 1938 and another by B. L. Iarovinskii (1922–2000) in 1970.

Rebellion – and from the perspective of the respective rulers, revolutions and uprisings are nothing other than a rebellion against an order they regard as legitimate – is not unusual for a city like Sevastopol' with its heavy military presence: the populations of port cities are generally considered "turbulent and uncontrollable".[11] But what did 1905 look like in the rest of Crimea? What participation was there among peasant and intellectual Tatars – there were no industrial workers in the classical sense in the largely agricultural peninsula – and among other national groups? In urban regions with mixed populations beyond Sevastopol', such as Feodosiia or Simferopol', there were some isolated instances of strikes, and in 1905 there were demonstrations on 1 May, while in the villages inhabited by Tatars there were no revolts to speak of.[12] Towards the end of 1905, however, the revolutionary events contributed to a hitherto unimaginable "organization of society":[13] led by local actors, and largely without interference by outside agitators, peasant organizations formed. There were isolated strikes by rural workers, and Tatar small-scale farmers, who traditionally argued with Slav and Muslim landowners over their long-established land usage privileges, felt encouraged to demand their rights with greater vigour.[14] As in other parts of the Empire, in the course of events there were also anti-Semitic acts of violence, some of them initiated by the local state authorities.[15]

The Empire-wide movement of Russia's Muslims, which had received considerable impulses since the 1880s from Gasprali and Jadidism (cf. Chapter 28), gained further momentum in 1905. Kazan' or Orenburg would soon become the real centres of a Muslim movement. Irrespective of these developments, in Crimea unprecedented debates began among the Muslim elites on the nature of Crimean Tatar identity beyond religion and language. There was also a generational aspect to these debates: while older, more established actors were satisfied with successes in the field of education policy such as the establishment of over 350 schools in the peninsula with instruction in Tatar and Russian,[16] younger players posed more fundamental questions about how the Crimean Tatars were related to Russia's Muslims, the Russian Empire and the Ottoman Empire. Were the Crimean Tatars a group distinct from the other Russian Tatars or the Turks? Was one specific variant of the Crimean Tatar language to be privileged or another? How were the Crimean Tatar populations' economic and political problems to be solved – within the tsarist empire, under the rule of Istanbul or independently of both powers?[17] And what was the nature of the manifold pan-Turkic elements to the debates?[18]

It became apparent that these intellectual discourses were no longer primarily about the significance of Islam as an identity-shaping factor, as had been the case some decades earlier and as it remained for Gaspıralı, who fundamentally saw the religion as an important reference point.[19] In the most important city in Crimea after Bağçasaray, Qarasuvbazar, the actors of a group often dubbed the Young Tatars (Genç Tatarlar) came together and defined the 'Crimean Tatar question' in social, political and indeed national terms, expressing doubts as to whether the autocratic Russian system offered a solution. Their central figure was the later mayor of Qarasuvbazar, Abdurreşit Mehdi (also known in the Russian form Reshid Medievich Mediev, 1880–1912), who was a member of the Second Duma that met between February and June 1907 before being disbanded. Some thirty-six of its 450 representatives were Muslims, who had originally formed their faction before some emanating from the Caucasus and the Volga region split off due to differences of opinion on the question of agriculture.[20] In electoral wards in which they were unable to put up a candidate of their own, they had cooperated with the liberal party of the Constitutional Democrats ("Cadets"). The Duma, a concession by the tsar in response to Empire-wide pressure, was dominated by left-wing politicians, which was one of the reasons it did not last long.[21]

Mehdi too leant towards social revolution. He was particularly concerned about the plight of the Crimean Tatar farmers, who had little land, and he demanded their situation be improved by giving them a share of the land held by the landowners, the state or the Muslim community.[22] Despite his comparatively radical views, he became one of the Muslim faction's deputy speakers in the Duma, whose programme was otherwise oriented around that of the Cadets.[23] In retrospect, Mehdi plays a role in the history of the formation of Crimean Tatar national identity primarily because he was probably the first to define Crimea as an entity *sui generis*: he considered it "not a province of the Russian Empire, segment of the Dar al-Islam [house of Islam, i.e. all the territories under Muslim rule] or adjunct of a larger Turkish homeland, but as the rational patrimony of the Crimean nation".[24] Although he and his supporters regarded the established Muslim clerics as their main enemies, he used language with religious overtones in order to win over the Crimean Tatar peasants. However, this was just linguistic adaptation; ultimately, the movement's tactics can be compared to those of the earlier Russian socialists, the Narodniks (Populists or Friends of the People), in terms of both their anti-religious stance and their antimonarchism.[25]

This development was preceded by the first Muslim Congress, attended by Muslim delegates from all parts of the Empire, in Nizhnii Novgorod in 1905. It would be followed by another in 1906 in St Petersburg. The congress considered how to improve the education system as well as discussing legal, juridical and religious problems faced by Russia's Muslims. Gaspıralı was initially successful in sharing his ideas on the necessity of integration into and orientation towards the Russian system.[26] Expecting the installation of a state duma, they agreed to form a Muslim party. In the end, they 'only' formed the Union of the Muslims in Russia (*Rusiya Musulmannarynyng Ittifaky* or the *Rusiya Musulmanlarının İttifakı*, abbreviated to Ittifak). Ittifak was nevertheless "on the way to [becoming] a party", observes Christian Noack.[27] However, the differences within the union, reflecting those of an entire demographic group erroneously conceived of as a single entity, soon became evident. In Crimea, Gaspıralı's supporters and the Young Tatars led by Mehdi with their journal *Vatan Hadimi* (Servant of the Nation) were soon joined by a third group sometimes referred to as "nationalists" (Fisher) or "separatists" (Vozgrin).[28] In any case, this current was typical of the age; national movements sprang up everywhere in the decades leading up to the First World War, driven by the conviction they could fulfil what they defined as their 'national fate' beyond the large empires.

The heads of this movement among the Crimean Tatars were the lawyer and later mufti Noman Çelebicihan (1885–1918) and Cafer Seydahmet Qırımer (1889–1960), who also had a degree in law; both would play important roles during the revolutionary events in Crimea in 1917 and 1918 (cf. Chapter 30).[29] The two men presumably got to know each other in 1908 in Istanbul, where, like many other Muslims from Russia, they completed their education.[30] The experience of the Young Turk Revolution during this period may have contributed to the politicization of these two actors and the rest of the Crimean Tatar diaspora in the Ottoman Empire, where the reintroduction of the constitution granted new liberties, which also extended to Russia's Muslims, including the Crimean Tatars, manifested in journalistic activities, for instance. They also formed political societies, some secret, others open. Their aim was ultimately the 'liberation of the Crimean Tatar nation'.[31] In 1911, a pamphlet entitled *Yirminci Asırda Tatar Milleti Mazlumesi* (The Oppressed Crimean Tatar nation in the Twentieth Century), written by Seydahmet in the Ottoman capital, even led to diplomatic intervention by St Petersburg after the Ottoman authorities demanded his arrest by their tsarist counterparts. Seydahmet fled to Paris, however.[32]

The Russian imperial authorities had already been paying close attention to the activities of their Muslim subjects in the Ottoman Empire, suspecting potential problems for domestic and foreign policy constellations.[33] In 1909, the Vatan Society (*Vatan Cemiyeti*) had formed in Istanbul under the aegis of Seydahmet and Çelebicihan, which scholars agree was an important step towards the genesis of a Crimean Tatar national political identity tied to the peninsula: "The Members of the Fatherland Society were proposing nothing less than independent Crimean Tatar statehood in their Crimean homeland", writes Williams, for instance.[34] The returning Crimean Tatars who had been politicized during their exile succeeded in forming an illegal communication network that distributed 'national' materials, founded reading circles and were able to influence multipliers such as teachers in the Gaspıralı's reformed schools. However, it would be incorrect to think that the majority of Crimean Tatars embraced this national consciousness at this point; in this respect too, the Crimean Tatar case is comparable to other non-dominant nationalities in the Eastern European land empires. The mobilized elites were not able to say whether their ultimate aim was independence or stronger pan-Turkic ties among the Tatars in the Russian Empire based on the example of the Young Turks. After 1905, some activists expressed disappointment with Gaspıralı; he was too 'flexible', rejected revolutionary currents and was above all too loyal "to the tsar, the Imperial Duma and the existing societal order". The fact that he "enjoyed the trust of the Ministry of the Interior" made them suspicious of him.[35] The younger generation pursued more extensive goals that seemed achievable after 1917 at the latest. Gaspıralı, a figure who remains highly regarded by Muslims to this day, despite all the criticism, would not live to see these developments; he died in September 1914 after a short and severe illness.

30

The First World War and the Revolution on the Periphery:

The Crimean Peninsula, 1917–20

Let us consider an early assessment of Soviet control in the peninsula:

> Fundamentally, the national question has never been solved properly [. . .]: 1) in the bourgeois capitalist system, the Tatars had the opportunity to lease property and earn their bread; in the Soviet system their lack of land increased; 2) earlier, the Crimean Tatars had their national military units: the Tatar cavalry squadrons in Simferopol' and Bağçasaray, who guarded Crimea, were found in the best barracks; the Soviet government has shorn not only the national military units but also the battle-tested international units of the Red Army of Tatar volunteers [. . .]; 4) in the bourgeois system, the Tatar population enjoyed freedom of movement, and today they are denied this opportunity [. . .]; 5) in the old regime, the Tatars could [. . .] freely exchange their products for bread and finished goods – the Soviet government, however, took all their stocks of wine, tobacco and fruits and gave them nothing in return. Those are the bare facts on which the Crimean Tatars base their assessment of the Soviet regime.[1]

This gloomy description of the situation in Crimea and the mood among the Crimean population was penned not by an enemy of the Bolsheviks, but by the convinced communist of Volga Tatar provenance Mirsäyet Soltangäliev (Tatar; Russian: Mirsaid Sultan-Galiev; 1892–1940[?]). And Soltangäliev was even clearer in his criticism of Soviet Russian policy towards the Crimean Tatars: it was an expression of the "Soviet regime's institutionalized but hidden colonization policy", which was driven by distrust of "the

East"/"the Orient" ("k Vostoku"). For the Soviets, he wrote, Crimea was a land full of petty bourgeois and hence their aim was "the complete economic and political demoralization of the Turko-Tatars". The Soviet regime and communism were ultimately just a new form of European imperialism that "is based on the denial of the right to private property and is thus even more powerful and more violent than before". Hence the Crimean Tatars harboured "poisonous thoughts" and died, moreover, "of hunger and tuberculosis".[2]

These withering lines were addressed to the then people's commissar of nationalities, Joseph Stalin. They were written in the spring of 1921, a few months after the final conquest of the peninsula by the Bolsheviks. They had only succeeded in taking the peninsula after the mass evacuation of the loyalist White troops under General Pëtr N. Vrangel' (1878–1928) with the assistance of British ships; Crimea was the part of the tsarist empire in which the enemies of Soviet power had been able to hold out the longest – with the exception of a few small enclaves in Siberia.

In November 1920, the prospects of a friendly reception for the Bolsheviks by the peninsula's inhabitants were looking good, since the predecessor to Vrangel', the White general Anton I. Denikin (1872–1947), had ruled with great brutality.[3] Vrangel' himself sought to restore law and order. He suspended martial law and installed military courts in its stead. However, some of his fellow combatants, shaped by years of violence, favoured making short work of opponents and took the law into their own hands, to the detriment of the local population: a particularly notorious figure was the White officer Ia. Slashchëv (1885/86–1929), who occasionally shot enemies himself, even if they had been acquitted by the court.[4]

The Soviet regime that established itself in the peninsula in the autumn of 1920 under the former *de facto* head of the short-lived Hungarian Soviet Republic and later victim of the Stalinist purges Béla Kun (1886–1938) and Rozaliia S. Zemliachka (actually: Rozaliia S. Zalkind; 1876–1947) did not prove an alternative, however. As during the brief existence of the Sovetskaia Sotsialisticheskaia Respublika Tavridy (Taurida Soviet Socialist Republic), which lasted a mere few weeks in the spring of 1918, violence was the method of choice.[5] The new regime indiscriminately persecuted its enemies, be they captive soldiers of the Volunteer Army, members of the so-called bourgeoisie or Crimean Tatar partisans fighting for an independent Crimean state, known as the Greens. Scholars estimate there were at least 25,000 and possibly as many as 120,000 victims of the Whites and the Reds in Crimea alone.[6]

It is probably for this reason that Crimea in the twentieth century – like the northern Black Sea region and large parts of Eastern Europe – has been identified as a peripheral area of a defined space of violence that recent research has occasionally labelled "bloodlands"[7] or a region of "sociogeographical exclusivity", as Felix Schnell puts it.[8] There have been some objections to this view,[9] some of them quite substantial, since this part of the former Russian Empire is not characterized solely by unrestrained violence and unchecked terror. The same holds for the peninsula: the period from 1917 to the late 1930s is marked by several caesurae distinguished by more than the extent of the violence they involved. In Crimea, as in other parts of the Soviet Union, the relentless terrorizing of the population could not be sustained. There were phases of consolidation, although they were admittedly followed by new waves of repressions – but that is only clear in retrospect. The population of Crimea thus experienced 'good' and 'bad' years, irrespective of their nationality: the First World War gave rise to the February Revolution, the October Coup and the Civil War. The years between 1917 and 1921 claimed the lives of around eight million former tsarist subjects – that is, more than the First World War, which 'only' saw the deaths of around 1.7 million soldiers and around two million civilians,[10] which are of course unfathomable tolls in themselves. For Manfred Hildermeier, world war, revolutions and civil war must be considered a single entity, and the civil war functioned as a "catch-up revolutionary war".[11] These years were undoubtedly a time of terror and violence for the population of Crimea too. Economic and social stabilization then set in, however, with the New Economic Plan (*Novaia Ėkonomicheskaia Politika*; NĖP), which lasted until around 1928, and its decentralized and partially liberalized economy, which included elements of a market economy. The Union-wide policy of "rooting" (Russian: *korenizatsiia*) also promoted the Crimean Tatar elites and culture. Hence to this day, Crimean Tatar memory policy refers to the 1920s as the "Golden Years".[12]

At first glance, this pattern reflects developments across the entire Soviet Union. Upon closer inspection, however, we can see the specifics that Martin Aust has pointed out in his book on the Russian Revolution, in which he stresses the plurality of the world-historical caesura emanating from the Russian Empire in 1917 and in the years that followed.[13] In Crimea, as in other peripheries of the Empire, there were both parallels and differences to the developments in the capital cities and the core territories inhabited by Eastern Slavs, some of which saw separate peasant revolutions. The imperial experiences of the local actors and their historical ties with the regions also shaped the course of events in different ways.

Incidentally, Soltangäliev was one of the early victims of the Soviets' persecution of their own nomenklatura that began in the mid-1920s: considered a Muslim national communist and pro-Turkish agent, he was first arrested and expelled from the Communist Party in 1923.[14] Prior to this, however – in 1921 – he had recommended in his letter to Comrade Stalin that the Kremlin radically change policy in Crimea in order to win over the local population for the Bolshevik cause: he advocated putting an end to the terror, temporarily pausing the introduction of state-run large-scale farms, a project the peasants rejected, and allocating them land. He argued that Crimea should become a separate territorial body with autonomous rights in order to make the socialist project more attractive to

Crimean intellectuals too.¹⁵ Moscow embraced Soltangäliev's proposals out of pragmatism, seeking to bind national minorities in the peripheries to the new regime following the destruction caused by the Civil War. Other factors were the geography of Crimea and the close ethnic and cultural relations between the Tatars and the Turks; the policy of détente adopted by Soviet Russia or the USSR (from December 1922 on) towards the Ottoman Empire or Turkey (from 1923 on) was not to be risked.¹⁶ A positive Tatar policy would also advertise the benefits of the new socialist order to neighbouring countries. In this phase, the Kremlin pursued an inclusive policy in general, not just in Crimea. The aim of privileging non-Russian nationalities – *korenizatsiia*¹⁷ – led to the establishment of the Crimean Autonomous Soviet Socialist Republic (Crimean Tatar: *Qırım Muhtar Sotsialist Sovet Cumhuriyeti*; Russian: *Krymskaia Avtonomnaia Sotsialisticheskaia Sovetskaia Respublika*; ASSR) in Crimea in 1921. It was followed by the Tatarization of the party apparatus and the use of Crimean Tatar in the republic's institutions from February 1922 onwards.¹⁸ Autonomous republics were always part of a union republic – for instance, the Crimean ASSR belonged to the Russian Socialist Federative Soviet Republic (Russian: *Rossiiskaia Sovetskaia Federativnaia Sotsialisticheskaia Respublika*; RSFSR), which ensured that the Union's laws were observed and influenced the appointments of important local personnel. Unlike the union republics, such as Georgia, Ukraine or Kazakhstan, autonomous republics did not have the right to leave the Soviet Union. This right, established by the union constitutions, was not a serious option for the union republics anyway. Nationalities considered to have local roots, like the Crimean Tatars, were nevertheless guaranteed certain autonomous rights within the ASSRs. Thus began the abovementioned "Golden Years", which would not have been possible without the end of the Russian Empire and the Bolshevik takeover.

However, the development had begun with the conflict contemporaries called the "Great War", which only turned into the "World War" in the course of the fighting and later became the "First World War". Events in the peninsula since the summer of 1914 had essentially resembled those in most of the other territories of the Russian Empire removed from the front. That is not to say that the war was not felt: daily life in the peninsula was also hampered by the usual wartime restrictions – there were restricted liberties and conscription, and inflation surged. Moreover, in the late October of 1914, Sevastopol' and other cities on the northern Black Sea coast were bombarded by German ships sailing under Ottoman flag. Some sea battles ensued, whereupon the tsarist empire declared war on the Ottoman Empire. Thenceforth, Crimea primarily served as a place of embarkment for tsarist troops heading for the Caucasian Front and as a military hospital. And a large number of Armenians and Greeks who had fled the massacres in the Ottoman Empire found refuge in the peninsula.¹⁹

Symptomatic of the imperial periphery was the mistrust of the 'Other' – be it ethnic, religious or 'just' confessional – that had been growing since the Crimean War. In Crimea, these tensions initially affected the Tatars, who had traditionally been considered disloyal in wartime. The descendants of the colonists who had arrived from the German-speaking lands from the late eighteenth century onwards were also under suspicion, however, particularly the remaining Mennonites, who traditionally rejected military service. Many of them had already left Russia following the introduction of universal conscription in 1874. In Crimea, some subsidiary colonies had nevertheless emerged in the second half of the nineteenth century, founded by people who had left the original settlements, which over time had become too small. From 1914, settlers of German origin and Crimean Tatars were accused – sometimes openly, sometimes implicitly – of being a kind of fifth column of Russia's enemies, specifically the German and the Ottoman Empires.[20] While this was true only of certain individuals, the tsarist regime took measures against its own subjects. Interestingly, it was the authorities far away in the centre that feared 'treason', not the local representatives of imperial power: after the war broke out, both the governor, Nikolai Kniazhevich (1871–1950) and his deputy assured Moscow that the Crimean Tatar population was exemplary and loyal to the tsar.[21] The traditionally admired Crimean Tatar cavalry, to which Soltangäliev would later refer in his letter to Stalin, served on the Western Front and elsewhere without any complaints about a disproportionate number of desertions.[22]

As in other peripheries far from the frontlines, in the Crimean experience it was not the outbreak of war in 1914 that was the real caesura, but 1917: the upheavals in the capital cities Petrograd and Moscow were echoed on the edges of the Empire – with some delay, and sometimes less intensively, but ultimately following a similar course, as comparatively late research on the revolutions in the provinces has shown.[23] In Crimea too, after the tsar had fallen power was seized by a Provisional Government of constitutional democrats led by N. Bogdanov (1875–1930) – without a great deal of friction. The establishment of an independent Crimean state was not initially on the agenda for the various nationalities, but they certainly wanted greater opportunities for participation.[24] The equal status of the nationalities and the freedom of speech and freedom of assembly declared in Petrograd were also upheld in the peninsula and led to the political mobilization of further sections of the population, the majority of whom had largely welcomed the end of the monarchy irrespective of their nationality.

In the areas beyond the core Russian territories, the boundaries between social and national revolution were blurred, since there was often (but not always exclusively) a connection between social situation and belonging to a certain nationality.[25] In the Baltic region, for instance, the Estonian peasantry went up against German landowners, or Ukrainian peasants in Volhynia took on the Polish landed gentry, lending a national element to the social. In multiethnic Crimea, as a consequence of tsarist Crimea policy, the situation was even more complicated: the Crimean Tatar peasantry's expectations of the new regime were different to those of a Russian or Ukrainian sailor in Sevastopol', but not to those of peasants with small patches of land in Central Russia. Conversely, the interests of large landowners, be they of Russian or Tatar descent, could be identical, irrespective of nationality and faith. This was also a result of the Empire's co-option of the elites.

In any case, like many non-Russian ethnicities in 1917, the Crimean Tatar population showed greater political and social activation than before, even if we do not have more precise details on the extent of their mobilization. Crimean Tatar but also Soviet authors note the remarkable influence of the Tatar party Milliy Fırqa (Crimean Tatar; People's Party), founded in 1917, which at this point only demanded Crimea's territorial autonomy within a federal and democratic Russian state. This group left of the Constitutional Democrats is said to have gained up to 60,000 supporters by the end of the year.[26] A more sensational claim (and hence one that should be taken with a pinch of salt) holds that "a good third of all Tatars inhabiting Crimea [*c.* 180,000] both male and female [!] were direct or indirect supporters of the [. . .] Milli Firka [. . .]".[27]

However popular this group may have been, the fact is that at a congress in early April 1917 Crimean Tatars discussed various political-national options, and a key role in the debate was played by two exponents of the Crimean Tatar national movement who had returned from Ottoman exile – Noman Çelebicihan and Cafer Seydahmet Qırımer (cf. Chapter 29).[28] The two activists had grown apart since their politicization during their student days in Istanbul. During the years of the Revolution, they embodied starkly different stances typically adopted by the national actors of the age – and not only by the Muslim population of Crimea: the 'camp' represented by Çelebicihan, who had been elected grand mufti of the Muslims in Crimea, Poland and Lithuania (and hence had a religious function), advocated fundamental equality with the Slav population in the peninsula. Çelebicihan even countenanced collaborating with the Bolsheviks if they proved in favour of a federal Russian state. In contrast, Seydahmet supported the restoration of a modernized Crimean Khanate with close ties to the Ottoman Empire. However, both were dissatisfied with the status quo, which explains why since the summer of 1914 they had turned both to Russia's allies and to Berlin and Vienna, pointing to the oppression they felt was faced by the Crimean Tatars and requesting support.[29] A Crimea liberated from the claws of Russia, argued a memo to the Axis powers, would benefit the German Reich due to the favourable geopolitical location; the Crimean Tatars also possessed a "healthy Volkskörper" and were better partners than the Slavs, since "alcohol and sodomy are forbidden by the laws of the religion, [and] diseases resulting from those vices are fewer among the Mohammedans than among the Russians".[30]

To take this as evidence of the disloyalty of 'the' Crimean Tatars during the First World War – and hence understand it as a prelude to Tatar collaboration during the Second World War (cf. Chapter 32) – is a gross oversimplification. Even if there were isolated cases of warm welcomes for the German occupiers, these were still primarily the activities of a small elite with nationalist leanings whose thinking had not yet taken root among the majority of the Tatar population. Moreover, enemy forces have always welcomed 'offers' of cooperation from national or religious representatives of their opponents, or have initiated them themselves.[31] This is especially the case when a region is considered to be of strategic significance – which is how both the Axis and the Entente saw Crimea.[32] However, Crimean Tatar nationalists' grovelling lent weight to the idea already circulating in German intellectual circles that Crimea was 'actually' a former Germanic territory; after all, for a long time the Goths had lived there (cf. Chapter 1). It also encouraged the associated fantasies within the imperial German general staff and admiralty. For instance, Erich Ludendorff (1865–1937), who as deputy chief of the Third Supreme Command (German: *Oberste Heeresleitung*, OHL) had a large influence on how Germany conducted the war, dreamt of establishing a German colony in Crimea well before Hitler's "Gotengau" plans.[33] For the time being, these were just ideas, however; it would be months before the Axis powers occupied the peninsula.

As in other parts of the Empire, social tensions intensified in Crimea during the course of the summer of 1917: besides the primarily social dissent between the Provisional Government and the soldiers' and sailors' soviets that had emerged in the naval port of Sevastopol' (largely consisting of Russians and Ukrainians), there were also national actors in the form of the Crimean Tatars, who had become alienated from the Russian state *per se*. But let us consider matters in chronological order: since the early summer of 1917, Milliy Fırqa had been demanding of the Provisional Government clear commitment to implementing autonomous territorial rights for Crimea.[34] However, the Provisional Government, mostly comprising Slavs, adhered to the idea of maintaining a Greater Russian unity state, drawing polemical responses from the Crimean Tatar press. Other topics were the development of a Crimean Tatar education system and the return of the Tatar formations fighting on the Western Front, who would form the core of a national army. This irritated those who supported the idea of a 'unified, indivisible Russia'. The arrest in July 1917 of figures who could unify Crimean Tatars, such as Çelebicihan, who was soon released again, however, did little to improve the atmosphere between the nationalities. Allied to this were the social demands of the Crimean Tatar actors, some of which matched those of the soldiers' and sailors' soviets in Sevastopol' – for instance, the call to abolish aristocratic privileges and the redistribution of land to the peasants, or for the war to end. However, these were proposals that neither the Provisional Government in Petrograd nor its branch in Simferopol' were willing to fulfil.[35]

While in the metropolises the months after the February Coup can be accurately called the phase of dual rule (the Provisional Government versus soldiers' soviets), the admittedly illogical term 'tripolar' rule is more appropriate for the situation in Crimea: the Provisional Government in Simferopol' and the soldiers' and sailors' soviets in Sevastopol' formed two poles, while Milliy Fırqa, Crimean Tatar formations and the Qurultay (People's Assembly) formed the third. In the autumn, the prospects of Petrograd calling an All-Russian Constituent Assembly led all parties to start preparing; potential delegates were determined, and the Qurultay in Bağçasaray got to work. Both its make-up – on the basis of equal voting rights for men and women – and the results were remarkable.[36] On the one hand, the Qurultay declared itself the representative of the national and cultural interests of the entire Crimean population, which would indicate that a national Crimean state had yet to become an issue. On the other hand, other decisions suggest the very opposite: Cafer Seydahmet Qırımer was made supreme commander of the Crimean Tatar units in the peninsula, which were referred to as the core of a national army. A constitution was drafted for a Crimean Republic conceived of as a parliamentary democracy "on the basis of the separation of powers (§7) and the 'absolute equality of men and women (§18)'".[37] With its recognition of equal rights for men and women, which had already been postulated by Russia's Muslim reformers (Jadidists) but was still disputed within the Muslim community, it was ahead of most of the other constitutions of its time.[38]

Another remarkable aspect is the explanations on the status of the nationalities; it stipulated that each should govern their own affairs and that the "form of the Crimean administration be established only via the Constituent Assembly of all inhabitants of Crimea".[39] Even if this wording recognizing the multinational character of the peninsula was motivated by realism – since without the non-Tatar majority "a Crimean state could not be achieved",[40] the Crimean Tatars constituting just a quarter of the population – Soviet publications' characterization of the draft as nationalist is unjustified. Beyond Simferopol' and Bağçasaray, the Democratic Crimean Republic had little power and was soon swept aside by the advancing Bolsheviks. Exponents of the Crimean Tatar national movement nevertheless consider it a milestone.[41]

Parallel to this, the Bolsheviks, hitherto marginalized by the events in Petrograd in the October, had grown in strength in the naval port of Sevastopol' and were further reinforced by the arrival of land troops and naval forces. The Provisional Government had silently disappeared, and the remaining Slav population that did not support Bolshevism formed a Constituent Assembly in which the Social Revolutionaries had a majority.[42] Fearing the strengthened Bolsheviks, the (Tatar) Crimean Republic collaborated with the (Slav) Constituent Assembly. Initially, the Red Guards, who with their long experience of fighting were prepared to commit violence, established the first short-lived Crimean state under the Bolsheviks. A first wave of 'Red violence' swept through the peninsula. It peaked in what became known as Bartholomew's Night, when members of the Qurultay were shot dead in Sevastopol' in February 1918. They included Noman Çelebicihan, who had also composed the Crimean Tatar national anthem and whom today's Crimean Tatars consider a national martyr.[43] Soviet publications saw this first phase of rule over Crimea as a success, since the work of the Revkom (Revolution Committee) had shown the population's "great love" for the Communist Party.[44] This didn't last long, for after the Germans had taken the peninsula in April 1918 (further devaluing the already problematic treaty of Brest-Litovsk between the Axis and the Soviet regime, which had not provided for an advance on Crimea) there were lynchings targeting people who had served on the Revkom. Crimean Tatars also took part in the reprisals.[45]

The various actors among the German occupiers pursued different plans. The OHL, especially Ludendorff, had far-reaching imperial ideas: establishing a German colonial state in the peninsula was at the very top of his wish list. It was to be formed by Russian Germans from all parts of the former tsarist empire.[46] That was the long-term goal. The short-term aim was to prevent the transfer of what remained of the tsarist navy to the Soviet regime, stipulated by the Treaty of Brest-Litovsk, by taking Crimea.[47] Compared with the OHL's visions for Crimea, the German Ministry for Foreign Affairs under Richard von Kühlmann (1873–1948) was less ambitious. It had firmly opposed occupying the peninsula, but Ludendorff had ultimately persuaded the Kaiser. Kühlmann quite justifiably feared problems with the Ottoman Empire, which was part of the Axis and had energetically sought Berlin's support for the establishment of a Muslim Crimean state under the aegis of Istanbul, which Seydahmet was now advocating too.[48] For the near future, German foreign policy intended to create an interim Crimean state that would be ruled by Ukraine in the long term. In this connection, it is important to note that the German Empire had no intention of recognizing the Ukrainian Het'man State under the former tsarist general and member of an old Cossack dynasty, Pavlo Skoropads'kyi (1873–1945), which was also under German occupation.[49] The plan was to keep both territories as puppet states. There are certainly a number of parallels between Ukraine and Crimea, and not only with respect to the quasi-colonial role German politicians envisaged for them in an Eastern Europe dominated by the Kaiserreich after the "Great Victory" they hoped for.

Sections of both the Ukrainian and the Crimean Tatar population had welcomed the Axis invasion, erroneously expecting the occupiers would lend support to their own national or social agendas. (They assumed the same thing during the Second World War, incidentally.) For the Germans, furthering national movements was a matter of pragmatism. Their support included symbolic manifestations, for instance by promoting national cultures in the education sector in both Crimea and Ukraine, which also involved founding a university in Simferopol', or funding the press.[50] But they refused to recognize an independent Tatar Crimean government – and its presumptive head, Seydahmet, had to spend a few days under arrest, albeit in luxury, as he later proclaimed.⁵¹

Instead, reflecting their policy in Ukraine, the Germans installed as prime minister a former member of the tsarist army with a regional connection to the occupied territory: the Lipka Tatar lieutenant general and later chief of the general staff of the short-lived Azerbaijan Democratic Republic (1981– 1920) Maciej Sulkiewicz (1865–1920). Like the Ukraïns'ka Derzhava (Ukrainian; Ukrainian State) under Skoropads'kyi, the Crimean state was the Germans' puppet. Today, the Crimean Tatar national movement looks back on it as independent, however, since it was not tied to Russia. This vision was further confirmed by the introduction of a distinct Crimean citizenship embracing all nationalities.

The government, formed by parties rather conservative in orientation, contained many of the nationalities living in the peninsula: after the Tatars, there were Russians – the individuals were apparently unconscious of a separate Ukrainian nationality, which nevertheless constituted around a quarter of the Slavs in Crimea – as well as representatives of German colonists and one Armenian.⁵² From the Crimean Tatar perspective, it was something of a blemish that the majority of the ministers were for reintegration into a new, indivisible Russia while Tatar actors dreamt of an independent Crimean state. In the later Soviet historiography, however, the period of German occupation between April and November 1918 is often adapted to fit an unbroken narrative on the revolutionary potential of Sevastopol': the city's population is claimed to have put up stern resistance to the "German imperialists", with strikes rendering the port useless to the imperial navy and Russian workers forging revolutionary alliances with sailors from the German battlecruiser sailing under Ottoman flag, SMS *Goeben*.⁵³

The ambitious foreign policy pursued by the Ukraïns'ka Derzhava put the German occupiers in something of a predicament. This was due not so much to Het'man Skoropads'kyi as to his foreign minister, Dmytro Doroshenko (1882–1952), who had strong Ukrainian nationalist leanings.⁵⁴ Doroshenko was one of the first Ukrainian politicians to express claims to Crimea as part of Ukraine.⁵⁵ He argued not so much from the perspective of a purported historical right as in terms of strategy and demographic policy, stressing that Sevastopol' was the key to the Black Sea and a large proportion of the Russian-speaking population of Crimean was Ukrainian, around 25 per cent.⁵⁶ He was happy to overlook the fact that the Ukrainians in Crimea were heavily Russified and were not particularly interested in the Ukrainian cause. In turn, Berlin ignored Doroshenko, partly in order to avoid upsetting the Soviet Russian government, which had not given up on Crimea itself. The Ukrainian het'man too, himself more Russian than Ukrainian in outlook, considered the restoration of an all-Russian state more realistic than a Ukrainian Crimea. Nevertheless, between the late summer and the October of 1918, various conversations on the future status of the peninsula were held by representatives of Kyiv, Berlin, Istanbul and Simferopol'. In the

Crimean government, the Tatar ministers argued, not surprisingly, for a Crimean Tatar state, which they had asked Istanbul to recognize, while the others preferred a non-socialist Russian state. Georgii V. Chicherin (1872–1936), people's commissar for foreign affairs of Soviet Russia and later the USSR between 1918 and 1930, made it clear to the Axis powers that Crimea "was, like the Don region, part of the Soviet Republic".[57]

The German troops' retreat in November 1918 meant that finding a solution to the issue of Crimea's future status was no longer Berlin's responsibility. If we consider the events of the Second World War and the situation facing Crimea's German inhabitants, the following aspect is interesting, however: unlike the nationalist leagues (*völkische Verbände*) in the German Empire, such as the Pan-German League (*Alldeutscher Verband*),[58] official policy before 1914 had taken little interest in instrumentalizing colonists with German ancestors in the tsarist empire.[59] The situation changed, however, during the First World War, leading to ambitious 'plans' such as Ludendorff's. Immediately after the invasion, the occupying forces overturned the discriminatory orders the Russian government had given after 1914,[60] and in the months that followed a common space of communication developed between the occupying administration and the Crimean Tatars, which had a sustained impact beyond 1918 and into the Second World War. Some Crimean Germans ultimately attempted to 'return' to their (purported) actual homeland, Germany, during the German retreat in the autumn of 1918. The German authorities curbed their expectations, however, insisting that Crimea was the place "where the colonist must undertake every effort to help Germany to its victory".[61] They pointed out that they urgently needed the railways to withdraw their troops and materiel, and colonists of German descent who "wanted to take their chattels (including their livestock) with them"[62] were merely a hindrance.

After the occupiers had left, another short-lived government was set up, headed by Solomon Krym (1864–1936), a former member of the First Duma and a Constitutional Democrat of Crimean Karaite descent. This government, opposed to both the Bolsheviks and the Russian Whites loyal to the tsar, was swept aside by the Red Guards in the spring of 1919.[63] Its most famous figure was Minister of Justice Vladimir D. Nabokov (1870–1922), father of the renowned writer Vladimir V. Nabokov (1899–1977). The Nabokov family had sought refuge in Crimea following the October Coup. Nabokov, Krym and other members of the government were evacuated with their families in early 1919 on board the *Hope*, one of the Allied ships that had been docked in Crimea since late 1918. Krym went to France, the Nabokovs to England.[64] Vladimir D. Nabokov was murdered three years later by Russian right-wing extremists during a meeting of exiled Constitutional Democrats in Berlin.

And in Crimea too, there began a phase of violence – the 'Red' and 'White' Terror.

31

The Crimean Peninsula, 1920–41

Oh really, forever this Crimea. Dust. Heat. Mountains rise dully into the sky. [. . .] Thus I have no particular interest in going there. But in the autumn I will go perhaps. But generally, it would be preferable if the entire tour of Crimea took two–three hours. And when stratospheric aeroplanes are flying, that is how it will be. You board in Leningrad at twelve – and at three you're bathing in the Black Sea. And you're home at six in the evening. That will be interesting. But essentially I do not intend to wait for this age, and three days' travel aren't really holding me back. Anyhow, cordial regards to travellers to Crimea. And however one may complain about this Crimea, it is a wonderful pearl when it comes to spas. And as far as its setting is concerned, it will constantly get better and better.[1]

In his commentary of 1935 entitled "Poritsanie Krymu" (Rebuke of Crimea), Mikhail M. Zoshchenko (1894–1958), a writer who had great success in the Soviet Union during the 1920s and 1930s before falling out of favour under neo-Stalinism,[2] complains half seriously about Crimea's popularity during the Soviet era. The peninsula had become a place of yearning for Soviet workers. In the summer, writes Zoshchenko, many Soviet citizens were drawn to the Black Sea in the belief that by bathing in it "they would be young and beautiful again". Young people travelled "with the slightest cause to Crimea" with very little money in their pockets, and "many people" generally liked the place.[3] The journey there was exhausting and the transport overcrowded, but "as far as the setting is concerned, it will constantly get better and better",[4] he ended his piece half ironically, half in hope.

The fledgling RSFSR sought to latch onto the tourism and spa industry that had begun to develop in the peninsula in the second half of the nineteenth century (cf. Chapter 27). And it did so with gusto. However, this was possible only because things had calmed down – that is, there was an absence of large-scale direct violence: the Civil War was over, the Whites were in exile and most of the remaining opponents such as the Social

Revolutionaries or the Mensheviks had been driven out or arrested.[5] Union-wide peace was achieved economically by the NĖP and politically by the targeted privileging of non-Russian nationalities in the early Soviet Union, a strategy that has been analysed by Terry Martin.[6]

An examination of the history of the post-revolutionary phase in the former Russian Empire shows that in the early years of their rule, the Bolsheviks were supple and flexible in their policies concerning the national minorities. For instance, the assumption that the new regime oppressed the Tatar minority in Crimea from the outset[7] is quite wrong. Initially, neither in the peninsula nor in the Soviet Union was there "a straight-forwardly asymmetric relationship between Moscow and the periphery", as Grégory Dufaud has meticulously demonstrated for Crimea; rather, the non-Russian territories were about to witness complex processes of negotiation. This gave the local actors room for manoeuvre which Crimean Tatar Communists, for instance, and even national actors outside the party were able to exploit. However, that the Kremlin allowed this room for manoeuvre in the first place was not a manifestation of altruism. Dufaud observes:

> The new rulers had no intention of sanctioning the existence of a national movement which might have rivalled or disputed their authority. Nonetheless these rulers urgently needed local executives and individuals ready to help them strengthen their hold on a population alienated by Bolshevik harassment and persecution.[8]

Like the tsarist government in the late eighteenth century, then, the new rulers had to secure the support of local actors and hence make concessions at the cost of pure ideology – and not only with an eye on the Crimean Tatars: the regional branch of the Bolsheviks in Crimea set up Armenian, Jewish and German sections in addition to its Muslim section.[9]

In many respects, Soviet national policy, which we have already discussed – and of which there is no unanimous assessment – represents a series of ad-hoc decisions until *c.* 1923 and the Twelfth Party Congress.[10] Despite the commitment to the peoples' right to self-determination Lenin expressed during the phase of the Revolution, much had remained vague, partly for propaganda reasons; the respective actors could interpret the phrase however they liked. Following Friedrich Engels' assumption that the nationalities issues would solve itself in the course of revolutionary development, the Bolsheviks had not spent much time examining the problem systematically. Famously, Joseph Stalin's treatise *Marxism and the National Question*, commissioned by Lenin and written in exile in Vienna in 1913 (and actually merely intended as criticism of the national theories of Austrian socialists such as Otto Bauer (1881–1938) and Karl Renner (1870–1950)) came to establish the guiding principles of national policy in the early Soviet Union. From today's perspective, his definition of a nation is simple, but typical of the age: "[. . .] a nation is not a racial or tribal, but a historically constituted community of people" that has emerged on the basis of community of language, community of territory, community of economic life and community of psychological make-up manifested in a community of culture. This definition "exhausted the characteristic features of a nation".[11] Like the Austro-Marxists he criticized, then, Stalin was of the opinion that every nationality needed a common language and culture and possessed a common "psychological make-up". Above all, however, a nation needed a territory. For many of the nationalities ruled by Moscow, this meant that they found themselves in nationally denominated administrative units – such as the aforementioned ASSR or the so-called autonomous regions (which were actually subordinate). This was ultimately the case for the Crimean Tatars too, even if this ethnonym was not included in the republic's title.[12] Unlike during the tsarist era, when the Tavricheskaia guberniia, formed in 1802, was larger than Crimea itself, the ASSR remained restricted to the peninsula.

In the eyes of both Moscow and the local actors, the policy of rooting (*korenizatsiia*) or indigenization was about catching up with modernization in an attempt to overhaul an anticipated backwardness.[13] The idea was also to allow the wounds of tsarist rule to 'heal' and to give the new regime the opportunity to present itself as an anti-colonial force, including abroad. For instance, the Crimean Tatars were treated with an eye on the Turks in the Ottoman Empire[14] and the Ukrainian population with an eye on Ukrainians living under Polish rule. These peoples were to be impressed with the positive situation of their conationals in Soviet Russia or the USSR.

From 1922 onwards, the national minorities in Crimea as a whole, but especially the Crimean Tatars, were particularly promoted in the fields of language, education and culture. Prior to this, in August 1921, Tatar had been granted the status of local state language, alongside Russian.[15] In the tsarist era, the Muslim clerics had had great influence over the Tatar schools; Gaspıralı's reformed schools had not been able to change this (cf. Chapter 28). The Bolsheviks, on the other hand, secularized education, although the Islamic schools were not eliminated completely until the 1930s.[16] This too can be seen as a pragmatic decision by the Kremlin in order to bind non-Russian nationalities to the new regime. On the whole, the successes in the school system and the increase in literacy were impressive. Almost 400 primary schools were created for the Crimean Tatar population alone. Overall illiteracy in the peninsula dropped to around 3 per cent, and several universities were founded.[17] Unsurprisingly, however, what was taught reflected the aims and views of the new regime.

The establishment of the ASSR did not lead to the Tatarization of Crimea's administration immediately. Rather, it was composed of several elements: a workers' soviet, a peasants' soviet and a sailors' soviet, the central Executive Committee and the Council of People's Commissars. The rural Tatar population was disadvantaged, since the most influential of these bodies was the workers' soviet, in which one delegate represented 500 inhabitants of a town or city – and that meant primarily Russians or Ukrainians. A rural delegate, on the other hand, spoke for 2,500, most of them Tatars.[18] The first Soviet constitution of 1924 put an end to this disadvantage for the Crimean Tatars or the rural population as a whole insofar as the actual federal representatives – the soviets – had no power.[19] This strengthened non-Slavic groups, at least in Crimea. Despite resistance from local communists or those sent from the centre, most of them Slavs, 'Tatar personnel' had to be found and trained. This proved difficult,[20] which explains the initial recruitment of 'bourgeois' or 'petty bourgeois' elements, for instance from the ranks of the former supporters of Milliy Fırqa. Ultimately, it was possible to turn the ASSR on the Black Sea into a kind of shop window for indigenization. As Chantal Lemercier-Quelquejay observes, "[The Crimean ASSR] was one of the few Muslim territories of Soviet Russia where the political importance of the native element was greater than its numerical value."[21]

Nevertheless, like the annexation of the Crimean Khanate by the Russian Empire in 1783 (cf. Chapter 21), the history of Crimea under Soviet aegis is not a special case. As an ASSR within the RSFSR and in keeping with the heavily centralist structure of the USSR, despite all federal propaganda it was firmly integrated into the fabric of the state as a whole. All significant developments and caesurae were also implemented in the ASSR, for better and for worse. Some of the positives were Crimea's status as an autonomous republic in and of itself, the blessings of indigenization and the stabilization of the economy, especially in the agricultural sector and in tourism. The negatives included famines and the persecution of political dissidents (or those who were declared such) and ultimately religious institutions and their representatives.

The famine of 1920/21 had mainly affected the Volga region and the areas south of the Urals, but it also affected the Black Sea territories, including the peninsula. It was caused by the consequences of the First World War, the revolutionary upheavals and the Civil War, but also by the Bolsheviks themselves, who were already making their first attempts at collectivization, which Soltangäliev had of course criticized (cf. Chapter 30). The situation was acerbated by a period of drought. However, unlike in the case of the "Great Famine" of 1932/33, which also cost lives in many parts of the Union,[22] the Kremlin leadership reacted pragmatically after some initial hesitation. They allowed foreign aid into the country[23] and implemented the NĖP, which had already been projected.[24] The famine's impact was nevertheless dramatic: the famine itself and its consequences, such as a higher mortality rate due to diseases, claimed many lives.[25]

The Union-wide famine of 1932/33 was even more devastating than that of 1921/22, and Crimea was not spared. Since the 1980s, the famine has been the subject of sustained debate largely initiated by the North American Ukrainian diaspora. With respect to Crimea, however, there is no discussion of whether the Great Famine was a deliberate – that is, a genocidal – attack on the Ukrainian nation by the Kremlin.[26] This is partly because Crimean Tatar actors discuss the topic of 'genocide' in connection with the deportations of 1944 (cf. Chapter 33).[27] The reason there was a famine with a higher death toll than in 1921/22[28] is unanimously considered to be the renewed collectivization or, in the case of the Kazakh nomads, the attempt to make them sedentary.[29] Unlike in the early 1920s, collectivization was pushed through much more vigorously from 1929 onwards. In Crimea, as in other parts of the Soviet Union, the peasants resisted, unwilling to give up the land they had been allocated only a few years earlier without a fight.[30] The Soviet regime reacted with a firm hand; peasants were executed, deported or died of starvation. Fisher estimates that between 1917 and 1933, around 50 per cent of the Crimean Tatar population – according to his calculations some 150,000 people – died in some way or other or left the peninsula either voluntarily or because they were forced to.[31]

However, what remained a multiethnic Crimea was rocked not only by primarily man-made disasters such as famine but also by a genuine natural disaster: the earthquake of 1927. In fact, there were two earthquakes: the first, which was not as strong, on 26 June, and second in the night between 11 and 12 September, which was also accompanied by a seaquake on the peninsula's southern coast that released gases from the seabed, causing fires.[32] Although Crimea is not considered a region particularly at risk from earthquakes, there had been smaller and larger ones over the years, such as during the Third Mithridatic War in 63 BC.[33] There were no deaths during the June quake, but there were injuries along with widespread destruction and panicked tourists who made a mad dash to leave Crimea. The September tremors were much stronger, being felt all over the peninsula, and three deaths were reported.[34] Even if it was a relatively small earthquake in terms of the number of victims, it caused considerable damage. Nigel A. Raab writes that the tremors on the coast in the September registered 9 out of 10 on the Rossi–Forel scale; unlike the Richter scale, for instance, which depends on the instruments used, the Rossi–Forel scale measures the impact on the landscape, streets or buildings.[35] Disasters such as earthquakes are profound caesurae for collectives, as the events in Lisbon in 1755 demonstrate.[36]

The global significance accorded to the earthquake in Crimea in 1927 certainly doesn't compare to that of 1755 or other great disasters, but in Soviet literature it nevertheless received considerable attention, for example in the famous satirical novel *Dvenadtsat' stul'ev* (*The Twelve Chairs*, 1928) by the Soviet writers Ilia Ilf (Iekhiel Leib Fainzil'berg; 1897–1937) and Evgenii Petrov (Evgenii Petrovich Kataev; 1903–42). The event also features in one of Zoshchenko's (see above) ironic short stories, "Zemletriasenie" ("Earthquake", 1930), in which the Yalta cobbler Snopkov sleeps through the great event in a drunken state behind a cypress tree in his courtyard. Lacking orientation and not knowing there was an earthquake in the night, he wanders through a city he no longer recognizes and wonders whether he is in Batumi or Turkey. After falling asleep again, he wakes up without his trousers and decides to travel to Kharkiv (Ukrainian; Russian: Khar'kov), where he intends to undergo withdrawal treatment. Zoshchenko ironically asks what the author's intention was behind his story: "The author is raising his voice energetically against drunkenness". He also points out – again ironically – the dangers of alcohol in the class struggle by citing a Soviet placard: "Do not drink! Under the influence of liquor you may embrace your class enemy!"[37]

But beyond this humoristic treatment, it is also interesting to consider the political and social implications of natural disasters in the Soviet context. Since the "idea of the controllability of the elements by science and technology" played a key role in the USSR, "disasters were an event alien to the system of really existing socialism".[38] They nevertheless happened, as a Soviet scientist remarked in a contemporary German-language scholarly journal: the earthquake had not taken "an inordinately stormy catastrophic course" but its unpredicted occurrence was of concern to him, especially since the population's "belief in scientific prognosis" had been "shaken".[39] Both the central and the local Soviet administration had their hands full managing the crisis; they had to calm the local population and the tourists who remained in Crimea in the late September, since, as Raab observes, "chaos was in the air".[40] The damage had to be dealt with quickly, since the authorities feared that the tourism industry would collapse and the Kremlin did not want unrest and dissatisfaction in an area of such military-strategic importance. The aid that arrived in the form of money, materials and labour came from various sources: the RSFSR, to which the Crimean ASSR of course belonged, provided loans and financial support, the Soviet Red Cross helped on the ground, and there were also donations from other parts of the Union – not overwhelming amounts, "but help did trickle in".[41]

The earthquake occurred just as the winds of change were blowing through Soviet politics and there were indications of the beginning of the end of the so-called Golden Years, at least in retrospect. Stalin had already consolidated his power at this point and could thus act without the threat of rivals. He had always understood the Union-wide indigenization policy as accelerating the belated process of nation-building, which was supposed to be finished within a few years – and in the late 1920s he considered this point to have arrived. Consequently, there was an extensive, albeit not total abandonment of *korenizatsiia*. The struggle against so-called national communists, the first sign of which had been nullifying Soltangäliev in 1923 (cf. Chapter 30), was continued with great fanfare. In 1928, the Crimean party leader Veli İbraimov (also Ibragimov; 1888–1928), originally a member of Milliy Fırqa before switching to the Bolsheviks, was charged with national communism and conspiring with Turkey, and was executed together with sixteen of his followers.[42] Even before the Shakty trial (also in 1928) in the Ukrainian SSR, frequently considered a turning point in Soviet national policy, a precedent had been set in Crimea.[43]

The trials, held in camera, were discussed by the press, probably in the interests of discipline. The reasons for this prelude to further purges, including in other parts of the Soviet Union, lay both beyond and within the Crimean ASSR. While Stalin's departure from the policy of promoting the nationalities as a means of accelerating the country's modernization can be considered the most important external factor, there were a number of internal factors in Crimea itself. The Kremlin had arrived at the conclusion that the party apparatus in the peninsula was dysfunctional.[44] Indeed, there had been upheavals since 1924, when the then commissar responsible for the workers and peasants, İbraimov, and other Crimean Tatar comrades had protested against the influence of the Volga Tatars whom Moscow deployed in Crimea. As Dufaud observes, the local forces had "a maximalist vision of korenizatsiia" and sought to install their own people in key positions.[45] Initially, the Kremlin and even Stalin himself had backed this position, above all supporting İbraimov,[46] but when the situation became chaotic and rumours about different factions working against each other reached Moscow, things changed.[47]

That was not all, however: İbraimov had been vehemently opposing the so-called productivization of Soviet Jews, a campaign hatched in Moscow which involved the allocation of large amounts of land to Jewish settlers in Crimea. Local objections were not necessarily connected to anti-Jewish resentment on the part of Crimean Tatar communists;[48] rather, they were more to do with local comrades' desire to compensate for the disastrous decline in the Crimean Tatar population since the tsarist era. Crimean Tatars from the diaspora, especially from the former regions of the Ottoman Empire, such as Dobruja, were supposed to return to their old homeland. Indeed, two dozen new Crimean Tatar settlements had been established between 1925 and 1927.[49] In order to prevent large-scale Jewish settlement, İbraimov also 'blocked' selected territories by settling Crimean Tatar peasants from southern Crimea in them.[50] What from his and other actors' perspective was redressing the injustice Russia had inflicted on Crimea's Muslim population and also corresponded to the indigenization policy that had been propagated hitherto was no longer considered opportune by the Kremlin in the spring of 1928. The trial and execution of İbraimov and his fellow functionaries put an end to Muslim immigration.

There would be no resettlement of Crimea with 'productivized' Jews on a large scale, however, since the project of a Jewish territory within the Soviet Union was realized in the Jewish Autonomous Oblast' of Birobidzhan in the Amur region, although this plan too was only moderately successful. In the peninsula on the Black Sea, two Jewish raions were nevertheless formed between 1931 and 1935 with the colonies of Fraydorf and Larindorf, along with thirty-two other smaller regional entities.[51] The Jewish population, considered a distinct nationality in the Soviet Union, had increased to around 60,000 due to immigration that would last until the late 1930s;[52] this is a situation to which we will return in the context of the Shoah in Crimea (cf. Chapter 32).

Repressions following accusations of national communism, the instalment of new elites, collectivization, resistance and famines – between the events of 1917 and the German Reich's invasion of the Soviet Union, Crimea must clearly be seen as part of the Soviet state structure as a whole. The Muslim clerics, long treated well in comparison to the Orthodox Church, had been persecuted since the 1930s, since the authorities thought they had supported kulaks, as the Soviet regime termed allegedly wealthy peasants.[53] Williams estimates that between 30,000 and 40,000 Crimean Tatars were victims of various purges;[54] there have been no corresponding studies on other nationalities in the peninsula. The largest wave of persecution began in 1936, as it did throughout the USSR. The party apparatus was ruthlessly 'purged', in the Stalinist terminology, and Tatar functionaries such as the head of the party in Crimea, İlyas Tarhan (1900–38), who had been in office since 1931, were executed. When Stalin's Soviet constitution of 1936 reduced the autonomous republics' political room for manoeuvre, the impact was also felt in the peninsula. Ultimately, limitations were imposed on the freedoms of non-Russian nationalities too; the number of Crimean Tatar newspapers, for instance, fell from twenty-three in 1935 to nine in 1938.[55]

Nevertheless, the indigenization policy did not come to a complete standstill; instead, it was largely staged for propaganda purposes. There was symbolic representation in that identification papers continued to state "Nationality" as "Crimean Tatar", "German", "Armenian", etc. (as was the practice in the USSR). 'National' topics remained obligatory in the educational establishments, and the folklore of the various nationalities was studied and cultivated – and in some cases invented.[56] Soviet national policy had promoted constructions of national identity that took on lives of their own, albeit not as the Kremlin had intended, and the Crimean Tatar identity was no exception;[57] in the peninsula too, the Soviet regime had fostered a secular national consciousness. Unlike most of the other nationalities in the peninsula, the Crimean Tatars lived exclusively on its territory, which reinforced the connection between ethnicity and the region.[58]

In 1934, the Crimean ASSR received special recognition: it received the highest Soviet accolade, the Order of Lenin, for its achievements in the field of culture.[59] In the Soviet era, at least from the mid-1930s on, the peninsula's multiethnic character and the Union's shifting positive and negative policies towards the non-Slavic population remained evident. This situation changed with the Second World War.

32

Crimea in the Second World War

Aleksei A. Surkov (1899–1983), best known for his patriotic rhymes and as a war correspondent during the Second World War was one of the most highly decorated writers in the USSR. He even served as president of the Writers' Union of the USSR from 1953 to 1959, succeeding the greatly admired Maksim Gorki (1868–1936) in the role. In the poem "Sevastopol'tsy" (The Sevastopol'ians) of 1943, the first two strophes of which are cited here, we have the convergence of two temporal levels – which his contemporary Soviet readership would have had no trouble understanding: the time of the Crimean War of 1853–6 and that of the Second World War:

> From below the nasal accordion whines "Die Wacht am Rhein".
> Darkness. Shadow of a German bayonet.
> At midnight the old sailor from the Black Sea Fleet wakes Koshka the sailor of the Red Fleet Shevchuk.
>
> And they go from Inkerman,
> through dark deathly silence
> up Malakhov Hill
> past the Korabel'noi Quarter[1]

Here Surkov "wakes" one of the most famous heroes of the Crimean War, Pëtr M. Koshka (1828–82), a sailor in the Red Fleet, in order to walk with him "through dark deathly silence" past the enemy, up Malakov Hill, one of the bloodiest sites of the Crimean War, before finally arriving in a district of Sevastopol' known as Korabel'noi; in the distance, the song "Die Wacht am Rhein" can be heard, considered a kind of unofficial national anthem in the German Empire and a symbol of the German will to conquer abroad. For the Soviet Union as a whole and for the population of Crimea, the Second World War began with the initial raid on Sevastopol' by the *Luftwaffe* in June 1941. A focal point of the struggle for the peninsula, both militarily and in terms of the culture of remembrance, was the 250-day siege of

Sevastopol' by the Wehrmacht, from 30 October 1941 to early July 1942. It was only then that German troops could report to Berlin that they had implemented the plan – to occupy the entire peninsula – before they were forced to withdraw in early 1944. In the twentieth century, the 'Hero City' of Sevastopol' held out for almost a hundred days less than their predecessors during the Crimean War, but the sacrifices of the Soviet people, at least equally brave, are heralded in heroic terms – especially in the constructed simultaneity of Surkov's poem.

The heroic Sevastopol' narrative survived the caesura between the tsarist and the Soviet empires, and has ultimately remained intact to this day. For instance, a Russian website entitled *Wargaming.net* contains an entry on Pëtr M. Koshka stating that the only people who don't know this sailor are those who have never heard of the "heroic defence" of the city in the years 1854–5, which, the anonymous author assumes, is impossible.[2] To return to Surkov's poem: it is remarkable that the Soviet writer named not only the common sailor Koshka and hence the workers at the centre of the ideology, but also figures from the upper echelons of society and the military who were nevertheless deserving heroes: the commander of the Black Sea Fleet, circumnavigator of the globe and researcher Mikhail P. Lazarev (1788–1851), or two officers who fell in the Crimean War, Vladimir A. Kornilov (1806–54, vice admiral) and Vladimir I. Istomin (1809–55, rear admiral), both of whom were fatally wounded on Malakhov Hill. The convergence of different temporal levels (in this case the Crimean War and the Second World War) helps to construct a linear historical narrative. This is a stylistic device employed in the politics of memory of both the Soviet Union and the Russian Federation, but it also features in other national contexts. It is also significant – as Serhii Plokhy pointed out years before the annexation of Crimea in 2014 – that these narratives make Sevastopol' an exclusively Russian city; even the Ukrainian population remains unmentioned.[3]

The German occupation regime brought the entire spectrum of the war of annihilation the National Socialists waged against the Soviet Union to Crimea too: violence; the attempt to exterminate the Jews; forced labour; collaboration; exploitation; passivity and Partisan activities. The first victims were the Crimean Germans. According to the first census in the tsarist empire in 1897, they had constituted 5.78 per cent of the population in the Taurida Governorate, which, as already mentioned, was larger than the peninsula itself,[4] and hence it is difficult to estimate precise figures. When war broke out, there were presumably over 53,000 Germans living in Crimea. In August 1941 – before the Wehrmacht had reached the peninsula, then – Stalin ordered their resettlement to the east of the Soviet Union, away from the front, in order to prevent their collaboration with the German invaders – reflecting fears during the First World War (cf. Chapter 30). Many of them ended up in what was known as the *trudarmiia* (Russian; actually *trudovaia*; the labour army), a form of forced labour that had first been introduced in the 1920s and was revived during the Second World War.[5]

In the autumn of 1941 (when the German army invaded) there were only 1,000 so-called Crimean Germans in the peninsula, and hence they were of limited use to the National Socialists as a nucleus for the planned Germanization programme. The paucity of local Germans thus influenced the National Socialists' foolhardy plans to establish a so-called "Gotengau" (cf. Chapter 1).

Initially, despite pipe dreams of a 'German Crimea', the peninsula had not played a key role in the war to annihilate the Soviet Union, since it had been considered a military "cul-de-sac".[6] Due to the advance east, which soon stalled, the German strategists soon came to regard this as an advantage, however. Significance was also attached to it as a base for launching the conquest of oil fields in the northern and southern Caucasus, which were very important for the war effort. Additionally, Berlin hoped that it would serve as a bargaining chip that would help bring officially neutral Turkey closer to the German Reich. That the Turks did not consider "Crimea a first-choice region of interest"[7] disappointed not only the Germans but also exiled Crimean Tatars such as Seydahmet, who pursued firmly anti-Soviet aims in Poland[8] and Romania, but also in Istanbul, Ankara and even in Lebanon.[9] They hoped in vain that Ankara would support the cause of the Crimean Tatars. After the summer of 1941, national actors in Berlin, such as the Dobruja-born Müstecib Ülküsal (1899–1996) or Mustafa Edige Qırımal (= Edige Kirimal; 1911–80), who had fled the peninsula after the execution of İbraimov and his supporters (cf. Chapter 31), even attempted to obtain permission to organize the Crimean Tatar population and to have the Crimean Tatar members of the Red Army released from German prisoner of war camps. As in the First World War (cf. Chapter 30), it would prove that the Germans were only open to offers of collaboration if they suited their own ends. They certainly didn't support the idea of an independent Crimean Tatar state.[10] However, after the war such actions gave the Soviet government cause[11] to claim that the Crimean Tatar population couldn't be trusted, as we will see in the context of the deportations of 1944 (cf. Chapter 33). Certainly, both for Hitler and for his many subordinate authorities, the occupation of Crimea was not about the liberation of the Crimean Tatars.

A factor that should not be underestimated was Sevastopol's nimbus; both the Soviets and the Germans considered it one of the best-fortified military facilities in the world; as Norbert Kunz succinctly observes, for the Germans "considerable prestige was at stake" in their attempt to take the city.[12] Indeed, the men and women of Sevastopol' did not make it easy for the assailants, holding out for 250 days, which then made the German triumph seem all the greater.

The Wehrmacht's march on Crimea had begun after victory in the Sea of Azov in the autumn of 1941. Together with the 3rd Romanian Army, the 11th Army under the command of the newly installed General Erich von

Manstein (1887–1973)[13] advanced on the peninsula via the Isthmus of Perekop. In the late October, they laid siege to Sevastopol', again with the assistance of Romanian forces. In the east too, in the Kerch Peninsula, the Wehrmacht initially stalled, the Red Army having returned at the turn of 1941/42. Unternehmen Trappenjagd (Operation Bustard Shoot) finally ended in May 1942, when the German and Romanian forces took Kerch.[14] Some 100,000 Red Army soldiers were taken prisoner. Unternehmen Störfang (Operation Sturgeon Catch), which the medieval historian Percy Ernst Schramm (1894–1970) documented from the perspective of the leadership in his role as war diarist to the Wehrmacht Supreme Command,[15] finally led to the fall of Sevastopol' in the early June of 1942. But the Germans paid a high price: Manstein, the Romanian forces and the Italians who had subsequently joined them[16] lost over a third of their offensive capacity.

In Crimea too, the deadly threat to the local Jewish population was already evident during the German advance: *Einsatzgruppen* (EGs) – in the Soviet Union, EG D under the command of Otto Ohlendorf (1907–51) – were deployed as the army's vanguard or rearguard. Besides eliminating alleged or actual Partisans and communist functionaries, their 'tasks' included murdering Jews and Roma. *Einsatzgruppe* D had already achieved notoriety during what became known as the Simferopol' Massacre of December 1941. Immediately after Sevastopol' was taken, over 4,000 Jews were massacred.[17] This was just the prelude, however, to the systematic racist extermination policy.

For Manstein, the Crimean campaign was a hard-won victory for which he was rewarded with the rank of general field marshal (equivalent to the rank of army general). And for the surviving Wehrmacht soldiers, the army leadership created a special decoration, the Krimschild (Crimea Shield). The conquest of the supposedly undefeatable fortress of Sevastopol' was milked for propaganda purposes: representatives of the press and diplomats from the Reich and the Axis countries visited the destroyed city, and a visit was even paid by King Michael I of Romania (1921–2017).[18]

In his meritorious study of the years 1941–4 in Crimea, Kunz finds that under Manstein, the occupation regime was "in many respects more moderate" than in other Soviet territories taken by the Germans.[19] On the whole, this assessment does not stand up, given the Third Reich's criminal policies. Especially if one rejects the apologetic self-stylization put forward with great success after the war by General Field Marshal Manstein. (Incidentally, he enjoyed a second career as an unofficial advisor on the development of the Federal Republic's army (the Bundeswehr) after his release as a prisoner of war in the early 1950s). Manstein was able to present himself to the West German public as a military expert while stylizing himself as a 'clean' Wehrmacht soldier unbesmirched by the less savoury aspects of politics – unlike the 'criminal' SS or the *Einsatzgruppen*.[20] Both were interpretations the majority of people in the post-war Federal Republic were only too happy to follow.

After the invasion of the Soviet Union in June 1941, the Wehrmacht received a friendly reception in some regions (e.g. in Eastern Galicia, which had been under Soviet administration since late 1939) from a population which misjudged the actual aims of the National Socialist state. In the peninsula too, some of the remaining population – that is, Crimean Tatars who were not serving in the Soviet army or the few ethnic Germans who had not been deported – welcomed the Wehrmacht with positive expectations. This may be explained by the persecution they had suffered since the mid-1930s, which had also extended to representatives of the formerly promoted Crimean Tatar culture such as the Turkologist and writer Bekir Çobanzade (1893–1937).[21] Another factor was the concessions the Germans made – at least in the first months of the occupation – out of pragmatism. On the whole, Johannes Hürter's assessment of National Socialist policy towards the non-Russian nationalities in the occupied territory is persuasive: it was merely "half-hearted wooing of the local population", who were not sufficiently accommodated in terms of agricultural policy, self-governance and religion, and hence these efforts did not come to anything.[22]

National Socialist policy was essentially shaped by racist views and guidelines that prevented more extensive concessions to the nationalities regarded as inferior. National Socialist Crimea policy was not motivated solely by racial ideology or strategy, however: Berlin was well aware of the peninsula's beauty and its location was important to the war economy in the context of the Reich Security Main Office's "Generalplan Ost" ("General Eastern Plan"). Hitler's "Gotengau" fantasies were a further factor.

> The partialy less restrictive policy towards the Crimean Tatar population (for instance the partial promotion of Tatar cultural activities or concessions in self-governance) must be seen as part of an offer of cooperation necessary in occupation regimes, not as a positive Tatar policy. Ultimately, the National Socialist resettlement plans envisaged a similar fate for the Crimean Tatars in the medium term as it did for the other 'non-Tatar' groups [23]

This ultimately meant deportation, even if Hitler's deportation order of early July 1942 – before Sevastopol' had been taken, then – only stipulated that "all Russian, Armenians and other Bolshevists" were to be resettled, not Crimean Tatars or Crimean Germans, although a first draft had mentioned Crimean Muslims.[24] Local actors had their work cut out persuading the "Führer" to abandon these plans; resettling around three-quarters of the entire population of Crimea would have been a huge logistical challenge, all the more so during wartime. Furthermore, depopulation would have been counterproductive; for one thing, the peninsula played a prominent role in the National Socialist policy of looting and appropriating food for the Reich. They could not afford to lose a large section of the harvest labour force – and the order was indeed withdrawn for practical reasons.[25] It was not only the military leaders on the ground who wished for more pragmatism in the policy towards the local population, the ultimate aim of which was disenfranchisement if not extermination. Similar reservations were expressed by Reich envoy Werner Otto von Hentig (1886–1984); in April 1942, he informed the Ministry for Foreign Affairs of the negative consequences of the murder of the Jews: he reported the mass shootings of Jews – 12,000 in a very short time in Simferopol' alone – to Berlin, and complained about the "effects of such butchery". These were

> of course by no means [limited] to the victims themselves; they affect the entire population of the occupied territory, because naturally no one thought it possible that we kill women and children. But they also affect the morale of the troops and, furthermore, our economic position too. Quite apart from the effects further abroad of course.

Economically, he thought it a poor move because Jews had often been employed in trades in the region's cities and now their abilities and labour were lacking.[26] Such rare voices went unheard, however; in Crimea too, the Shoah was executed ruthlessly: after just six months, Berlin received reports that the peninsula was now "free of Jews". This had been preceded by the 'usual' disenfranchisement, stigmatizing and humiliation of the Jewish population and the dressing-up of the occupiers' extermination policy as "resettlement". In Crimea too, the Wehrmacht supported *Einsatzgruppen* in committing genocide. There were also some differences to the other sites of the National Socialist genocide, however:[27] due to the geography of the peninsula, the local Jews were not taken to concentration camps first, but were murdered and burnt on the spot. This was probably also to minimize the psychological burden on the perpetrators – not surprisingly, that of the victims was of no consequence in the National Socialist logic of extermination – since in Crimea, extensive experiments were conducted with killing machines, referred to by the local population as "dushegubka" (Russian; "soul killers"). Besides the use of gas wagons, barges full of people were sunk on the Black Sea; more than 1,000 died this way. Unlike in Eastern Galicia,[28] for instance, there were no local pogroms against Jewish neighbours in Crimea, although isolated anti-Semitic acts were carried out by Tatar and Slav inhabitants.[29]

The most significant difference to the Shoah in the rest of the occupied territories was the probably "muddle", to use Kunz's lax but apt term, that confronted both the National Socialist actors in the peninsula and the ethnogenists in Berlin.[30] The National Socialists' claim to be the defining authority meant they could decide who was a Jew and who was not. The one-dimensional reduction to the obscure characteristic of 'race' overlooked the diversity of Judaism. While they were aware of the differences between Ashkenazim and Sephardim and members of both groups were victims of the Shoah, the many forms of Jewish life in Crimea posed something of a dilemma. Besides the Talmudic Jews (c. 60,000), most of whom were Ashkenazim and were promptly murdered, there were three other groups: Mountain Jews, the Krymchaks (c. 6,400) and Karaites (cf. Chapter 24), who with a population of 8,300 constituted the largest of these smaller branches.[31]

The Mountain Jews, originally from the Caucasus, had arrived in Crimea only in the late 1930s due the efforts of the American Jewish Joint Distribution Committee – which was also active in the Soviet Union between 1924 and 1938 – in the context of the so-called productivization campaign. The German perpetrators had no doubts about their 'Jewishness', and hence they became victims of the Shoah.[32] Things were a little different in the case of the Krimchaks, a linguistically Tatarized Jewish group, and the Karaites. Ohlendorf himself provisionally excluded both groups from extermination in December 1941 and turned to the head of the Reich Ministry for the Occupied Eastern Territories, Alfred Rosenberg, who was responsible for "racial matters", asking him to check which race they belonged to. In Berlin, it was found that the Krymchaks were definitely Jews. Their extermination promptly began; as in other parts of occupied Europe, only a few of them were able to save themselves by going into hiding.[33] In the case of the Karaites, on the other hand, like the tsarist authorities the Germans ultimately assumed that they were not Jews. As Kiril Feferman observes, German racial politicians and scholars were already grappling with the Karaite question in the 1930s – and there was some divergence in their findings. Fortunately for the Crimean Karaites, during the occupation the prevailing view was that they were not Jews; the Germans relied on 'scientific' assessments as well as statements by Karaites themselves.[34] The literature repeatedly points out that members of the other Jewish communities supported their brethren – by confirming that the Karaites were not Jews.[35] Be that as it may, the "Reichsführer SS" himself, Heinrich Himmler (1900–45), decided in their favour, which Feferman takes as evidence that the Nationalist Socialist state attached great importance to the Karaite question.[36] Individual Karaites did nevertheless fall victim to the National Socialists, in some cases simply due to mistakes made by the latter. Certainly, the German policy to spare the Karaites seems to have been driven by pragmatic considerations; they "enjoyed the backing of their Tatar neighbours in particular, that is, of partners who from the German perspective were indispensible".[37] Had the German Reich achieved the "Endsieg" ("final victory") and no longer had to worry about such matters, it is possible that the Karaite's 'race' would have been reassessed. For the time being, however, they were useful, especially since some of them fought for the Germans and headed westward with the Wehrmacht when it retreated in April 1944.[38]

We will consider the support the occupying forces received from the local population in the context of the deportations that ensued after the Soviet army had retaken the peninsula in Chapter 33. Here it is worth mentioning, however, that the enthusiasm shown by the early collaborators quickly turned to disappointment. Even the groups who were not targeted *per se* by the Wehrmacht and *Einsatzgruppen* soon came to experience the regime's brutality. Everyday life was characterized by raids, controls and food shortages. Since the fertile peninsula played a large role in supplying the German war effort, many foodstuffs were diverted to the Eastern Front.[39] Due to security concerns, Crimea was under strict military administration until the Wehrmacht finally withdrew: fierce partisan warfare, or "gang warfare" ("Bandenkrieg"), in the National Socialist terminology, raged in the peninsula, especially in the mountains, where conditions were not conducive to conventional combat. Although the occupiers were occasionally successful in harrying the resistance fighters, ultimately the German forces were no match for them or, above all, for the Soviet troops. In April 1944, the Germans were forced to retreat. And Crimea became Soviet once again.[40]

33

The Deportations of 1944/45 and Their Background

In May 2016, Susana Camaladinova, born in what was then the Kirghiz Soviet Socialist Republic in 1983, achieved overnight fame: the lyrical soprano from a Crimean Tatar-Armenian family represented Ukraine in the internationally popular Eurovision Song Contest in Stockholm under her stage name Jamala (Crimean Tatar: Camala; Ukrainian/Russian: Dzhamala):

> I could not spend my youth there
> Because you took away my land
> I could not spend my youth there
> Because you took away my land[1]

Her song "1944", sung in English and Crimean Tatar, won first prize despite relatively close competition from Australia and the Russian Federation, which made the result all the more sensational. She thus brought Eurovision to Kyiv for the second time; in 2004, the contest was won by the western Ukrainian Ruslana Lyzhychko (*1973), and hence it was held in the Ukrainian capital for the first time in 2005. Both Ruslana and Jamala thus performed in times in which the eyes of the world were on Ukraine: the 2005 Song Contest became a joyful celebration of the so-called Orange Revolution that had taken place just months earlier. Jamala's performance in Sweden in 2016, on the other hand, was shaped by a gloomier mood – for two reasons: firstly, Russia had annexed Crimea just over two years earlier, in March 2014, and secondly, Jamala sang about an event that must certainly be considered 'the' traumatic turning point in recent Crimean Tatar history and is known in Crimean Tatar as *sürgün*. The term translates as "deportation" or "exile" and denotes the forced resettlement of the Crimean Tatar population from the peninsula in May 1944. It is no surprise, then, that observers considered Ukraine's contribution in itself and Jamala's victory to be politically motivated. In the lead-up to the contest, the Russian Federation complained to the organizers, pointing out that the forum forbids clearly political statements. However, the organizers followed Jamala's explanation that the song was about the personal fate of her grandmother, who was deported to the eastern Soviet Union in 1944 with her five children – one of whom died in transit. She claimed it was not a statement on the tense situation between Ukraine and the Russian Federation due to the annexation or the situation in eastern Ukraine.[2]

Even if the Crimean Tatar community had had plenty of experience as a diaspora since the late eighteenth century, the events surrounding 18 May 1944 – to which Jamala's song refers – are of particular significance to the Crimean Tatar collective, shaping its culture of remembrance to this day.[3] Only around two weeks after the German military had retreated and the Red Army had completely retaken the peninsula, the Soviet regime deported practically the entire Crimean Tatar population then living there to Central Asia and Siberia or to the Urals. At the time, they numbered around 220,000; some 20,000 of the men were serving in the Soviet army and hence were not in Crimea but with their units. The Crimean Tatars were not the only group to be deported to the east. In the peninsula, they shared this fate with the Crimean Germans, who had been transferred to the eastern regions after the German invasion of the Soviet Union (cf. Chapter 32), as well as with Armenians, Greeks and Bulgarians. In other parts of the Soviet Union, victims of the policy included the Chechens or Ingush of the northern Caucasus or the descendants of German colonists in the Volga region.[4]

In the case of the Crimean Tatars, the Stalinist regime justified the deportation via their alleged mass collaboration with the German and Romanian occupiers and a disproportionately large number of desertions by Crimean Tatar soldiers in the Red Army. For instance, the relevant Russian-language literature repeatedly claimed – and in some cases continues to claim – that there were 20,000 deserters of Crimean Tatar descent. However, the Ukrainian historian Serhiy Hromenko has examined this figure in his opinionated and generally very readable book #CrimeaIsOurs. History of the Russian Myth, supported by the Ministry of Information Policy of Ukraine. Understandably, he arrives at a different figure: since an approximate total of only 20,000 male Crimean Tatars served in the army during the Second World War, the number of deserters cannot be correct, since every Crimean Tatar soldier would have had to have deserted. He estimates an approximate total of four-thousand deserters of Crimean Tatar descent.[5] Most scholars agree that the accusation of mass collaboration with the occupying troops is unjust, and not only in the case of the Crimean Tatars. In his famous "secret speech" at the Twentieth Party Congress of the CPSU in 1956, Nikita Khrushchev (1894–1971) arrived at the following assessment:

> Not only a [sic; "no" – K.S.J.] Marxist-Leninist but also no man of common sense can grasp how it is possible to make whole nations responsible for inimical activity, including women, children, old people, Communists and Komsomols, to use mass repression against them, and to expose them to misery and suffering for the hostile acts of individual persons or groups of persons.[6]

However, he specifically avoided referring to the Muslim population of Crimea – his speech did not mention them at all, and they were not rehabilitated either. That did not happen until 1967, under his successor Leonid Brezhnev (1906–82), although this collective 'exoneration' did not include the right to return. This also explains why it wasn't until after the collapse of the Soviet Union that Crimean Tatars returned in large numbers to a homeland younger generations only knew from the stories of their older relatives.

But how should we assess the collaboration by Crimean Muslims during the Second World War? It is not disputed that "[a]s in other territories" the Wehrmacht "also made use of the ethnic circumstances on the Black Sea" and all in all seemed satisfied with the support received from the Crimean Tatars.[7] The remaining Crimean Germans who had escaped the precautionary resettlement by the Soviet authorities in the summer of 1941, Crimean Bulgarians and the few Romanians or Italians living in the peninsula had also collaborated with the German or Romanian authorities and received certain privileges in return.[8] It was pointed out decades ago that a nuanced understanding of the term "collaboration" is called for,[9] since for many inhabitants of Crimea, cooperation with the occupiers was a matter of sheer necessity due to the looting and diversion of food supplies alone (cf. Chapter 32), not to mention the permanent (unspoken) threat of violence that the Shoah must have brought home to the non-Jewish population too. Nevertheless, as in 1918, there were also indigenous actors who hoped to gain more from collaboration than easier access to scarce food supplies. Given the persecution of large groups during what have become known as the Great Purges, it hardly surprising, however, that many inhabitants of Crimea harboured the desire to be free from Soviet rule. Many even dreamed of an independent Crimean state; it goes without saying, however, that the National Socialists were the worst 'partners' imaginable for such an aim. Of course, they were not interested in liberating repressed nationalities and coexisting with them on equal terms; rather, they anticipated exploiting them in order to establish German dominance in Eastern Europe.

As is so often the case with controversial historical questions, there is considerable divergence regarding the estimated number of Crimean Tatar collaborators. It is hard to say for certain how many "volunteers" ("Hilfswillige" – literally people prepared to help) assisted the occupiers, be it as members of the self-defence units established in the peninsula, as auxiliary police, as interpreters or in other institutions supporting the occupation regime. Estimates range from around 6,000[10] to 15,000[11] or 20,000.[12] It is certainly impossible to speak of the mass collaboration by 'the' Crimean Tatar population that Moscow ultimately gave as the reason for the deportations in the spring of 1944. Moreover, some Crimean soldiers in the Red Army received the highest decorations.[13] But that was not enough to save the Crimean Tatar population from banishment and decades in exile.

There is some controversy surrounding how thoroughly the Kremlin and the NKVD planned and executed the deportation; the American historian Norman Naimark claims that "every single Tatar had to go, whatever their position in society, whether married to a Russian or not",[14] while other scholars believe that Crimean Tatars who took up the Partisan struggle against the Germans or fought on the front escaped deportation. Some also say that Crimean Tatars married to members of other nationalities were not removed or could return to Crimea after a short time.[15] Whatever the case may be, the fates of some individuals are repeatedly mentioned in this context, such as that of Amet-Han Sultan (Russian/Ukrainian: Amet-Khan Sultan; 1920–71), a flying ace considered the USSR's most highly decorated soldier of non-Slavic descent. Several street names, busts and monuments commemorate this hero of the Soviet Union, and not only in Crimea. A museum to him was even set up in the town of his birth, Alupka.[16] There are several variations on his fate and that of his family, none of which can be conclusively verified; for the sake of simplicity, let us follow the Russian and English *Wikipedia* entries: he is supposed to have experienced the deportations in Alupka while taking leave from the front. According to one version, he used his status as a hero to prevent his parents' deportation; another has it that the family escaped deportation because Amet-Han's father was a member of the Lak ethnicity from Dagestan and only his younger brother Imran, who had been a Tatar auxiliary policeman during the German occupation, was punished. A dramatic version relates that when an NKVD officer wanted to take Amet-Han and his parents to the deportation site, a fight ensued and Amet-Han was eventually able to show he was a hero of the Soviet Union. This is said to have been confirmed by other soldiers, and the secret policeman apologized. Finally, it is also claimed that the family did not have to resettle to Central Asia but 'only' had to go to Dagestan, and was also given more time to pack than other Crimean Muslims.[17]

It is not surprising that *sürgün* has also featured in art and culture as the most important remembrance resource concerning the Crimean Tatar people. In a recent study, Swetlana Czerwonnaja and Martin Malek have pointed out that the "trauma of deportation and the outlawry collectively perceived as a tragedy"[18] implicitly or explicitly pervades Crimean Tatar literature. For authors such as Ėmil' Amit (1938–2002) or Ėrvin Umerov (1938–2007), *sürgün* remained their lifelong subject matter. As recently as 2013, the Crimean Tatar director and actor Akhtem Seitablaev (*1972) made the first film on the subject, entitled *Haytarma* (Crimean Tatar; The Return). Seitablaev also played the lead role, that of Amet-Han Sultan. For Gerhard Gnauck writing in *Die Welt*, *Haytarma* is a "rather conventionally filmed but coherently narrated and moving film" with good special effects when the German and Soviet pilots engage in dogfights over the Crimean Mountains. After the annexation of Crimea by the Russian Federation in 2014, the film seemed "like an epitaph for a lost landscape and homeland".[19]

FIGURE 33.1 *Amet-Han Sultan – two-time hero of the Soviet Union, photograph from 1945.*

The film certainly attempts to interpret the collective catastrophe as a new beginning, ending with the birth of a child in one of the railway wagons in which the deportees are ferried into exile and with the question as to what name the child should be given. Even in times of great need and despair, new life begins, then – and the life of the Crimean Tatar collective thus continues.[20]

In his above-mentioned polemical debunking of the Russian Crimea myths, Serhiy Hromenko dedicates a chapter to the notion that "Crimean Tatars Are a 'Traitor People'".[21] In it, he considers this idea, virulent in Russia, by examining the Soviet debates after 1944. After the Second World War, this older stereotype gained a new lease of life in order to justify the deportations. Prince Potemkin's wish for a Crimea that would be so much better without Tatars was 'fulfilled' under Stalin. Moreover, for the first time in the recorded history of Crimea, the peninsula was largely ethnically homogenized; it had become almost entirely Slav – that is, Russian and Ukrainian. Multiethnic Crimea no longer existed.

34

Crimea after the Second World War

The novel *Medea and Her Children* (*Medeia i ee deti. Semeinaia Khronika*), first published in Russian in 1996, was penned by the writer and Putin critic Liudmila Ulitskaia, who moves back and forth between Moscow and Israel. The work tells of the life of a Soviet – that is, multinational – family spread out between the centres of the USSR and one of its peripheries, the Crimean Peninsula:

> Medea Mendez had the maiden name of Sinoply and was, if we disqualify her younger sister Alexandra who moved to Moscow in the late 1920s, the last remaining pure-blooded Greek of a family settled since time immemorial on the Tauride coast, a land still mindful of its ties with Ancient Greece. She was also the last member of the family who could speak passably the medieval Pontic Greek which survived only in the Tauride colonies and lagged one thousand years behind modern Greek, the same length of time it was separated from the language of antiquity.
> There had long been no one for her to talk to in this wornout, resonant language [. . .] The other Tauride Greeks of Medea's generation had either died or been deported, but she had lived on in the Crimea by the grace of God, as she supposed, but partly no doubt also because of the Spanish surname bequeathed by her late husband, a jolly Jewish dentist with vices which were minor but not insignificant, and virtues which were great but meticulously concealed.[1]

The novel's emotional focal point is the eponymous hero Medea, who is descended from Pontic Greeks. She escaped the fate of the other Crimean Greeks, who, like the peninsula's Tatars or Bulgarians, had been deported after the Second World War, due to her marriage to a Soviet Jew. In the Soviet Union, the Jewish population were of course considered a separate nationality, and hence she lived in a mixed marriage that protected her from banishment. The protagonist's forename – Medea – takes us back to Classical Antiquity and the realm of myth associated with the region: Medea was the daughter of King Aeëtes of Kolchis, located on the eastern shore of the Black Sea, on the territory of today's Georgia. In Classical mythology, Medea fell in love with Jason and helped him and the Argonauts steal the Golden Fleece protected by her father. Medea and Jason thus both had to flee Kolchis before marrying and having two sons, whom she killed after Jason left her for Kreon's daughter.

The Medea theme has received a lot of attention from writers, including Euripides, Seneca (c. 1–65 AD), the Austrian Franz Grillparzer (1791–1872) and the Germans Hans Henny Jahn (1894–1959) and Christa Wolf (1929–2011), who have all subjected it to very different treatment. Ulitskaia's Medea has little in common with her mythical namesake, however; for the Slavonic studies scholar Wolfgang Kasack, she is primarily a "force field toward which a countless crowd of relatives are oriented", a crowd consisting of "people of many nations". For Kasack, Medea symbolizes "the connectedness of people *per se*".[2] At the same time, however, she represents the Soviet multinational family that was not only propagated by the Soviet leaders but also truly existed to some extent: people married or entered into other relationships with each other beyond ethnic boundaries and communicated in the *lingua franca* of the USSR, Russian. The novel reflects the fate of a handful of relatives during the twentieth century without making the ruptures and caesurae – the Revolution, building socialism, the Second World War, the deportations – the story's focus; these events can nevertheless be felt in terms of their impact on the characters. Their connection not only to Medea but also to the peninsula itself becomes evident: we feel their joy at being able to spend their holidays in this beautiful place even if its polyethnicity no longer existed in the twentieth century, 'relicts' such as the Crimean Greek Medea notwithstanding.

Crimea was a difference place after the Second World War, not only due to the widespread devastation but also because of the loss of its people to combat, massacre and deportation – in today's terms, genocide (in the case of the Shoah) and ethnic cleansing, which also involves genocidal elements. There were other changes too: the peninsula had a new status within the state structure; a good year after the deportation of the Tatar population, the Autonomous Soviet Socialist Republic was disbanded on 30 June 1945, having existed since the early 1920s. In the years that followed, Crimea was an *oblast'* (an administrative region) within the Russian Socialist Federative Soviet Republic (RSFSR). This change in status was not announced until a year later, however, in late June 1946. The reason given for this change and for the resettlement of the Tatars was, once again, purported collaboration, this time with the National Socialists. And again there was no mention of the role Tatars played in liberating the peninsula from the invaders as members of the Red Army or as Partisans.[3]

It is telling, then, that the Soviet leadership and the local administration sought to obliterate all memory of the deported peoples, especially the Crimean Tatars: the Crimean Tatar schoolbooks printed during the *korenizatsiia* (cf. Chapter 31) campaign of the 1920s were burnt, mosques, cemeteries, etc. were destroyed and place names of Crimean Tatar (and occasionally pre-Tatar) origin had to make way for new ones. This policy of eradicating older, now undesirable historical traces is nothing new: whereas under Catherine II Hellenized names were still preferred (cf. Chapter 22), now Russification was the watchword; for instance, Qarasuvbazar became "Belogorsk" and Bağçasaray became "Pushkinskii", which nevertheless alluded to Alexander Pushkin and his poem "Bakhchisaraiskii fontan" (Chapter 1). This cultural and administrative Russification, as Brian G. Williams has labelled the procedure,[4] was accompanied by the targeted immigration of Russian and Ukrainian settlers in an attempt to revive the depopulated rural regions and provide the urgently needed labour force. Ultimately, this move appears to be a repeat of the policy tsarist Russia pursued just under a century earlier, after the Crimean War, when it replaced the Tatar population that had emigrated with Slavs (cf. Chapter 27). It is estimated that around 90 per cent of the Slav population of Crimea only arrived in the peninsula after the Second World War.[5] It was only then that it had 'become Russian' in the true sense of the word.

It wasn't necessarily these ethnopolitical upheavals that made the world take notice of Crimea; it was rather the Yalta Conference of 4–11 February 1945. This diplomatic meeting of the Allied heads of state of the USA (Franklin D. Roosevelt, 1882–1945), Great Britain (Winston Churchill, 1874–1965) and the Soviet Union (Joseph Stalin) in the Livadiia Palace was mainly held to decide the future of the German Reich, which was already on its last legs and would finally capitulate three months later. Other topics of discussion in Yalta were the European post-war order, France's incorporation into the circle of the victorious powers and the Soviet Union's joining the war with Japan, which it would do after Germany had been defeated.

The agreement the Allies reached in Yalta concerning the so-called spheres of influence in Europe made the conference a *lieu de mémoire* (albeit it one with negatives associations) only for Poland, as Stefan Troebst has persuasively argued. For example, while in the German collective memory the three-power conference[6] with the most sustained impact would be the Potsdam Conference (August 1945), barely associated with Yalta, for Polish ears the name is a cipher for an unjust post-war order that surrendered Poland – an ally in exile, no less – to the Soviet Union.[7] What was this view based on? In Yalta it was decided that the eastern territories of the Second Polish Republic that had gone to Russia following the Additional Secret Protocol to the Hitler–Stalin pact of 1939 would remain part of the USSR. As compensation, the new Poland received parts of East Prussia and the hitherto German territories east of the Oder and Neisse rivers. Poland's bourgeois government in exile was replaced with a pro-Soviet one and it was decided to resettle other sections of the population. While the deportation of the German population from the new Polish territories was less controversial in the Polish discourse, the expulsion of local Poles from the territories that now formed part of the USSR – which had not been openly announced at Yalta – was of course a bone of contention. In both respects, then, for some sections of the Polish population, Yalta – and with it Crimea – stands for the West's betrayal of their homeland. Along with the (positive) Sarmatian myth (cf. Chapter 1), a negative myth is associated with the peninsula.

The next event that might have drawn attention to Crimea abroad but went unnoticed due to the Soviet propaganda strategy took place in 1954, a year after the death of Stalin, then: the transfer of the Crimean *oblast'* to the Ukrainian Soviet Republic, frequently – but wrongly – referred to as Khrushchev's gift to Ukraine. This transfer was made public against the backdrop of extensive celebrations to mark the 300th anniversary of the Pereiaslav Agreement of 1654, when the Ukrainian Cossacks under Khmel'nyts'kyi subordinated themselves to Tsar Alexis Mikhailovich. Ukrainian historiography considers this to have merely been a case of establishing temporary, pragmatic ties to the Polish king. Russian historiography prefers to interpret the treaty with recourse to the first Eastern Slavic state, Kyivan Rus', as a reunification of 'Great' and 'Little Russians' (= Ukrainians).[8] At any rate, the transfer of Crimea to Ukraine in 1954 was presented as a token of the 'unswerving friendship' between the Union's two largest nationalities.

FIGURE 34.1 *Group photo at the Yalta Conference, 1945 (from left to right: Winston Churchill, Franklin D. Roosevelt and Joseph Stalin).*

The political background to the celebration of the events of 1654 and Crimea's transfer to Ukrainian jurisdiction is complex and, it must be stressed, it has not been fully explained to this day. And for a long time, it would seem no attempts were made to explain it, as the political scientist Gwendolyn Sasse established some years ago. She herself presents various versions and potential explanations that shed a little light on the affair.[9] What is beyond doubt is that Khrushchev did not act on his own, and for this reason alone, one cannot speak of a 'gift'. Probably because of his close personal ties to Ukraine, it has often been argued that he wanted to honour the country by presenting it with Crimea or – as Vladimir Putin put it less elegantly – by handing over the peninsula "like a sack of potatoes".[10] The political constellation in the Kremlin and the ongoing power struggle to succeed Stalin contradict this interpretation; at this point, Khrushchev did not have the necessary influence. At the very least, the Presidium of the Central Committee of the CPSU under Georgii M. Malenkov (1901–88) would have had to have been involved in the decision, the Ukrainian historian Iurii Shapoval presumes.[11] There has also been debate as to whether the transfer to Ukraine was meant to pass on a considerable part of the logistical and financial burden of the reconstruction of Crimea following its destruction during the war. Another not entirely implausible explanation is that Ukraine thereby had to accept part of the responsibility for the morally and legally reprehensible mass resettlement of nationalities with roots in Crimea.[12] It is also possible that it was for wholly pragmatic reasons; due to the lack of a land link between the peninsula and the RSFSR (until the summer of 2017), it was easier to supply and reconstruct the peninsula from Ukraine.[13] Presumably, as is so often the case in history, a number of factors played a role.

Whatever the case may be, Crimea's incorporation into the Ukrainian Soviet Republic must also be examined in connection to Russian–Ukrainian relations and in the context of the Soviet Union as a whole. Crimea was undoubtedly a "lavish gift" from Moscow to Kyiv, to cite Plokhy,[14] and would reinforce the 'reunification' of Russia and Ukraine on the symbolic level. The same holds, incidentally, for another measure: when the United Nations was founded, Ukraine and the Byelorussian SSR both received their own seats in the General Assembly of the United Nations, which was only possible with the approval of the Western Allies. After the Second World War, the second-largest Eastern Slavic nationality became *secunda inter pares* after the Russians. The non-Slavic nationalities took this to be a clear message, since despite every insistence on Soviet patriotism, politically and demographically, the Slav element dominated in the USSR. The 'gift's' signals to the Ukrainian SSR and its nomenklatura were also complex: Khrushchev could be relatively certain he had the backing of the Ukrainian political elite, but it didn't hurt to have Crimea as an additional dowry from Moscow. At the same time, it also meant that there was now a Ukrainian territory in which most people were Russian and even more were Russian-speaking;

most ethnic Ukrainians spoke Russian as their first language (and still do). Given that the Kremlin feared so-called Ukrainian National Bolshevists as early as the 1920s,[15] increasing the Russian population in this Soviet republic might have been a desired side effect.

The most plausible explanation, however, is that at the time of the 'gift', after victory in the Second World War and its rise as a super and nuclear power, the Soviet Union was at its zenith. The collapse of the Soviet empire seemed unthinkable to all. And given the centralist state structure, despite proclamations of a federal system, whether or not a certain territory belonged to one Soviet republic or another was of limited relevance. Or to put it another way: the notion that the beautiful peninsula would ever become 'abroad' for Russians was simply unthinkable, both in 1954 and in the decades thereafter. In 1991, however, the deck was reshuffled (cf. Chapter 35).

Even though there has yet to be a satisfactory examination of Crimea's political and economic development after the Second World War and its incorporation into the Ukrainian SSR,[16] what we can say is that the peninsula's development remained dependent on that of the state as a whole, although use was made of local options, which was even possible in the Soviet Union. The situation thereafter was ambivalent: as in 1921/22 and 1932/33, in 1946/47 Crimea was affected by a famine, brought on by drought and destruction, although there were fewer victims this time due to access to fresh fish.[17] Like other territories retaken by the Soviet army, Crimea saw destruction on a large scale, particularly in urban areas such as Sevastopol' (along with Kerch in the eastern peninsula), where only 3 per cent of what had been built before the war remained intact in 1944. This was compounded by the Wehrmacht's tactic of causing as much damage as possible when retreating from an area. In the case of Crimea, this included destroying the water supply.[18] Since the peninsula had always struggled with severe water shortages, this had a heavy impact; there were a number of epidemics in the immediate post-war years. Projects such as the construction of the North Crimean Canal, begun in 1961, which supplied mainly the northeastern regions with water,[19] brought longer-term relief.

Besides reconstructing destroyed buildings and infrastructure, one of the biggest problems was repopulating the peninsula. The shortage of people and hence a labour force was not only due to the occupation policy, the Shoah and the National Socialist system of forced labour but was also a product of the deportations (cf. Chapter 33). Russian historiography estimates that the population decreased from over 1.2 million before 1941 to around 350,000 in the summer of 1944.[20] As already mentioned, during the resettlement following the deportations, preference was given to Russian and Ukrainian families working in agriculture, which was a prominent sector of the peninsula's economy along with tourism. Despite various setbacks, such as the departure of dissatisfied new settlers, in 1959 the population had already surpassed its pre-war level by around 75,000.[21] The labour shortage nevertheless remained a pressing problem. It was just one of many; Crimea fell behind the other regions of the Ukrainian SSR or the RSFSR due to a lack of investment by the central authorities and bad planning. In this connection, Sasse points to the problematic nature of Soviet data, which makes calculating the actual economic capacity in the peninsula a difficult task. The fact is that the reports on qualitative and quantitative increases in productivity often had little to do with reality. They were part of the propaganda drive to convince the socialist world (and ideally the world outside it) that the Soviet system was superior. It cannot be fully established where the funds for reconstruction and further economic development came from – from Moscow or from Kyiv?[22] It would be useful to know this, however, if we are to assess the extent to which Crimea's transfer to Ukraine was a success. Sasse ultimately comes to the conclusion that in relation to large-scale projects such as the North Crimea Canal, a "hierarchy of decision making" developed, instructions passing from Moscow and the all-powerful state economic planning committee Gosplan (*Gosudarstvennyi planovyi komitet*) to Kyiv before reaching Simferopol'.[23]

A certain degree of freedom in decision-making was enjoyed by Sevastopol' after 1965 onwards. when it was awarded the official title of "Hero City": from 1948 to the 1990s, it remained a closed territory; due to its military strategic importance, even Soviet citizens required a special permit to visit, and it was responsible for its own budget.[24] Moreover, it was one of only three cities in the Soviet Union of "federal rank", the other two being Moscow and Leningrad. According to a popular Russian myth, the city was awarded this status not only because of its efforts during the Crimean War and the Second World War but also for the rather banal reason that Stalin realized during a visit in 1948 that reconstruction was stalling, whereupon the Extraordinary Administration made more funds available.[25] The legal status of Sevastopol' can only be outlined briefly here, but it is important to note that in the debates on the assumed illegality of Crimea's transfer to the Ukrainian SSR in 1954, Russians occasionally argue that as a city of federal rank, Sevastopol' has always been Russian and never Ukrainian (cf. Chapter 36).

Sevastopol' was founded as a naval port and was thus primarily intended to meet the military requirements of the Russian and later the Soviet fleet. However, there were economic expectations from the very outset, although over the years they would be only partially fulfilled.[26] In line with its location, the local economy was dominated by shipbuilding, fishing, wine production and smaller textile and food production. Development of heavy industry was hindered by the rocky terrain of the city's environs.[27] In rebuilding the destroyed city, the inhabitants displayed agency, and perhaps even a collective stubbornness that certainly had heroic elements to it in the immediate post-war years with the revival of Stalinism. As Karl Quall has demonstrated, the local actors refused, for instance, to follow the architectural tendencies in the "wedding cake" urban architecture typical of the era.

Instead, the city was reconstructed more or less in line with its historical image. Indeed, to this day Sevastopol's architecture has combined a primarily Russian style with Soviet elements – the agitation that accompanied the reconstruction drive "(re)created a glorious past and present and combined them with the future promise of the great Soviet utopia".[28]

That such a large number of former Soviet citizens have such positive associations with Crimea irrespective of their ethnic origins is due not only to the popular narrative of the "Hero City" of Sevastopol' but also to the peninsula's rapid development into one of the most important places in Soviet mass tourism. As we have seen, Crimea had always attracted tourists, and virtually became a place of yearning, but it was not until the second half of the twentieth century that it became a destination for the masses.[29] A wide range of types and contexts of travel developed: in addition to the sanatorium culture established in the tsarist era, there were tours run by trade unions and other societal organizations (often with their own homes and lodgings) as well as individual tourism, which was also possible in the Soviet Union. A specific phenomenon came closest to realizing the "great Soviet utopia": the Soviet Pioneer camp culture, the undisputed 'capital' of which was the Artek complex founded near Hurzuf.[30] It was the most famous and most prestigious of the many camps for the Pioneer youth organizations in the USSR and the so-called Eastern Bloc, and still exists today, albeit under different auspices.[31] In the Soviet Union, Artek was synonymous with the collective dreams of several generations of young Soviet people. They did not come true for all of them, since only those

FIGURE 34.2 *The Artek Pioneer camp, 1986.*

children who had proven particularly deserving at school and in youth organizations were allowed to spend their holidays there. Or at least in theory, since in practice the less talented offspring of the Soviet nomenklatura also made it to the holiday camp. Artek was supposed to demonstrate the superiority of the Soviet system to the outside world and hence it also became a centre for international children's and youth exchanges. The Pioneer camps were part of a programme intended to mould the child into the so-called New (= socialist) Man, a system of education that was to take place as early as possible and was removed from the nuclear family. Some of the ideological indoctrination by education was certainly tailored to children,[32] young talents were searched for and promoted, and famous personalities such as the cosmonaut Iurii Gagarin (1934–68) or Soviet and foreign heads of state such as Walter Ulbricht (GDR, 1893–1973), Georgi Dimitrov (Bulgaria, 1882–1949) or Ho Chi Minh (Vietnam, 1890–1969) visited Artek. The sprawling facility consisting of several main and satellite camps also set architectural standards, particularly its expansion between 1957 and 1966, which also raised the capacity to the extent that from the mid-1960s on, it could host the annual holidays of over 20,000 children and adolescents at any one time.[33]

Overall, however, the peninsula's economic development after the Second World War was not a success story, despite the important tourism sector, the food industry (e.g. fish canning) and a few large industrial plants such as the iron ore combine in Kerch (the Kamysh Burunskii Iron Ore Combine). Ultimately, the same holds for the traditionally important agricultural sector. Along with tobacco,[34] the main products were fruit, vegetables and wine – sectors that repeatedly suffered setbacks that were less to do with the Ukrainian administration than with the Soviet context as a whole.[35] Beyond the so-called Eastern Bloc, the peninsula's economy received special international attention in the mid-1980s due to the anti-alcohol campaign launched by the last general secretary of the CPSU, Mikhail Gorbachev (1931–2022). This was one of various initiatives combating excessive drinking during the Soviet era, but the campaign between 1985 and 1987 caused the biggest stir. Abstinence was supposed to raise productivity and life expectancy, particularly for men, and lower the crime rate. The campaign, whose motto was "Sobriety – life's norm" (Russian: "Trezvost' – Norma zhizni"), consisted of a number of measures that included raising the price of alcohol and limiting where and when it was sold but also a drastic reduction in the cultivation of the relevant crops. For Crimea, with wines that had attained world renown in the nineteenth century, such as Massandra, the programme was simply catastrophic. Some ancient and precious grape varieties were lost forever.[36]

No study of the history of the Crimean Peninsula would be complete without consideration of the deported Crimean Tatars, the majority of whom were forced to live in Central Asia from 1944 onwards. Far away from their homeland, few of them had forgotten Crimea; strong memories were preserved for generations, as the ethnologist Greta Lynn Uehling has demonstrated.[37] Despite all repressions during the Soviet era, Crimean Tatars did not merely dream of a "return" (Crimean Tatar: *avdet*) to the peninsula but also attempted to achieve it by mostly legal means. Like so many Soviet citizens, the Crimean Tatar population had hoped for some respite after Stalin's death. They were disappointed in that they were not mentioned in Khrushchev's so-called secret speech of 1956 and were only rehabilitated a decade later. All the same, in the course of the 1950s there were improvements to conditions in the so-called special settlements where Crimean Tatar and other deported nationalities lived. Prior to this, the death rate was very high, even going by the official Soviet figures, which record that around 18 per cent of the Crimean population died within the first eighteen months of the deportations in the spring of 1944. Unsurprisingly, Crimean Tatar sources give a much higher figure – some 46 per cent.[38] A significant feature of ethnic cleansing, also evident in the case of the Crimean Tatars, is the relatively high number of victims among women and children.[39] In the post-war years, the Crimean Tatar diaspora attempted to adapt to their new environment and get on with the local population, with varying levels of success, as Williams has established via a series of interviews: whereas in Kazakhstan relations between new and old settlers were generally amicable, this cannot be said of the Mari Republic or the main region of deportation, the Uzbek SSR.[40]

A real caesura was the Crimean Tatar's partial rehabilitation by the Supreme Soviet of the USSR in 1967. They were exonerated of the charge of mass collaboration, although they still had no right to return to Crimea. The wording chosen was interesting: tellingly, the decree referred to them as the "Tatar nationality that previously lived in Crimea". The term "Crimean Tatar" was avoided and there was nothing to suggest that the "Tatar nationality" would ever inhabit the peninsula again. Additionally, the text exonerating them was not published throughout the Soviet Union; it only appeared in the regions to which they had been deported.[41] For many Soviet citizens outside these regions, the Crimean Tatars thus remained a nation of traitors. Individual Crimean Tatar families who made it back to Crimea under their own steam after 1967 were usually sent back by the authorities.[42]

In the dispute over the legacy and consequences of Stalinism and its huge number of victims, a dissident movement had emerged during the late 1950s. By reproducing and distributing their own texts (Russian: *samizdat*), writers were able to circumvent state censorship, leading to the emergence of a counter public sphere, albeit it a small one, that was anti-Stalinist but overall operated within the logic of the system. From the mid-1960s on, but especially in 1968, the year that changed so much around the world, the dissidents increasingly entered the spotlight. As members of a group particularly affected by the Stalinist repressions, the Crimean Tatars also played a role in this movement. One of them was Mustafa Cemilev (Crimean Tatar; Ukrainian: Mustafa Dzhemiliev, Russian: Mustafa Dzhemilev), to this day the most important and best-known figurehead of the Crimean Tatar movement. Born near Sudak in 1943, as an infant the later activist was deported with his parents to Central Asia. From the late 1950s on, he campaigned for the Crimean Tatar cause with petitions, and hence came into conflict with the Soviet regime. A number of career obstacles were put in his way; for instance, he was not allowed to pursue his interest in Oriental studies at university. He was first arrested in 1966, for so-called anti-Soviet agitation, and he spent a total of fifteen years in Soviet prisons and camps, which earned him a "Mandela-like" status. In imprisonment, he repeatedly went on hunger strike for several months, only surviving due to the prison authorities' decision to force feed him.[43] The Soviet authorities were quite clearly afraid his countrymen would regard him as a martyr. In 1969, he and other Soviet activists such as Viktor Krasin (1929–2017) became founding members of the Initiative Group for the Defence of Human Rights in the Soviet Union. One of its activities was providing international organizations with information on human rights violations.[44]

Along with Andrei Sakharov (1921–89) and the former high-ranking military officer Petr Grigorenko (Russian; Ukrainian: Petro Hryhorenko; 1907–87), Cemilev became one of the most popular figures in the dissident scene. The connection between Grigorenko and the Crimean Tatar movement demonstrates that *sürgün* – the deportation of 1944 – was also felt to be unjust beyond Tatar or Muslim discourse groups. Grigorenko, who later became a founding member of the Moscow Helsinki Group for Human Rights and at times was seen as its unofficial chairman, was quite explicit about it too: in 1968, in a speech in Moscow before Crimean Tatars protesting for their return to Crimea, he declared that their deportation had been unconstitutional. He also encouraged them not to give in. "So begin to demand. And demand not just parts, pieces, but all that was taken from you unlawfully – demand the reestablishment of the Crimean Autonomous Soviet Socialist Republic! [Stormy applause and cries of 'Hail the Crimean Autonomous Soviet Socialist Republic']".[45]

The Crimean Tatar audience's response to Grigorenko – who later emigrated to the USA, where he lived until his death – and his proclamation "Hail the Crimean Autonomous Soviet Socialist Republic" demonstrate that for a long time, most dissidents, including Crimean Tatars, operated within the system. Well into the Gorbachev era, the Crimean Tatars' political aim was not the dissolution of the USSR, an independent state or the revival of the Crimean Khanate with more or less close ties to Turkey, but the restoration of the ASSR. But the Soviet leadership did not exploit this situation. Since the early 1980s, the authorities had been considering creating a substitute Tatar homeland far away from the northern coast of the Black Sea, in the dry steppe regions south of Samarqand (Uzbek; Russian: Samarkand) and Buxoro (Uzbek; Russian: Bukhara); the future inhabitants protested.[46] Clearly, most Russian members of the Soviet nomenklatura did not understand the Crimean Tatar population's close emotional bond with the peninsula – despite the fact that the Russians themselves had developed such a close connection to it, considering it an indispensible Russian territory and speaking of "our Crimea" (Russian: "Krym nash"). However, it also shows just how little the political elites had departed from the early Soviet Union's strategy of national territorialization, according to which each ethnicity was to receive its 'own' territory. For the Crimean Tatars, however, it was clear that their sole territory was Crimea. The end of the Soviet Union brought them closer to this goal.

The rule that had often applied to Crimea as an imperial periphery – that events in the centre usually echoed (sometimes more faintly) in the peninsula – was proven again when the Soviet Union came to an end, although it may not have been clear to people at the time that they were living in an empire that was breaking up. It was not so much Gorbachev's "restructuring" (*perestroika*) as his desire for "transparency" (*glasnost'*) that opened up to Soviet citizens a greater sphere of communication. For the Crimean Tatar diaspora, the new freedom of speech enabled mass mobilization. But the situation also changed for the largely Slav population in Crimea itself. The Chornobyl' nuclear disaster in April 1986 had led to the formation of civil society, principally in Ukraine, where national and environmental demands merged, the latter soon being eclipsed by the former.[47] Crimea too saw the formation of a 'green' movement that primarily took aim at Moscow's plans to build a nuclear power station in the peninsula. Even the local Communist Party adopted this stance, and held a moratorium in the spring of 1989 – without consulting the responsible authorities in Moscow. (Kyiv had no say in the matter.)[48]

The party elite in the peninsula had already been departing from Moscow's official course since the mid-1980s. However, this was not because Gorbachev's plans to restructure the Soviet system didn't go far enough for them, but because they thought they went *too far*; the Russian-speaking nomenklatura, trenchant structural conservatives, adhered to Soviet social and political ideas – and continue to do so to this day. This was not least because beautiful Crimea had become a favourite spot for retired functionaries who remained well connected. Hence it is not surprising that in the late 1980s these circles were already voicing plans reminiscent of the supposedly good old days of the Soviet Union – namely the pre-Stalinist era: they wanted Crimea to return to its pre-war status of an Autonomous Soviet Socialist Republic (ASSR), perhaps as a separate economic area within the Soviet Union. At the same time, they hoped this would allow them to channel the growing influx of Tatars. Pragmatically exploiting Gorbachev's policies, which they otherwise rejected, in January 1991 they held a referendum on the restoration of the Crimean ASSR, which was supported by an astounding 93 per cent of participating voters. There was great disappointment, then, when the Supreme Soviet of Ukraine, which was formally responsible for Crimea, only approved the "re-establishment of the Crimean ASSR" as part of the Ukrainian SSR.[49] The majority of the Crimean population had of course been hoping to be connected to the Russian Soviet Republic. While neither the Soviet constitution of 1977 nor the constitution of the Ukrainian SSR made provisions for such an autonomous structure, in the generally chaotic end times of the USSR the ASSR plan was adopted by Kyiv.[50] In the years that followed, this caused problems between Simferopol', the peninsula's old and new political centre, and Kyiv, as well as between Ukraine and the Russian Federation.

It is telling of the peculiar pro-Russian/pro-Soviet stance held even by Crimea's Ukrainian population that the civil society movements that sprang up in Ukraine after Chornobyl' did not manifest themselves in the peninsula, or did so only briefly. Notwithstanding the exception of the anti-nuclear movement that was 'hijacked' by Crimea's old communist cadres, dissident groups such as Narodnyi Rukh Ukraïny (the National Movement of Ukraine, abbreviated to Rukh), which played a large role in Ukraine itself, appeared only temporarily.[51] And the Helsinki movement, which left its mark on the entire Soviet Union in the late 1970s, found hardly any resonance among Crimea's Slav population – in contrast to its reception among the Crimean Tatars, most of whom still lived outside the peninsula at this point, however.[52]

35

After the Dissolution of the Soviet Union:

Crimea as Part of Independent Ukraine

The Communist Party of Ukraine's newspaper article in 2007 reporting the visit by the mayor of Moscow, Iurii Luzhkov (*1936), who held the post from 1992 to 2010, indicates some of the political problems Crimea faced after the dissolution of the Soviet Union in 1991:

> "Fetch us back!" – the Sevastopol'ians shouted to Moscow's mayor [...] In Sevastopol', Iurii Luzhkov was welcomed with Russian flags and banners [emblazoned with] "Russian Sevastopol' ". Around a thousand members of pro-Russian organizations gathered in Nakhimov Square and shouted to the Moscow mayor, "We're with Russia!", "Fetch us back!" After the ceremonial opening of the Moscow Business and Cultural Centre, already abbreviated in Sevastopol' to "Moscow House", Luzhkov announced to the Sevastopol'ians that "the processes that tore Sevastopol' and Crimea from Russia have created wounds in the hearts of the Russian people". Then the crowd broke out in applause. After the rally, a boat of the commander of the Russian Federation's Black Sea Fleet took Luzhkov to the cruiser Moskva, where dinner awaited him. It was announced that the esteemed guest was served suckling pig, as is the fleet's custom.[1]

A considerable section of the peninsula's Russian and Ukrainian majority (and by no means only in Sevastopol') refused to accept that the peninsula was part of independent Ukraine – and were thus "with Russia". Likewise, the majority of people in the Russian Federation were not willing to accept a 'Ukrainian Crimea' either. Luzhkov, very popular in Russia since 2000 as a sporadic supporter of Vladimir Putin and a vocal opponent of homosexuality, was one of those politicians who had taken a strong stance against a Ukrainian Crimea since the early 1990s and had actively supported anti-Ukrainian forces in the peninsula. He would later lose his position as mayor due to accusations of corruption, but not before he had declared the peninsula a "Russian Palestine"[2] and Sevastopol' a Russian city, for which he received a temporary ban on entering Ukraine in 2008.[3] Despite his and other protests against Ukraine's possession of 'our Crimea', as it was soon referred to in the Russian debates from the 1990s onwards, on the international stage the Kremlin committed itself to recognizing the borders resulting from the breakup of the Soviet Union: in the Budapest Memorandum of 1994, the USA, the United Kingdom and the Russian Federation recognized the sovereignty and the existing borders of Ukraine, Kazakhstan and Belarus in return, *inter alia*, for the handover over their nuclear arsenals; this would again be relevant in the context of the events of 2014 (cf. Chapter 36).[4] However, Moscow undoubtedly signed more as a result of its political powerlessness in the difficult circumstances of the early 1990s than out of conviction.

Sevastopol' – to cite Charles King in 2010 – "is in Ukraine and is not really part of it".[5] Indeed, after 1991 the city became the centre of pro-Russian groups and remained a base for the Russian Federation's Black Sea Fleet. At the same time, it was also home to the Ukrainian navy. In the early years of independence, the status of the former Soviet naval facilities and the Red Fleet had been a bone of contention between Kyiv and Moscow. A treaty of 1997 ultimately governed the allocation of ships and the Russian forces' right to remain in Sevastopol' – and was supposed to have been valid until 2017. But as early as 2010, the pro-Russian Ukrainian president Viktor Ianukovych (*1950) extended it until 2042 with the Kharkiv Agreement. In return, then President Dmitrii Medvedev (*1965) granted Ukraine better terms for Russian gas supplies – always a point of dispute between the two countries – and further financial compensation.[6]

A further issue was the return of Crimean Tatar people to the peninsula, which had been on the rise since the late 1980s despite some setbacks. The migration grew to the extent that Tatars constituted around 12 per cent of the entire population by the annexation of 2014.[7] Incidentally, Moscow had planned their repatriation during the last years of the USSR and had drawn up a "State Programme for the Return of the Crimean Tatars to the Crimea Oblast'". In 1989, the Soviet government had officially guaranteed their right to return, which had only become possible under Gorbachev. The Crimean Tatar activist Cemilev, who had spent years of his life in camps and prisons, had already been released in 1986, and since 1987 there had been several protest campaigns by the Tatars heard throughout the Soviet Union.

The state's return programme was supposed to assist the new arrivals with practical and financial problems; however, not without irony, the end of the Soviet Union – the very state that had executed the deportations – also meant the end of this support.[8] The returnees faced further difficulties; it proved expensive and complicated to swap citizenship of one state (e.g. Uzbekistan) for that of another (Ukraine), entailing high fees and lots of travel. Many had missed the deadline Ukraine had set for easier access to citizenship. But even when these problems had been solved and people had managed to resettle and possessed identification papers, they still faced difficulties: the Russian-speaking majority in Crimea were not enthusiastic about the new arrivals. They feared claims to their land and property as well as competition in a tense labour market. Additionally, traces of the distrust of the Crimean Tatars as 'alien', 'dangerous' and 'traitorous', cultivated during the tsarist and Soviet eras, remained among the Slav population. Perhaps some Russian or Ukrainian inhabitants of Crimea also felt something approaching a guilty conscience, since the deportations had undoubtedly been unjust. Whatever the case may be, particularly after 2003 there were a series of violent clashes between the Tatar and the Slav populations over symbolic and financial recompense for suffering, land and housing as well as over the generally sparse economic resources.[9]

The so-called Orange Revolution in late 2004,[10] which led to a largely peaceful protest movement against the corrupt system following vote rigging in the presidential elections and ultimately helped Viktor Iushchenko (*1954) to deserved victory, had relatively few supporters in Crimea. This was reflected by the votes Iushchenko received in the two disputed ballots there, in contrast to other regions of Ukraine: 14.59 per cent in November (7.61 per cent in Sevastopol') and 15.41 per cent in December (7.96 per cent in Sevastopol'). His pro-Russian opponent Ianukovych had a clear lead.[11] Crimea (as well as eastern Ukraine, also heavily influenced by Russian Soviet sentiment) generally voted differently to the rest of Ukraine, as demonstrated by the referendum held in December 1991 over recognition of the declaration of independence of 24 August: a total of 90 per cent of voters were for an independent state, meaning that it was not only Ukrainians that chose independence; they constituted only 73 per cent of the population. In Crimea, on the other hand, far fewer were in agreement: only 54.2 per cent chose to leave the dissolving Soviet Union.[12]

While a significant number of the Slav majority population took a conservative stance, then, the Crimean Tatars who had returned to the peninsula were interested in a making a fresh start – while clearly harking back to a past considered "golden" (cf. Chapter 31). Political organization was a significant part of this project. In June 1991, before the declaration of independence and in the presence of Cemilev, who quickly became a universally recognized leader, they founded a national assembly in Simferopol'. They again chose to call it the Qurultay, drawing on the name used during the revolutionary phase of 1917/18. A "Declaration On the National Sovereignty of the Crimean People" claimed that the peninsula was a "national territory" and determined their own flag and national anthem. Relations with the non-Tatar nationalities were to be governed on the basis of universal human and civil rights. A representative body comprising thirty-three delegates was formed – the Meclis of the Crimean Tatar People (Crimean Tatar: *Qırımtatar Milliy Meclisi*) – which was to represent their interests to the central government and communicate with international bodies. Cemilev was the obvious choice as chairman. Refat Çubarov (*1957), today a figurehead himself, made his first appearance on the political scene as his deputy. A functional network of local representatives quickly developed throughout much of the peninsula.[13]

Not surprisingly, Soviet and later Russian forces both within the peninsula and beyond were disturbed by the Crimean Tatar population's claim to Crimea as a national territory and repeatedly demanded the dissolution of the Meclis;[14] ultimately, it was about more than the symbolic question of to whom Crimea actually 'belonged'. Formally, it was established that it was part of Ukraine. But for a long time, Kyiv did not recognize the Meclis. It was only under President Leonid Kuchma (*1938, president 1994–2005) that a "Council of Representatives of the Crimean People" was installed, consisting of the same members of the Meclis. However, whether or not this amounted to legal recognition was controversially discussed.[15]

After the declaration of independence, Kyiv had difficulties implementing real power in the peninsula and thus made concessions to the region insofar as it was the only one to be granted autonomous status within the central administrative structure. In 1992, the Crimean parliament (Ukrainian: *Verkhovna Rada Avtonomnoï Respubliky Krym*; Russian: *Verkhovnyi Sovet*

FIGURE 35.1 *The flag of the Crimean Tatars.*

Avtonomnoi Respubliki Krym; Crimean Tatar: *Qırım Muhtar Cumhuriyetiniñ Yuqarı Radası*), dominated by pro-Russian parties, passed a Crimean constitution, thereby taking a clearly separatist stance. A key player in this move was the Respublikanskoe dvizhenie Kryma (RSD, Republican Movement of Crimea) headed by Iurii Meshkov (*1945), which openly called for Ukraine's secession from Ukraine and annexation to Russia or for an independent Crimean state as part of the Community of Independent States (CIS).[16] In the short term, however, Crimea managed to calm the centrifugal forces, in part via a Crimean constitution that corresponded to Ukraine's. This constitution made Crimean Tatar an official language alongside Ukrainian and Russian. Sasse considers Kyiv's response to have been clever, since it was able to keep the "region (Crimea), the state (represented by the institutions in Kyiv) and the international environment (shaped by the political actors in Moscow)" in balance with incentives and restrictions.[17]

For some time, this proved a successful strategy, as long as there were hopes in Crimea, as in the rest of Ukraine, for normalization – for instance, prosperity and a significant reduction in the corruption omnipresent in all parts of the former Soviet Union. These hopes were not fulfilled, but there were different reactions in different parts of the country: while in western and central Ukraine there was a desire for internal reform, during both the Orange Revolution and Euromaidan in 2013/14 (cf. Chapter 36), eastern Ukraine and Russian Crimea focused on a solution from outside – by the Russian Federation. With Iushchenko favouring joining not only the European Union but also NATO, the suspicion had grown in Russian circles that Ukraine was a kind of Trojan horse for the West. The conflict's echo was keenly felt in Sevastopol', for instance in early 2006, when Ukrainian representatives of Yalta's port authorities seized the Ya-13 lighthouse, which had hitherto been used by the Russian fleet but to which Ukraine now laid claim. When in the late summer of 2008 the South Ossetia crisis gave rise to widespread fears that Ukraine could be Russia's next victim, many in Simferopol' and Sevastopol' responded with anti-NATO demonstrations. And by no means were the demonstrators limited to those who had spent their youth in the USSR and hence might be suspected of a certain nostalgia. On the contrary, "[i]t was above all young people with mobile phones and designer T-shirts, who performed creative street theatre to protest against the US presence [in the form of a US command ship before the coast – K.S.J.]", reported Charles King.[18] The ban on Ukrainians accepting Moscow's offer of dual citizenship also led to anti-Kyiv and anti-NATO demonstrations in Crimea.[19]

Despite all these problems, it was not foreseeable that the peninsula would be annexed in early 2014. Certainly, Sasse's assessment in 2010 that Ukraine's Crimea policy was a "model of successful conflict prevention" proved incorrect.[20]

36

Russian Again?! Crimea After the Second Annexation of 2014

The following dialogue might be considered somewhat prescient:

> "What's going on down in the Crimea? Is the Ukrainian military ready for a Russian invasion?"
>
> Bixby shrugged. "I can only give you an unclassified answer. I know you retain clearance, but I haven't figured out what the fuck your deal is yet."
>
> "Hey, like I said, I'm not asking for anything sensitive. I'm just an American tourist thinking of going on holiday in Odessa."
>
> Bixby shook his head. "Okay. Well . . . I would suggest you go to Maui, instead. Maybe you could get a senior discount on a hotel room there. Crimea is going to blow up soon. The Russians are ready to invade, just looking for an excuse. The Ukrainians are moving troops into the region to dispel them – that's in the local news, so I'm not giving you anything TS there – and it's as likely as not the Russians will use the Ukrainians' movements as a provocation for them to go in."
>
> "Because of all the Russian nationals living in the Crimea."
>
> "Yep. [. . .]"[1]

One might expect this exchange to be from a conversation between two American secret service men shortly before the Russian Federation began "working on returning Crimea to Russia",[2] beginning in February 2014. In fact, it is an excerpt from the thriller *Command Authority* by Tom Clancy (1947–2013), the creator of several popular detective stories and the immensely successful figure of the agent Jack Ryan, played on screen by Harrison Ford and others. In *Command Authority*, Jack Ryan has become president of the United States, and his opponent is the president of the Russian Federation, Valeri Volodin, who is clearly based on Vladimir Putin. Literary renderings of historical events of varying artistic merit are nothing new, of course, even for a writer like Clancy, who operated in the field of "body bag literature" and was "in literary terms no more than a third-rate Le Carré", as a reviewer put it somewhat unflatteringly in the German newspaper *Die Welt*.³ What is remarkable about the novel is the date of its publication, however: 3 December 2013 – months before Euromaidan had gathered steam. As is well known, the citizens' protests throughout Ukraine took aim at pro-Russian President Ianukovych's surprising decision not to sign the Association Agreement and his cleptocratic regime, setting in motion a chain of events that culminated in Ianukovych's taking flight to Russia, his ultimately illegal removal from office by the parliament in Kyiv (the Rada), the beginning of combat in eastern Ukraine and Russia's annexation of Crimea, a conflict that continues to this day (winter 2018) and has cost over 10,000 lives.

Clancy himself did not live to see either the publication of his book or the "return of Crimea to Russia"; he died at the age of sixty-six in October 2013. He nevertheless displayed a better nose for the Kremlin's plans than most experts and political analysts, who were wrong-footed by Russia's intervention in Crimea and eastern Ukraine. In Clancy's novel, the "return of Crimea to Russia" becomes a highly controversial military matter – "long-range missile batteries devastated Ukrainian defensive positions, and fighter bombers flew inland to destroy airfields in the eastern Crimea" – after "tanks rolled west over the border, much as they had done in Estonia"; we read of "pitched battles of tanks and Grad multiple rocket launcher systems".⁴ In reality, fortunately, it wasn't quite like that: the NATO state Estonia was not invaded by Russian troops, which would have triggered Article 5 of the NATO Treaty, presumably resulting in a war between the Russian Federation and the Western alliance. And the occupation of Crimea also played out differently to how Clancy portrayed it: it involved comparatively low levels of violence, even if the act itself was belligerent, amounting to the first occupation of another state's territory by a great power since the end of the Second World War. The Ukrainian state, which had managed to bring about a change in power via a "spontaneous civil society mass movement"⁵ for the second time, lacked the power and capacity to prevent the annexation. A compounding factor was that in eastern Ukraine, and to an extent in the south, and certainly in Crimea, there was less agreement with Kyiv and less enthusiasm for a national project than in western or central Ukraine. Especially in Crimea, diffuse Russian Soviet sentiment, the country's largest proportion of people of Russian descent (over 68 per cent) and dissatisfaction with a socio-economic situation the Ukrainian state was unable to fix meant that many pinned their hopes on Moscow. The inhabitants of Crimea were not interested in the new wave of civil society protests in other parts of the country. On the contrary, in the course of February 2014, several pro-Russian demonstrations took place in the peninsula. In the parliament of the Autonomous Republic of Crimea, representatives openly advocated re-annexation by Russia. The Crimean parliament's then president, Vladimir A. Konstantinov (*1956), even flew to Moscow for political discussions "and was extensively quoted as making statements [. . .] that the Kremlin could interpret as a 'cry for help' at any time", as the *Frankfurter Allgemeine Zeitung* reported on 20 February 2014.⁶ And that is just what the Kremlin did.

Moscow had been very worried from the outset by the events in Kyiv over closer ties with the EU; Russia considered Ukraine (like other parts of the former Soviet Union) part of its own sphere of influence or (in the official terminology) its "Near Abroad" (Russian: *Blizhnee zarubezh'e*). And many Russians felt particularly 'near' to Ukrainians, whose decision to take their own path as a nation many 'Greater Russians' still cannot fathom. Both the Orange Revolution and Euromaidan had Russia worried it could now lose Ukraine for good. After the Winter Olympics in Sochi ended on 23 February 2014 and the situation in Ukraine had not calmed down in a way that reflected Moscow's interests, Russia intervened on 27 February: well-trained and heavily armed fighters without nationality markings or rank insignia occupied important strategic facilities in Crimea, such as the airport in Simferopol', Ukrainian army bases and the parliament. These troops were not combatants according to the Law of War and were referred to as "little green men" (Ukrainian: *zeleni cholovichki*) by the Ukrainians or as "friendly people" (Russian: *vezhlivye liudi*) by the Russians. In fact, however, they were members of the Russian military and its special units, who were joined by the soldiers stationed legally in Crimea. They were soon reinforced by a considerable number of troops who were actually in the Ukrainian military.⁷

At the same time, Sergei V. Aksenov (*1972), who had been the chairman of a largely insignificant party called Russian Unity (Russian: *Russkoe Edinstvo*) since 2010, was declared president by some members of the parliament under military occupation in Simferopol', something they were not authorized to do. He has since become a member of the dominant party United Russia (Russian: *Edinaia Rossiia*) and president of the republic within the Russian Federation.⁸ His 'government' immediately called on Moscow, requesting "protection against Ukrainian nationalists and extremists prepared to commit violence";⁹ in tried and tested Soviet fashion (see for instance Hungary in 1956, the CSSR in 1958 and Afghanistan in 1979), Moscow provided this 'assistance'. On 16 March, a referendum was held at very short notice, yet an alleged 90 per cent of participating inhabitants of Crimea – some 82 per cent of all eligible to vote, according to official figures – backed annexation by Russia. This vote was not in line with the Ukrainian constitution, which was still valid, as even the Russian-language *Wikipedia* page notes.¹⁰ A day later, Crimea's independence from Ukraine was declared and on 18 March Putin and representatives of the illegitimate Crimean government signed a treaty confirming the peninsula's membership of the Russian Federation. To be precise, two new so-called subjects of the union joined – the Republic of Crimea and the city of federal rank Sevastopol', its special status of the 'Hero City' again being reflected in its receiving its own administration.

The speech President Putin gave to the Federation Council and the State Duma on 18 March 2014 to mark the official completion of the annexation

– or, as Putin put it, "reunification" – was quite remarkable: he began by emphasizing the legality of the referendum, claiming it had met international legal norms – a view shared by few experts outside Russia.[11] Not for the first time, and not for the last, Putin delved into the repertoire of historical legitimation for a Russian Crimea (cf. Chapter 1): "everything in Crimea speaks of our shared pride and history". It was the site of the baptism of Rus', it was sacred and full of symbols of Russian military glory and outstanding valour.[12] He didn't ignore the traditional diversity in the peninsula – "Russians and Ukrainians, Crimean Tatars and people of other ethnic groups have lived side by side" – but he made it clear that Russians constituted the absolute majority of the 2.2 million inhabitants. He also stated that the 350,000 ethnic Ukrainians were Russian-speaking and that even the Crimean Tatar population "lean towards Russia". That could simply not be true, however; most Crimean Tatars had boycotted the referendum and clearly opposed annexation. He mentioned the Stalinist deportations in the vaguest of terms: the Crimean Tatar population, "just as a number of other peoples in the USSR", had been "treated unfairly", but millions of others had suffered, "primarily Russians".

The president's offer to grant three languages equal status – Russian, Ukrainian, the use of which had been marginal in Crimea even before the annexation, and Crimean Tatar – may be seen as a concession to the Muslim and Ukrainian inhabitants, but this status had already been in place before 2014. Not surprisingly, Putin said that the transfer of Crimea to Ukraine in 1954 and its remaining Ukrainian territory until 1991 had been illegal: the peninsula had been "handed over like a sack of potatoes" ("kak meshok kartoshki"), which he considered an outrageous historical injustice Russia had not been able to prevent at the time. What he considered a chaotic situation in Ukraine due to the "coup", as he called it (referring to Euromaidan) had moved the Russian-speaking inhabitants of Crimea to request Moscow to defend their rights and their lives. "Naturally, we could not leave this plea unheeded", he declared. The president of the Russian Federation also promised, or threatened, that Russia would always represent the interests of the "millions of Russians and Russian-speaking people" in Ukraine by "political, diplomatic and legal means".

Moscow's claims to protect Russians in the so-called Near Abroad had first been manifested after the breakup of the Soviet Union in August 2008 during the Georgian War over South Ossetia and Abkhazia. The thriller writer Clancy was clearly thinking of this when he had one of his characters explain Russia's actions in his novel:

"You probably know those Russian nationals only got their citizenship because Moscow handed out passports to Ukrainians of Russian heritage. It was an FSB [Federal'naia sluzhba bezopasnosti Rossiiskoi Federatsii (Federal Security Service of the Russian Federation) – K.S.J.] op all the way, setting the stage for the invasion. [...] they will say, 'We have to come in to protect our citizens.' They did exactly the same thing in Georgia a few years ago."[13]

Indeed, in 2008 the Ukrainian administration under Iushchenko had banned dual citizenship for Ukrainian citizens for this very reason.[14] In 2014, Putin and others took a slightly different line of argument, mostly speaking of the Russian-speaking population of Ukraine that had to be protected. And in so doing, Moscow went a step further with its claims; it was no longer just a case of allegedly protecting ethnic Russians. Incidentally, after the Georgia crisis, Russia had formally adapted a key document in order to realize its aims concerning the "Near Abroad": the "Military Doctrine 2020", which was passed in 2010 under President Dmitrii A. Medvedev and is hence sometimes named after him. *Inter alia*, this doctrine expanded Russia's options for deploying its forces abroad, including for the 'protection' of Russian citizens living in one of the former Soviet republics. In this way, the Kremlin had retrospectively attempted to justify its actions in Georgia.[15]

It is not only Putin's speech that repeatedly refers to a threat to national minorities – in this case, to Russians in Ukraine – and thereby portrays the annexation as an act of self-defence. In codified international law, a nation's right to defend itself is an important principle. In reality, however, it often collides with a principle that is probably considered even more important – the territorial integrity of states. In the case of Crimea's annexation, Ukraine's territorial integrity was certainly violated – of that there can be no doubt. And do Russian people in the peninsula need Moscow's protection – were they harassed or threatened? This was "not at all recognizable", according to the expert on international law Bruno Simma, a former judge at the International Court in The Hague and professor of international law at Munich's Ludwig Maximilian University, who condemns the Russian intervention. At the same time, he voiced criticism that international law's prohibition of the use of force and intervention has been "repeatedly punctured and weakened" in the recent past, including by the USA and sections of the European Union, for instance in the case of Kosovo[16] (also frequently cited by Russia). Most experts agree that the Russian Federation's annexation of Crimea represents a violation of the general prohibition of the use of force by the United Nations Charter, Article 2(4), which stipulates:

> All Members shall refrain in their international relations from the threat or use of force against the territorial integrity or political independence of any state, or in any other manner inconsistent with the Purposes of the United Nations.[17]

There are few Russian lawyers who subscribe to this argumentation.[18] Even if individual politicians such as the former chairman of the German Socialist Democrat Party (SPD) Matthias Platzeck (*1953) or the highly respected former federal chancellor Helmut Schmidt (1918–2015) showed great understanding for Putin's course regarding Crimea and eastern Ukraine,[19] the European Union reacted by imposing extensive sanctions on the Russian Federation. The sanctions have repeatedly been extended to this day (i.e. late 2018). While 'Russian Crimea' currently exists *de facto*, the military conflict in eastern Ukraine continues. The great hopes many Ukrainians pinned on Poroshenko (*1965) were not fulfilled.

The same holds not least for the Crimean Tatars, the overwhelming majority of whom expressed their desire for Crimea to remain part of Ukraine. Crimea's re-incorporation into a Russian state, which has negative associations in the Tatar collective memory, confronted them with further challenges. They feared losing their homeland once more – and for some of them, this fear has already become reality. One of them is the selfsame national hero, Cemilev (cf. Chapter 34), who was elected a pro-Western member of the Ukrainian parliament in 1998. Russia denied him and Refat Çubarov entry to Crimea for five years. Crimean Tatars faced further oppression, although this can be interpreted as exposure to the generally problematic situation concerning politics and civil society in the Russian Federation rather than genuinely anti-Tatar measures. After the so-called referendum, Crimean Tatar representatives rightly feared conflicts with the new Crimean government headed by Aksenov and Russian nationalists buoyed by their success. And hence several thousand of the *c.* 280,000 Crimean Tatars left the peninsula immediately after the Russian takeover, according to the calculations of the Society for Threatened Peoples.[20] Hundreds fled to L'viv (Ukrainian; Polish: Lwów; German: Lemberg) in western Ukraine, for instance, despite the fact that Tatar actors called for people to stay in the peninsula.[21] The Qurultay (cf. Chapter 35) recommended refraining from violence and also advocated partial cooperation with the Russian regime, hoping, somewhat naively, for the reestablishment of national territorial autonomy for their nationality. At the same time, however, it declared the referendum illegal and sought to make contact with international organizations (the United Nations, the Council of Europe, the OSCE, the Organization of Islamic Cooperation).[22] Turkey, with its close historical, cultural and linguistic ties to the Crimean nation and a large Crimean Tatar diaspora, did remarkably little for its brothers and sisters, probably to avoid risking relations with Moscow.[23]

As in Putin's speech of 18 March 2014, the Russian leadership initially made certain concessions to the Crimean Tatar movement. But there were repeated clashes between the Tatars, Russian militia and the official authorities; trusting coexistence could hardly develop, if only due to historical experience. Cases of "having people disappear", kidnappings and politically active Crimean Tatars standing trial with dubious standards of justice are rife.[24] In early 2015, the closure of the TV station ATR, which also broadcasts in Crimean Tatar, caused a furore, including in the Western media, which had quickly lost interest in Crimea. The broadcaster is owned by the Crimean Tatar businessman Lenur Edem oğlu İslâmov (*1966) and had opposed the Russian annexation. The station was searched several times by the police before being closed for good, accused of not being properly registered.[25] Meanwhile, it continues to broadcast from non-occupied Ukraine.

House searches and repressions were also noted by the Meclis (cf. Chapter 35), the evening newspaper *Avdet* and other Crimean Tatar institutions.[26] Russia accuses the Meclis of political and religious extremism or even proximity to the Islamic State organization, and hence it has been forbidden since 26 April 2016. True to the motto "Divide and Rule", Moscow had formed pro-Russian alternative organs such as *Qırım birligi* (Unity of Crimea).[27] There are already individual Crimean Tatar politicians who have come to an arrangement with the Russian regime, as have some of the high clerics.[28] In late 2014, Uwe Halbach, an expert on the Muslim regions on the (post-)Soviet space, pointed to the ethno-political challenges between the Russian, Ukrainian and Tatar populations resulting from the annexation. He also identified the risk that "Islamist networks active in Russia and in other parts of the post-Soviet space [might] take up the Crimean question – under the slogan of the fight against the oppression of Muslims. [. . .] With its annexation of Crimea, Russia potentially [runs] the risk of opening up a new Islamist front". He further observed that some Crimean Tatar fighters had already left for Syria.[29]

Far more Crimean Tatars, however, fight in the Ukrainian armed forces, including in contested eastern Ukraine and in a volunteer unit established in 2015, the Noman Çelebicihan Batalyonı, named after the First World War activist and creator of the Crimean Tatar national anthem Noman Çelebicihan (cf. Chapter 30), who was executed by the Bolsheviks during the Civil War. The battalion was organized by İslâmov (see above), and is stationed in the Kherson region west of Crimea. With at least 500 men, the plan, according to İslâmov in 2015, is "to defend the borders of the Crimea inside Crimea";[30] so far, however, they have not managed to drive Russia out of the peninsula.

On the contrary, in many respects ties between Crimea and Russia are growing ever closer. As in 1783, in 2014 the Russian administration went about "swiftly integrat[ing] Crimea into the Russian state"[31] and reinforcing connections between the mainland and the peninsula – in the literal sense too, since until recently there was a lack of transport connections enabling Russia to supply Crimea, the ferry across the Kerch Strait notwithstanding. Many goods as well as energy had to be brought in from the north via the Isthmus of Perekop – that is, via Ukraine. And Ukraine flexed its only 'muscle' in the Crimea question more frequently by closing the border. Moscow quickly responded with plans to build a "patriotic bridge" between Kerch and Taman; plans had long existed[32] – and were indeed implemented. The bridge, around 19 kilometres in length (Russian: Krymskii most) was built with immense speed in May 2018, when it opened for road travel. In a well-staged ceremony, it was opened by a visibly proud President Putin, who personally drove a lorry over the bridge, thereby demonstrating to the world not only Russian engineering prowess but also that he can drive a lorry. The bridge is supposed to open for rail transport in 2019. It is too early to predict its ecological and economic consequences.[33]

However things turn out, the Crimean Bridge gives Moscow better opportunities for controlling the Kerch Strait and the Sea of Azov, the location of two important hubs for Ukraine: Berdians'k and the crucial deepwater port and steel city of Mariupol'. Kyiv opposed the bridge not just for political but also for economic reasons: large ships over 33 metres in height cannot pass under it, and Russia increasingly conducted elaborate and expensive checks despite the fact that it had been agreed in 2003 that both states could navigate these waters. On 25 November 2018, there was then a serious incident which underlined that while Crimea had largely been forgotten in recent decades, it was still a significant trouble spot: the Russian navy took control of three of the Ukrainian navy's ships, one of which it is said to have rammed beforehand, and arrested their crews. Some sailors were wounded. Russia spoke of provocation by Kyiv, claiming that the Ukrainian ships had illegally crossed the border between Ukraine and Russia.[34] The Ukrainian president, Petro Poroshenko, promptly had martial law declared for the first time since the outbreak of the conflict in 2014, although the Rada made clear to him his constitutional limitations, suspecting that the beleaguered president was seeking to present himself as a 'hard man' once again in the lead-up to the elections in the spring of 2019.[35] The election of the new president, Volodymyr Zelens'kyi (*1978), in May 2019 showed that this strategy did not win over voters.[36]

FIGURE 36.1 *The Crimean Bridge under construction, 13 October 2017.*

Kyiv has repeatedly criticized Russian policy, with respect to the Crimean Tatars for instance – and this criticism was much more vehement and much faster than the EU's eventual response.[37] However, until the Ukrainian naval ships were taken, it was hard to deny the impression that Kyiv was resigned to losing Crimea and considered the threat of finally losing eastern Ukraine to be much more serious.

Has Crimea really become Russian – "Krym nash", as the slogan has claimed since 1991? Does it belong to Russia? Halbach answers this question with an analogy well worth thinking about: "In reality this region belongs to Russia as self-evidently as Algeria belongs to France – namely as a historical colony."[38]

Postscript

This postscript was written in the summer of 2023. All further developments in this ongoing war could not be taken into account.

The Russian invasion of Ukraine began on 24 February 2022. As I write these lines, the war has been fought for over a year, with no end in sight. Some observers consider this date a "Zeitenwende",¹ a profound caesura that must persuade even the last of the pro-Putin Europeans, including many Russians, that he presides over an unjust regime. But this has only been partly the case: Putin's ratings and advocacy of Russia's merciless bombardment of its Ukrainian neighbour, labelled a "fraternal people", are still supposed to be close to 80 per cent.² This figure cannot be verified, however, since many Russians have withdrawn into inner emigration. Others, attempting to escape conscription, political repression and the war, are trying their luck in Russia's "Near Abroad" (that is, neighbouring states such as Georgia or Kazakhstan) or in the West, which isn't easy given the entry restrictions. And what about the inhabitants of Crimea, a suspiciously high majority of whom celebrated its annexation in 2014? What is their stance on the brutality of the Russian troops in the areas north of the Isthmus of Perekop connecting Crimea to the mainland? As we have seen, this is something the exiled Soviet writer Vasillii P. Aksënov already thought about in his novel *The Island of Crimea* (cf. the Introduction). What has been Moscow's policy towards the peninsula since late 2020? How have the living conditions changed for the local population, for instance due to the Crimean Bridge, opened in 2018 (cf. Chapter 36), which was supposed to facilitate the transport of people and goods? That was indeed the great hope harboured by most inhabitants, and not only those of Russian extraction . . . To be clear: the situation has drastically worsened for the Crimean population since February 2022, even if it is much better than the conditions faced by those living north of the Isthmus. But let us examine things in sequence.

Over the past two or three years even, the Russian state has once again persecuted alleged or actual opponents of the system – including in Crimea – and has restricted political rights and civil liberties: in a worldwide comparative survey by the NGO Freedom House, the Russian Federation received 19 out of 100 points in the combined categories "Civil Liberties" and "Political Rights". The democracy scores recorded separately for Crimea in 2021 are even worse, standing at just 7; Ukraine, by comparison, received 61 points and is thus labelled "partly free".³ As in the eighteenth century (cf. Chapter 22), the peninsula has been aligned structurally, economically and politically with the core Russian territories. As in the tsarist era, the idea of creating a *corpus separatum* or a special status reflecting the special circumstances was anathema to the Kremlin decision-makers.⁴ Indeed, as early as 2014, Crimea had largely been brought into line with the Russian Federation and all opposition had been eliminated. In part, this was achieved by deploying a large number of officials from the centre in the peninsula, many of whom have embraced the opportunity to advance their careers. This too emphasized claims to a Russian Crimea – to "nash Krym".

Inside Russia itself, but also for the inhabitants of Crimea, the Crimean Bridge, opened in 2018, quickly became an unquestioned matter of national sanctity. The explosions and the damage they caused in the early hours of 8 October were nothing less than another heavy blow to Russia's already battered collective self-esteem: the attacks on the other Ukrainian territories were anything but a success. The Ukrainians, led by their president Volodymyr Zelens'kyi, stood up to their assailants with great determination and great courage. They were aided by the logistical and military assistance of, *inter alia*, the UK, the USA and the European Union. To date, it is impossible to speak of a Russian walkover. The death toll, however, is already immense, both for the military and civilians; it is already approaching 200,000. In Crimea itself, things largely remained quiet after the war broke out, although young men were conscripted and the Russian security services are keeping a close eye on a population Russia has traditionally considered untrustworthy, including the remaining Crimean Tatars. The latter's situation has deteriorated further; for one thing, a disproportionately large number of young Tatar men are being selected for conscription.⁵ Some weeks after the explosion on the Crimean Bridge, it remains unclear who was responsible. Was it an accident, a boat drifting under the bridge? The Ukrainian security service, the SBU? For Putin, it was immediately quite clear: he labelled it a Ukrainian attack, an act of aggression. Zelens'kyi is keeping eloquently silent on the matter, although such a measure would have been a legitimate act of self-defence; the bridge carries Russia's supplies for its annihilation of the Ukrainian people, power stations and infrastructure, and Ukraine's armed forces are defending the country via precision attacks on Russian military targets. In the summer of 2022 there had already been a series of explosions in Crimea causing deaths and injuries, and drones had been sighted above several spots in the peninsula. Russia pointed the finger at the British military.⁶ More precise details are not known . . .

Like his predecessor Poroshenko, Zelens'kyi has emphasized Ukraine's claim to Crimea, for instance on 23 August 2022, on the eve of his speech marking Independence Day. Speaking via video link in international forums, he and many others support an initiative launched by the Ukrainian foreign ministry in 2021 called the Crimean Platform. Its aim is to use diplomatic means to reverse Crimea's annexation by Russia in 2014: "The Crimean Platform will become a foreign policy instrument of the de-occupation strategy. This flexible international format is aimed at consolidating international efforts and achieving synergy of intergovernmental, parliamentary, and expert levels. The ultimate goal of the platform is eventual de-occupation of Crimea and its return to Ukraine by peaceful means."[7]

Presently, an end to the war is certainly not in sight, although international law clearly supports the Ukrainian position – but how long will this remain the case? Since the spring of 2023, the Ukrainian army has been using drones to hit back at the Russian invaders in the peninsula. Are these much-cited game changers in the fight for Crimea? A likelier outcome is that the future negotiators will follow the established narrative of a Russian Crimea.

NOTES

Orientation: Terminology and Spelling

1 Maiakovskii (1998), 17.

Introduction

1 Aksyonov (1983), 339–40. The Russian original, *Ostrov Krym*, was published in 1981 in Ann Arbor – that is, during the author's exile in the USA. Cf. also Slobin (1992).
2 Cit. Höller (2015).
3 Veser (2015).
4 Aksyonov (1983), ix.
5 Aksyonov (1983), 340.
6 Veser (2017).
7 Ascherson (2015), 26.
8 Cf. for instance Schuller (2007).
9 As I entitled my habilitation treatise: Jobst (2007b).
10 Cf. e.g. Luchterhand (2014).
11 A.L. Jakokson's works on the history of Crimea in the Middle Ages remain unsurpassed: Jakobson (1964); Jakobson (1973). All other specialist literature will be cited in the respective chapters.
12 Magocsi (2014) has produced a well-written and appealingly designed album, but it only partially meets academic standards – although that was not the intention of this expert on the history of Carpatho-Ukraine. The most comprehensive study in Russian, at least of the history of the Crimean Tatars, is by Vozgrin (2013). However, the work does not consider the pre-Tatar times and is also written from a clearly pro-Tatar perspective, occasionally lacking scholarly objectivity. Since the annexation of Crimea, several works have appeared in Russian; cf. the *Istoriia* (2015) by a historians' collective. The survey by Kent (2016) is not very convincing, particularly since he devotes scant attention to the time before the peninsula's annexation by Russia in 1783.
13 In the Soviet era, this sparkling wine was known as 'Sovetskoe", however.

14 Cf. in particular Kunz (2005).
15 Kuhn (2001).
16 Cf. Troebst (2007); Özveren (1997). Other important studies are: King (2004); Ascherson (2015).

Chapter 1

1   Goethe (2005), Act 1 Scene 2, 4–5.
2   Cf. *inter alia* Christoph Willibald Gluck's (1714–87) opera *Iphigénie en Tauride*, which premiered in 1779. Goethe published his first prose version of his *Iphigenia* the same year, followed by further versions in 1781 and 1786.
3   On this topos, cf. Hall E. (1989), for whom this way of thinking was an established ideology stabilizing rule in the fifth century BC and emerged in the context of the Persian Wars.
4   Herodotus (2008), Book IV, 103.
5   For a representative account of the Iphigenia topos, cf. Engert (2007)
6   Weber (1998), 71.
7   Germer (1998), 35.
8   Germer (1998), 33.
9   For a detailed account, cf. Jobst (2007b), especially 131–76.
10 For the British context, see the discussion of the Crimean War in Chapter 27.
11 Ascherson (2015), 12.
12 Sulimirski (1970). This work was first published in 1979 in Polish.
13 My discussion here and below draws on Augustynowicz (2017), 38–45. Cf. also Długosz and Scholz (2013), however.
14 Augustynowicz (2017), 38.
15 Augustynowicz (2017), 39.
16 Wiederkehr (2007).
17 Molnár and Magyar (2001), 6.
18 In the nineteenth century, this myth saw travellers head to the region in search of traces of 'Hungarian' life; cf. e.g. Besse (1838).
19 Littleton and Malcor (1994).
20 For an account that does not claim to be exhaustive, cf. Jobst (2007b), 435–41.
21 For a linguistic perspective, cf. Anderson T. (2012), especially 224 and 229.
22 For an introduction, cf. Neutatz (1993), especially 204–20.
23 For further details, cf. Chapter 3 in the present volume.
24 Here I draw on Stearns Jr. (2012), who also provides Busbecq's report in the original Latin and in German translation.
25 Cf. Stearns Jr. (2012), 176–8.
26 Vinogradov and Korobov (2015).

27 Here and below Kunz (2005), especially 41–73.
28 See the critical edition of Hitler's table talk with an introduction and commentary by Werner Jochmann: Jochmann (1980), especially 39, 48, 90–1 and 124.
29 For a full discussion, cf. Albrecht (2016), 369–70, fn. 98, and Vinogradov (2020).
30 Kunz (2005), 234.
31 See the relevant chapters for other myths associated with the peninsula, such as the military myths tied to the impressive defensive efforts in the Crimean War and the Second World War, renowned beyond the Russian-speaking world.
32 Cf. especially Jobst (2019).
33 Cf. Chapter 7.
34 Carter (2003); Jobst (2013a).
35 Kozelsky (2010).
36 Cf. here Stender-Petersen (1986), 37–8; Vinogradov (1999).
37 Primary Chronicle (1953), 53–4.
38 Müller L. (2001), 8.
39 Zhitie (1999).
40 The correct translation of "rus'sky pismeny" would be "Old East Slavic" and not "Old Russian", as is often encountered. The best source on the complex field of translating these and similar terms remains Müller L. et al. (1992).
41 Zhitie (1999), passage 3.
42 Iastrebov (1883), 36–7.
43 Kliutschewskij (1925 ff.), vol. 1, 99.
44 Jobst (2007b), 303, note 74.
45 For an overview, cf. Stökl (1983), 59; Haumann (1996), 45–6.
46 Cf. Kawerau (1967).
47 Cf. Jobst (2007b), 296–8.
48 Primary Chronicle (1953), 113.
49 Putin (2014).
50 Cf. the anthology edited by Rudiakov and Kazarin (1989).
51 In the Ukrainian context, a name particularly associated with Crimea is Lesia Ukraïnka (1871–1913), since this important author repeatedly stayed in the peninsula and recorded her impressions in her poetry. There is a museum dedicated to her in Yalta. Regarding Crimean Tatar literature, one might think of a 'negative myth': the literary depictions of the deportation of the Crimean Tatars; cf. Czerwonnaja and Malek (2017).
52 Cf. for instance Liusyi (2003).
53 On the Pushkin cult in Russia and the Soviet Union, cf. Sinyavski (1995).
54 Cf. Jobst (2007b), 256 f.
55 Hokanson (1998), 127.

56 Pushkin's poem was published in 1824. Here I cite the translation by William D. Lewis in Pooshkeen (i.e. Pushkin) (2012 [1849]).
57 Pooshkeen (i.e. Pushkin) (1849] 2012), 26.
58 Pooshkeen (i.e. Pushkin) (1849] 2012), 27.
59 Pushkin to Anton Delvig, no date (1824), cit. Keil, (2001), 111.
60 Köck et al. (1995), 121.
61 Hammer-Purgstall, (1970), 101–103.
62 Cf. Keil, 183.
63 Mickiewicz (1928 [1826]), 19. The translation privileges content over form.
64 Cadot (1987), 149 f.
65 However, between the World Wars there were plans for a confederate, primarily Slavic state stretching from the Black Sea to the Baltic Sea, based on the concept of the "Międzymorze" (Intermarium) proposed by Marshal Józef Piłsudski (1867–1935). Cf. Troebst (2002).
66 Kostomarov (1967), 56. I thank Alois Woldan (Vienna) for bringing my attention to this poem of twelve strophes. The translation privileges content over form.

Chapter 2

1 Herodotus (2008), Book IV, 46.
2 Herodotus (2008), Book IV, 59–66.
3 The categories of 'the Self' and 'the Other' and their mutual dependence have long been discussed in the field of cultural studies. For an introduction, cf. Craanen and Gunsenheimer (2006).
4 Herodotus (2008), Book IV, 67.
5 For instance Asheri, Lloyd and Corcella, who reject this view held by scholars such as F. Hartog (1980); cf. Asheri et al. (2007), 560, note. 33. On essentialization in Greek Antiquity, cf. also Hall E. (1989). On Herodotus's ethnographic descriptions, cf. Bichler (2000).
6 Note that in his histories, Herodotus distinguishes between three kinds of Scythians: the nomad Scythians, the Royal Scythians and the agricultural Scythians.
7 Ivantchik (2005), 33.
8 Parzinger (2004), 123. For a recent survey of the literature, cf. Chochorowski (2004).
9 Many scholars have followed Wenskus's (1977) proposal of instead speaking of gentile entities.
10 On the Cimmerians, cf. Sauter (2000), who assesses the written reports and archaeological finds.
11 Parzinger (2004), 24.
12 Parzinger (2004), 18. Ivantchik also distinguishes between territorial and literary "Cimmerians".

13 Cf. Gossel-Raeck and Busch (1993); Rolle (1991).
14 Parzinger (2004), 111 f., speaks of "impaired conclusions" due to the work of expert grave robbers.
15 Chrapunow (1999), 21 f. These are primarily remains from the seventh to fifth centuries BC, named Kisil-Koba culture after the site of their discovery southeast of Simferopol'. Ceramics indicating a Tauri settlement have also been discovered on the south coast of Crimea and in Bağçasaray.
16 For more detail, cf. Chrapunow (1999), 22. This interpretation is shared, with some qualification, by Magocsi (2014), for instance, who writes of the Tauri: "The Taurans were a tribal group of unknown origin, who, at least from the first millennium BCE, lived in the mountainous zone of the Crimea where they engaged in animal husbandry, some agriculture, and fishing along the coasts" (11).
17 Herodotus, Book IV, 103.
18 Cf. Hall J. (2003), *inter alia* 45 f.
19 Yntema (2010), 99.
20 Cf. Dougherty (1994).
21 Bengtson (1979), 67.
22 After Crimea was retaken by the Red Army in 1944, it was not only Crimean Tatars who were deported. Their fate was shared by other groups that had long had roots in the peninsula, such as the Bulgarians and the Crimean Greeks.
23 Heinen (2006); Maslennikov (1981). Cf. also the older but still valuable study by Gajdukevič (1949).
24 Cf. for instance Selov-Kovedjaev (1986).
25 Gajdukevič (1949), 70.
26 This finding has been substantially informed by Soviet investigations of the necropolises; cf. Gajdukevič (1949), 233–297. On the excavations from 1949 to the 1960s, cf. the expanded German edition: Gajdukevič (1971).
27 Here I follow my essay Joost (2015a).
28 Rostovtzeff (1922), 7.
29 Including Fedor Dostoevskii or in the twentieth century the so-called Eurasians. For an introduction, cf. Vucinich (1972); Hauner (1990).
30 D'iakov and Nikol'skii (1952), 401 f.
31 He supported this thesis *inter alia* with the results of archaeological excavations of Scythian grave mounds; cf. Rostovtzeff (1922), 20–5. The Black Sea region including Crimea thus offers historians excellent opportunities for comparing historical civilizations or entangled history; cf. Kaelble (1999); Werner and Zimmermann (2004).
32 Leder (2005), 22.
33 For instance by Kürşat-Ahlers (1994).
34 Kushko (2014), 9.
35 Cf. for instance Stepanchuk (1999).
36 Ascherson (2015), 17.

37 Cf. the foundational work by Baeque (1993).
38 Rostovtzeff (1922), 64 f.
39 Cf. Moreno (2007), especially the chapter "Ex Ponto. The Athenian Grain Supply and Black Sea Archaeology", 144–208.
40 Ascherson (2015), 19 f.

Chapter 3

1 Herodotus (2008), Book IV, 113–14.
2 Herodotus (2008), Book IV, 116.
3 In the nineteenth century, Johann Jakob Bachofen's theory of gynaecocracy based on the analysis of Classical mythology proved particularly popular: Bachofen (1997). Concerning the (in)validity of archaeological evidence for the existence of Classical matriarchies, cf. the positions taken by Röder et al. (1996).
4 Ascherson (2015), 104–15.
5 Lysenko (2006).
6 For a foundational work on the Sarmatians, cf. Brzezinski and Mielczarek (2002).
7 Dan (2017), 101. This view is shared by other authors; cf. for instance Jankowski (2006), 25.
8 Parzinger (2004), 17.
9 Radt (2003).
10 Dan (2017), 97.
11 Aibabin (1999), 36, assumes that Sarmatian groups withdrew to the southwestern mountainous region beneath Mount Ai-Petri in the third century AD.
12 Neapolis Scythian (2017). Cf. also the further information presented there on the excavations and photographs of the settlement. On the settlement's history, cf. Zaitsev (2003).

Chapter 4

1 Strabo (2001), Book VII, Chapter 4, Paragraph 4.
2 For an introduction, cf. Jung-Kaiser (2013).
3 Zhukov (1955), 411, cit. Neubauer H. (1960), 147.
4 Cf. Højte (2009).
5 Cf. Højte (2006).
6 Rostovtzeff (1922), 155: "[I]t was no longer a real Greek city. Hellenism in Panticapaeum was perishing daily."
7 Rostowzew (1902), 85.

8 Sarnowski and Zubar (1996).
9 The term used for several military conflicts between the Dacians – presumably more of an umbrella term than a homogenous ethnos – and the Roman Empire under Domitian (81–96) and Trajan (98–117) which ended with Dacia's annexation by the Romans. For an introduction, see Strobel (1989).
10 Rostowzew (1902). 87.
11 Rolle and Brenow (2006); Rolle (1980), 150.

Chapter 5

1 Jordanes (1939), 111. Cf. also Jordanes (1915), 85–6.
2 Jordanes's *Getica* is bound up with more scholarly controversies than it would be possible to discuss in detail here. One of the questions that remains concerns the extent to which Jordanes drew on the older but lost writings of the late Classical Roman statesman and scholar Cassiodor (*c*. 485–580); cf. Christensen (2002). On the claim often traced back to Jordanes that the Goths were originally from Scandinavia, cf. Chapter 2.
3 For instance according to Aleksandr A. Vasil'ev (1870–1952), considered one of the most important Byzantinists of the twentieth century. Vasiliev (1936), 30
4 Other terms are Ostrogoths, Ostrogot(h)i, Ostrogotae or Greut(h)ungi; cf. also Greule (2003).
5 Rosen (2007), 7.
6 Kulikowski (2007), who considers the "Gothic storm" in the time before 200 AD fictive.
7 Stickler (2007), 118.
8 On the etymology, cf. Vasiliev (1936), 52–7.

Chapter 6

1 Zhitie (1999), Chapter 3.
2 For an introduction, cf. Schmitt J. (2016).
3 Pillinger (1996), 310 f.
4 Cf. for instance Vasiliev (1936), 5 f. Reference is usually made to Eusebius of Caesarea, Eusebius (2007), for instance 319.
5 For an introduction, cf. Plontke-Lüning (2012), 347.
6 Cf. for instance Vasiliev (1936), 15, who considers this likely. Cf. also Schaferdiek (1979), 287–9.
7 Vasiliev (1936), 7.
8 Plontke-Lüning (2012), 348.
9 Gertsen and Mogarichev (1992).

10 Cf. for instance Jakobson (1964), 32.
11 Romančuk (2005), 88.

Chapter 7

1   Primary Chronicle (1953), 84.
2   Cf. for instance Pletnjowa (1978); Zhivkov (2015). Cf. also the analysis of relations between the Khazars and Kyivan Rus': Petrukhin (2007).
3   On the economy, cf. Noonan (2007), on Crimea especially 219–28.
4   Noonan (1992).
5   Cf. Albrecht and Herdick (2013), 31.
6   Altschüler (2006), 190.
7   Artamonov (1962), 266 f.
8   For a recent survey of the research, cf. Alikberov et al. (2010). Cf. also Bujnoch (1972), especially 54–106.
9   Golden (2006), 85; a somewhat divergent interpretation is offered by Altschüler (2006), 237 f., who refers to the Khaganate as a "monarchy with division of powers", stating that there were two khagans, one for the legislature and one for the exectutive.
10 For Justinian II's biography, cf. the introduction by Dieten (1976); Leontsine (2012).
11 Albrecht and Herdick (2013), 29.
12 For instance Pletnjowa (1978), 37.
13 Vasiliev (1936), 83.
14 Noonan (2007), 219 f.
15 Cf. the extensive discussion in Albrecht and Herdick (2013).
16 Cf. for instance Brook (2006), 136 f.
17 Jobst (2013a).
18 Brandes W. (1988), here 187 f.
19 On the history and status of the excavations, cf. Mack and Carter (2003). Jakobson's study (1959) remains a useful survey of excavations in the tsarist empire, especially 5–16.
20 Albrecht and Herdick (2013), 31.
21 Vasiliev (1936), 80.
22 Cf. for instance "Ioann Gotskii", in: Kogonashvili (1995), 93 f. This has probably given rise to the view that John took part in the Council of Hieria called by Emperor Constantine V in 754, at which iconodulism was condemned. Vasiliev (1936), 89 f. takes a different position.
23 Pletnjowa (1978), 125.
24 Albrecht and Herdick (2013), 31.

25 For the French translation, cf. Auzépy (2006). For the Russian version, cf. for instance Vasil'evskii (1878).
26 Cf. Vinogradov (2010), who points to many uncertain elements in this source, with respect to both the reconstruction of events and the translation from the Greek.
27 Primary Chronicle (1953), 84.
28 Constantine (1985), 65.

Chapter 8

1 Constantine (1985), 53.
2 Pritsak (1975), 228.
3 Constantine (1985), 49.
4 Constantine (1985), 51.
5 Pritsak (1975), 232.
6 Primary Chronicle (1953), 85.
7 Primary Chronicle (1953), 90. We have already encountered the motif of making drinking vessels out of the heads of enemies in Herodotus's description of the Scythians (cf. Chapter 3).
8 Pritsak (1975), 231.
9 Pletnjowa (1978), 133–5.
10 Albrecht and Herdick (2013), 34. Cf. too the lively description of the waterborne incursions by the warriors of Rus' under the heading "Of the coming of the Russians in 'monoxyla' from Russia to Constantinople" in *De administrando imperio*. Constantine (1985), 57–63.
11 Primary Chronicle (1953), 134.
12 For an overview, cf. Chkaidze (2010).
13 For instance by the Russian polymath Mikhail V. Lomonosov (1711–65), who in the mid-eighteenth century even believed he could prove that the Sarmatians had actually been Slavs; in this understanding, 'Slavs' already inhabited the region in the centuries BC. Cf. Slezkine (1997), 50 and 57. On Stalin's attempts to prove the region had had an autochthonous Slav population, cf. Ascherson (2015), 42–43 f.
14 Vasiliev (1936), 118–26.
15 Kliutschewskij (1925 ff.), Volume 1, 99.

Chapter 9

1 *Tale of the Armament of Igor* (1915). See also a later verse translation by Robert Mann, *Song of Prince Igor* (1979), 13.
2 Cf. for instance Filip (1990).

3   Cf. for instance Likhachëv (1985).
4   Zalizniak (2008).
5   In the Old East Slavic version, the Slavic variant of Sudak "Surozh" is used; cf. for instance Song of Prince Igor (1979), 42. Another variant of the time was "Soldaia" or "Sougdaia" (Greek).
6   We use this term in the following.
7   For an introduction, cf. Golden (2003).
8   Cf. the interpretation of the Slavic–Asian encounter offered by George Vernadsky, a historian belonging to the Eurasian Movement in Russian intellectual history: Vernadsky (1969).
9   Magocsi (2014), 27 f., is of the opinion that this battle gave the Mongol Tatar troops important knowledge which served them well in the late 1230s: "This time they came with a massive military force estimated at between 120,000 and 140,000 troops under the supreme command of Chinggis Khan's grandson, Khan Batu."
10 Williams (2001), 11.
11 Haumann (1996), 98 f.
12 Williams (2001), 11.

Chapter 10

1   The literature also refers to the Golden Horde as the Khanate.
2   Mission of Friar William (1990), 63–4.
3   The common equation of the Horde with the "Mongol Empire" is inaccurate, since the Mongols were by no means in the majority in this very fluid 'state'. Islam was adopted in the first half of the fourteenth century. Cf. also Klein D. (2014). Magocsi (2014), 29, writes that for reasons that remain unclear to this day, the term "Tatars" quickly became established for the inhabitants of the entire Horde, even though the term actually meant the subaltern Turkic-speaking groups.
4   Pritsak (1991).
5   Abu-Lughod (1989).
6   Ascherson (2015), 87.
7   Albrecht and Herdick (2013), 35.
8   For an overview, cf. Jaspert (2004); Lilie (2004). On the Fourth Crusade, cf. Phillips (2004).
9   Karsten (2012), 31.
10 Cf. Norwich (2000), 202 f.
11 Norwich (2000), 203–15.
12 Cf. for instance Külzer (2006).
13 Karsten (2012), 33; cf. also Norwich (2000), 215.

14 Cf. in detail Epstein (1996), 141–3.
15 Brătianu (2014), 171.
16 King (2004), for instance 65.
17 This cooperation involved, for instance, joint maintenance of the trading post of Tana (today: Azov) on the Don Estuary and frequent joint resistance to the demands of the Horde. Cf. Rösch (2000), 77 f.
18 Epstein (1996), 230.
19 Albrecht and Herdick (2013), 39.
20 For extensive discussion on the basis of a wealth of sources, cf. Brătianu (2014), 171–9.
21 Cf. Balard (1987); Jobst (2015a).
22 Wenskus (1973). The Alans, who spoke an Iranian language, were evidently descendants of the Sarmatians.
23 On its history, cf. Karpov (2007); Bryer (1980).
24 Litavrin (1967), 29–49. Albrecht and Herdick (2013), 35 f., argue that local rulers had greater influence.
25 Here I follow Bulgakova (2008), especially 263 and 274.

Chapter 11

1 Schmitt C. (1942), 5–6.
2 Schmitt C. (1981), 12.
3 Jobst et al. (2008), here 29.
4 A standard work on the Golden Horde, despite some problematic terminology, is Spuler (1965); other standard works include Fedorov-Davydov (1973); Weatherford (2004); Halperin (1987); Ostrowski (1998). Ostrowski's study in particular most persuasively re-examines the idea of the Horde's backwardness that pervades Western discourses.
5 Hartog L. (1996), 164 f.
6 These views were heavily influenced by the work of the sociologist and sinologist Karl Wittfogel, which enjoyed many print runs: Wittfogel (1957).
7 Ostrowski (1998), 86. On the social strata, cf. Spuler (1965), 293–300.
8 Cf. Hobson (2004); Weatherford (2004).
9 Epstein (1996), 289.
10 Osterhammel (2003), 21.
11 Cf. Karsten (2012), 41.
12 Di Cosmo (2010), 99. An indicator of a certain amount of self-government on the part of the colonies in the Black Sea region is, for instance, the establishment of a kind of administrative office in 1113: "Eight officials regulated navigation to Tana, Caffa and the Black Sea [. . .]. The office of the Crimea soon had jurisdiction over all ships sailing beyond Sicily and Maiorca."

This *Officium Gazariae* also monitored the shipping regulations, writes Epstein (1996), 193 f.

13 The medieval historian Valentin Groebner quite rightly notes with reference to terms such as "mixing", "integration" or "acculturation": "It is that which arriving migrants do with the local population and the converse, conquerors with subjects, slave owners with their slaves: in short, sex between people of different origin." Groebner (2007), 432.
14 Di Cosmo (2010), 85.
15 Brătianu (1969), 262.
16 Cf. Rösch (2000), 77 f.
17 Cf. here for instance Hryszko (2004); Brătianu (1969), for instance 186, who considers the slave trade to have been a more important economic factor in Mongol society than in the feudal states of Europe.
18 From the tenth century onwards, Slav traders were also involved in the slave trade, although it is not known to what extent. Cf. Fisher (1972b), 576.
19 Epstein (2001); Quirini-Popławska (2002).
20 Cf. King (2004), 116, and the literature he lists there.
21 It has not been possible to establish how many people each ship carried.
22 Cf. Fisher (1972b), 577.
23 Fisher (1972b), 576.
24 For a more detailed account of this later period, cf. Kizilov (2007).
25 Rösch (2000), 138.
26 Brătianu (1969), 225.
27 Cf. Bernstein (2009), on the Great Plague 138 f.
28 For an introduction, cf. Fouquet u. Zeilinger (2011), on the Great Plague especially 107–10. There is no consensus concerning the number of victims: for instance, Brătianu (1969), 237, thinks it was around a third of Europe's then population, which would suggest twenty million to twenty-five million deaths, while a higher estimate is provided by Benedictow (2004), 380 f., who considers some 60 per cent to have been likely.
29 Meier M. (2005).
30 Ascherson (2015), 90.
31 Bulst (1979), here 46.
32 Gerste (2004). For different opinions on the infection pathways, cf. Wheelis (2002) and Dean et al. (2018).
33 Cf. for instance Derbes (1966) or Brătianu (1969), 244, who writes of "[c]ette formule de guerre microbienne".
34 Ascherson (2015), 90, states that between December 1347 and September 1348, three-quarters of the European population in the Black Sea colonies died.
35 Albrecht and Herdick (2013), 41.
36 To cite the title of a work of popular scholarship: Kurowski (1986).

37 Gumilëv (1997), 173.
38 Spuler (1965), 120.
39 Nagel (1993).
40 For instance Soucek (2000), 123. The Timurid Empire existed between 1370 and 1507, its core territories roughly comprising today's states of Afghanistan, Iran and Uzbekistan. Its capital was initially Samarkand and later Herat.

Chapter 12

1 Erzählung (2003), 47, 49 and 51. Henceforth based on Beyer's discussion and his German translation.
2 For his biography, cf. Erzählung (2003), 28 f.
3 An interpretation already proposed by Vasiliev (1936), 188.
4 Erzählung (2003), 41 and 43.
5 Erzählung (2003), 31.
6 On the early history of Lithuania, cf. Rowell (1994).
7 Not to be confused with Timur Lenk (cf. Chapter 12), who supported him and Edigü, however, against Toktamış.
8 Albrecht and Herdick (2013), 42.
9 Cf. Bunar and Sroka (1996).
10 "Evrei [Jews – K.S.J.]", in: Kogonashvili (1995), 82 f.
11 Albrecht and Herdick (2013), 43.
12 Vasiliev (1936), 182.
13 Albrecht and Herdick (2013), 43.
14 Brătianu (1969), for instance 321.
15 Here and in the following I draw primarily on the pioneering history of the Crimean Goths by Vasiliev (1936), 194. Albrecht and Herdick (2013), 44, go even further, with reference to sources from the Genoese tradition, in describing Theodoro as one of the important powers in the entire Black Sea region – naming the Empire of Trebizond, which existed until 1461, in addition to those mentioned by Vasiliev.
16 On the borders and conflicts between Theodoro and the Genoese territories over Cembalo, cf. Bocharov (2017).
17 Vasiliev (1936), 204.
18 Cf. Vasiliev (1936), 205: "Alexis did not abandon his cherished dream of taking possession of this important fortress and port."
19 Albrecht and Herdick (2013), 44.
20 For a detailed account, cf. Vasiliev (1936), 205–07.
21 Cf. the extensive discussion in Epstein (1996), 273 f.

Chapter 13

1. Broniovius (1867), 352–3. Stefan Albrecht (2011) has produced the first complete translation of this most important Latin source into German. Cf. also older, incomplete translations into Russian in the nineteenth century: Shershenevich (1867); or into English in 1625: Collections (1906).
2. On Broniewski's biography and the text's publication history, cf. Albrecht (2011).
3. Albrecht (2011), 3.
4. Contrary to Abrecht (2011), 1, Broniewski was not the first to proclaim Crimea's beauty; the fourteenth-century Exarch Matthew (cited extensively in Chapter 13), for instance, was writing considerably earlier.
5. Here it must suffice to mention only the efforts of the Muscovite Grand Prince Ivan IV (Groznyi; usually mistranslated into English as "the Terrible"), who commissioned the sixteenth-century Book of Degrees (Russian: *Stepennaia kniga*), a collection of hagiographic lives of princes intended to lend the ruling dynasty the dignity of an honorable lineage. Cf. for instance Lenhoff (2005).
6. Broniovius (2011), 97, note 151.
7. Broniovius (2011), 97.
8. Alan Fisher, who remains the authority on the history of the Crimean Tatars, writes that "the origins of the Crimean Tatars are as obscure as the origins of most peoples", Fisher (1978), 1. Williams (2001), 7–38 essays an "ethnogenesis" of the Crimean Tatars in the context of the peninsula's multiethnic development throughout the ages.
9. Gaivoronskii (2007); on the biography of Hacı I Giray, cf. especially 13–30.
10. Fisher (1978), 3.
11. Cf. Smirnov (1887), 210–12.
12. Cf. Tyszkiewicz (1989); Tyszkiewicz (2002).
13. On Smirnov's life and his *magnum opus* on the history of the Khanate under Ottoman rule, cf. the brief examination by Cwiklinski (2014).
14. Smirnov (1887), 227
15. Another example from Eastern Europe is the myth of the foundation of Kyivan Rus' related by the Primary Chronicle, according to which the inhabitants of Rus' requested three brothers from Scandinavia to rule over their land. Unlike the East Slavic context, which has been the subject of a very intensive controversy since the eighteenth century, on which there is not space to dwell here – cf. Lichačev (1970); Kaminskii (2012) – the Crimean Tatar version is not particularly disputed.
16. Vasiliev (1936), 206.
17. Williams (2001), 45.
18. Cf. Lebedev (1990). Here we draw on the English translation available online at: http://byzantinebronzes.ancients.info/page31.html (accessed 19 January 2018). Cf. the illustrations at http://byzantinebronzes.ancients.info/page45.html (accessed 19 January 2018) showing early use of the national symbol the Crimean Tatars use to this day, including on their flag. (Cf. Figure 36.1.)

19 Williams (2001), 45.
20 Fisher (1978), 4.
21 Ivanics (2012). The Kıpçak clan grew out of the Turkic-speaking ethnos of the Kumans/Kipchaks (cf. Chapter 3).
22 Ivanics (2012), 27: in the eighteenth century, the most influential clans, besides the Barın and Şirin, were the Mansur and Siciut.
23 Cf. Vásáry (2012), especially 15, where he elaborates his theory of the *translatio imperii* from the Horde to the Khanate.
24 Fisher (1978), 2. According to other studies, Shaykh Ahmad did not die until 1528/29.
25 Vásáry (2012), 15.
26 Cf. the extensive discussion by Kusber (1998). Cf. also Conermann and Kusber (1997).
27 Cf. for instance Kolli (1913), 108: "In Caffa itself, given that the majority of the population consisted of Tatars, all commercial matters were conducted in the Tatar language. In the bazaar and in the urban shops and counting houses the Tatar language sounded almost everywhere."
28 Williams (2001), 27 f.; Jobst (2011b), 14.

Chapter 14

1 Evliyâ (1934), 93.
2 Hillebrand (2017), 42, on whom I also draw in the following.
3 The first partial translation into English was produced by Joseph Freiherr [Baron] von Hammer-Purgstall (1774–1856), an Austrian diplomat and one of the founders of the scholarly study of the Ottomans. The above quotation is also from his translation. On the publication and translation history of Evliyâ's Crimean report, cf. Hillebrand (2017), 45–7; on the translations into Polish and Russian, cf. *idem*, 61, note 74.
4 UNESCO (2013).
5 For instance by Matuz (1996), 67.
6 Cf. also Zaytsev (2010).
7 Matuz (1964) expounds on one event on the basis of a source discovered in the *Rigsarkivet* (Danish National Archive) in Copenhagen, which may have influenced his conclusions on the Crimean Khanate's "vassal relationship". In specific, the source relates to the appointment and removal of Âdil Çoban Giray as Crimean khan in the mid-seventeenth century.
8 Jobst (2011b), 15.
9 Epstein (1996), 281–3. The sale of women from the Black Sea region was indeed more lucrative than that of men; women from the Caucasus in particular were in high demand.
10 Cf. Brătianu (1969), 311–14.

11 Kreiser and Neumann (2008), 93.
12 For a more extensive discussion, cf. Fisher (1978), 5.
13 Brătianu (1969), 315.
14 Matuz (1996), 57.
15 Fisher (1978), 10.
16 Gajvoronskij (2007), 50.
17 Jobst (2011b), 15.
18 Fisher (1978), 12.
19 Cf. Hathaway and Barbir (2008), 8 f.
20 Cf. the standard work by Burak (2015).
21 On the term "caliph", cf. Heine (1990).
22 Cf. Denny (2000).
23 Ottoman and Crimean Tatar are Turkic languages, the former belonging to the Oghuz language family, the latter to the Kipchak (Tatar).
24 Fisher (1978), 13.
25 Cf. Khoroshkevich (2000).
26 For a history of the Grand Duchy that takes into consideration the time before the Union of Lublin, cf. Niendorf (2010)
27 Völkl (1975).
28 Cf. Binder-Iijima and Dumbrava (2005).
29 King (2004), 121.
30 Brătianu (1969), 321 f.
31 Cf. Vasiliev (1936), 266.
32 The term is incorrect, since the Ottoman Empire did not consist only of Turkic peoples and Muslims. It is also important to avoid equating the Empire with the Republic of Turkey, which did not exist until 1923.
33 Delumeau (1985).
34 Cf. for instance Feichtinger and Heiss (2013), especially the editors' introduction (7–23); Barbarics-Hermanik (2009)
35 Meuthen (1983), 1–6.
36 Cf. Vasiliev (1936), 254–65, who names and cites several Ottoman and Arabian, but also European, sources.
37 On his work and his biography, cf. Pretzel (1987).
38 Löwe (1896), 221.
39 Jörg von Nürnbergk, cit. Löwe (1896), 222.
40 Löwe (1896), 222, where he also discusses the "three kings", whom he considers to be two princely brothers and one of their sons.
41 Cf. for instance Vasiliev (1936), 278; Löwe (1896), 223 f.
42 Cf. the standard work by Braude and Lewis (1982).
43 Matuz (1996), 112.

44 On the conquest and on European Christian expansion in general, cf. Sievernich (2011).
45 On this, for the following discussion and on the motif of "Orthodox Crimea", which we have also encountered in the stylization of the baptism of Chersonesus (cf. Chapter 2), cf. Jobst (2007b), 289–311.
46 Khartakhai (1866/1867), 2, 150.

Chapter 15

1 Kleemann (1771), 155.
2 For the few known biographical details, cf. Nikolaus Kleemann (2018).
3 Kleemann (1771), 150.
4 Papp (2012).
5 Cf. for instance Andreev (1997), 123.
6 Cf. Barkey (2008).
7 Here, the dichotomy metropolis–periphery is used not in uncritical subscription to so-called dependence theory, world system theory and the like but in order to denote spatial and cultural disparities without value judgment. For an introduction to the terminology, cf. Boeckh (1993); Nölke (2006).
8 Jobst (2011b), 16.
9 Papp (2012), 77, on whom I mostly draw in the following.
10 Cf. Papp (2012), 83 f.
11 Papp (2012), 76.
12 Cf. Hillebrand (2017), for instance 54.
13 Matuz (1964), 134.
14 Cf. Papp (2012), 79.
15 Papp (2012), 79 f.
16 Cf. Matuz (1964), 135.
17 Matuz (1964), 135.
18 Faroqhi (1994), 419, defines them as "mercenaries of peasant background".
19 For more precise details, cf. Fisher (1972a).
20 Cf. for instance Petritsch (1983).
21 Cf. Kołodziejczyk (2012), 50. On the autochtonous population's perception of Crimean Tatar soldiers in 1683 in particular, cf. Augustynowicz (2012).
22 Barker (1967), 220. For most historians, it is an established fact that Crimean Tatar troops participated in the Second Siege of Vienna. However, Kołodziejczyk, considered the leading authority on Crimean Tatar foreign policy in the early modern period, states that the then Crimean khan Murad Giray (1627–96) refused to participate in the decisive battle; cf. Kołodziejczyk (2012), 51. What is beyond dispute is that he rejected the move, considering it unlikely to succeed; cf. Cardini (2004), 234. For what remains an important

study on the background to Grand Vizier Kara Mustafa's decision, cf. Leitsch (1981).
23 For an overview based on eye-witness reports, cf. Augustynowicz (2012).
24 Schwarcz (2017), 208. Schwarcz puts this down to the complicated situation regarding the sources; they are located in Istanbul, Vienna, Moscow, Moscow, Paris and Teheran and are mostly unedited.
25 Cf. Andreev (1997), 123.
26 Cf. Arens and Klein (2004), 497. The Principality of Transylvania could also claim the status of a privileged vassal of the Sublime Porte, "firstly due to the domestic- and foreign-political scope it was granted by Istanbul and secondly with respect to its tribute payments". Moldavia and Walachia had to pay much higher tribute than the Crimean Khanate or Transylvania.
27 Cf. the extremely meritorious edition and study by Matuz (1976).
28 Cf. Augustynowicz (2005).
29 The reciprocal contact between Moscow and Bağçasaray not only served the delivery of tribute, but can probably also be interpreted as 'normal' diplomatic contact, complete with the usual conflicts. Cf. also Zertsalov (1890).
30 Cf. Hottop-Riecke (2017), especially 69 f.
31 On the specific event, cf. Kołodziejczyk (2012), 52.
32 Cf. Fisher (1977).
33 Smirnov (1887), 555.
34 Matuz (1996), 139.
35 Fisher (1978), 45.
36 Karamzin (2013).
37 The clear reservations concerning Ivan IV expressed by Karamzin, who fundamentally justifies the autocratic system, may have been informed by the violence of the Oprichniki, a special military unit of the tsar. Hosking (1997), 55, is of the opinion that Ivan's troops, "[c]orrupted and enfeebled by their own impunity, [...] proved incapable in 1571 of repelling Devlet-Girei".
38 Cf. the standard work by Hoffmann P. (1991).
39 Cf. Fisher (1978), 40 f.
40 Zaytsev (2010), 25.
41 As demonstrated by, for instance, the travel report by the Ottoman subject Evliyâ Çelebi, examined by Hillebrand (2017).
42 Zaytsev (2010), 25.
43 Fisher (1978), 17.

Chapter 16

1 Opisanie (1879), 470.
2 Krymskaia oblast' (1953).

3 Jobst (2007b), 206. On the male gaze in assessments of the Crimean Tatar population, cf. 206–18.
4 Opisanie (1879), 480.
5 Broniovius (2011), 119.
6 Cf. Jobst (2011a).
7 Broniovius (2011), 119.
8 Cf. Kusber (1998).
9 Cf. also Chapters 3 and 5.
10 Cf. the list of "Tatar Raids for Captives" from 1468 to 1694 in Fisher (1972b), 580–3.
11 Jobst (2011b), 21.
12 Skorupa (1994), especially 263 and 285.
13 Khodarkovsky (2002), 223.
14 Cf. Lavrov (2009).
15 Khodarkovsky (2002), 223 f.
16 Cf. Lavrov (2009), 443, who notes that only the Vatican and Catholic orders made efforts to buy captives' freedom.
17 Cf. the findings of the Polish Ottoman scholar Dariusz Kołodzieczyk: Kołodzieczyk (2006), 151. Cf. the discussion of the various positions taken by scholars in Davies B. (2007), 23–7.
18 According to Kołodziejczyk (2011), xiv. On the other hand, it should be noted that around 12 million people were taken from West, Central and Southern Africa to the Americas as slaves: Segal (1995), 4. Another hotspot of the slave trade was the Mediterranean, where business was often conducted at 'private' initiative – that is, by pirates – however. Cf. Davies R. (2004), who estimates that between 1 million and 1.5 million people entered into slavery in the region between 1500 and 1800.
19 Cf. Albrecht (2011).
20 Broniovius (2011), 115.
21 Fisher (1972b), 582 f., on whom I largely draw in the following.
22 Kefe was the central shipping port. Captives from Muscovy were generally transported there from Azov via the Black Sea, while those from the Polish-Lithuanian Commonwealth had to take a diversion via Özi/Özü, today's port of Ochakiv (Ukrainian; Russian Ochakov) in Ukraine, before being taken to Kefe by ship.
23 Broniovius (2011), 115.
24 Fisher (1972b), 584.
25 Cf. the collected edition Witzenrath (2016), in which many contributions deal with the role played by slaves, both as 'victims' and as 'perpetrators'.
26 On the history of slavery, cf. for instance Lavrov (2009), 425–43.
27 Russkii Krym (2003), 1.
28 Kizilov (2007), 30.

29 Kizilov (2007), 30.
30 Kizilov (2007), 30 f.
31 Fisher (1972b), 577.
32 Fisher (1972b), 583 and 584. According to Fisher, the slave trade in Istanbul was conducted "[w]ithout exception" by Jews. However, cf. also the nuanced treatment of the roles of perpetrators and victims in Kizilov (2007), 25–30.
33 For examples, cf. Spuler (1965), 386.
34 Hellie (1982), 73 f. and 82 f. The differences between slavery and serfdom, which was not abolished in the tssarist empire until 1861, cannot be examined in detail here. In short, serfs possessed some legal rights and their owners also had certain legal obligations. Slaves, on the other hand, had the status of speaking objects. In both cases there were indisputably discrepancies between theory and practice.
35 Cf. some examples in Fisher (1972b), 589.
36 In 1641, the Don Cossacks conquered Ottoman Azov on the lower course of the Don in 1641 and participated in various tsarist campaigns against the Crimean Khanate in the late seventeenth century.

Chapter 17

1 Thounmann (1786), 63 f. The original German, Thunmann (1784), was not available.
2 Eberhard J. (1779).
3 Thunman (1774). The work presented the "Universal History of the Peoples who Lived on the Black Sea and Lake Maeotis Until the Invasion By the Mogols [sic]". In the chapter "On some aspects of Russian history", one of his foci was the role played by ethnicities of Scandinavian origin in the history of Kyivan Rus', and he also took a stance on what was known as the Varangian question or the Norman theory; 367–406, here especially 371–90.
4 Cf. Jobst (2007b), 90 f., 156 f.
5 Opisanie (1879), 487.
6 For greater detail, cf. Williams (2001), 88 f., on whom I draw here.
7 Wine was produced and consumed in the Crimean Khanate era too, including by the Muslim Crimean Tatars. Cf. Halenko (2004), 507–47.
8 Cf. Williams (2001), 58 f.
9 Jobst (2007b), for instance 220.
10 Markov (1994), 212. This is a prime example of the applicability of the concept of similarity, which also plays a role in colonial contexts. Cf. Bhatti and Kimmich (2015).
11 Windt (1917), 187.
12 Fisher (1978), 24.
13 Fisher (1977), 69 f.

Chapter 18

1. Beauplan (1993 [1780]), 10–11. The French original was first published in Rouen in 1650, entitled *Description d'Ukraine qui sont plusieurs Provinces du Royaume de Pologne contenuēs depuis les confins de la Moscouie, iusques aux limites de la Transilvanie, ensemble levrs moevrs, façons de viuns, et de faire la guerre.*
2. For an overview of the Cossack communities, cf. Kappeler (2013). The study by Stökl (1953) is still useful. There are other Cossack communities besides the abovementioned, the first two of which are of particular importance for our focus, for instance the Iaik Cossacks or the Siberian Cossacks.
3. The Cossack communities were indeed originally purely male, understanding themselves to be a military "brotherhood that upholds male values such as honour, courage, physical strength and stamina and reminiscent of the medieval orders of knights", writes Andreas Kappeler. Later, Zaporog Cossacks usually had families; their wives were sometimes Tatars stolen from the Ottoman Empire from the Caucasus. Kappeler (2013), 51.
4. Kappeler (2013), 14.
5. Cf. the standard work by Kumke (1993a).
6. Besides the Khmel'nyts'kyi Uprising by the Dnipro Cossacks, to which we will return later, mention must be made of another rebellion: that of the Cossack leader Ivan I. Bolotnikov (?– 1608), a former serf who had been captured by the Crimean Tatars, returned to his homeland after years as a galley slave and led a large revolt against tsarist power. Cf. Crispin (2006).
7. Pausz (2017), 15.
8. Kappeler (2013), 12.
9. On the Ottoman military's response to the Cossack attacks, cf. the article and translation of source material by Ostapchuk (1990).
10. Cf. Jobst (2015b), 106–15.
11. Smirnov (1887), 546.
12. Skorupa (1994), 261.
13. Ascherson (2015), 103.
14. Since the breakup of the Soviet Union, several Cossack leagues have been reconstituted in the territories of the Community of Independent States (CIS). This so-called Neo-Cossackhood is often characterized by strong (Russian or Ukrainian) nationalism. Cf. for instance Skorik (1995); Toje (2006); Ganzer (2005); Schorkowitz (2008).
15. Cf. the standard work by Plokhy (2001).
16. Cf. Kumke (1993b), 84 f.

Chapter 19

1. Broniovius (1867), 356–7.
2. Broniovius (2011), 79.

3   As Edward Said pointed out with reference to the example of professionalized Oriental studies, for instance in Said (1978). On the role of "Orientalism" in Eastern European history, cf. for instance Jobst (2000); Schimmelpenninck van der Oye (2010).
4   Peter Simon Pallas, *Bemerkungen auf einer Reise in die südlichen Statthalterschaften des Russischen Reiches in den Jahren 1793 und 1794*. First published in 1799 in German, the work was translated into almost all European languages – including Russian. References are henceforth to the English translation, Pallas (1812). On Pallas himself, cf. Wendland (1992). Pallas not only travelled around Crimea but also undertook extensive expeditions to other parts of the Russian Empire, including the Urals and Siberia.
5   Cf. Jobst (2007b), 117–22.
6   Pallas (1812), Volume 2, 262.
7   Pallas (1812), Volume 2, 346 f.
8   Cf. the reader containing canonical texts on the debate: Bronfen (1997).
9   According to Williams (2001), 124, nothing is known about marriages between Christians and Tatars during the tsarist era; he interprets this as an act of defining Muslim identity on the part of the Crimean Tatar population. In contrast, cf. Jobst (2007b), 212–15, where I have documented a number of such cases on the basis of Russian sources.
10 At least in the interpretation of Fisher (1981), 141, on the situation in the city of Kefe in the Ottoman Empire.
11 Jobst (2007b), 192–5.
12 On the history and architecture of the palace, which was built in several phases, presumably commencing around 1540, cf., besides Fisher (1978), 29 f., the official website *Bakhchisaraiski zapovednik* (2018). The Russian-language *Wikipedia* entry is also interesting: the palace is not considered a low-quality construction, as was long the prevailing view in the Russian and Soviet discourse; on the contrary, it is described as a monument of universal importance. Cf. Khanskii dvorets (2018).
13 Broniovius (2011), 79.
14 Cf. Hillebrand (2017), 53.
15 Fisher (1978), 16.
16 On agricultural production in Crimea under the Khanate, cf. Vozgrin (1992), 156–8.
17 Jakobson (1973), 148.
18 Khartakhai (1866/1867), 1, 207.
19 Collins (1975), 259.
20 For an overview, cf. Papke (1983).
21 Collins (1975), 259 f.
22 Collins (1975), 262–4.
23 Magocsi (2014), 43.

24 Fisher (1978), 30.
25 On the ethnogenesis of the Crimean Tatars, cf. Williams (2001), 7–39; Voitovych (2009). The distinction between "Tat" and "Yaliboyu" is linguistic; the latter speak an Oghuz – that is, Southwestern Turkic – dialect.
26 Cf. Magocsi (2014), 43, who writes that the population did not increase until well into the eighteenth century; cf. the comparison of the various estimations in Williams (2001), 69 f.
27 Davies B. (2007), 23, is of the opinion that the many slave raids undertaken to the north were ultimately also a result of the disproportionate power held by the clans in the Khanate: "The khan had to offer them frequent opportunities to raid for prisoners to ransom", otherwise they would have acted on their own initiative.
28 Fisher (1978), 21.

Chapter 20

1 Binhack (1869), 41–2.
2 His textbook on Latin cases is still available from antiquarian bookstores: Binhack (1877).
3 Binhack (1869), 42. The translation privileges content over form.
4 Binhack, born in 1836, retrospectively saw the final end to the "long night" – that is, Ottoman dominance – in Greece's independence, achieved in 1830. The Greeks' struggle, lasting almost a decade, was supported by all the European Great Powers, including the Russian Empire. However, Binhack warned the Orthodox Greeks about the ties to the tsarist empire, "that bear / That waits at your gates", or the Habsburg "eagle who / Sits in the reeds in the Danube sand"; Binhack (1869), 44.
5 Cf. Collins (1975), 274 f.
6 Davies B. (2007), 191.
7 Cf. Matuz (1996), 143–64.
8 Vozgrin (1992), 216–20
9 Davies B. (2007), 192. He also points to the parallel rise of the Kalmycks as a steppe power that repeatedly advanced into the territories of the eastern Nogai in the Azov region.
10 Inalcik (1969); Rodinson (1966). An economic history of the Crimean Khanate is lacking, unfortunately.
11 Taagepera (1988).
12 According to Fisher (1973), 50, actors around Ivan IV were already thinking about a large-scale campaign against the Khanate. These plans were abandoned, however, due to their futility.
13 Here and in the following, I draw on Heller (1992).

14 Berezhkov (1891).
15 Subtelny (1993), 96.
16 Hoensch (1983), 150. Ultimately, it had been clear that the Cossacks would split since 1654. Ukrainian historiography usually sees this as the painful division of a protonational Ukrainian state and refers to it as the "Ruïna" (Ukrainian; ruin). Cf. Jobst (2015b), 111.
17 Vozgrin (1992), 226.
18 For the full chain of events, cf. Davies B. (2007), 159–72.
19 For the details, cf. Subtelny (1993), 96–8.
20 Cf. Davies B. (2007), 171 f.
21 Hammer-Purgstall (1970), 171.
22 On the khan's rule from 1678–83, before he was removed by the sultan at the clans' request, cf. Hammer-Purgstall (1970), 169–71. It can be presumed that one of the reasons Murad Giray was deposed was that he weakened the Sharia court, which had previously been the preserve of a mufti appointed by the clerical authorities in Istanbul, in favour of a court that answered to the khan. This reinforcement of the khan's position is likely to have displeased both the *mirza*s and the sultan.
23 The Khanate chose not to secure the entire length of its borders with its northern neighbours, probably because it would have been too expensive to do so. Cf. Arens and Klein (2004), 494.
24 Cf. the contemporary report of a Polish envoy to the Muscovite court of Zapiski, translated from the French in Zapiski (1891).
25 Cf. Fisher (1973).
26 Hammer-Purgstall (1970), 22, names a total of fifty-four different reigns of khans.
27 Cf. Fisher (1977); Fisher (1978), 50.
28 To cite the Turkologist Barbara Kellner-Heinkele at a conference on the history of the Crimean Khanate in Munich in 2008. Cf. the conference programme: Krimkhanat (2008).
29 Cf. Hammer-Purgstall (1970), 194–8.
30 On the assessment of the rebellion of 1699–1701 in Tatar and Ottoman historiography, cf. Klein D. (2012b). On the peace of 1699, cf. Molnár (2013).
31 Here I draw primarily on Vozgrin (1992), 238–44.
32 Vozgrin (1992), for instance 240 f., anticipated the position of Ukrainian nationalist historiography, according to which the Zaporog Cossacks represented a protonational state, and writes of a Crimean Tatar–Ukrainian rapprochement.
33 Vozgrin (1992), 245 f.
34 According to Hosking (1997), 48, the Crimean Tatars had "providently burnt their granaries and poisoned their wells".
35 We will return to the topic of disease and quarantine measures later. Cf. also Robarts (2017), especially the chapter "Instruments of Despotism (II):

Epidemic Disease, Quarantines, and Border Control in the Russian Empire", 139–168.

36 Hammer-Purgstall (1970), 205; Kliutschewskij (1945), Volume 2, 66; Seymour (1855), 28. Seymour's work, published in the context of the Crimean War, served to undermine Russia.
37 Cf. Iaremchuk and Bezverkhyi (1994), 21, who mention the collection and burning of Crimean Tatar books and documents by order of the administration in 1833.
38 Cf. the literature listed in Fisher (1978), 213, note 3.
39 For Fisher (1978), 51, the partial reconstruction of the palace within just three years' of the withdrawal of Russian troops was an impressive achievement.
40 Baumgart (1972) remains essential reading on the subject. Cf. also Figes (2010) – note his programmatic subtitle "The Last Crusade".
41 Here I mostly draw on the older but still relevant study by Anderson M. (1966), as well as on Bitis (2007) and Frary and Kozelsky (2014). Cf. also their introduction (3–34) with a recent survey of the literature, although it doesn't take into account the studies written in German.
42 Particularly Britain and the Habsburg Empire long preferred a balance of power and wanted to uphold the territorial integrity of the Ottoman Empire, at least *de jure*; none of the Great Powers had anything against exercising strong economic and political influence over the Ottoman Empire, however. After the Crimean War, the Oriental Question increasingly became the Balkan Question.
43 King (2004), 5.
44 Hösch (1964), 196.
45 Hösch (1964), 196.
46 On this factor and Ladygin's report, cf. Jones (1996), 125 f.
47 Hösch (1964), 202.
48 Hösch (1964), 133 f.
49 Panin – as part of an older tradition – considered Russia a 'Nordic' power; this was an opinion frequently encountered within Russia until the end of the Crimean War. He thus rather rejected the imperial ambitions in the south. On the shift in the Russian collective self-perception from a 'Nordic' to an 'eastern power', cf. Lemberg (1985).
50 Vorontsov (1915).
51 Vorontsov (1916), 191 f.
52 Fisher (1970), 41.
53 Fisher (1978), 54. Cf. the complete text: Forma manifesta (1896).
54 Cf. Druzhinina (1955), still a standard work. Anderson M. (1966), xi, considers the piece one of the most important in the history of European diplomacy as a whole.
55 Cf. the different positions in Davison (1976) or Weisband (1973), 211.

Chapter 21

1. Kliuchevskii (1903), 52–4.
2. Müller M. (1984) remains the standard work on the partitions.
3. Jobst (2012), 213.
4. Voltaire to Catherine II, Ferney, 13th February 1773, in: Lentin (1974), 147–9, here 148.
5. Voltaire's slightly ironic reference to the partition of Poland is certainly interesting: "You are well used to partitions."
6. Vozmushchenie (1872). According to Fisher (1970), 61, Devlet III Giray freed the Russian envoy (see below) in order to secure Russia's support.
7. Hammer-Purgstall (1970), 229–32.
8. For details, cf. Fisher (1978), 56–9.
9. Fisher (1978), 59.
10. Vozgrin (1992), 265. Vozgrin is wrong here, since it was Devlet IV not Devlet III, who reigned from 1716 to 1717.
11. Fisher (1970), 69.
12. Cf. the transcript of a talk by Il'ia Zaitsev in which despite the misleading title the Crimean Khanate is recognized as a high-level political entity: Sochnev (2016).
13. Catherine II to Voltaire, 23 March/3 April 1772, in: Reddaway (1971), 159–61.
14. Cf. Gajda (2002).
15. Fisher (1978), 55; Williams (2001), 77, note 8.
16. Lazzerini (1988), 124.
17. Bennigsen and Broxup (1993), 17 f., for instance, interpret this as a sign of respectful treatment of Islam.
18. Fisher (1970), 90 f.
19. Vozgrin (1992), 267 f., writes that according to official figures, over 12,000 inhabitants died.
20. Fisher (1978), 66.
21. Jena (2001), 180 f.
22. Potemkin to Catherine II, Before 14.12.1782, in: Smith (2004), 124.
23. Cf. the Russian text in Polnoe sobranie (1830), 897 f., and the English translation "The Manifesto on the Annexation of the Crimea, April 8, 1783" in Vernadsky et al. (1972), 412 f.

Chapter 22

1. Here I follow Jobst (2007b), especially 105–17, and Jobst (2017c).
2. Catherine II to Potemkin, 20–21 May 1787, in: Smith (2004), 178–99.
3. Cf. for instance Schama (1995), Pokhody (1896).

4   Cf. Jobst (2007b), 107 f.
5   Zorin (2001), 108.
6   Potemkin to Catherine II, 7 January 1787, in: Smith (2004), 176.
7   Jena (2001), 278.
8   Joseph II to Field Marshall Lascy, 3 June 1787, in: Arneth (1869), 363.
9   Joseph II to Lascy, 3 June 1787, in: Arneth (1869), 363 f
10 On her life and work, cf. Franke (1995).
11 Craven (1970 [1789]), 183 f.
12 Craven (1970 [1789]), 191.
13 Only some of the place names desired at the very top became established: Catherine II's son, Paul (1754–1801), decreed the re-Tatarization of the place names in Crimea, but his successor, Alexander I, undid the measure; Aqmescit, for instance, officially became Simferopol' once more. In 1826, Nicholas I then issued the "Highest Order" "from now on to no longer call Sevastopol' Akhtiar, but always Sevastopol'". Vysochaishee povelenie (1902), 87. The term "Taurida" (instead of "Crimea") only survived insofar as the "Tavricheskaia oblast'" was created, an administrative unit that extended beyond the territory of Crimea.
14 Ségur (1926). The Crimean Journey is described in the third volume.
15 Ligne (1989).
16 Helbig (1804).
17 Jena (2001), 18–27.
18 For extensive discussion, cf. Jobst (2001a), 140.
19 Elbin (1979), 64.
20 Elbin (1979), 57–60.
21 Cf. in detail Jobst (2007a); Jobst (2001a).
22 V.V. Kokhovskii to V.S. Popov, 12 March 1787, in: Mursakovich (1877–9), 262. On other stagings in this context, cf. Jobst (2017c).
23 Vernadsky et al. (1972), 412. Cf. also the survey in Conermann (1998).
24 Jobst (2012), 215.
25 Gabaev (1913); O'Neill (2008). O'Neill writes of c. 250 Crimean Tatar soldiers who deserted. O'Neill (2017).
26 Cf. Jobst (2007b), especially the chapter "Der zeitgenössische Orient III. Exodus, Nützlichkeit und Illoyalität" (The Contemporary Orient III. Exodus, Utility and Disloyalty), 219–53.
27 On the position of Muslim soldiers in the tsarist army, cf. Davies F. (2016). I thank Franziska Davies for allowing me to take a look at her work prior to its publication.
28 Cf. Jobst (2017b); Qualls (2009).
29 Semin (1955), 33.
30 For details, cf. Jobst (2017b).
31 Cf. Lashkov (1886) and Potemkin to Catherine II, 16 July 1783, in: Smith (2004), 143–4.

32 Cf. for instance Osterhammel (2008).
33 Jobst (2017a), 95.
34 Lashkov (1886), 91.
35 Cf. Fisher (1979), 78.
36 Cf. Igelström (2018).
37 Fisher (1968), especially 548–52.
38 Cf. O'Neill (2010), who places this phenomenon in the wider imperial context.
39 Cf. O'Neill (2008), 6 f. I thank Ricarda Vulpius (Berlin) for confirming that this was the normal procedure for subjugated groups swearing oaths before the eighteenth century.
40 This classification of high-ranking positions in the state government, at the court and in the military, introduced by Peter I, remained until 1917.
41 Fisher (1978), 83.
42 Cf. Jobst (2017a), 96. Cf. also O'Neill (2010), 403.
43 Gavril (1844).
44 Jobst (2017a), 98 and 110.
45 Fisher (1978), 74–5.
46 Cf. the survey by Brandes D. (1998).
47 Potemkin to Catherine II, 29 July 1783, in: Smith (2004), 145–7, here p. 146.
48 The correspondence between Catherine and Potemkin in 1783 contains information on the problem of disease.
49 For a comprehensive study, cf. Robarts (2017).
50 Pallas (1967), Volume 2, 32 f.
51 Jobst (2012), 224.
52 Cf. Brandes D. (1993) and Auerbach (1965).
53 Zorin (2001), 102 f.
54 Cit. Billbassof (1897), Volume 1 (Die Literatur bis zu Katharina's Tode), 504. Cf. other odes and poems in the same volume.
55 Cf. Wolff (1994), 127.
56 On the genesis of this idea, cf. the standard work by Wolff (1994). A very influential discussion with an economic basis was Gerschenkron (1962). Latterly, scholars have departed from this dichotomy, emphasizing the concept of multiple modernity's: Eisenstadt (2007).

Chapter 23

1 Holderness (1823); Anonyma (1855), 140 f. For her biography, cf. Mary Holderness (2017).
2 Gazley (1956), 360.

3   On women travellers in the imperial context, cf. Marbo (1991), 163; Pratt (1992). In the case of Crimea, cf. Jobst (2001d).
4   Holderness (1823), 2.
5   Holderness (1823), for instance 122 f.
6   Holderness (1823), 141.
7   This is the author's observation. Cf. also Fisher (1978), 82.
8   Jobst (2007b), 209.
9   Holderness (1823), cf. for instance 223 f.
10 Melman (1992), 52.
11 Holderness (1823), 225.
12 Holderness (1823), 225.
13 Cf. Jobst (2007b), 208–12. Cf. also some illustrations in the reprint (with commentary) of a work by the naturalist and member of the St Petersburg Academy Gustav Ferdinand Richard Radde (1831–1903) that first appeared in 1856 and 1857.
14 Williams (2001), 124, is unaware of any documented cases, unlike Jobst (2007b), 216.
15 Jobst, for instance (2008), 45.
16 In the following, I draw on, *inter alia*, Jobst (2014); Jobst (2017a).
17 On this calculation, cf. the tsarist historian Lashkov (1886), 91.
18 Fisher (1979), 84–5.
19 Tavricheskaia oblast' (Taurida Province), formed in 1784, became Tavricheskaia guberniia (Taurida Governorate) in 1802.
20 Diulichev (2002), 241.
21 The term denotes religious foundations governed by Islamic law. Muslims thereby supported religious institutions (for instance mosques, madrasahs or mausoleums) or general facilities important for a community (for instance wells): Hartung (2005).
22 Lazzerini (1988), 131 f.
23 For a study on the Russian Empire that takes into account imperial history in general, cf. Burbank (2008). Another example on the Empire's western border is presented by Ganzenmüller (2013).
24 Cf. for instance Lemercier-Quelquejay (1967). A study of the wave of apostasy in the nineteenth century is provided by Frings (2010).
25 Cf. Kozelsky (2010).
26 Bennigsen (1972), 147.
27 Rudakov (1903).
28 Cf. Jobst, for instance (2008), 45.
29 Herlihy (1986), 79 f.
30 Rhinelander (1990), 89 f.
31 Here I draw on Noack (2000), especially 49–77.

32 Jobst (2017a), 93.
33 Cf. Meier F. (1991); Masud (1990).
34 Karpat (1984/1985) and Karpat (1986).
35 Lynch (1965), 162. In particular, the peninsula's wine, which attained world renown in the last quarter of the nineteenth century, was initially unsuccessful, since the prestigious grape varieties imported by foreign vintners had poor yields.
36 Neubauer H.-J. (1998), 13.
37 Lazzerini (1997), here 170.
38 Bloch (1963), here 43.

Chapter 24

1 Holderness (1823), 144.
2 Holderness (1823), 144 f.
3 Zelepos (2015).
4 Cf. for instance Meyer A. (2013).
5 Goethe (2005), Act 1 Scene 1, p. 1.
6 Filélliny (2018).
7 Cf. the very persuasive study by Zorin (2001), here the chapter "Russkie kak Greki" (Russians as Greeks), 31–64.
8 Here I draw on, *inter alia*, Zelepos (2007) and Jobst (2007b), 243–7. See also Chapter 21.
9 This figure too is only an estimate, since there are no valid statistics and contemporary counts do not distinguish between the peninsula itself and the regions to its north. The first census in the Russian Empire was not conducted until 1897. Here I draw on Magocsi (2014), 50 f.
10 Zelepos (2007), 619.
11 Safonov (1844), here 219.
12 Zelepos (2007), 619.
13 Jobst (2007b), 247.
14 Naimark (2008), 132.
15 Holderness (1823), 163.
16 Holderness (1823), 178: besides the autocephalous and Roman Catholic Armenians, Crimea was also inhabited by Arian Christians with roots in the peninsula.
17 Cf. Brandes D. (2007a), 433. The literature usually ignores the role the Gagauz played in this 'Bulgarian' immigration to Crimea. Brandes, on the other hand, expressly points to this group. We might ask to what extent the Russians were actually aware that they were distinct from Bulgarians, since Gagauz are also Orthodox Christian. However, this Turkic people speaks Gagauz, which is closely related to Ottoman Turkish.

18. This area roughly comprises the south of today's Ukraine, including historical Bessarabia and parts of eastern Ukraine and southern Russia bordering the Sea of Azov and the Black Sea. At the time, it included the Governorates of Kherson (with Odesa), Ekaterinoslav and Taurida.
19. Neutatz (1993), 23 f.
20. Neutatz (1993), 258 f.
21. Myeshkov (2008), 24 f.
22. Brandes D. (2007b), 514, states that only 0.75 per cent of the Germans in the tsarist empire converted to Orthodoxy; the German settlers were thus particularly unwilling to integrate. However, this certainly did not mean a lack of loyalty to the dynasty and the empire.
23. Holderness (1823), 162.
24. Myeshkov (2008), 348.
25. Cf. for instance the travel report Elpat'evskii (1998), 62 f.
26. Brandes D. (2007c), 1065.
27. Holderness (1823), 126.
28. Holderness (1823), 178. Due to the abovementioned lack of data, this figure cannot be verified, but it seems to be extremely generous.
29. Here I draw on Kizilov (2007/2008).
30. Holderness (1823), 178.
31. For an introduction, cf. Schur (1992); Szyszman (1989).
32. Ascherson (2015), 22.
33. Perevodshchikov (1853), 16.
34. Jobst (2007b), 244.
35. Williams (2001), 177 and 173 f.
36. Neutatz (1993), 31–33.
37. Pinson (1970), 4 f. Neutatz (1993), 32, on the other hand, writes of successful settlement by Bulgarians.
38. Kratkii otchet (1868), 354.
39. On the economic aspirations immediately after the annexation, cf. Jobst (2007b), 118 f. On the economic situation in the first decades of tsarist rule, cf. Lynch (1965).
40. Cf. Ezhov et al. (2016) and Mal'gin (2006).
41. Baumgart (1972), 122.
42. Petrov (2004).
43. Diulichev (2006), 145.

Chapter 25

1. Tolstoï (1888 [1855–6]), 32–4. Cf. also the more recent translation, *The Sebastopol Sketches*, by David McDuff (Tolstoy (1936 [1855–6]).

2   Tennyson (1910), 267–8.
3   Krahé (1998); Tate (2003).
4   Iron Maiden (2009).
5   Cf. the proceedings of the conference "Der Wiener Kongress und seine Folgen" (The Congress of Vienna and Its Consequences) held in Coburg in 2015: Tagungsbericht (2015).
6   German remembrance policy also prioritizes the World Wars – especially the Second World War started by the German Reich – due to the civilizational rupture of the Shoah.
7   There is an extraordinary abundance of research on the Crimean War – and it has been significantly influenced by German-speaking historians such as Winfried Baumgart: Baumgart (1972) and his several volumes of edited documents: Baumgart (1979 ff.). Cf. also Seaton (1977); Wetzel (1985); Tarle (1959); Goldfrank (1994); Palmer (1987) and Figes (2010), who emphasizes the conflict's religious aspect.
8   While one of Britain's claims was that it was protecting the Ottoman Jews and other groups, France claimed to protect the Catholics, while the Russian Empire claimed it was protecting the Orthodox subjects of the sultan.
9   Treue (1980), 137.
10 Daniel U. (2006), 44.
11 Keller (2001), xii.
12 On Russell, cf. Royle (1987).
13 Gernsheim and Gernsheim (1954).
14 For instance Schieder (1977), 88.
15 Cf. Edgerton (1999), 1–3. The Crimean War was the first to see the use of steamships and mines, and the first plans were made to use chemical weapons and submarines. Moreover, until the First World War, no war had involved so many losses.
16 Nieuważny (2011).
17 Wetzel (1985), 159.
18 Keller (2001), 177.
19 For an introduction, cf. Curtiss (1966); Mienert (2000).
20 Cf. Machaev (1914). On today's veneration for Bakunina as the "pride of the soil of Tver", cf. Morozov (2016).
21 Jobst (2007b), on the panorama as an artform in general and on the Sevastopol' panorama in particular, 373–6, here 374.
22 Cf. the standard work by Wegner (2002).
23 A period of reforms throughout the Ottoman Empire had begun in 1839.
24 Cf. for instance Beyrau et al. (1996).

Chapter 26

1. Twain (1869), n.p.
2. On Twain's tour of Russia and his attitude on the tsarist empire, cf. Fuchs (2011).
3. On the genesis of the myth of Sevastopol' in the Russian and Soviet politics of memory, cf. Plokhy (2000).
4. Cf. Semin (1955), 152–69, who provides an overview of the remembrance measures begun from within the ranks of "the people" immediately after the "oborona" (defence) had ended. In terms typical of the times, he described the measures to honour the fallen initiated by the administration and the tsarist dynasty as "hypocritical", 154 f.
5. Tarle (1954).
6. Vaneev (1983), 22.
7. Sasse (2007), 229.
8. Jena (2001), 188; on Potemkin's involvement in the city's founding, cf. especially 188–90.
9. According to Seaton (1977), 106, the population had even increased to 45,000 by 1854. This is presumably due to the higher number of military men stationed there in wartime.
10. Cf. Jobst (2007b), 354–67 and 380–406.
11. Viazmitinov (1882), 62.
12. Schweiger-Lerchenfeld (1887), 204.
13. Markevich (1994). This did not change until the work of Mara Kozelsky, on which I draw in the following. Cf. especially Kozelsky (2018).
14. Kozelsky (2014), 168 f.
15. Kozelsky (2014), 168 f.
16. Gertsen (1861), 973.
17. Figes (2010), 339.
18. Gertsen (1861), 973 f. Cf. also Jobst (2007b), 239–43.
19. Kozelsky (2010), 168 f.
20. Jobst (2007b), 236.
21. Markevich (1994), 18–23.
22. Gertsen (1861), 974.
23. Figes (2010), 344.
24. Cf. Trustam (1984), 175, and Edgerton (1999), 142.
25. For discussion of the topos of rape, cf. Burgess-Jackson (1996), especially 43–64. For a systematization of the categories of nationalism, sexuality and rape in war, cf. Pryke (1998).
26. Senner (1999), here 137 and 145.
27. Baumgart (1972), 11.

28 Baumgart (1972), 116
29 According to Wegner (2002), xxiv, this is the reason behind many peace agreements.
30 Baumgart (1972), 123.
31 Gorizontov (2012), 66.
32 Cf. the text of the Treaty of Paris and its appendices in: Traité (1856).
33 Figes (2010), 432.
34 Treaty of Paris (1856).
35 Pinson (1970).

Chapter 27

1 Kinsky and Chalmers (2015), 81.
2 Cf. besides Wolff (1994) and Jobst (2013b).
3 Moon (2001).
4 On the consequences in the field of law, cf. Kirmse (2013).
5 Cf. Jobst (2007b), 403–06.
6 Baumgart (1972), 122.
7 Cf. Jaworski (2014), 19.
8 On the many travel reports on Crimea in Russian, cf. Nepomniashchii (1999).
9 Telesko (2014).
10 For an overview, cf. Usyskin (2000); McReynolds (2003).
11 Mal'gin (2006), 100.
12 On the first decades under Russian rule, cf. Lynch (1965).
13 Cf. the contemporary report Kratkii otchet (1868).
14 Cf. Böröcz (1992).
15 Apart from Russians, the majority of them were probably German and French, but Poles such as K. Kaczkowski also toured the peninsula and left us with reports: Kaczkowski (1829).
16 Oliphant (1854). Cf. also his biography by Taylor (1982).
17 N. Kalinin and Zemlianichenko (1993), 122–4.
18 For the decree's wording, cf. Dekret SNK (1920).
19 Fisher (1978), 99.
20 Cf. Jobst (2007b), 340.
21 Cf. Mal'gin (2006), 95–6.
22 Mal'gin (2006), 105.
23 Fuhs (1992), 173.
24 Mazurevskii (1845), here 27.
25 Markov (1994), 245.

Chapter 28

1. Vesti (1863), 242 f.
2. Vesti (1863), 245.
3. Vesti (1863), 242.
4. Lazzerini (1988), 136.
5. Fisher (1978), 96 f.
6. Kirimli S. (1990), 29–39.
7. Cit. Kirimli S. (1990), 39.
8. Cf. Davies F. (2013), 165 f.
9. For instance Platon A. Zubov, governor general of Novorossia and confidant of Tsarina Catherine II (1767–1822). Cf. Kirpenko (1897)
10. Cf. Fisher (1978), 88, and Zenkovsky (1960), 124 f.
11. Jobst (2010).
12. Cf. Jobst (2007b), 202–04.
13. Gol'denberg (1883), 84 f.
14. On the history of literacy in the Russian Empire, cf. Brooks (1985).
15. For a detailed account, cf. Noack (2000).
16. Lazzerini (1997), 177.
17. Meyer J. (2014), 21.
18. On Gaspıralı' biography, cf. Lazzerini (1973).
19. Most recently Tuna (2015).
20. Hofmeister (2017), especially 124 and 135.
21. First edition: Gasprinskii (1881).
22. Terciman also had subscribers in the Ottoman Empire and even in India; cf. Fisher (1978), 103.
23. Cf. Bennigsen and Lemercier-Quelquejay (1964), 35–46.
24. Noack (2000), 147 f.
25. His daughter Şefiqa Gaspıralı (Crimean Tatar; Russian: Shefika Gasprinskaia; 1886–1975) was one of his closest colleagues and the editor of several magazines devised for a female readership. Unfortunately there are no satisfying studies in Western and Slavic languages, but cf. Gankevich (1994); Hablemitoğlu and Hablemitoğlu (1998).
26. Noack (2000), 150.
27. Cf. for instance Gankevich and Shendrikova (2008).
28. Hofmeister (2017), 124–8.
29. Kirimli H. (1993), here 534.
30. Kappeler (1993), 196.
31. Williams (2001), 190.
32. Jobst (2017a), 101.

33 According to international law, then still in its infancy, the Crimean Tatar population is to be considered an indigenous or autochthonous nationality. Cf. United Nations (2007). Cf. also United Nations (2013), 6: "Indigenous communities, peoples and nations are those which, having a historical continuity with pre-invasion and pre-colonial societies that developed on their territories, consider themselves distinct from other sectors of the societies now prevailing on those territories, or parts of them. They form at present non-dominant sectors of society and are determined to preserve, develop and transmit to future generations their ancestral territories, and their ethnic identity, as the basis of their continued existence as peoples, in accordance with their own cultural patterns, social institutions and legal system."

34 Slocum (1998).

Chapter 29

1 Pis'mo (1983), 107.
2 Cf. for instance Vaneev (1983), 12.
3 Smolin (2012), 165 f.
4 For an example of a positive assessment of Golikov, cf. Tiuliakov (2014).
5 The scene can be watched at: http://cinema.arte.tv/de/artikel/die-treppenszene-aus-panzerkreuzer-potemkin (accessed 14 March 2018).
6 On the status of research on the revolution of 1905, cf. especially Kusber (2007). Cf. also Ascher (1988/1994).
7 On the various sites of the revolution, cf. the edited collection Frings and Kusber (2007) and for instance Tych (1990).
8 Cf. the publication by Melvin (2017), which is more suitable for military history enthusiasts.
9 Cf. for instance Polkanov (1936). Cf. also Jobst (2017b), 166.
10 Without claiming to be exhaustive, the Russian *Wikipedia* entry on Smidt names over fifty cities in the former Soviet Union in which he is commemorated with a street name, a monument or a plaque: Shmidt (2018). Cf. also Qualls (2009), 138.
11 Osterhammel (2009), 402.
12 Vozgrin (1992), 362.
13 Neutatz (2013), 111.
14 Tatar peasants in the Volga region took a similar stance; cf. Noack (2000), 235.
15 Vozgrin (1992), 363 f., emphasizes that Crimean Tatars were not involved in anti-Semitic excesses, adding that in one case, a Tatar cavalry unit was deployed to break up the "Pogromshchiki" (pogromists).
16 Fisher (1978), 104.
17 Magocsi (2014), 75 f.

18 Pekesen (2014).
19 Lazzerini (1997), 177.
20 For detailed discussion, cf. Noack (2000), 256 f.
21 The elections for the Third Duma were also restructured to the disadvantage of national minorities.
22 Williams (2001), 320.
23 Noack (2000), 258.
24 Williams (2001), 320.
25 Williams (2001), 321 f.
26 Fisher (1978), 104.
27 Noack (2000), 254.
28 Fisher (1978), 106; Vozgrin (1992), 381.
29 Cf. the two short biographies in Kogonashvili (1995), 252 and 310.
30 Cf. the standard work by Adam (2002).
31 For more extensive discussion, cf. Kirimli S. (1990), 102–4.
32 Bowman (2005).
33 Cf. Adam (2002), 194 f. and 428–48.
34 Williams (2001), 325.
35 Adam (2002), 94.

Chapter 30

1 Sultan-Galiev (1997).
2 Sultan-Galiev (1997).
3 Jobst (2001c), here 103.
4 Zhiromskaia (2004).
5 It was committed in April 1918 by the German imperial army and troops of the Ukrainian People's Republic (UNR), which was also short-lived.
6 Cf. Litvin (1995), 81, who refrains from naming more specific figures due to the paucity of sources.
7 Snyder (2010).
8 Schnell (2012), 12.
9 There is not space here to present the plethora of opinions on Snyder's *Bloodlands*. For a representative account, cf. Forum (2012); Hagen (2014).
10 Opfer (2014); Overmans (2014), 665, estimates that the tsarist army lost some 1.8 million soldiers.
11 Hildermeier (2017).
12 For extensive discussion, cf. Jobst (2017a).
13 Cf. the blurb to Aust (2017).

14 He was arrested again in 1928 and spent six years in prison. In 1937 he was remanded once more in the course of the Great Purges, and was executed in 1940: Bucher-Dinc (1997).
15 Sultan-Galiev (1997).
16 Cf. the solid study by Pusat (2017).
17 Cf. Martin (2001).
18 Cf. Guboglo and Chervonnaia (1992); Dekret (1918); Postanovlenie (1922).
19 Magocsi (2014), 81. It is striking that for most studies, the years between 1914 and 1916 are hardly worth mentioning. The First World War usually 'begins' with the February Revolution; cf. for instance the discussion under the heading "Zatish'e' pered burei" (The Calm Before the Storm) in Vozgrin (1992), 382 f.
20 On the situation of the Russian Mennonites during the First World War, which has only been researched in part to date, cf. Nelipovič (2016), 361 f. During the war, Mennonites, including those from the Taurida Governorate, were primarily deployed in building roads and as medics.
21 Davies F. (2016), 215 f.
22 Davies F. (2016), 254.
23 Cf. for instance Suny (1972); Raleigh (1986); Figes (1989); Penter (2000).
24 Here I primarily draw on Jobst (2001c).
25 Cf. for instance Penter (2000).
26 Korolev (1993), 25.
27 Jobst (2001c), 90.
28 Cf. the nationalist text Kirimal (1952), 35–9.
29 For details, cf. Jobst (2001c), 90–2.
30 Aktschura Oglu (1916), 3 and 11.
31 This also holds for the tsarist empire, which sought the support of the so-called Russophiles in the Austrian crown land of Galicia and Lodomeria in the years leading up to the First World War, although it considered the Austrian Ukrainians part of the Russian people. On the corresponding policy of the German Empire, cf. Zetterberg (1978). Çelebicihan and Seydahmet Qırımer were also active in this organization funded by Berlin's Ministry for Foreign Affairs (*Auswärtiges Amt*).
32 Berlin had significant plans concerning Crimea; cf. for instance Golczewski (2010), 27–346.
33 Baumgart (1966).
34 There had been controversies at a congress of Muslims in Russia held in May 1917: representatives (around 200 of the *c*. 900 delegates were female) of the closed territories such as Crimea argued for national territorial regional bodies, while others preferred extra-territorial cultural autonomy within a reformed Russia. For detailed discussion of the congress, cf. Fenz (2000), 100–14.
35 Jobst (2001c), 92–4.
36 Here I draw on Jobst (2001b), 216 f.
37 Jobst (2001b), 216.

38 Presumably this will not have changed the Crimean Tatars' lifeworlds, however. At the congress itself, women remained heavily underrepresented, with four female delegates out of a total of seventy-six.
39 Cf. the full-length text in German and Turkish in Kirimal (1952), 107–14.
40 Jobst (2001b), 217.
41 Cf. for instance Seïdahmet (1921), 75.
42 Fisher (1978), 118.
43 Magocsi (2014), 86.
44 Vaneev (1983), 19.
45 Pipes (1997), 186 f.
46 Baumgart (1966), 532.
47 On the issue of the fleet, cf. the contemporary assessment of Pavlo Skoropads'kyis: Skoropads'kyi (1999), 209 f., especially notes 338 and 339.
48 Cf. Jobst (2001c), 96.
49 The Het'man State was the successor state to the UNR.
50 On the German occupation of Ukraine, cf. Mark (1993), 181–7; Jobst (2001b), 222–4; Kirimal (1952), 181 f. and note 731.
51 Seidahmet Krym (1930), 110.
52 Arslan-Bej (1932), here 249.
53 Cf. for instance Vaneev (1983), 16 f. The Turkish name for the *Goeben* was the *Yavuz Sultan Selim*.
54 Here and in the following I draw primarily on Jobst (2001b), 223–8.
55 Earlier, a – socialist – Ukrainian state had been demanded by Iuliian Bachyns'kyi in 1897, in the journal *Ukraïna Irredenta* in 1897: Jobst (1997).
56 Doroshenko (1923), 35.
57 Ansprüche (1918).
58 For an introduction, cf. Puschner (2013).
59 Neutatz (1993), 437.
60 Jobst (2001c), 100.
61 Deutsche Zeitung (1918).
62 Jobst (2001c), 101.
63 The Crimean Soviet Socialist Republic (*Krymskaia Sovetskaia Sotsialisticheskaia Respublika*) existed for around eight weeks before the Whites' Volunteer Army put an end to it.
64 Éndel' (2014).

Chapter 31

1 Zoshchenko (1937), 231.
2 Scatton (1993).

3   Soschtschenko (2010), 266.
4   Soschtschenko (2010), 271.
5   Cf. Liebich (1997).
6   Martin (2001), 183: "By encouraging the growth of national identity and resolutely opposing assimilation, the Soviet government showed an ostentatious and unthreatening respect for the national identity of all non-Russians." Cf. also Slezkine (1994).
7   Uehling (2015). Cf. also Uehling (2004), who begins her examination with the observation that "The Soviet authorities began committing crimes against Crimean Tatars from the time they got control of Crimea."
8   Dufaud (2012b), 258 f.
9   Dufaud (2012a), 105: Formally, all national sections were on the same level below the local committee of the Communist Party, but "[i]n reality, the Tatar office enjoyed pre-eminence because of the activity of Tatar spokesmen who had succeeded in having 'the indigeneity' of their home group admitted".
10 Pipes devoted considerable attention to this subject in the 1950s; on the development of the nationalities question from Marx and Engels to Lenin and Stalin via the Austro-Marxists, cf. especially Pipes (1997) 29–49.
11 Stalin (1942 [1913]), 9–10.
12 There were over twenty autonomous republics before the Second World War. Besides the Crimean ASSR, republics without ethnonyms were the Naxçıvan ASSR (Azerbaijani; Russian: Nakhichevan'), Turkestan (until 1924) and Dagestan (until 1991).
13 Cf. Martin (2001), 5.
14 Dufaud (2012b), 267.
15 Dufaud (2012b), 264.
16 Cf. Bogomolov et al. (2010), especially 77–88.
17 Cf. Williams (2001), 355 f.; Magocsi (2014), 107.
18 Cf. Fisher (1978), 136.
19 Cf. Hildermeier (1998), 203.
20 Cf. Williams (2001), 351 f.
21 Cf. Lemercier-Quelquejay (1968), 23.
22 Today, the famine of the early 1930s is often incorrectly portrayed as an event that exclusively affected Ukraine; the Holodomor (Ukrainian; death by starvation) is one of the country's core sources of remembrance. Cf. Jobst (2015b), the chapter "Das ukrainische 'Traumagedächtnis'. Holodomor und Čornobyl'" (The Ukrainian 'Trauma Memory'. Holodomor and Chornobyl'"), 234–52.
23 Contrary to Kirimal (1952), 288, who assumes that the Bolsheviks didn't allow any foreign aid into Crimea.
24 Cf. for instance Patenaude (2002).
25 It is difficult to say how many victims there were, insofar as actors usually state the highest possible figures in order to emphasize the enemy's cruelty. It is

estimated that up to 10 million died of starvation Union-wide; Fisher (1978), 137, writes that Crimea lost around 21 per cent of its population, but this includes not only deaths but also refugees. It is not possible to state this percentage in numbers, since the first Soviet census took place in 1926 and for a number of reasons, the last ones in the tsarist empire cannot be used as comparative figures. According to the census of 1926, some 713,823 people lived in Crimea: Vsesoiuznaia perepis' (2006).

26 There are countless publications on the Holodomor. Here it must suffice to mention just two works examining different aspects, including in relation to the politics of memory and transethnic issues: Kas'ianov (2010); Sapper et al. (2004).

27 Cf. also Seydahamet (2005).

28 The number of victims in the context of the famine of 1932/33 is still controversially discussed. However, there is not sufficient space to discuss the debate here; the figures range from seven to eleven million deaths Union-wide.

29 Kindler (2018).

30 For greater detail, cf. Fisher (1978), 143–5, on whom I draw in the following.

31 Fisher (1978), 145.

32 Yalçiner et al. (2004).

33 Blavatskii (1977).

34 On the destruction and reconstruction of Alushta, cf. Zemletriasenie (2009).

35 Raab (2017), 40.

36 Breiden (1994).

37 Zoshchenko (1965 [1930]), 219.

38 Guski (2008), 73 f.

39 Brussilowski (1928), 442 f.

40 Raab (2017), 44, on whom I draw in the following (39–50).

41 Raab (2017), 47.

42 Dufaud (2012a), 123, reports that İbraimov was also charged with murder.

43 Cf. Jobst (2015b), 185 f.

44 Dufaud (2012a), 117.

45 Dufaud (2012a), 108.

46 For instance, in a dispute with the local secret police, then the (O]GPU (Ob"edinënnoe gosudarstvennoe politicheskoe upravlenie; Joint State Political Administration). Stalin personally intervened in İbraimov's favour after the GPU had ordered the execution of two Tatar peasants; cf. Dufaud (2012b), 269.

47 This is discussed extensively in the two cited studies by Dufaud.

48 As the Crimean Tatar diaspora politician Kirimal (1952), 29, argued, emphasizing the long tradition of Jewish–Tatar coexistence in Crimea. Indeed, there is no indication of an anti-Jewish stance on the part of İbraimov.

49 Fisher (1978), 141; Williams (2001), 360–8.

50 Williams (2001), 365.
51 Cf. the standard work by Kuchenbecker (2000), on the role of Crimea, cf. especially 91–112.
52 Magocsi (2014), 105 f.
53 Bogomolov et al. (2010), 88. These repressions peaked in 1937 with the arrest of 100 Muslim clerics, ninety-nine of whom are believed to have been executed.
54 Williams (2001), 368.
55 Kirimal (1952), 297–9.
56 Cf. Hirsch (2005).
57 Martin (2001), 13, points to the aggressive promotion "of symbolic markers of national identity".
58 For extensive discussion, cf. Williams (2001), 368 f.
59 Fisher (1978), 148.

Chapter 32

1 Surkov (1989), 137. The translation privileges content over form.
2 Koshka (2017).
3 Plokhy (2000), 372.
4 Pervaia perepis' (2018).
5 Cf. for instance Eisfeld and Herdt (1996). Cf. also the report by a Crimean German subjected to these repressions: Riss (2007/2008).
6 Kunz (2005), 16.
7 Kunz (2005), 27.
8 Crimean Tatar exiles were also involved in the anti-Soviet Prometheus movement supported by Poland; Copeaux (1993). Cf. also Gasimov (2011).
9 On the Crimean Tatar diaspora's transnational networks between the wars, cf. Gasimov (2017).
10 On this trip to Berlin, cf. Aydin (2002); Williams (2001), 377 f.
11 For instance, Kirimal, who remained in the Federal Republic of Germany after the war, had been, among other things, a member of the Waffen-SS. Cf. Roman'ko (2004). Cf. also Roman'ko (2011).
12 Kunz (2005), 18.
13 The previous commanding officer, Eugen Siegfried Erich Ritter von Schobert (1883–1941), had recently been killed in an accident.
14 Cf. for instance the apologetic interpretation by Erich von Manstein: Manstein (2004), 256–61.
15 Schramm (1982). For an assessment of Schramm, cf. Messerschmidt (2004).
16 In his military-historical, nationalist and apologetic study, the Russian author A.B. Shirokorad (2006), 233–48, examines Italy's role in the Crimean campaign, mainly by listing the material deployed. This chapter has an

interesting title: *Neobyknovennye prikliucheniia ital'iantsev v Rossii* (The Unusual Adventures of the Italians in Russia), recalling a comedy of 1974 that was very popular in the Soviet Union: *Neveroiatnye prikliucheniia ital'iantsev v Rossii* (The Unbelievable Adventures of the Italians in Russia).

17 Cf. Angrick (2003), especially 324–60.
18 Kunz (2005), 18 f.
19 Kunz (2005), 236.
20 For extensive discussion, cf. Wrochem (2006).
21 Cf. Bowman (2003).
22 Hürter (2012), 25.
23 Jobst (2017a), 106.
24 Cit. Kunz (2005), 65.
25 Kunz (2005), 66.
26 Hentig (2018).
27 Here I primarily draw on Kunz (2005), 179–204.
28 Cf. Struve (2015).
29 On this and on the occupation regime's anti-Semitic propaganda in Crimea, cf. Tyaglyy (2011).
30 Kunz (2005), 191.
31 Here I draw on Green (1984), 171. All figures refer to the period before 1941.
32 Feferman (2007), especially 104.
33 Cf. Green (1984), 172 f.
34 Feferman (2011), 283 f.
35 Cf. for instance Ascherson (2015), 23.
36 Feferman (2011), 284.
37 Kunz (2005), 190.
38 Feferman (2011), 285, writes of "hundreds of Karaites".
39 Kunz (2005), especially 133–54.
40 Kunz (2005), especially 109–32.

Chapter 33

1 I cite BertBrac's English translation of the original refrain in: Jamala (2017). The original goes: "Yaşlığıma toyalmadım/Men bu yerde yaşalmadım/ Yaşlığıma toyalmadım/Men bu yerde yaşalmadım".
2 Adler (2016). Cf. also Bayer (2016).
3 Cf. Uehling (2004).
4 Cf. besides Naimark (2008) Pohl (1999); Nekrich (1978); Deportationen (2012). All of these works also deal with the Crimean Tatar case.
5 Hromenko (2017), 97–106.

6 Khrushchev (1976 [1956]), 58.
7 Kunz (2005), 205.
8 Kunz (2005), 207. Kunz points out that little is known about collaboration by the non-Tatar population.
9 Hoffmann S. (1968), for instance, distinguished between involuntary collaboration (as reluctant recognition of its necessity) and voluntary collaboration (as an attempt to exploit the necessity of collaboration for one's own overarching ends).
10 Magocsi (2014), 111.
11 Hromenko (2017), 120.
12 Kreindler (1986), 391.
13 According to an article published in the Russian newspaper *Kommersant* after the annexation of 2014, some 35,000 Crimean Tatars served in the Soviet army between 1941 and 1944: Galustian et al. (2015). Hromenko (2017), 100, considers such a figure exaggerated, since as a rule only ten per cent of a nationality were mobilized.
14 Naimark (2002), 102.
15 Cf. for instance Krugosvetov (2016).
16 The museum's website was not accessible in October 2018, perhaps because it now serves as part of the Crimean Tatar Museum of Cultural Heritage (Simferopol'): https://krtmuseum.ru/muzej-dvazhdy-geroya-sovetskogo-soyuza-amet-hana-sultana-g-alupka/
17 Amet-Khan (2018).
18 Czerwonnaja and Malek (2017), 219.
19 Gnauck (2015).
20 The film *Haytarma* has been made available on YouTube by the Consulate of Ukraine in Edinburgh: https://www.youtube.com/watch?v=f181jS4_egs (accessed 9 September 2018).
21 Hromenko (2017), 107–17.

Chapter 34

1 Ulitskaya (2002 [1996]), 3.
2 Kasack (1997), 732.
3 Cf. for instance Fisher (1978), 167 f.
4 Williams (2001), 404.
5 Guboglo and Chervonnaia (1995), 39.
6 The first three-power conference had taken place in Teheran in 1943.
7 Here I draw on Troebst (2017), 344 f.
8 Plokhy (2017), 282, quite rightly points out the different assessments in Soviet historiography: while in the 1920s this agreement was still considered to have

strengthened the Tsardom and was thus seen in a negative light, later there were more positive assessments of the Russian Empire.

9 In the following I draw on Sasse (2007), especially 107–28, and on Plokhy (2017), 280–84.
10 Cf. Hromenko (2017), 198–203.
11 Shapoval (2009).
12 Potichnyj (1975), here 308.
13 Cf. for instance Subtelny (2000), 500.
14 Plokhy (2017), 283.
15 Cf. for instance (2015b), 199–201.
16 This does not hold for Sevastopol' after 1944; Qualls (2009) has largely closed this gap. Hitherto unmined source material on Moscow's economic policy towards Crimea in interplay with Kyiv has been concisely examined and assessed by Sasse (2007), especially 121–6.
17 Siegelbaum (2018); Qualls (2009), 109 f.
18 Qualls (2009), 1 f
19 Cf. Tymchenko (2014).
20 Diulichev (2006), 196 f.
21 Maksymenko (1990), 58.
22 Sasse (2007), 122 f.
23 Sasse (2007), 124.
24 Vaneev (1983), 22.
25 Cf. the discussion in Hromenko (2017), 178–203.
26 Cf. Jobst (2017b), 172 f.
27 Cf. Qualls (2009), 13.
28 Cf. Qualls (2009), 5.
29 On the development of Soviet tourism in general, cf. Koenker (2013).
30 For an introduction, cf. Furin and Rybinski (1975).
31 Cf. the website Artek (2018), which currently advertises the camp with the slogan "In the sunny city" ("V solnechnom gorode").
32 Cf. Kelly (2007), 548 f.
33 Winkelmann (2003).
34 During occupation, German companies were also involved in the brutal exploitation of local labour for tobacco production: Roth and Abraham (2011).
35 Cf. Sasse (2007), 123.
36 For an assessment of the campaign's consequences, cf. Latysh (2010).
37 Uehling (2004).
38 Marples and Duke (1995), 277.
39 Naimark (2008), 132.

40 Williams (2001), 391.
41 For the full-length text, cf. Fisher (1978), 179.
42 Naimark (2008), 133.
43 For Cemilev's biography, cf. for instance Williams (2001), 427–30, cit. 427.
44 Daniel A. (2016).
45 For the full-length speech in English translation, cf. Grigorenko (2018).
46 Cf. Williams (2001), 430–3.
47 For Ukraine, excluding the peninsula, cf. for instance Jobst (2011c). On the Soviet phenomenon of "eco-nationalism", cf. Dawson (1996).
48 Sasse (2007), 131 f.
49 For further details, cf. Sasse (2007), 133–40.
50 Cf. Magocsi (2014), 134 f.
51 On the role of the *Rukh* in the breakup of the USSR, cf. Haran and Prokoptschuk (2013).
52 Cf. Saal (2014); Peter and Wentker (2012).

Chapter 35

1 Pupchenko and Dremova (2007).
2 Luzhkov (2000), 5.
3 Kalnysh and Solov'ev (2008).
4 Kappeler (2014), 355. For the corresponding text, cf. for instance Memorandum (2014).
5 King (2010), here 319.
6 Klußmann (2014). In accordance with the treaty of 1997, Moscow had paid Kyiv only 98 million US dollars per annum, and hence the latter had demanded recompense.
7 Cf. the table (Appendix 1) in Sasse (2007), 275.
8 Cf. Williams (2001), 451.
9 Spannung (2003). For a detailed account, cf. Malek (2017), here 168–77.
10 Cf. for instance D'Anieri (2011).
11 Cf. Sasse (2007), 263.
12 Kappeler (2014), 253.
13 Here I draw on Malek (2017), especially 181–91.
14 Pro-Russia Groups (2010).
15 Malek (2017), 182 f.
16 Marples and Duke (1995), 276.
17 Sasse (2010), 115.
18 King (2010), 328.

19 Cf. Jobst (2015b), 260 f.
20 Sasse (2010), 105.

Chapter 36

1   Clancy and Greaney (2013), 200–1. Clancy often collaborated with a co-author, in this case Greaney
2   In the words of President Putin in the programme *Krym* (2017), first broadcast by the Russian station Rossiia 1 on 15 March 2015.
3   Krekeler (2014).
4   Clancy and Greaney (2013), 464.
5   Kappeler (2014), 346. Cf. also *idem* 338–51 on Euromaidan.
6   Schmidt (2014).
7   Kappeler (2014), 352, assumes that over half of the Ukrainian soldiers stationed in Crimea had entered into Russian service by 24 March 2014.
8   For a profile of Aksenov, cf. Shuster (2014).
9   Kiew (2014)
10 Krymskii krizis (2018).
11 For an assessment of the appropriation of Crimea in 2014 by experts on international law, cf. Luchterhandt (2014).
12 Here and in the following Putin (2014).
13 Clancy and Greaney (2013), 201 f.
14 Jobst (2015b), 260 f.
15 For an overview, cf. Klein M. (2010).
16 Hipp (2014).
17 Charter (2021), Article 2(4).
18 Gall (2015).
19 Russland-Politik (2014); Krim-Krise (2014).
20 Gesellschaft für bedrohte Völker (2017), 7.
21 Eichhofer (2014).
22 Halbach (2014).
23 On Turkey's stance in the Crimean crisis, cf. Gasimov (2014).
24 Cf. Gesellschaft für bedrohte Völker (2017), 7 f.
25 Krymskii telekanal (2015).
26 I draw on Malek (2017), 192–196, and Halbach (2014).
27 Rubljow (2017).
28 Malek (2017), 196 f.
29 Halbach (2014).
30 Crimea blockade (2017).

31 Kappeler (2014), 354.
32 Birger (2015). Building a bridge was discussed before the First World War. In the Second World War, both German and later Soviet actors attempted to build one. The German bridge was blown up by the Wehrmacht in 1943, and the hastily erected Soviet construction collapsed in February 1944 under the pressure of ice masses. Cf. for instance Hoppe (2016).
33 Romashchenko et al. (2018).
34 Esch (2018).
35 On the sequence of events, cf. for instance Ballin (2018). Cf. also the piece by Stomporowski (2018), who observes "prejudgment" of the Russian side by German politicians and media; on the whole, the article is well-researched and knowledgeable but clearly seeks to promote understanding for Russia, also attacking the critical stance towards Moscow adopted by the German green party (Die Grünen) and NATO's activities in the region.
36 It is not yet clear what strategy Zelens'kyi will ultimately pursue with regard to Crimea, although he has repeatedly offered dialogue with Russia without deviating from his demands that Crimea be returned to Ukraine.
37 Krim (2016).
38 Halbach (2014).

Postscript

1 The Gesellschaft für deutsche Sprache (Society for the German Language, GfdS) in Wiesbaden chose "Zeitenwende" as its "Word of the Year"; cf. Gerke (2022). The term, originally denoting the beginning of the AD period, was used by German federal chancellor Olaf Scholz in his speech to the Bundestag on 27 February 2022 with reference to the historical caesura represented by Russia's invasion of Ukraine and the war in Eastern Europe. It is not the first military conflict in the region since the 1990s, although Russia's President Putin has euphemistically termed it a "special operation" ("Spetsoperatsiia").
2 Statistica (2022), ratings as of 20 December 2022.
3 By way of comparison: the UK scored 93, the USA 83. Only three countries in this global ranking received all 100 points: Sweden, Norway and Finland. Cf. Freedom House (2022).
4 Tyshchenko (2017).
5 Barth (2022).
6 Klug (2022). For the backstory, cf. Latschan (2022).
7 Ukraine Analytica (2021).

SOURCES AND BIBLIOGRAPHY

Sources

Aktschura Oglu (1916): Jussuf Aktschura Oglu (i.e. Yosıf Aqçura), *Die gegenwärtige Lage der mohammedanischen Turko-Tataren Russlands und ihre Bestrebungen*, Berne.

Anonyma (1855): Anonyma, *The Crimea. Its Towns, Inhabitants and Social Customs by a Lady, Resident near the Alma*, London.

Ansprüche (1918): "Ansprüche der Sowjetregierung", *Der Neue Orient*, 2, 4:21.

Arneth (1869): Alfred Ritter von Arneth (ed.), Joseph II. und Katharina von Rußland. Ihr Briefwechsel, Vienna.

Auzépy (2006): M.-F. Auzépy, "La vie de Jean de Gothie (BHG 891)", in: C. Zuckermann (ed.), *La Crimée entre Byzance et le Khaganat khazar*, Paris, 69–85.

Baumgart (1979 ff.): Winfried Baumgart (ed.), *Akten zur Geschichte des Krimkriegs*, Munich/Vienna.

Beauplan (1993 [1780]): Guillaume Le Vasseur, Sieur de Beauplan, *A Description of Ukraine,* translated and with an Introduction by Andrew B. Pernal and Dennis F. Essar, Cambridge, MA. (French: Guillaume Levasseur de Beauplan, *Description d'Ukraine qui sont plusieurs Provinces du Royaume de Pologne contenuës depuis les confins de la Moscouie, iusques aux limites de la Transilvanie, ensemble levrs moevrs, façons de viuns, et de faire la guerre*, Rouen, 1650).

Berezhkov (1891): *Mikhail N. Berezhkov, Plan zavoevaniia Kryma, sostavlennyi v tsarstvovanie Gosudaria Alekseia Mikhailovicha uchenym slavianinom Iuriem Krizhanichem* [Plan for the Conquest of Crimea, Drawn Up During the Reign of the Ruler Aleksei Mikhailovich by the Learned Slav Iurii Krizhanich], St Petersburg.

Besse (1838): Jean-Charles de Besse, *Voyage en Crimée, au Caucase, en Géorgie, en Arménie, en Asie-Mineure et à Constantinopel en 1829–1833. Pour servir à l'histoire de Hongrie*, Paris

Billbassof (1897): B. von Billbassof (i.e. Bil'basov), *Katharina II. Kaiserin von Rußland im Urtheile der Weltliteratur*, 2 vols., Berlin.

Broniovius (1867): Martinus Broniovius, "Opisanie Kryma (Tartariae Descriptio) Martina Broneskago" [A Description of Crimea (Description of the Tatars) by Martinus Broniovius], translated by I.G. Shershenevich and I.I. Murzakevich, in: ZIOOIiD, 24, Volume 6, 333–67.

Broniovius (2011): Martinus Broniovius, *"Tartariae descriptio". Text und Übersetzung*, in: Albrecht and Herdick (2011), 45–122.

Brussilowski (1928): L. Brussilowski, "Beeinflussung der neuropsychischen Sphäre durch das Erdbeben in der Krim 1927", in: *Zeitschrift für die gesamte Neurologie und Psychiatrie*, 18, 116:1, 442–70.

Collections (1906): "Collections out of Martin Broniovius de Biezerfedea Sent Ambassadour from Stephen King of Poland, to the Crim Tatar. Contayning a Description of Tartaria, or Chersonesus Taurica, and the Regions Subject to the Perecop or Crim Tatars, with their Customs Private and Public in Peace and War", in: Samuel Purchas, *Hakluytus Posthumus or Purchas His Pilgrims. Contayning a History of the World in Sea Voyages and Lande Travells by Englishmen and Others*, Volume 13, Glasgow, 461–91.

Constantine (1985): Constantine Porphyrogenitus, *De Administrando Imperio*, Greek text edited by Gy. Moravcsik, English translation by R.J.H. Jenkins. New, revised edition, 2nd imprint. Dumbarton Oaks Center for Byzantine Studies, Washington, DC.

Craven (1789): Elizabeth Craven, *A Journey through the Crimea and Constantinople*, Dublin (reprint New York 1970).

Dekret (1918): "Dekret vserossiiskogo tsentral'nogo ispolnitel'nogo komiteta i soveta narodnykh komissarov RSFSR ob avtonomnoi krymskoi sovetskoi sotsialisticheskoi respublike" [Decree of the All-Russian Central Executive Committee of the Council of People's Commissars of the RSFSR on the Crimean Autonomous Soviet Socialist Republic], 18 October 1918, in: Guboglo and Chervonnaia (1992), 37–9.

Dekret SNK (1920): "21 dekabria. Dekret SNK ob ispol'zovanii Kryma dlia lecheniia trudiashchikhsia" [Decree of the SNK on the Use of Crimea for the Medical Treatment of the Workers], in: *Izvestiia* [News], No. 288, 22 December 1920, 59–61. Online: http://docs.historyrussia.org/ru/nodes/12796 - 21-dekabrya-dekret-snk- ob-ispolzovanii-kryma-dlya-lecheniya-trudyaschihsya#mode/inspect/page/3/zoom/4 (accessed 21 August 2018).

Deutsche Zeitung (1918): *Deutsche Zeitung für die Krim und Taurien*, 11 September 1918, No. 9.

Doroshenko (1923): *Dmytro Doroshenko, Moi spomyny pro nedavne-mynule. Doba Het'manshchyny 1918* [My Memories of the Recent Past. The Time of the Het'manate in 1918], L'viv.

Eberhard (1779): Johann August Eberhard, *Lobschrift auf Herrn Johann Thunmann, Prof. der Weltweisheit und Beredsamkeit auf der Universität zu Halle*, Halle. Online: http:// digitale.bibliothek.uni-halle.de/vd18/content/titleinfo/1657901 (accessed 20 February 2018).

Elbin (1979): Günter Elbin (ed.), *Literat und Feldmarschall. Briefe und Erinnerungen des Fürsten Charles Joseph de Ligne*, Stuttgart.

Elpat'evskii (1998): *Sergei Elpat'evskii, Krymskie ocherki god 1913-i. Vstupitel'noe slovo, primechaniia Dmitriia Loseva* [Crimean Sketches from the Year 1913. Introduction and Notes by Dmitrii Losev], Feodosiia.

Erzählung (2003): "Die Erzählung des Matthaios von der Stadt Theodoro, übersetzt und eingeleitet von Hans-Veit Beyer. Mit einer Appendix zum Vat.gr. 952 von Peter Schreiner", in: *Byzantinische Zeitschrift*, 96:1, 25–57.

Eusebius (2007): Eusebius von Caesarea, *De vita Constantini. Über das Leben Konstantins*, with an introduction by B. Bleckmann. Trans. and commentary by H. Schneider, Turnhout.

Evliya (1934): Evliya Çelebi, *Narrative of Travels in Europe, Asia, and Africa, in the Seventeenth Century. Translated from the Turkish by the Ritter Joseph von Hammer*, Volume 1. London.

Forma manifesta (1896): "1771 god. No. 2044. Marta 21. Forma manifesta k krymskim tataram ot imeni kn. Dolgorukova, po povodu vstupleniia v Krym ego armii" [Year 1771. No. 2044. 21 March. Form of the Manifest to the Crimean Tatars in the Name of Prince Dolgorukov, On the Occasion of His Army's Entry into Crimea], in: SIRIO, March 97, St Petersburg, 245 f.

Gabaev (1913): Georgii Gabaev, "Krymskie tatary pod russkimi znamenami. Kratkaia istoricheskaia spravka" [The Crimean Tatars under Russian Flags. A Brief Historical Letter], in: ZhIRVIO, 68:3, 131–7.

Gasprinskii (1881): Ismail Gasprinskii, Russkoe musul'manstvo. Mysli, zametki i nabliudeniia [Russian Islam. Thoughts, Notes and Observations], Simferopol'.

Gavril (1844): Arkhiepiskop Khersonskii i Tavricheskii Gavril, "Pereselenie grekov iz Kryma v azovskuiu guberniiu i osnovanie Gotfiiskoi i Kafiiskoi eparkhii" [The Resettlement of the Greeks from Crimea to the Azov Governorate and the Foundation of the Gotfisk and Kafisk Eparchy], in: ZIOOIiD, 1, 197–204.

Gertsen (1861): Aleksandr Gertsen, "Gonenie na krymskikh Tatar" [The Persecution of the Crimean Tatars], in: KOL, 22 December 1861, No. 117, 973–977.

Glavnoe Arkhivnoe upravlenie (1983): Glavnoe Arkhivnoe upravlenie pri sovete ministrov USSR et al. (eds.), *Sevastopoliu 200 let 1783–1983. Sbornik dokumentov i materialov* [200 Years of Sevastopol' 1783–1983. Collection of Documents and Materials], Kyiv.

Gol'denberg (1883): M. Gol'denberg, Krym i krymskie tatary [Crimea and the Crimean Tatars], in: VE, 18 No. 11, 67–89.

Grigorenko (2018): "Speech of Petro Grigorenko to Crimean Tatars. 1968", in: International Committee for Crimea. Online: http://www.iccrimea.org/surgun/grigorenko.html (accessed 5 August 2018).

Guboglo and Chervonnaia (1992): M.N. Guboglo and S.M. Chervonnaia (eds.), *Krymskotatarskoe natsional'noe dvizhenie* [The Crimean Tatar National Movement], Volume 2: *Dokumenty, materialy, khronika* [Documents, Materials, Chronology], Moscow.

Hammer-Purgstall (1970): Joseph von Hammer-Purgstall, *Geschichte der Chane der Krim unter osmanischer Herrschaft vom 15. Jahrhundert bis zum Ende des 18. Jahrhunderts. Als Anhang zur Geschichte des Osmanischen Reichs zusammengetragen aus türkischen Quellen, mit Literatur- Übersetzungen und Anmerkungen, mit der Zugabe eines Gasels von Schahingerai, Türkisch und Deutsch*, St. Leonards/Amsterdam (Reprint of the edition published in Vienna in 1856).

Helbig (1804): G.A W. von Helbig, *Potomkin. Ein interessanter Beitrag zur Regierungsgeschichte Katharinas der Zweiten*, Leipzig.

Hentig (2018): "Dok. 07–156, Werner Otto von Hentig an das Auswärtige Amt in Berlin, 8. 04. 1942. Ich fürchte, daß ich Sie mit dem ersten Bericht enttäuschen muß", in: *Die Quellen sprechen. Die Verfolgung und Ermordung der europäischen Juden durch das nationalsozialistische Deutschland 1933–1945. Eine dokumentarische Höredition* (audio file). Online: http://die-quellen-sprechen.de/07 – 156.html (accessed 9 September 2018).

Herodotus (2008): *The History of Herodotus*. Translated into English by G.C. Macaulay. Volume 1. Online: http://www.gutenberg.org/files/2707/2707-h/2707-h.htm#link42H_4_0001 (accessed 11 April 2023).

Holderness (1823): Mary Holderness, *New Russia. Journey from Riga to the Crimea by Way of Kiew with some Account of the Colonization, and the Manners and Customs of the Colonists of New Russia, to Which are Added Notes Relating to the Crim Tatars*, London.

Iastrebov (1883): V. Iastrebov, "Khersones Tavricheskii" [Tauric Chersonesus], in: KS, 2:5 30–8.

Jochmann (1980): Werner Jochmann (ed.), *Adolf Hitler. Monologe im Führerhauptquartier 1941–1944. Die Aufzeichnungen Heinrich Heims*, Hamburg.

Jordanes (1915): *The Gothic History of Jordanes*, in English Version with an Introduction and a Commentary by Charles Christopher Mierow, Princeton, 1915. Online: http://ia800303.us.archive.org/1/items/gothichistoryofj00jord/gothichistoryofj00jord.pdf (accessed 11 April 2023).

Jordanes (1939): *Romanii in izvoarele istorice medievale* [Romanians in Medieval Historical Sources], edited and translated by Gheorghe Popa-Lisseanu, Bucharest.

Kaczkowski (1829): K. Kaczkowski, *Dziennik podróży do Krymu* [Diary of a Journey to Crimea], Warsaw.

Karamzin (2013): N.M. Karamzin, "Glava III. Prodolzhenie tsarstvovaniia Ioanna Groznogo. 1569–1527 g." [Chapter III. Continuation of the Rule of Ivan "the Terrible". 1569–1527], in: *idem, Istoriia gosudarstva Rossiiskogo* [History of the Russian State], Volume 9, London (ebook).

Khartakhai (1866/1867): F. Khartakhai, "Istoricheskaia sud'ba krymskikh tatar" [The Historical Fate of the Crimean Tatars], in: VE, 1(1866), 182–236; 2(1867), 140–74.

Khrushchev (1976 [1956]), Nikita Sergeyevich Krushchev, *The 'Secret' Speech: Delivered to the closed session of the Twentieth Congress of the Communist Party of the Soviet Union*, with an introduction by Zhores A. Medvedev and Roy A. Medvedev, translated by Tamara Deutscher, Nottingham 1976.

Kirpenko (1897): K. Kirpenko, "Ordera Kniazia Platona A. Zubova" [The Order of Prince Platon A. Zubov], in: ITUAK, 26, 1–10.

Kleemann (1771): *Nikolaus Ernst Kleemanns Reisen von Wien über Belgrad bis Kilianova, durch die Butschiack-Tartarey über Cavschan, Bender, durch die Nogeu-Tartarey in die Crimm, dann von Kaffa nach Konstantinopel, nach Smirna und durch den Archipelagum nach Triest und Wien, in den Jahren 1768, 1769 und 1770. Nebst einem Anhange von den besondern Merkwürdigkeiten der crimmischen Tartarey in Briefen an einen Freund*, Vienna.

Kliuchevskii (1903): Vasilii O. Kliuchevskii, *Lektsii po russkoi istorii* [Lectures on Russian History], Volume 3, St Petersburg

Kliutschewskij (1925 ff.): W. Kliutschewskij (i.e. V.O. Kliuchevskii), *Geschichte Rußlands*, 4 volumes, Stuttgart/Berlin.

Kliutschewskij (1945): W. O. Kliutschewskij (i.e. V.O. Kliuchevskii), *Russische Geschichte von Peter dem Großen bis Nikolaus I*, 2 volumes, Zurich.

Kolli (1913): L.P. Kolli, "Khadzhi-Girei khan i ego politika (po genuėzskim istochnikam). Vzgliad na politicheskie snosheniia Kaffy s Tatarami v XV veke" [Khan Khadzhi-Girei and his Politics (According to Genoese Sources). A Look at Caffa's Political Relations with the Tatars in the 15th Century], in: ITUAK, 27, Volume 50, 99–139.

Kratkii otchet (1868): "Kratkii otchet o poezdke v techenie leta 1861 g. (s 10 maia po 15 sentiabria) Iu. E. Iansona. Chlena ekspeditsii po issledovaniiu iugo-zapadnogo raiona" [Short Report on a Journey in the Summer of 1861 (from 10 May to 15 September) by Iu. E. Ianson. Member of the Expedition to Research the Southwestern Raion], in: IIRGO, 4, 349–59.

Lashkov (1886): Fedor F. Lashkov, "Statisticheskie svedeniia o Kryme, soobshchennye kaimakanami v 1783 godu" [Statistical Particulars About Crimea, Provided by Kajmakanen in the Year 1783], in: ZIOOIiD, 43, Volume 14, 91–99.

Lentin (1974): A. Lentin (ed.), *Voltaire and Catherine the Great. Selected Correspondence*. Translated, with commentary, notes and introduction by A. Lentin. Cambridge.

Ligne (1989): Prince de Ligne, *Mémoires et Mélanges historiques*, Paris (first published in 1827 in Paris).

Lopatin (1997): Viacheslav S. Lopatin (ed.), *Ekaterina II i G.A. Potemkin. Lichnaia perepiska 1769–1791* [Katharina II and G.A. Potemkin. The Personal Correspondence 1769–1791], Moscow.

Luzhkov (2000): Iurii Luzhkov, "Russkaia Palestina" [Russian Palestine], in: *Krymskii Al'bom* [Crimean Album], 1999, Feodosiia/Moscow.

Makhaev (1914): Sergei K. Makhaev, *Podvizhnitsy miloserdiia. Russkie sestry miloserdiia. Kratkie biograficheskie ocherki* [Fighters for Compassion. Russian Nurses. Short Biographical Sketches], Moscow.

Manstein (2004): Erich von Manstein, *Verlorene Siege*, 17th edition, Bonn.

Markevich (1994): Arsenii Markevich, *Tavricheskaia guberniia vo vremia krymskoi voiny po arkhivnym materialam* [The Taurida Governorate at the Time of the Crimean War According to Archive Material], Simferopol' (reprint of the edition ITUAK, 19 [1905], Volume 37).

Markov (1994): Evgenii Markov, *Ocherki Kryma. Kartiny krymskoi zhizni, istorii i prirody* [Crimean Sketches. Pictures of Life in Crimea, of History and Nature], Simferopol'/Moscow (reprint of the third edition of 1902).

Mazurevskii (1845): G. Mazurevskii, "Sel'sko-khoziaistvennaia storona iuzhnogo berega Kryma" [The Agricultural Side of the Southern Coast of Crimea], in: BdCh, 12, No. 10, 17–28.

Mission of Friar William (1990): William of Rubruck, *The Mission of Friar William of Rubruck: His Journey to the Court of the Great Khan Möngke 1253–1255*, translated by Peter Jackson, edited and with a commentary by Peter Jackson and David Morgan, London.

Mursakovich (1877–1879): N. Mursakovich, "Pis'ma pravitelia tavricheskoi oblasti Vasiliia Vasil'evicha Kokhovskogo pravitelui kantseliarii V.S. Popovu, dlia doklada ego svetlosti kniaziu Grigoriiu Aleksandrovichu Potemkinu-Tavricheskomu" [Letters of the Administrator of Tavricheskaia oblast', Vasilii Vasil'evich Kokhovskii, to the Administrator of the Chancellery V.S. Popov for Submission to his Serene Highness Prince Grigorii Aleksandrovich Potemkin von Taurien], in: ZIOOIiD, 34–36, Volume 10/11, 235–364.

Oliphant (1854): Laurence Oliphant, *The Russian Shores of the Black Sea*, London (Reprint New York 1970).

Opisanie (1879): "Opisanie perekopskikh i nogaiskikh Tatar, Cherkesov, Mingrelov i Gruzin. Zhana De-Liuka, monakha dominikanskogo ordena 1625" [Description of the Perekop and Nogai Tatars, the Circassians, the Mingrelians and Georgians by Zhan-de-Liuk, Monk of the Dominican Order in 1625], in: ZIOOIiD, 36, Volume 2:11, 473–93.

Pallas (1812): Peter Simon Pallas, *Travels Through the Southern Provinces of the Russian Empire in the Years 1793 and 1794. Translated from the German of P. S. Pallas, Counsellor of State to His Imperial Majesty of All the Russias, Knight, &c. Second Edition, Illustrated with One Hundred and Twenty-One Plates In Two Volumes. Vol. I.* Online: https://wellcomecollection.org/works/wtfwhr9g (accessed 11 April 2023) (German: Peter Simon Pallas, *Bemerkungen auf einer Reise in die südlichen Statthalterschaften des Russischen Reiches in den Jahren 1793 und 1794*, Graz 1967 [1799]).

Perevodshchikov (1853): D.M. Perevodshchikov, "Poezdka iz Peterburga v Krym i obratno" [A Journey from St Petersburg to Crimea and Back], in: SOV, 12:1, Section 6, *Smes'*, 1–38.

Pervaia perepis' (2018): "Pervaia vseobshchaia perepis' naseleniia Rossiiskoi Imperii 1897 g. Raspredelenie naseleniia po rodnomu iazyku i uezdam 50 gubernii Evropeiskoi Rossii. Tavricheskaia Guberniia" [First General Census of the Russian Empire in 1897. Classification of the Population By Mother Tongue and the Uezds of the 50 Governorates of European Russia. Taurida Governorate], in: *Demoskop weekly*. Online: http://demoscope.ru/weekly/ssp/rus_lan_97_uezd.php? reg=1420 (accessed 9 September 2018).

Pis'mo (1983): "Pis'mo P.P. Shmidta s pros'boi posle kazni pokhoronit' ego riadom s zhertvami rasstrela demonstratsii v Sevastopole 18 oktiabria 1905 g., 26. 12. 1905" [Letter by P.P. Schmidt With the Request to Bury Him After His Exection Next to the Shot Victims of the Sevastopol' Demonstration of 18 October, 26. 12. 1905], in: *Glavnoe Arkhivnoe upravlenie* (1983), 107 f.

Pokhody (1896): "Pokhody Ekateriny II po Volge i Dnepru" [Catherine II's Travels Over the Volga and the Dnepr], in: RS, 27, Volume 88:10–12, 423–45.

Polnoe sobranie (1830): *Polnoe sobranie zakonov Rossiiskoi Imperii. S 1781 po 1783* [The Complete Collection of the Laws of the Russian Empire. From 1781 to 1783], Volume 21, St Petersburg.

Postanovlenie (1922): "Postanovlenie tsentral'nogo ispolnitel'nogo komiteta i soveta narodnykh komissarov Kryma o tatarizatsii gosudarstvennykh apparatov i o primenenii tatarskogo iazyka v uchrezhdeniiakh respubliki" [Decision of the Central Executive Committee and the Council of People's Commissars of Crimea On the Tatarization of the State Apparatus and On the Use of Tatar Language in the Institutions of the Republic], 10 February 1922, in: Guboglo and Chervonnaia (1992), 40–1.

Primary Chronicle (1953): *The Russian Primary Chronicle. Laurentian Text*. Translated and edited by Samuel Hazzard Cross and Olgerd P. Sherbowitz-Wetzor, Cambridge 1953, 53–4. Online: http://www.mgh-bibliothek.de/dokumente/a/a011458.pdf

Radde (2008): Gustaf Radde, *Krymskie Tatary. Vstupitel'naia stat'ia, obshchaia redaktsiia i kommentarii G. Bekirovoi* [The Crimean Tatars. An Introductory Article, Edited and With a Commentary by G. Bekirova], Kyiv.

Reddaway (1971): W. F. Reddaway (ed.), *Documents of Catherine the Great. The Correspondence with Voltaire and the Instruction of 1767, in the English Text of 1768*, New York.

Riss (2007/2008): Hilda Riss, "Deutsche von der Krim in Arbeitslagern im Bezirk von Swerdlowsk", in: *Landsmannschaft der Deutschen aus Russland Heimatbuch*, 58–91.
Rudakov (1903): V.E. Rudakov, "Shirinskii-Shikhmatov. Platon Aleksandrovich", in: *Ėntsiklopedicheskii slovar' Brokgauza i Efrona* [Brockhaus's and Efron's Encyclopaedic Lexicon], Volume 39a, St Petersburg, 591.
Safonov (1844): S. Safonov, "Ostatki grecheskikh legionov v Rossii, ili nyneshnee naselenie Balaklavy" [The Remains of the Greek Legions in Russia or the Present Population of Balaklava], in: ZIOOIiD, 1, 205–56.
Schmitt C. (1942): Carl Schmitt *Land und Meer. Eine weltgeschichtliche Betrachtung*, Stuttgart.
Schöll (1829): Adolf Schöll (ed.), *Herodot's von Halikarnaß Geschichte*, Stuttgart. Online: http://www.mdz-nbn-resolving.de/urn/resolver.pl?urn=urn:nbn:de:bvb:12-bsb10236268-8 (accessed 16 November 2017).
Schramm (1982): Percy Schramm (ed.), *Kriegstagebuch des OKW, 1942*, Volume 1 and 2, Augsburg.
Schweiger-Lerchenfeld (1887): Armand Freiherr v. Schweiger-Lerchenfeld, *Zwischen Donau und Kaukasus. Land und Seefahrten im Bereiche des Schwarzen Meeres*, Vienna/Pest/Leipzig.
Ségur (1926): M. le Comte de Ségur, *Mémoires ou souvenirs et anecdotes*, three volumes, second edition, Paris.
Seïdahmet (1921): Djafer Seïdahmet (i.e. Cafer Seydahmet Qırımer), *La Crimée. Passé – Présent. Revendication des Tatars de Crimée*, Lausanne.
Sejdahmet Krym (1930): Dżafer Sejdahmet Krym (i.e. Cafer Seydahmet Qırımer), *Przesłość, terazniejszość. Dążenia niepodległościowe Tatarów krymskich* [Past, Present. The Crimean Tatar's Striving for Independence], Warsaw.
Seydahamet (2005): Cafer Seydahamet, "Famine in Crimea", translated into English by Inci Bowman, in: International Committee for Crimea, 13 March 2005. Online: http://www.iccrimea.org/historical/famine1931.html (accessed 10 February 2016).
Seymour (1855): H.D. Seymour, *Russia on the Black Sea and the Sea of Azof. Being a Narrative of Travels in the Crimea and Bordering Provinces. With Notices of the Naval, Military, and Commercial Resources of those Countries*, London.
Skoropads'kyj (1999): Pavlo Skoropads'kyj, *Erinnerungen 1917 bis 1918*, ed. by Günter Rosenfeld, Stuttgart (= Quellen und Studien zur Geschichte des östlichen Europa, 55).
Smirnov (1887): Vasilii D. Smirnov, *Krymskoe Khanstvo pod verkhovenstvom Otomanskoi Porty do nachala XVIII veka* [The Crimean Khanate Under the Rule of the Ottoman Porte Up To the Early Eighteenth Century], St Petersburg.
Smith (2004): Douglas Smith (ed.), *Love & Conquest: Personal Correspondence of Catherine the Great and Prince Grigory Potemkin*, DeKalb, Illinois.
Song of Prince Igor (1979): *The Song of Prince Igor. Russia's Great Medieval Epic*, translated by Robert Mann, Eugene, Oregon.
Stalin (1942 [1913]): Joseph Stalin, *Marxism and the National Question. Selected Writings and Speeches*, New York.
Strabo (2001): Strabo, *Geography*, Books 6–7, translated by Horace Leonard Jones, Cambridge, MA (reprint of the first edition of 1924). Online: https://archive.org/details/Strabo08Geography17AndIndex/Strabo%2003%20Geography%20 6-7/page/238/mode/2up (accessed 11 April 2023).

Sultan-Galiev (1997): M. Sultan-Galiev, "Narodnomu komissaru po delam natsional'nostei tov. Stalinu. Kopiiu ZK RKP(B). Doklad o polozhenii v Krymu" [To the People's Commissar of Nationalities, Comrade Stalin, in Copy to the Central Committee of the RCP[B]. Report on the Situation in Crimea], in: Gasyrlar avazy. Ėkho vekov [Echo der Jahrhunderte], 3/4. Online: http://www.archive.gov.tatarstan.ru/magazine/go/anonymous/main/?path= mg:/numbers/1997_3_4/03/03_2/ (accessed 9 August 2017).

Tale of the Armament of Igor (1915): *The Tale of the Armament of Igor. A.D. 1185. A Russian Historical Epic*, translated by Leonard A. Magnus, London.

Thounmann (1786): *Description de la Crimée par M. Thounmann* [Thunmann], *Professeur à Halle. Traduite de l'allemand*, Strasbourg.

Thunmann (1784): Hans Erich Thunmann, *Der krimsche Staat*, Troppau.

Thunman (1774): Johann Thunman, *Untersuchungen über die Geschichte der östlichen europäischen Völker*, Leipzig.

Vasil'evskii (1878): V.G. Vasil'evskii, "Zhitie Ioanna Gotskogo" [Life of John of Gothia], in: ZhMNP, 195, Ianvar', Otd. II, 25–34. (Reproduced in: Trudy V.G. Vasil'evskogo [The Works of V.G. Vasil'evskii], Volume 2, 351–427).

Vernadsky et al. (1972): George Vernadsky et al. (eds.), *A Source Book for Russian History from Early Times to 1917*, Volume 2, New Haven.

Vesti (1863): "Vesti iz Simferopolia", in: ZhMNP, 39 (March), Part CXVII, 241–245.

Viazmitinov (1882): A.A. Viazmitinov, "Sevastopol' ot 21 marta po 28 avgusta 1855 g." [Sevastopol' from 21 March to 28 August in the Year 1855], in: RS, 13, 34:4–6, 1–70.

Vorontsov (1916): Mikhail I. Vorontsov, "Doklad imperatritse Ekaterine II-oi po vstuplenii Eia na Prestol, izobrazhaiushchii sistemu Krymskikh Tatar, ikh opasnost' dlia Rossii i pretenziiu na nikh. O Maloi Tatarii" [Report to Empress Catherine II After Her Ascension to the Throne, Depicting the System of the Crimean Tatars, Their Dangerousness for Russia and the Demands [Put] to Them. On Lesser Tataria], in: ITUAK, 43, 190–3.

Vozmushchenie (1872): "Vozmushchenie Tatar" [The Tatar Upheaval], in: ZIOOIiD, Volume 8, 188–190.

Vsesoiuznaia perepis' (2006): "Vsesoiuznaia perepis' naseleniia 1926 g. SSSR, respubliki i ikh osnovnye regiony. Naselennye mesta. Nalichnoe gorodskoe i sel'skoe naselenie" [All-Union Census of 1926 of the USSR, the Republics and Their Main Regions. The Inhabited Places. The Available Urban and Rural Population], in: *Demoskop Weekly*, 5 November 2006. Online: http://www.demoscope.ru/weekly/ssp/ussr_26.php?reg=12 (accessed 9 August 2018).

Vysochaishee povelenie (1902): "Vysochaishee povelenie ne imenovat' Sevastopolia Akhtiarom i Evpatorii – Kozlovom. Predlozhenie ministra iustitsii Senatu 5-go fevralia 1826" [The Most Sublime Order to Not Name Sevastopol' Akhtiar and Not Name Evpatoriia Kozlov. Bill of the Ministry of Justice to the Senate of 5 February 1826], No. 1947, in: RS, 33, 112:1–3, 87.

Windt (1917): Harry de Windt, *Russia as I Know it*, Philadelphia.

Zapiski (1891): "Zapiski de-la Nevillia o Moskovii 1689 g. Pokhod Moskvitian na Krym 1689 goda" [The Reports By de la Neville On Moscovy in the Year 1689. The Muscovites' Campaign in Crimea of 1689], in: RS, 22, 72:10–12, 241–81.

Zertsalov (1890): A.N. Zertsalov, *Ob oskorblenii tsarskikh poslov v Krymu v XVII veke* [On the Insult to the Tsarist Ambassador in Crimea in the XVIIth Century], Moscow.

Zhitie (1999): "Zhitie Konstantina-Kirilla. Pamiat' i zhitie blazhennogo uchitelia nashego Konstantina Filosofa, pervogo nastavnika slavianskogo naroda. Podgotovka teksta i perevod L.V. Moshkovoi i A.A. Turilova, kommentarii B.N. Flori" [The Life of Constantine-Cyril. Memoir and Life of Our Late Teacher Constantine Filosof, the Slavic People's First Teacher. Edited and Translated by L.V. Moshkovaia and A.A. Turilov, Commentary by B.N. Flori], in: D.S. Likhachev et al. (eds.), *Biblioteka literatury Drevnei Rusi* [Library of the Literature of Old Rus'], Volume 2: XI–XII veka [11th–12th Century], St Petersburg. Online: http://lib.pushkinskijdom.ru/Default.aspx?tabid=2163#_edn61 (accessed 20 November 2017).

Literary sources

Aksyonov (1983): Vassily Aksyonov (i.e. Vasilii P. Aksënov), The Island of Crimea, translated by Michael Henry Heim, New York (Russian: Ostrov Krym, Ann Arbor 1981)

Binhack (1877): Franz Binhack, *Zusammenhängende deutsch-lateinische Übersetzungsstücke für den Schul- und Hilfsunterricht. Casuslehre*, Amberg.

Binhack (1869): Franz Binhack, "Die orientalische Frage", in: *idem, Reime und Träume*, Neuburg.

Clancy and Greaney (2013): Tom Clancy and Mark Greaney, *Command Authority*. Tom Clancy, Mark Greaney, Command Authority, London.

Goethe (2005): Johann Wolfgang von Goethe, *Iphigenia in Tauris*, translated by Anna Swanwick. Online: https://www.gutenberg.org/files/15850/15850-h/15850-h.htm (accessed 11 April 2023) (German: Johann Wolfgang von Goethe, *Iphigenie auf Tauris. Kritische Studienausgabe*. Ed. by Rüdiger Nutt-Kofoth, Stuttgart (= Reclams Universal-Bibliothek, 19258), 2014).

Kinsky and Chalmers (2015): Esther Kinsky and Martin Chalmers, *Karadag Oktober 13. Aufzeichnungen von der kalten Krim*, Berlin.

Kostomarov (1967): M.I. Kostomarov, "Do Mar'ï Potots'koï" [To Mariia Potots'ka], in: Tvory v dvoch tomakh [Works in Two Volumes], Bd. 1, Kyiv, 56.

Maiakovskii (1989): V.V. Maiakovskii, "Krym" [Crimea], in: Rudiakov and Kazarin (1989), 17 f.

Mickiewicz (1928 [1826]): Adam Mickiewicz, *Sonety i sonety Krymskie*, Łódź, 1928.

Pooshkeen (2012 [1849]): Alexander Pooshkeen (i.e. Aleksandr Pushkin), "The Bakchesarian Fountain", in: *The Bakchesarian Fountain. And Other Poems, by Various Authors*. Translated by William D. Lewis, Philadelphia 1849, n.p. Online: http://www.gutenberg.org/files/8192/8192-h/8192-h.htm (accessed 11 April 2023).

Rudiakov and Kazarin (1989): A.N. Rudiakov and V.P. Kazarin (eds.), *Krym. Poėticheskii atlas* [Crimea. A Poetic Atlas], Simferopol'.

Sinyavski (1995): Andrei Sinyavski (i.e. Abram Terz), *Strolls with Pushkin*. Translated by Slava I. Yastremski and Catherine Theimer Nepomnyashchy, New Haven/New York.

Song of Prince Igor (1979): *The Song of Prince Igor. Russia's Great Medieval Epic*. Translated by Robert Mann. Eugene, Oregon.

Surkov (1989): Andrei A. Surkov, "Sevastopol'tsy" [The Sevastapol'ians], in: Rudiakov and Kazarin (1989), 137.
Tennyson (1910): Alfred Tennyson, *The Poems of Alfred Tennyson: 1830–1863*, ed. by Ernest Rhys, London.
Tolstoï (1888 [1855–1856]): Count Lyof N. Tolstoï, *Sevastopol*, New York. Translated from the Russian by Isabel F. Hapgood, New York.
Tolstoy (1986 [1855–1856]): Leo Tolstoy, *The Sebastopol Sketches*, Translated with an Introduction and Notes by David McDuff, London.
Twain (1869): Mark Twain, *The Innocents Abroad. Or The New Pilgrims' Progress*, Hartford. Online: https://www.gutenberg.org/files/3176/3176-h/3176-h.htm
Ulitskaya (2002 [1996]): Ludmila Ultiskaya, *Medea and Her Children*, translated from the Russian by Arch Tait, New York.
Zoshchenko (1937): Mikhail Zoshchenko, "Poritsanie Krymu" [Rebuke of Crimea], in *idem, Rasskazy, povesti, fel'etony, teatr, kritika 1935-1937* [Stories, Novels, Feuilletons, Plays, Criticism], Leningrad, 229–32.
Zoshchenko (1965 [1930]), Mikhail Zoshchenko, "Earthquake", in: Mirra Ginsburg (ed.), *The Fatal Eggs and Other Soviet Satire*, New York/London, 215–219 (Russian: Mikhail Zoshchenko, "Zemletriasenie" [The Earthquake], in: *idem, Rasskazy, fel'etony, povesti* [Stories, Feuilletons, Novels], Leningrad, 71–4).

Secondary sources

Abu-Lughod (1989): Janet I. Abu-Lughod, *Before European Hegemony. The World System A.D. 1250–1350*, New York.
Adam (2002): Volker Adam, *Rußlandmuslime am Vorabend des Ersten Weltkrieges. Die Berichterstattung osmanischer Periodika über Rußland und Zentralasien*, Frankfurt am Main.
Aibabin (1999): A.I. Aibabin, *Ėtnicheskaia istoriia rannevizantiiskogo Kryma* [An Ethnic History of Early Byzantine Crimea], Simferopol'.
Albrecht (2011): Stefan Albrecht, "Die 'Tartariae descriptio' des Martinus Broniovius", in: Albrecht and Herdick (2011), 1–10.
Albrecht (2016): Stefan Albrecht, "Cherson als Zentralort auf der südwestlichen Krim (6.-10. Jahrhundert)", in: Ivan Bugarski, Orsolya Heinrich-Tamaska, Vujadin Ivanisevic and Daniel Syrbe (eds.), *GrenzÜbergänge. Spätrömisch, frühchristlich, frühbyzantinisch als Kategorien der historisch-archäologischen Forschung an der mittleren Donau = Late Roman, Early Christian, Early Byzantine as categories in historical-archaeological research on the Middle Danube*, Remshalden (=Forschungen zu Spätantike und Mittelalter, 4), 355–84.
Albrecht and Herdick (2011): Stefan Albrecht and Michael Herdick (eds.), *Im Auftrag des Königs. Ein Gesandtenbericht aus dem Land der Krimtataren. Die "Tartariae descriptio" des Martinus Broniovius (1579)*, Mainz (= Monographien des Römisch-Germanischen Zentralmuseums, 89).
Albrecht and Herdick (2013): Stefan Albrecht and Michael Herdick, "Ein Spielball der Mächte. Die Krim im Schwarzmeerraum (VI.–XV. Jahrhundert)", in: *idem* and Falko Daim (eds.), *Die Höhlensiedlungen im Bergland der Krim. Umwelt,*

Kulturaustausch und Transformation am Nordrand des Byzantinischen Reiches, Mainz, 25–56.

Alikberov et al. (2010): K. Alikberov et al. (eds.), *Khazary. Mif i istoriia* [The Khazars. Myth and History], Moscow.

Altschüler (2006): Boris Altschüler, *Die Aschkenasim. Außergewöhnliche Geschichte der europäischen Juden*, Berlin.

Anderson M. (1966): M.S. Anderson, *The Eastern Question, 1774–1923. A Study in International Relations*, New York.

Anderson T. (2012): Thorsten Anderson, "Der nordgermanische Sprachzweig", in: Heinrich Beck, Dieter Geuenich and Heiko Steuer (eds.), *Altertumskunde – Altertumswissenschaft – Kulturwissenschaft. Erträge und Perspektiven nach 40 Jahren Reallexikon der germanischen Altertumskunde*, Berlin/Boston (= Ergänzungsbände zum Reallexikon der Germanischen Altertumskunde, 77), 215–44.

Andreev (1997): A.P. Andreev, *Istoriia Kryma. Kratkoe opisanie proshlogo krymskogo poluostrova* [History of Crimea. A Short Description of the Past of the Crimean Peninsula], Moscow.

Angrick (2003): Andrej Angrick, *Besatzungspolitik und Massenmord. Die Einsatzgruppe D in der südlichen Sowjetunion 1941–1943*, Hamburg.

Arens and Klein (2004): Meinolf Arens and Denise Klein, "Neues Forschungsprojekt am Ungarischen Institut München. Das frühneuzeitliche Krimkhanat zwischen Orient und Okzident. Dependenzen und autonome Entwicklungsmöglichkeiten an der Schnittstelle zwischen orthodoxer, lateinischer und muslimischer Welt", in: *Ungarn-Jahrbuch*, 27, 492–8.

Arslan-Bej (1932): Arslan-Bej (d.i. Leon Kryczyński), "Generał Maciej Sulkiewicz 1865–1920", in: *Rocznik Tatarski* [Tatar Yearbook], 1, 247–55.

Artamonov (1962): M.I. Artamonov, *Istoriia Khazar* [The History of the Khazars], Leningrad.

Ascher (1988/1994): Abraham Ascher, *The Revolution of 1905*, 2 vols., Stanford.

Ascherson (2015): Neal Ascherson, *Black Sea. Coasts and Conquests: From Pericles to Putin*, revised edition, London.

Asheri et al. (2007): David Asheri, Alan Lloyd and Aldo Corcella, *A Commentary on Herodotus Books I–IV*. Ed. by Oswyn Murray and Alfonso Moreno, Oxford.

Auerbach (1965): Hans Auerbach, *Die Besiedlung der Südukraine in den Jahren 1774–1787*, Wiesbaden.

Augustynowicz (2005): Christoph Augustynowicz, "Tatarische Gesandtschaften am Kaiserhof des 17. Jahrhunderts", in: Marlene Kurz et al. (eds.), *Das osmanische Reich und die Habsburgermonarchie. Akten des internationalen Kongresses zum 150-jährigen Bestehen des Instituts für Österreichische Geschichtsforschung, Wien, 22.–25. September 2004*, Munich, 313–38.

Augustynowicz (2012): Christoph Augustynowicz, "Begegnung und Zeremonial. Das Bild der Krimtataren bei Balthasar Kleinschroth und Johann Christian Lünig", in: Klein D. (2012a), 189–210.

Augustynowicz (2017): *Christoph Augustynowicz, Kleine Kulturgeschichte Polens. Vom Mittelalter bis zum 21. Jahrhundert*, Vienna.

Aust (2017): Martin Aust, *Die Russische Revolution. Vom Zarenreich zum Sowjetimperium*, Munich.

Aydin (2002): Filiz Tutku Aydin, "Crimean Turk-Tatars. Crimean Tatar Diaspora Nationalism in Turkey", International Committee for Crimea, 8 January 2002. Online: http://iccrimea.org/scholarly/aydin.html (accessed 9 September 2018).

Bachofen (1997): Johann Jakob Bachofen, *Das Mutterrecht. Eine Untersuchung über die Gynaikokratie der alten Welt nach ihrer religiösen und rechtlichen Natur. Eine Auswahl.* Ed. by Hans-Jürgen Heinrichs, ninth edition, Berlin.
Bade et al. (2007): Klaus J. Bade et al. (eds.), *Enzyklopädie Migration – Integration – Minderheiten seit dem 17. Jahrhundert*, Paderborn.
Baeque (1993) : Antoine de Baeque, *Le Corps de l'Histoire. Métaphores et politique (1770–1800)*, Paris.
Balard (1987) : Michel Balard, "Les Orienteux à Caffa au quinzième siècle", in : *Byzantinische Forschungen*, 11, 223–38.
Barbarics-Hermanik (2009): Zsuzsa Barbarics-Hermanik, "Reale oder gemachte Angst? Türkengefahr und Türkenpropaganda im 16. und 17. Jahrhundert", in: Harald Heppner (ed.), *Türkenangst und Festungsbau*, Frankfurt am Main et al., 43–78.
Barker (1967): Thomas M. Barker, *Double Eagle and Crescent. Vienna's Second Turkish Siege and Its Historical Setting*, New York.
Barkey (2008): Karen Barkey, *Empire of Difference. The Ottomans in Comparative Perspective*, Cambridge, UK.
Baumgart (1966): Winfried Baumgart, "Ludendorff und das Auswärtige Amt zur Besetzung der Krim", in: *Jahrbücher für Geschichte Osteuropas*, 14, 529–38.
Baumgart (1972): Winfried Baumgart, *Der Friede von Paris 1856. Studien zum Verhältnis von Kriegführung, Politik und Friedensbewahrung*, Munich/Vienna.
Benedictow (2004): Ole J. Benedictow, *The Black Death 1346–1353. The Complete History*, Woodbridge.
Bengtson (1979): Hermann Bengtson, *Griechische Geschichte. Von den Anfängen bis in die römische Kaiserzeit*, fifth edition, Munich.
Bennigsen (1972): Alexandre Bennigsen, "The Muslims of European Russia and the Caucasus", in: Wayne S. Vucinich (ed.), *Russia and Asia. Essays on the Influence of Russia on the Asian Peoples*, Stanford, 135–66.
Bennigsen and Broxup (1993): Alexandre Bennigsen and Marie Broxup, *The Islamic Threat to the Soviet State*, New York.
Bennigsen and Lemercier-Quelquejay (1964): Alexandre Bennigsen and Chantal Lemercier-Quelquejay, *La presse et le mouvement national chez les Musulmans de Russie avant 1920*, Paris/The Hague.
Bernstein (2009): William Bernstein, *A Splendid Exchange. How Trade Shaped the World*, London.
Beyrau et al. (1996): Dietrich Beyrau et al. (eds.), *Reformen im Rußland des 19. und 20. Jahrhunderts. Westliche Modelle und russische Erfahrungen*, Frankfurt am Main.
Bhatti and Kimmich (2015): Anil Bhatti and Dorothee Kimmich (eds.), *Ähnlichkeit. Ein kulturtheoretisches Paradigma*, Konstanz.
Bichler (2000): Reinhold Bichler, *Herodots Welt. Der Aufbau der Historie am Bild der fremden Länder und Völker, ihrer Zivilisation und ihrer Geschichte*, Berlin.
Binder-Iijima and Dumbrava (2005): Edda Binder-Iijima and Vasile Dumbrava (eds.), *Stefan der Große. Fürst der Moldau. Symbolfunktion und Bedeutungswandel eines mittelalterlichen Herrschers*, Leipzig.
Bitis (2007): Alexander Bitis, *Russia and the Eastern Question. Army, Government and Society, 1815–1833*, Oxford.
Blavatskii (1977): V.D. Blavatskii, "Zemletriasenie 63 goda do n. ė. na Kerchenskom polustrove" [The Earthquake of 63 BCE in the Kerch' Pensinsula], in: *Priroda* [Nature], 8, 55–9.

Bloch (1963): Marc Bloch, "Réflexions d'un historien sur les fausses nouvelles de la guerre", in: *idem*, Mélanges historiques, Volume 1, Paris, 41–57.
Bocharov (2017): S.G. Bocharov, "Zametki po istoricheskoi geografii Genuëzskoi Gazarii XIV–XV vv. Konsul'stvo Chembal'skoe" [Observations on the Historical Geography of Genoese Khazaria in the 14th–15th Centuries. Consulate of Chembalo], in: *Povolzhskaia Arkheologiia* [Archaeology of the Volga Region], 20, 2, 204–23.
Boeckh (1993): Andreas Boeckh, "Dependencia-Theorien", in: Dieter Nohlen (ed.), *Lexikon Dritte Welt*, completely revised new edition, Reinbek bei Hamburg, 165 f.
Bogomolov et al. (2010): Alexander Bogomolov et al., "Islamic Education in Ukraine", in: Michael Kemper, Raoul Motika and Stefan Reichmuth (eds.), *Islamic Education in the Soviet Union and Its Successor States*, London/New York, 67–106.
Böröcz (1992): József Böröcz, "Travel-Capitalism. The Structure of Europe and the Advent of the Tourist", in: *Comparative Studies in Society and History*, 39, 708–41.
Bowman (2003): Inci Bowman, "Çobanzade. A Crimean Tatar Poet and Turkish Scholar. Review", International Committee for Crimea, 10 August 2003. Online: http://www.iccrimea.org/literature/cobanzade.html (accessed 19 January 2016).
Bowman (2005): Inci Bowman, "Cafer Seydahmet Kirimer (1889–1960)", International Committee for Crimea, 12 March 2005. Online: http://www.iccrimea.org/historical/cskirimer.html (accessed 9 August 2018).
Brandes D. (1993): Detlef Brandes, *Von den Zaren adoptiert. Die deutschen Kolonisten und die Balkansiedler in Neurußland und Bessarabien 1751–1914*, Munich.
Brandes D. (1998): Detlef Brandes, "Die Ansiedlung von Ausländergruppen an der unteren Wolga und in Neurußland unter Katharina II. Plan und Wirklichkeit", in: Eckhard Hübner, Jan Kusber and Peter Nitsche (eds.), *Rußland zur Zeit Katharinas II. Absolutismus – Aufklärung – Pragmatismus*, Cologne/Weimar/Vienna, 303–14.
Brandes D. (2007a): Detlef Brandes, "Bulgarische und gagausische Siedler in Neurußland und Bessarabien seit dem 18. Jahrhundert", in: Bade et al. (2007), 433–6.
Brandes D. (2007b): Detlef Brandes, "Deutsche Siedler in Rußland seit dem 18. Jahrhundert", in: Bade et al. (2007), 514–21.
Brandes D. (2007c): Detlef Brandes, "Ukrainische und russische Siedler in Neurußland seit dem 18. Jahrhundert", in: Bade et al. (2007), 1063–5.
Brandes W. (1988): Wolfram Brandes, "Die byzantinische Stadt Kleinasiens im 7. und 8. Jahrhundert. Ein Forschungsbericht", in: *Klio*, 70:1, 176–208.
Brătianu (1969): Gheorghe I. Brătianu, *La mer Noire. Des origines à la conquête ottomane*, Munich.
Brătianu (2014): Gheorghe I. Brătianu, *Les Génois et les Vénitiens dans la mer Noire aux XIIIe– XIVe siècles*, édité par Victor Spinei et Ionel Cândea, Bucharest/Brăila (= Florilegium magistrorum historiae archaeologiaeque Antiquitatis et Medii Aevi, XV).
Braude and Lewis (1982): Benjamin Braude and Bernard Lewis (eds.), *Christians and Jews in the Ottoman Empire. The Functioning of a Plural Society*, New York et al.

Breiden (1994): Wolfgang Breiden (ed.), *Die Erschütterung der vollkommenden Welt. Die Wirkung des Erdbebens von Lissabon im Spiegel europäischer Zeitgenossen*, Darmstadt.
Bronfen (1997): Elisabeth Bronfen (ed.), *Hybride Kulturen. Beiträge zur anglo-amerikanischen Multikulturalismusdebatte*, Tübingen.
Brook (2006): Kevin Alan Brook, *The Jews of Khazaria*, Lanham.
Brooks (1985): Jeffrey Brooks, *When Russia Learned to Read. Literacy and Popular Literature 1861–1917*, Princeton.
Bryer (1980): Anthony A. M. Bryer, *The Empire of Trebizond and the Pontos*, London.
Brzezinski and Mielczarek (2002): Richard Brzezinski and Mariusz Mielczarek, *The Sarmatians 600 B.C.–A.D. 450*, Oxford.
Bucher-Dinc (1997): Gabriele Bucher-Dinc, *Die mittlere Wolga im Widerstreit sowjetischer und nationaler Ideologien. Eine Untersuchung anhand autobiographischer und publizistischer Schriften des Wolgatataren Mirsaid Sultan-Galiev*, Wiesbaden.
Bujnoch (1972): Josef Bujnoch (ed.), *Zwischen Rom und Byzanz. Leben und Wirken der Slavenapostel Kyrillos und Methodios nach den Pannonischen Legenden und der Klemensvita. Bericht von der Taufe Rußlands nach der Laurentiuschronik*, second edition, Graz (= Slavische Geschichtsschreiber, 1).
Bulgakova (2008): Viktoria Bulgakova, "Islamisch-christlicher Kulturkontakt im nördlichen Schwarzmeerraum. Sugdaia unter Herrschaft der Seldschuken", in: Michael Borgolte et al. (eds.), *Mittelalter im Labor. Die Mediävistik testet Wege zu einer transkulturellen Europawissenschaft*, Berlin (= Europa im Mittelalter, 10), 261–274.
Bulst (1979): Neidhard Bulst, "Der Schwarze Tod. Demographische, wirtschafts- und kulturgeschichtliche Aspekte der Pestkatastrophe von 1347–1352. Bilanz der neueren Forschung", in: *Saeculum*, 30:1, 45–67.
Bunar and Sroka (1996): Piotr Bunar and Stanisław A. Sroka, *Wojny, bitwy i potyczki w średniowiecznej Polsce* [Wars, Battles and Combat in Medieval Poland], Kraków.
Burak (2015): Guy Burak, *The Second Formation of Islamic Law. The Hanafi School in the Early Modern Ottoman Empire*, Cambridge.
Burbank (2006): Jane Burbank, "An Imperial Rights Regime. Law and Citizenship in the Russian Empire", in: *Kritika. Explorations in Russian and Eurasian History*, 7:3, 397–431.
Burgess-Jackson (1996): Keith Burgess-Jackson, *Rape. A Philosophical Investigation*, Aldershot et al.
Cadot (1987): Michel Cadot, "Exil et poésie. La Crimée de Puškin et de Mickiewicz", in: *Revue Études Slaves*, 59, 141–55.
Cardini (2004): Franco Cardini, *Europa und der Islam. Geschichte eines Missverständnisses*, Munich.
Carter (2003): J.C. Carter (ed.), *Crimean Chersonesos. City, Chora, Museum, and Environs*, Austin.
Chkhaidze (2010): V.N. Chkhaidze, "Tmutarakan'. Vladenie Drevnerusskogo gosudarstva v 80-e gg. X – 90-e gg. XI vekov" [Tmutarakan'. The Rule of an Old Russian State in the 980s and 1090s], in: *Vestnik Moskovskogo gorodskogo pedagogicheskogo universiteta. Seriia "Istoricheskie nauki"* [Messenger of the Moscow City Pedagogic University. Series "Historical Studies"], 5:1, 20–37.

Chochorowski (2004): Jan Chochorowski (ed.), *Cimmerians, Scythians, Sarmatians. In Memory of Professor Tadeusz Sulimirski*, Kraków.
Chrapunow (1999): Igor Chrapunow, "Taurer, Skythen, Sarmaten und Alanen", in: Thomas Werner (ed.), *Krim. Archäologische Schätze aus drei Jahrtausenden*, Heidelberg, 20–33.
Christensen (2002): Arne Søby Christensen, *Cassiodorus. Jordanes and the History of the Goths. Studies in a Migration Myth*, Copenhagen.
Collins (1975): Leslie J.D. Collins, "The Military Organization and Tactics of the Crimean Tatars during the Sixteenth and Seventeenth Centuries", in: V. J. Parry and M.E. Yapp (eds.), *War, Technology, and Society in the Middle East*, London, 257–76.
Conermann (1998): Stephan Conermann, "Expansionspolitik im Zeichen des Aufgeklärten Absolutismus? Katharina II. und die Krimtataren", in: Eckhard Hübner, Jan Kusber and Peter Nitsche (eds.), *Rußland zur Zeit Katharinas II. Absolutismus – Aufklärung – Pragmatismus*, Cologne/Weimar/Vienna, 337–59.
Conermann and Kusber (1997): Stephan Conermann and Jan Kusber (eds.), Die *Mongolen in Asien und Europa*, Frankfurt am Main (= Kieler Werkstücke. Series F. 4).
Copeaux (1993): Étienne Copeaux, "Le mouvement 'Prométhéen'", in: *Cahiers d'études sur la Méditerranée orientale et le monde turco-iranien*, 16, 9–46.
Craanen and Gunsenheimer (2006): Michael Craanen and Antje Gunsenheimer (eds.), *Das 'Fremde' und das 'Eigene'. Forschungsberichte (1992–2006)*, Bielefeld.
Crispin (2006): Martin Crispin "Der Bolotnikov-Aufstand 1606–1607", in: Heinz-Dietrich Löwe (ed.), *Volksaufstände in Rußland. Von der Zeit der Wirren bis zur 'Grünen Revolution' gegen die Sowjetherrschaft*. Wiesbaden, 27–68.
Curtiss (1966): John Shelton Curtiss, "Russian Sisters of Mercy in the Crimea 1854–1855", in: *Slavic Review*, 25, 84–100.
Cwiklinski (2014): Sebastian Cwiklinski, "Vasilij Dmitrievič Smirnovs Forschungen zur Geschichte des Khanats der Krim im Spannungsfeld von Wissenschaft und Politik", in: *Nauchnoe nasledie professora A.P. Pronshteina i aktualnye problemy razvitiia istoricheskoi nauki. K 95-letiiu so dnia rozhdeniia vydaiushchegosia rossiiskogo uchenogo. Materialy Vserossiiskoi (s mezhdunarodnym uchastiem) nauchno-prakticheskoi konferentsii, g. Rostov-na-Donu, 4–5 aprelia 2014 g.* The Scholarly Legacy of Prof. A.P. Pronshtein and the Current Problems in the Development of Historical Studies. On the Occasion of the 95th Birthday of the Outstanding Russian Scholar. Materials of the All-Russian Scholarly-Practical Conference (with Internaitonal Participation), Rostov-on-Don, 4–5 April 2014], Rostov-on-Don, 568–74.
Czerwonnaja and Malek (2017): Swetlana Czerwonnaja and Martin Malek, "Literarische Verarbeitungen der Deportation der krimtatarischen Bevölkerung. Eine 'vergessene' Quelle der Geschichtsforschung", in: *ÖZG*, 28:1: *Krimtataren* (ed. by Ulrich Hofmeister and Kerstin S. Jobst), 218–23.
Dan (2017): Anca Dan, "The Sarmatians. Some Thoughts on the Historiographical Invention of a West Iranian Migration", in: Felix Wiedemann, Kerstin P. Hofmann and Hans-Joachim Gehrke (eds.), *Vom Wandern der Völker. Migrationserzählungen in den Altertumswissenschaften*, Berlin (= Berlin Studies of the Ancient World, 41), 97–134.
Daniel A. (2016): Alexander Daniel, "Russland. Oppositionsgeschichte". Part 8. Translated from the Polish by Gero Lietz, in: Bundesstiftung Aufarbeitung (ed.),

Biografisches Lexikon. Widerstand und Opposition im Kommunismus 1945–1991. Online: https:// dissidenten.eu/laender/russland/oppositionsgeschichte/8/ (accessed 9 August 2018).
Daniel U. (2006): Ute Daniel, "Der Krimkrieg 1853–1856", in: *idem* (ed.), *Augenzeugen. Kriegsberichterstattung vom 18. bis zum 21. Jahrhundert*, Göttingen, 40–67.
D'Anieri (2011): Paul D'Anieri (ed.), *Orange Revolution and Aftermath. Mobilisation, Apathy, and the State in Ukraine*, Baltimore.
Davies B. (2007): Brian L. Davies, *Warfare, State and Society on the Black Sea Steppe 1500–1700*, New York.
Davies F. (2013): Franziska Davies, "Eine imperiale Armee. Juden und Muslime im Dienste des Zaren", in: *Jahrbuch des Simon-Dubnow-Instituts*, 12, 151–72.
Davies F. (2016): Franziska Davies, *Muslims in the Russian Army 1874–1917*, doctoral thesis, Ludwig Maximilian University of Munich.
Davies R. (2004): Robert Davies, *Christian Slaves, Muslim Masters. White Slavery in the Mediterranean, the Barbary Coast, and Italy, 1500–1800*, Basingstoke.
Davison (1976): R.H. Davison, "Russian Skill and Turkish Imbecility. The Treaty of Kutchuk Kainardji Reconsidered", in: *Slavic Revue*, 35, 463–483.
Dawson (1996): Jane I. Dawson, *Eco-Nationalism. Anti-Nuclear Activism and National Identity in Russia, Lithuania, and Ukraine*, Durham/London.
Deportationen (2012): *Deportationen in Stalins Sowjetunion. Das Schicksal der Russlanddeutschen und anderer Nationalitäten*, special issue of *Nordost-Archiv. Zeitschrift für Regionalgeschichte*, N.F. 21.
Dean et al. (2018): Katherine R. Dean, Fabienne Krauer, Lars Walløe and Boris V. Schmid, "Human ectoparasites and the spread of plague in Europe during the Second Pandemic", in: Biological Sciences, 115:6, 1304–1309. Online: https:// www.pnas.org/doi/abs/10.1073/pnas.1715640115
Derbes (1966): Vincent Derbes, "De Mussis and the Great Plague of 1348. A Forgotten Episode of Bacteriological Warfare", in: *Journal of the American Medical Association*, 196:1, 59–62.
Delumeau (1985): Jean Delumeau, *Angst im Abendland. Die Geschichte kollektiver Ängste im Europa des 14. bis 18. Jahrhunderts*, 2 vols., Reinbek bei Hamburg.
Denny (2000): Frederick Mathewson Denny, "Umma", in: Th. Bianquis et al. (eds.), *The Encyclopaedia of Islam. New Edition*, Volume 10, Leiden, 859b–63b.
Di Cosmo (2010): Nicola Di Cosmo, "Black Sea Emporia and the Mongol Empire. A Reassessment of the Pax Mongolica", in: *Journal of the Economic and Social History of the Orient*, 53, 83–108.
Dieten (1976): Jan Louis van Dieten, "Justinian II. Rhinotmetos", in: *Biographisches Lexikon zur Geschichte Südosteuropas*, Volume 2, Munich, 314–316.
D'iakov and Nikol'skii (1952): V.N. D'iakov and N.M. Nikol'skii (eds.), *Istoriia drevnego mira. Uchebnik* [The History of the Ancient World. A Textbook], Moscow.
Diulichev (2002): Valerii P. Diulichev, *Rasskazy po istorii Kryma* [Narratives on the History of Crimea], fifth edition, Simferopol'.
Diulichev (2006): Valerii P. Diulichev, *Krym. Istoriia v ocherkakh. XX vek* [Crimea. History in Sketches. 20th Century], Simferopol'.
Długosz and Scholz (2013): Magdalena Długosz and Piotr O. Scholz (eds.), *Sarmatismus versus Orientalismus in Mitteleuropa*, Berlin.

Dougherty (1994): Carol Dougherty, "Archaic Greek Foundation Poetry. Questions of Genre and Occasion", in: *Journal of Hellenic Studies*, 114, 35–6.

Druzhinina (1955): E.I. Druzhinina, *Kiuchuk-Kainardzhiiskii mir 1774 goda. Ego podgotovka i zakliuchenie* [The Peace of Kiuchuk-Kainardzha 1774. Its Preparation and the Conclusion], Moscow.

Dufaud (2012a): Grégory Dufaud, "La constitution d'une déviation nationaliste dans l'Union soviétique des années 1920. Les Tatars de Crimée et la veli-ibraïmovchtchina", in: *Genèses*, 86:1, 104–25.

Dufaud (2012b): Grégory Dufaud, "The Establishment of Bolshevik Power in the Crimea and the Construction of a Multinational Soviet State. Organisation, Justification, Uncertainties", in: *Contemporary European History*, 21:2, 257–72.

Edgerton (1999): Robert B. Edgerton, *Death or Glory. The Legacy of the Crimean War*, Boulder.

Eisenstadt (2007): Shmuel N. Eisenstadt, *Multiple Modernities. Der Streit um die Gegenwart*, Berlin.

Eisfeld and Herdt (1996): Alfred Eisfeld and Viktor Herdt (eds.), *Deportation, Sondersiedlung, Arbeitsarmee. Deutsche in der Sowjetunion 1941 bis 1956*, Cologne.

Engert (2007): Rolf Engert, *Iphigenie. Dichtungen von der Antike bis zur Gegenwart. Euripides – Jean Racine – Johann Wolfgang Goethe – Gerhardt Hauptmann*. Second edition expanded with an index of people and foreign words, Leipzig.

Epstein (1996): Steven A. Epstein, *Genoa and the Genoese 958–1528*, Chapel Hill.

Epstein (2001): Steven A. Epstein, *Speaking of Slavery. Color, Ethnicity and Human Bondage in Italy*, Ithaca.

Faroqhi (1994): Suraiya Farochi, "Crisis and Change 1590–1699", in: Halil İnalcık (ed.), *An Economic and Social History of the Ottoman Empire. 1300–1914*, Volume 2, Cambridge, 411–636.

Fedorov-Davydov (1973): German A. Fedorov-Davydov, *Die Goldene Horde*, Munich.

Feferman (2007): Kiril Feferman, "Nazi Germany and the Mountain Jews. Was There a Policy?", in: *Holocaust and Genocide Studies*, 21:1, 96–114.

Feferman (2011): Kiril Feferman, "Nazi Germany and the Karaites in 1938–1944. Between Racial Theory and Realpolitik", in: *Nationalities Papers*, 39:2, 277–94.

Feichtinger and Heiss (2013): Johannes Feichtinger and Johann Heiss (eds.), *Kritische Studien zur "Türkenbelagerung"*, Vienna.

Fenz (2000): Hendrik Fenz, *Vom Völkerfrühling bis zur Oktoberrevolution 1917. Die Rolle der aserbaidschanischen Elite bei der Schaffung einer nationalen Identität*, Münster et al. (= Hamburger Islamwissenschaftliche und Turkologische Arbeiten und Texte, 11).

Figes (1989): Orlando Figes, *Peasant Russia, Civil War. The Volga Countryside in Revolution*, Oxford.

Figes (2010): Orlando Figes, *The Crimean War. A History*, London.

Filip (1990): Ota Filip, "Das Igor-Lied", in: Karl Corino (ed.), *Gefälscht! Betrug in Politik, Literatur, Wissenschaft, Kunst und Musik*, Frankfurt am Main, 209–17.

Fisher (1968): Alan W. Fisher, "Enlightened Despotism and Islam under Catherine II", in: *Slavic Review*, 27, 542–53.

Fisher (1970): Alan W. Fisher, *The Russian Annexation of the Crimea 1772–1783*, Cambridge.

Fisher (1972a): Alan Fisher, "Les rapports entre l'Empire ottoman et la Crimée. L'aspect financier", in: *Cahiers du monde russe. Russie, Empire Russe, Union Soviétique*, 13, 368–81.
Fisher (1972b): Alan W. Fisher, "Muscovy and the Black Sea Slave Trade", in: *Canadian-American Slavic Studies*, 6 (Winter):4, 575–94.
Fisher (1973): Alan W. Fisher, "Azov in the Sixteenth and Seventeenth Centuries", in: *Jahrbücher für Geschichte Osteuropas*, 21, 161–74.
Fisher (1977): Alan W. Fisher, "Crimean Separatism in the Ottoman Empire", in: William W. Haddad and William Ochsenwald (eds.), *Nationalism in a Non-National State. The Dissolution of the Ottoman Empire*, Columbus/Ohio, 77–92.
Fisher (1978): Alan Fisher, *The Crimean Tatars*, Stanford.
Fisher (1979): Alan Fisher, "Social and Legal Aspects of Russian-Muslim Relations in the 19th Century. The Case of Crimean Tatars", in: Abraham Ascher, Tibor Halasi-Kun and Bela K. Kiraly (eds.), *The Mutual Effects of the Islamic and Judeo-Christian Worlds. The East European Pattern*, Brooklyn, 77–92.
Fisher (1981): Alan Fisher, "The Ottoman Crimea in the 16th Century", in: *Harvard Ukrainian Studies*, 5, 135–70.
Forum (2012): "Forum. Timothy Snyder's Bloodlands", in: *Contemporary European History*, 21:2, 115.
Fouquet and Zeilinger (2011): Gerhard Fouquet and Gabriel Zeilinger, *Katastrophen im Spätmittelalter*, Darmstadt.
Franke (1995): Susanne Franke, *Die Reise der Lady Craven durch Europa und die Türkei 1785/1786. Text, Kontext und Ideologien*, Trier (= Grenzüberschreitung, 4).
Frary and Kozelsky (2014): Lucien J. Frary and Mara Kozelsky (eds.), *Russian-Ottoman Borderlands. The Eastern Question Reconsidered*, Madison/Wisc.
Frings (2010): Andreas Frings, "Neukonstruktion von Lebenswelten im multiethnischen Wolga-Kama-Raum. Die Apostasiewelle von 1866", in: Victor Herdt and Dietmar Neutatz (eds.), *Gemeinsam getrennt. Lebenswelten der multiethnischen bäuerlichen Bevölkerung im Schwarzmeer- und Wolgagebiet vor 1917*, Wiesbaden, 143–64.
Frings and Kusber (2007): Andreas Frings and Jan Kusber (eds.), *Das Zarenreich, das Jahr 1905 und seine Wirkungen. Bestandsaufnahmen*, Münster et al.
Fuchs (2011): John Andreas Fuchs, "Ein Yankee am Hofe des Zaren. Mark Twain und die Friends of Russian Freedom", in: *Forum für osteuropäische Ideen- und Zeitgeschichte*, 15:2, 69–85.
Fuhs (1992): Burkhard Fuhs, *Mondäne Orte einer vornehmen Gesellschaft. Kultur und Geschichte der Kurstädte 1700–1900*, Hildesheim/Zurich/New York.
Furin and Rybinski (1975): Stanislaw Furin and Jewgeni Rybinski, *Das Pionierlager Artek*, Moscow.
Gajda (2002): Oliver Gajda, *Katharina II. von Russland im Diskurs der Sexualität. Mittelbare Einflüsse narrativer Fiktion auf Geschichtswissenschaft*, Berlin (ebook). Also as a Master's dissertation, Universität Hamburg, 2001.
Gaidukevich (1949): Viktor F. Gaidukevich, *Bosporskoe tsarstvo* [The Bosporan Kingdom], Moscow/Leningrad.
Gajdukevič (1971): Viktor F. Gajdukevič, *Das Bosporanische Reich, 2. neubearb. und wesentl. erw. Auflage in dt. Sprache mit den Ergebnissen der archäologischen Untersuchungen von 1949 bis 1966*, Vienna/Cologne/Graz.

Gaivoronskii (2007): Oleksa Gaivoronskii, *Poveliteli dvukh materikov. Krymskie khany XV–XVI stoletii i bor'ba za nasledstvo Velikoi Ordy* [Masters of Two Continents. The Crimean Khans from the 15th to the 16th Century and the Battle for the Heritage of the Golden Horde], Kyiv et al.

Gall (2015): Caroline von Gall, "Analyse. Ist die Krim wirklich russisch? Russische Juristen diskutieren über die Rechtmäßigkeit der Aufnahme der Krim", in: *Bundeszentrale für politische Bildung*, 11 May 2015. Online: http://www.bpb.de/internationales/europa/ russland/analysen/206618/analyse-ist-die-krim-wirklich-russisch-russische-juristen- diskutieren-ueber-die-rechtmaessigkeit-der-aufnahme-der-krim (accessed 14 March 2017).

Gankevich (1994): V.Iu. Gankevich, "Rol' I. Gasprinskogo i ego sem'i v razvitii narodnogo obrazovaniia sred. krymsko-tatarskikh zhenshchin na rubezhe XIX–XX vekov" [The Role of I. Gasprinskii and His Family for the Development of National Education Among Crimean Women Around the Turn of the XIXth–XXth Century], in: *Krym i Rossiia. Nerazryvnye istoricheskie sud'by i kul'tura. Materialy respublikanskoi nauchno-obshchestvennoi konferentsii* [Crimea and Russia. Inseparable Historical Fates and Culture. Materials of the Republican Scholarly and Public Conference], Simferopol', 19–21.

Gankevich and Shendrikova (2008): V.Iu. Gankevich and S.P. Shendrikova, *Ismail Gasprinskii i vozniknovenie liberal'no-musul'manskogo politicheskogo dvizheniia* [Ismail Gasprinskii and the Emergence of the Liberal Muslim Political Movement], Simferopol'.

Ganzenmüller (2013): Jörg Ganzenmüller, *Russische Staatsgewalt und polnischer Adel. Elitenintegration und Staatausbau im Westen des Zarenreichs 1772–1850*, Cologne et al.

Ganzer (2005): Christian Ganzer, *Sowjetisches Erbe und ukrainische Nation. Das Museum der Geschichte des Zaporoger Kosakentums auf der Insel Chortycja*, Stuttgart.

Gasimov (2011): Zaur Gasimov, "Der Antikommunismus in Polen im Spiegel der Vierteljahresschrift Wschód 1930–1939", in: *Jahrbuch für Historische Kommunismusforschung*, 18, 15–30.

Gasimov (2014): Zaur Gasimov, "Nahe Verwandte, so fern. Die Türkei, die Tataren und die Krim", in: *Osteuropa*, 64:5–6, 311–22.

Gasimov (2017): Zaur Gasimov, "Krimtatarische Exil-Netzwerke zwischen Osteuropa und dem Nahen Osten", in: *ÖZG*, 28:1, 142–66.

Gazley (1956): John G. Gazley, "The Reverend Arthur Young, 1769–1827. Traveller in Russia and Farmer in the Crimea", in: *Bulletin of the John Rylands Library*, 38:2, 360–405. Online: https://www.escholar.manchester.ac.uk/api/datastream?publicationPid=uk-ac-man- scw:1 m2797&datastreamId=POST-PEER-REVIEW-PUBLISHERS-DOCUMENT.PDF (accessed 7 May 2018).

Gertsen and Mogarichev (1992): A.G. Gertsen and M. Mogarichev, "Ikonoborcheskaia Tavrika" [Iconoclastic Taurida], in: *Antichnaia drevnost' i srednie veka* [Classical Antiquity and the Middle Ages], 26, 180–90.

Germer (1998): Stefan Germer, "Retrovision. Die rückblickende Erfindung der Nationen durch die Kunst", in: Monika Flacke (ed.), *Mythen der Nationen. Ein europäisches Panorama*, Berlin, 33–52.

Gernsheim and Gernsheim (1954): Helmut Gernsheim and Alison Gernsheim, *Roger Fenton. Photographer of the Crimean War. His Photographs and his Letters from the Crimea*, London.

Gerschenkron (1962): Alexander Gerschenkron, *Economic Backwardness in Historical Perspective*, New York.
Golczewski (1993): Frank Golczewski (ed.), *Geschichte der Ukraine*, Göttingen.
Golczewski (2010): Frank Golczewski, *Deutsche und Ukrainer*, Paderborn.
Golden (2003): Peter B. Golden, "The Qipčaqs of Medieval Eurasia. An Example of Stateless Adaptation in the Steppes", in: *idem, Nomads and their Neighbours in the Russian Steppe. Turks, Khazars and Qipchaqs*, Aldershot et al. (= Variorum collected Studies Series, 752), 132–57.
Golden (2006): P.B. Golden, "The Khazar Sacral Kingship", in: Kathryn L. Reyerson, Theofanis G. Stavrou and James D. Tracy (eds.), *Pre-Modern Russia and its World. Essays in Honor of Thomas S. Noonan*, Wiesbaden (= Schriften zur Geistesgeschichte des östlichen Europa, 29), 79–102.
Golden et al. (2007): Peter B. Golden, Haggai Ben-Shammai and András Róna-Tas (eds.), *The World of the Khazars. New Perspectives. Selected Papers from the Jerusalem 1999 International Khazar Colloquium hosted by the Ben Zvi Institute*, Leiden/Boston (= Handbuch für Orientalistik, Sektion 8, 17).
Goldfrank (1994): David M. Goldfrank, *The Origins of the Crimean War*, London/New York.
Gorizontov (2012): Leonid E. Gorizontov, "The Crimean War as a Test of Russia's Imperial Durability", in: *Russian Studies in History*, 51:1, 65–94.
Gossel-Raeck and Busch (1993): Berthild Gossel-Raeck and Ralf Busch (eds.), *Gold der Skythen. Schätze aus der Staatlichen Eremitage St Petersburg*, Münster.
Green (1984): Warren P. Green, "The Fate of the Crimean Jewish Community. Ashkenazim, Krymchaks, and Karaites", in: *Jewish Social Studies*, 46:2, 169–76.
Greule (2003): Albrecht Greule, "Ostgoten. §1 Namenkundliches", in: Heinrich Beck, Dieter Geuenich and Heiko Steuer (eds.), *Reallexikon der Germanischen Altertumskunde*, second edition, Volume 22, Berlin/New York, 344 f.
Groebner (2007): Valentin Groebner, "Mit dem Feind schlafen. Nachdenken über Hautfarben, Sex und 'Rasse' im spätmittelalterlichen Europa", in: *Historische Anthropologie*, 15, 431–8.
Guboglo and Chervonnaia (1995): M.N. Guboglo and S.M. Chervonnaia, "The Crimean Tatar Question and the Present Ethnopolitical Situation in Crimea", in: *Russian Politics and Law*, 33:6, 31–60.
Gumilëv (1997): L.N. Gumilëv, *Ot Rusi do Rossi. Sost. i obshch. red. A.I. Kurkchi* [From Rus' to Russia. Ed. by A.I. Kurkchi], Moscow.
Guski (2008): Andreas Guski, "Die Stimme der Opfer. Vom Umgang mit Katastrophen in Russland", in: *Osteuropa*, 58:4–5, 61–79.
Hablemitoğlu and Hablemitoğlu (1998): Şengül Hablemitoğlu and Necip Hablemitoğlu, *Şefika Gaspıralı ve Rusya'da Türk kadın hareketi, 1893–1920* [Şefika Gaspıralı and the Turkish Women's Movement in Russia, 1893–1920], Ankara.
Hagen (2014): Mark von Hagen, "Rezension zu Felix Schnell, Räume des Schreckens. Gewalt und Gruppenmilitanz in der Ukraine, 1905–1933. Hamburg, Hamburger Edition 2012", in: *Historische Zeitschrift*, 299:3, 822–4.
Halbach (2014): Uwe Halbach, "Analyse. Die Krimtataren in der Ukraine-Krise", in: *Bundeszentrale für politische Bildung*, 13 November 2014. Online: http://www.bpb.de/ internationales/europa/ukraine/195184/analyse-die-krimtataren-in-der-ukraine-krise (accessed 19 January 2018).

Halenko (2004): Oleksander Halenko, "Wine Production, Marketing and Consumption in the Ottoman Crimea 1520–1542", in: *Journal of the Economic and Social History of the Orient*, 47, 507–47.
Hall E. (1989): Edith Hall, *Inventing the Barbarian. Greek Self-Definition through Tragedy*, Oxford.
Hall J. (2002): Jonathan Hall, *Hellenicity. Between Ethnicity and Culture*, Chicago.
Halperin (1987): Charles J. Halperin, *Russia and the Golden Horde. The Mongol Impact on Medieval Russian History*, Bloomington.
Haran and Prokoptschuk (2013): Olexij Haran and Dmytro Prokoptschuk, "Die Ukraine und die Desintegration der UdSSR", in: Martin Malek and Anna Schor-Tschudnowskaja (eds.) *Der Zerfall der Sowjetunion. Ursachen – Begleiterscheinungen – Hintergründe*, Baden-Baden, 327–46.
Hartog F. (1980): François Hartog, *Le Miroir d'Hérodote. Essai sur la représentation de l'autre*, Paris.
Hartog L. (1996): Leo de Hartog, *Russia and the Mongol Yoke. The History of the Russian Principalities and the Golden Horde 1221–1502*, London/New York.
Hartung (2005): Jan-Peter Hartung, "Die fromme Stiftung (waqf). Eine islamische Analogie zur Körperschaft?", in: Hans G. Kippenberg and Gunnar Folke Schuppert (eds.), *Die verrechtlichte Religion. Der Öffentlichkeitsstatus von Religionsgemeinschaften*, Tübingen, 287–313.
Hathaway and Barbir (2008): Jane Hathaway and Karl K. Barbir, *The Arab Lands under Ottoman Rule 1516–1800*, Harlow.
Haumann (1996): Heiko Haumann, *Geschichte Rußlands*, Munich/Zurich.
Hauner (1990): Milan Hauner, *What is Asia to Us? Russia's Asian Heartland Yesterday and Today*, Boston.
Heine (1990): Peter Heine, "Khalif", in: Adel Theodor Khoury, Ludwig Hagemann and Peter Heine (eds.), *Islam-Lexikon*, Volume 2, Gütersloh, 441–4.
Heinen (2006): Heinz Heinen, *Antike am Rande der Steppe. Der nördliche Schwarzmeerraum als Forschungsaufgabe*, Stuttgart.
Heller (1992): Wolfgang Heller, "Križanić, Juraj", in: *Biographisch-Bibliographisches Kirchenlexikon*, Volume 4, Herzberg, Columns 670–674.
Hellie (1982): Richard Hellie, *Slavery in Russia 1450–1725*, Chicago/London.
Herlihy (1986): Patricia Herlihy, *Odessa. A History 1794–1914*, Cambridge, MA.
Hildermeier (1998): Manfred Hildermeier, *Geschichte der Sowjetunion. Entstehung und Niedergang des ersten sozialistischen Staates*, Munich.
Hildermeier (2017): Manfred Hildermeier, "Die Russische Revolution und ihre Folgen", in: *Aus Politik und Zeitgeschichte*, 34–36. Online: http://www.bpb.de/apuz/254458/ die-russische-revolution-und-ihre-folgen?p=all (accessed 9 August 2017).
Hillebrand (2017): Caspar Hillebrand, "Evliya Çelebis Krimbericht. Hintergrund, Sprache, Erzählweise", in: ÖZG, 28:1, 41–64.
Hirsch (2005): Francine Hirsch, *Empire of Nations. Ethnographic Knowledge and the Making of the Soviet Union*, Ithaca, NY.
Hobson (2004): John M. Hobson, *The Eastern Origins of Western Civilization*, Cambridge.
Hoensch (1983): Jörg K. Hoensch, *Geschichte Polens*, Stuttgart.
Hoffmann P. (1991): Peter Hoffmann, "Karamzins 'Geschichte des Russischen Reiches'. Bemerkungen zur Rezeption in der sowjetischen Historiographie", in: *Zeitschrift für Slawistik*, 35, 611–31.

Hoffmann S. (1968): Stanley Hoffmann, "Collaborationism in France during World War II", in: *The Journal of Modern History*, 40:3, 375–395.
Hofmeister (2017): Ulrich Hofmeister, "Ein Krimtatare in Zentralasien. Ismail Gasprinskij, der Orientalismus und das Zarenreich", in: ÖZG, 28:1, 114–41.
Højte (2006): Jakob Munk Højte, "From Kingdom to Province. Reshaping Pontos after the Fall of Mithridates VI", in: Tønnes Bekker-Nielsen (ed.), *Rome and the Black Sea Region. Domination, Romanisation, Resistance,* Aarhus (= Black Sea Studies, 5), 15–30.
Højte (2009): Jakob Munk Højte: "The Death and Burial of Mithridates VI", in: idem (ed.), *Mithridates VI and the Pontic Kingdom,* Aarhus, 121–30.
Hokanson (1998): Katya Hokanson, "Pushkin's Captive Crimea. Imperialism in The Fountain of Bakhchisarai", in: Monika Greenleaf and Stephen Moeller-Sally (eds.), *Russian Subjects. Empire, Nation, and the Culture of the Golden Age,* Evanston, Ill., 123–48.
Hösch (1964): Edgar Hösch, "Das sog. 'Griechische Projekt' Katharinas II. Ideologie und Wirklichkeit der russischen Orientpolitik in der zweiten Hälfte des. 18. Jahrhunderts", in: *Jahrbücher für Geschichte Osteuropas,* 12, 168–206.
Hosking (1997): Geoffrey Hosking, *Russia. People and Empire 1552–1917,* Cambridge, MA.
Hottop-Riecke (2017), Mieste Hottop-Riecke, "Tatarisch-Preußische Interferenzen im 17. und 18. Jahrhundert. Eine Beziehungsgeschichte in Zeugnissen der Militär- und Geistesgeschichte", in: ÖZG, 28:1, 65–90.
Hromenko (2017): Serhiy Hromenko, *#CrimeaIsOurs. History of the Russian Myth,* Kyiv.
Hryszko (2004): Rafał Hryszko, *Z Genui nad Morze Czarne. Z kart genueńskiej obecności gospodarczej na północno-zachodnich wybrzeżach Morza Czarnego u schyłku średniowiecza* [From Genoa to the Black Sea. On the Maps of Genoa's Economic Presence on the Northwestern Shore of the Black Sea at the End of the Middle Ages], Kraków.
Hürter (2012): Johannes Hürter, "Die nationalsozialistische Besatzungspolitik in der Sowjetunion", in: *Forum für osteuropäische Ideen- und Zeitgeschichte,* 16:1, 15–28.
Igelström (2018): "Igelström, Otto Heinrich Frh. v.", in: *Baltisches Biographisches Lexikon digital (BBLd). Digitalisierungsprojekt der Baltischen Historischen Kommission.* Online: http://www.bbl-digital.de/eintrag/Igelstrom%2C-Otto-Heinrich-Frh.-v.-seit-1792-Gf.- 1737-1823/ (accessed 17 May 2018).
Inalcik (1969): Halil Inalcik, "Capital Formation in the Ottoman Empire", in: *The Journal of Economic History,* 29, 97–140.
Istoriia (2015): *Istoriia Kryma* [History of Crimea], Moscow.
Ivanics (2012): Mária Ivanics, "Die Şirin. Abstammung und Aufstieg einer Sippe in der Steppe", in: Klein D. (2012a), 27–44.
Ivantchik (2001): Askold Ivantchik (i.e. Askol'd I. Ivanchik), *Kimmerier und Skythen. Kulturhistorische und chronologische Probleme der Archäologie der osteuropäischen Steppen und Kaukasiens in vor- und frühskythischer Zeit,* Mainz.
Ivantchik (2005): Askold I. Ivantchik, *Am Vorabend der Kolonisation. Das nördliche Schwarzmeergebiet und die Steppennomaden des 8. - 7. Jahrhunderts v.Chr. in der klassischen Literaturtradition. Mündliche Überlieferung, Literatur und Geschichte,* Moscow et al.

Iakobson (1959): A.L. Iakobson, *Rannesrednevekovyi Khersones* [Early Medieval Chersonesus], Moscow/Leningrad.
Iakobson (1964): A.L. Iakobson, *Srednevekovyi Krym. Ocherki istorii i istorii material'noi kul'tury* [Medieval Crimea. Treatises on the History and the History of the Material Culture], Moskva/Leningrad.
Iakobson (1973): A.L. Iakobson, *Krym v srednie veka* [Crimea in the Middle Ages], Moscow.
Iaremchuk and Bezverkhyi (1994): V.D. Iaremchuk and V.B. Bezverkhyi, "Tatary v Ukraïni. Istoryko- politolohichnyi aspekt" [Tatars in Ukraine. The Historico-Politocological Aspect], *Ukraïnskyi istorychnyi zhurnal* [Ukrainian Hisotrical Journal], 5, 18–29.
Jankowski (2006): Henryk Jankowski, *A Historical-Etymological Dictionary of Pre-Russian Habitation Names*, Leiden et al.
Jaspert (2004): Nikolas Jaspert, *Die Kreuzzüge*, Darmstadt.
Jaworski (2014): Rudolf Jaworski, "Einführung in Fragestellung und Themenfelder", in: Stachel and Thomsen (2014), 11–30.
Jena (2001): Detlef Jena, *Potemkin. Favorit und Feldmarschall Katharinas der Großen*, Munich.
Jobst (1997): Kerstin S. Jobst, "Marxismus und Nationalismus. Julijan Bačyns'kyj und die Rezeption seiner 'Ukraïna Irredenta' (1895/96) als Konzept der ukrainischen Unabhängigkeit?", in: *Jahrbücher für die Geschichte Osteuropas*, N.F. 45, 31–47.
Jobst (2000): Kerstin S. Jobst, "Orientalism. E.W. Said und die Osteuropäische Geschichte", in: *Saeculum. Jahrbuch für Universalgeschichte*, 51:2, 250–66.
Jobst (2001a): Kerstin S. Jobst, "Die Taurische Reise von 1787 als Beginn der Mythisierung der Krim. Bemerkungen zum europäischen Krim-Diskurs des 18. und 19. Jahrhunderts", in: *Archiv für Kulturgeschichte*, 83:1, 121–44.
Jobst (2001b): Kerstin S. Jobst, "Ein kleiner Ordnungsversuch im südlichen Rußland. Das Beispiel der Halbinsel Krim", in: Harald Heppner and Eduard Staudinger (eds.), *Region und Umbruch 1918. Zur Geschichte alternativer Ordnungsversuche*, Frankfurt am Main et al., 203–30.
Jobst (2001c): Kerstin S. Jobst, "Im Spiel mit großen Mächten? Nationale Konflikte nach dem Zerfall des Zarenreichs bis zum Beginn des Russischen Bürgerkriegs 1918/19 auf der Halbinsel Krim", in: Philipp Ther and Holm Sundhaussen (eds.), *Nationalitätenkonflikte im 20. Jahrhundert. Ursachen von inter-ethnischer Gewalt im Vergleich*, Wiesbaden (= Forschungen zur Osteuropäischen Geschichte, 59), 83–107.
Jobst (2001d): Kerstin S. Jobst, "'Übrigens lassen sich hier nur selten Weiber sehen'. Die Darstellung der Geschlechterverhältnisse in Reiseberichten über die Krim (18.-20. Jahrhundert)", in: Karsten Brüggemann, Thomas M. Bohn and Konrad Maier (eds.), *Kollektivität und Individualität. Der Mensch im östlichen Europa. Festschrift für Prof. Dr. Angermann zum 65. Geburtstag*, Hamburg, 212–23.
Jobst (2007a): Kerstin S. Jobst, "'Asien auf der Krim'. Die Kategorien 'Orient' und 'Okzident' im europäischen Krim-Diskurs vor dem Ersten Weltkrieg", in: Christophe Duhamelle, Andreas Kossert and Bernhard Struck (eds.), *Grenzen und Grenzräume im europäischen Vergleich*, Frankfurt am Main, 225–46.
Jobst (2007b): Kerstin S. Jobst, *Die Perle des Imperiums. Der russische Krim-Diskurs im Zarenreich*, Konstanz.
Jobst (2010): Kerstin S. Jobst, "Die Wahrnehmung von Assimilations- und Akkulturationsprozessen im russischen Krim-Diskurs vor dem Ersten

Weltkrieg", in: Victor Herdt and Dietmar Neutatz (eds.), *Gemeinsam getrennt. Lebenswelten der multiethnischen bäuerlichen Bevölkerung im Schwarzmeer- und Wolgagebiet vor 1917*, Wiesbaden, 181–94.

Jobst (2011a): Kerstin S. Jobst, "Bilder des indigenen Kriegers in der russischen Kultur", in: Stefan Bayer and Matthias Gillner (eds.), *Soldaten im Einsatz. Sozialwissenschaftliche und ethische Reflexionen*, Berlin (= Sozialwissenschaftliche Studien, 49), 185–204.

Jobst (2011b): Kerstin S. Jobst, "Das frühneuzeitliche Krim-Khanat", in: Albrecht and Herdick (201Ukra1), 11–22.

Jobst (2011c): Kerstin Jobst, "Ukraïns'ka travmatychna pamiat'. Holodomor i Chornobyl'" [The Ukrainian Traumatic Memory. Holodomor und Chornobyl'], in: *Krytyka*, 15:11–12. Online: https://krytyka.com/ua/articles/ukrayinska-travmatychna-pamyat-holodomor-i- chornobyl (accessed 14 March 2017).

Jobst (2012): Kerstin S. Jobst, "Vision und Regime. Die ersten Jahrzehnte russischer Krim-Herrschaft", in: Klein D. (2012a), 211–27.

Jobst (2013a): Kerstin S. Jobst, "Chersones", in: Joachim Bahlcke, Stefan Rohdewald and Thomas Wünsch (eds.), *Religiöse Erinnerungsorte in Ostmitteleuropa. Konstitution und Konkurrenz im nationen- und epochenübergreifenden Zugriff*, Berlin, 3–10.

Jobst (2013b): Kerstin S. Jobst, "Where the Orient Ends? Orientalism and its Function for Imperial Rule in the Russian Empire", in: James Hodkinson et al. (eds.), *Deploying Orientalism in Culture and History. From Germany to Central and Eastern Europe*, Rochester, NY, 190–208.

Jobst (2014): Kerstin S. Jobst, "Gefährliche Fremde und Titularnation? Partizipation der Krimtataren im Zarenreich und in der frühen Sowjetunion", in: Katrin Boeckh et al. (eds.), *Staatsbürgerschaft und Teilhabe. Bürgerliche, politische und soziale Rechte in Osteuropa*, Munich, 179–98.

Jobst (2015a): Kerstin S. Jobst, "Der nördliche Schwarzmeerraum", in: *Europäische Geschichte Online*, ed. by Leibniz-Institut für Europäische Geschichte (IEG), Mainz. Online: http://www.ieg-ego.eu/jobstk-2015-de (accessed 24 November 2017).

Jobst (2015b): Kerstin S. Jobst, *Geschichte der Ukraine*, second, updated edition, Stuttgart.

Jobst (2017a): Kerstin S. Jobst, "'Dunkle' und 'Goldene' Zeiten. Krimtataren unter zarischer und sowjetischer Herrschaft bis 1941", in: ÖZG, 28:1, 91–113.

Jobst (2017b): Kerstin S. Jobst, "'Einnahme unmöglich'? Sevastopol' als Geschichte eines (Miss-)Erfolgs", in: Oliver Auge and Doris Tillmann (eds.), *Kiel und die Marine. 150 Jahre gemeinsame Geschichte*, Kiel, 161–82.

Jobst (2017c): Kerstin S. Jobst, "Russländisch-imperiale Image-Produktionen im ausgehenden 18. Jahrhundert. Die Reise Katharinas II. in den 'russischen Süden'", in: Christoph Augustynowicz and Agnieszka Pufelska (eds.), *Konstruierte (Fremd-?)Bilder. Das östliche Europa im Diskurs des 18. Jahrhunderts*, Berlin/Boston, 94–107.

Jobst (2019): Kerstin S. Jobst, "Holy Ground. The (Re-)Construction of an Orthodox Crimea in 19th Century Russia", in: Liliya Berezhnaya and Heidi Hein-Kirchner (eds.), *Rampart Nations. Bulwarks Myths of East European Multiconfessional Societies in the Age of Nationalism*, Oxford/New York, 125–45.

Jobst, et al. (2008): Kerstin S. Jobst, Julia Obertreis and Ricarda Vulpius, "Imperiumsforschung in der Osteuropäischen Geschichte. Die

Habsburgermonarchie, das Russländische Reich und die Sowjetunion", in: *Comparativ. Zeitschrift für Globalgeschichte und vergleichende Gesellschaftsforschung*, 18:2: Ostmitteleuropa transnational (ed. by Peter Haslinger), 27–56.
Jones (1996): Robert E. Jones, "Opening a Window on the South. Russia and the Black Sea 1695–1792", in: Maria di Salvo (ed.), *A Window on Russia. Papers from the V. International Conference of the Study Group on 18th-Century Russia in Gargnano 1994*, Milan/Rome, 123–129.
Jung-Kaiser (2013): Ute Jung-Kaiser, "Mithridates", in: Peter von Möllendorff, Annette Simonis and Linda Simonis (eds.), *Historische Gestalten der Antike. Rezeption in Literatur, Kunst und Musik*, Stuttgart/Weimar (= Der Neue Pauly. Supplemente, 8), Columns 683–90.
Kaelble (1999): Hartmut Kaelble, "Der historische Zivilisationsvergleich", in: *idem* et al. (eds.), *Diskurse und Entwicklungspfade. Vergleiche in den Gesellschafts- und Sozialwissenschaften*, Frankfurt am Main, 29–52.
Kalinin and Zemlianichenko (1993): N. Kalinin and M. Zemlianichenko, *Romanovy i Krym* [The Romanovs and Crimea], Moscow.
Kaminskij (2012): Konstantin Kaminskij, "Der Normannenstreit als Gründungsschlacht der russischen Geschichtsschreibung. Zur Poetik wissenschaftlicher Anfangserzählungen", in: Thomas Wallnig et al. (eds.), *Europäische Geschichtskulturen um 1700 zwischen Gelehrsamkeit, Politik und Konfession*, Berlin et al., 553–80.
Kappeler (1993): Andreas Kappeler, *Rußland als Vielvölkerreich. Entstehung, Geschichte, Zerfall*, second edition, Munich.
Kappeler (2013): Andreas Kappeler, *Die Kosaken*, Munich.
Kappeler (2014): Andreas Kappeler, *Kleine Geschichte der Ukraine*, fourth, expanded edition, Munich.
Karpat (1984/1985): Kemal Karpat, "Ottoman Urbanism. The Crimean Emigration to Dobruca and the Founding of Mecidiye 1856–1878', in: *International Journal of Turkish Studies*, 3, 1–27.
Karpat (1986): Kemal Karpat, "The Crimean Emigration of 1856–1862 and the Settlement and Urban Development of Dobruca", in: Gilles Lemercier, S. Veinstein and Enders Wimbush (eds.), *Turco-Tatar Past, Soviet Present. Studies Presented to Alexandre Bennigsen*, Paris, 275–303.
Karpov (2007): Sergei P. Karpov, *Istoriia Trapezundskoi imperii* [The History of the Empire of Trebizond], St Petersburg.
Karsten (2012): Arne Karsten, *Geschichte Venedigs*, Munich.
Kasack (1997): Wolfgang Kasack, "Ljudmila Evgen'eva Ulickaja. Medea i ee deti. Semejnaja chronika", in: *idem* (ed.), *Hauptwerke der russischen Literatur*, Munich, 732 f.
Kas'ianov (2010): Heorhii Kas'ianov, *Danse macabre. Holod 1932–1933 rokiv u polityts, masovii svidomosti ta istoriohrafii (1980-ti-pochatok 2000-kh)* [Danse Macabre. The Famine of 1932–1833 in Politics, Collective Consciousness and Historiography. The 1980s to the 2000s], Kyiv.
Kawerau (1967): Peter Kawerau, *Arabische Quellen zur Christianisierung Rußlands*, Wiesbaden.
Keil (2001): Rolf-Dietrich Keil, *Alexander Puschkin. Ein Dichterleben*, Frankfurt am Main/Leipzig.
Keller (2001): Ulrich Keller, *The Ultimative Spectacle. A Visual History of the Crimean War*, Amsterdam et al.

Kelly (2007): Catriona Kelly, *Children's World. Growing up in Russia. 1890–1991*, New Haven.
Kent (2016): Neil Kent, *Crimea. A History*, London.
Khodarkovsky (2002): Michael Khodarkovsky, *Russia's Steppe Frontier. The Making of a Colonial Empire 1500–1800*, Bloomington/Indianapolis.
Khoroshkevich (2000): A.L. Khoroshkevich, *Rus' i Krym. Ot soiuza k protivostoianiiu. Konets XV – nachalo XVI vv.* [Rus' and Crimea. From Alliance to Hostility. The Late 15th–16th Century], Moscow. Kindler (2018): Robert Kindler, *Stalin's Nomads. Power and Famine in Kazakhstan*, Pittsburgh.
King (2004): Charles King, *The Black Sea. A History*, Oxford.
King (2010): Charles King, "Stadt am Rande. Sevastopol' – Europas nächster Krisenherd?", in: *Osteuropa*, 60:2–4, 319–329.
Kirimal (1952): Edige Kirimal, *Der nationale Kampf der Krimtürken mit besonderer Berücksichtigung der Jahre 1917–1918*, Emsdetten, Westf.
Kirimli S. (1990): Sirri H. Kirimli, *National Movements and National Identity Among the Crimean Tatars 1905–1916*, Ph.D. dissertation, University of Wisconsin, Madison, Wisc.
Kirimli H. (1993): Hakan Kirimli, "The 'Young' Tatar Movement in the Crimea 1905–1909", in: *Cahiers du Monde russe et soviétique*, 34:4, 529–60.
Kirmse (2013): Stefan B. Kirmse, "Law and Empire in Late Tsarist Russia. Muslim Tatars Go to Court", in: *Slavic Review*, 72:4, 778–801.
Kizilov (2007): Mikhail Kizilov, "Slave Trade in the Early Modern Crimea from the Perspective of Christian, Muslim, and Jewish Sources", in: *Journal of Early Modern History*, 11, 1–31.
Kizilov (2007/2008): Michail Kizilov, "Krymchaki. Sovremennoe sostoianie obshchiny" [Krymchaks. The Community's Present Situation], in: *Evroaziatskii evreiskii ezhegodnik* [Eurasian Jewish Yearbook], 5768. Online: https://web.archive.org/web/20151017142435/http://library.eajc.org/page70/news13498 (accessed 14 March 2018).
Klein D. (2012a): Denise Klein (ed.), *The Crimean Khanate between East and West (15th–18th Century)*, Wiesbaden (= Forschungen zur osteuropäischen Geschichte, 78).
Klein D. (2012b): Denise Klein, "Tatar and Ottoman History Writing. The Case of the Nogay Rebellion 1699–1701", in: Klein D. (2012a), 125–46.
Klein D. (2014): Denise Klein, "Zeichen und Wunder. Die Konversion der Goldenen Horde zum Islam im Blick ihrer Nachfahren (16.–18. Jahrhundert)", in: Andreas Helmedach et al. (eds.), *Das osmanische Europa. Methoden und Perspektiven der Frühneuzeitforschung zu Südosteuropa*, Leipzig, 381–404.
Klein M. (2010): Margarete Klein, "Russlands neue Militärdoktrin 2020. Unentschlossener Kompromiss zwischen Traditionalisten und Reformern", in: *SWP Aktuell*, 21. Online: https://www.swp-berlin.org/fileadmin/contents/products/aktuell/2010 A21_kle_ks.pdf (accessed 14 March 2017).
Köck et al. (1995): Dagmar Köck et al. (eds.), *Die Krim entdecken. Unterwegs auf der Sonneninsel im Schwarzen Meer*, Berlin.
Koenker (2013): Diane P. Koenker, *Club Red. Vacation Travel and the Soviet Dream*, Ithaca, NY.
Kogonashvili (1995): K. Kogonashvili, *Kratkii slovar' istorii Kryma* [A Concise Dictionary of the History of Crimea], Simferopol'.

Kołodzieczyk (2006): Dariusz Kołodzieczyk, "Slave Hunting and Slave Redemption as a Business Enterprise. The Northern Black Sea Region in the Sixteenth to Seventeenth Centuries", in: *Oriente Moderno*, n.s. 25, 149–59.

Kołodziejczyk (2011): Dariusz Kołodzieczyk, *The Crimean Khanate and Poland-Lithuania. International Diplomacy on the European Periphery (15th–18th Century). A Study of Peace Treaties Followed by Annotated Documents*, Leiden/Boston.

Kołodziejczyk (2012): Dariusz Kołodzieczyk, "Das Krimkhanat als Gleichgewichtsfaktor in Osteuropa (17.–18. Jahrhundert)", in: Klein D. (2012a), 47–58.

Korolev (1993): V.I. Korolev, *Vozniknovenie politicheskikh partii v Tavricheskoi gubernii* [The Emergence of the Political Parties in Taurida Governorate], Simferopol'.

Kozelsky (2010): Mara Kozelsky, *Christianizing Crimea. Shaping Sacred Space in the Russian Empire and Beyond*, DeKalb, Illinois.

Kozelsky (2018): Mara Kozelsky, *Crimea in War and Transformation*, Oxford.

Kozelsky (2014): Mara Kozelsky, "The Crimean War and the Tatar Exodus", in: Mara Kozelsky and Lucien J. Frary (eds.), *Russian-Ottoman Borderlands. The Eastern Question Reconsidered*, Madison/Wisconsin, 165–92.

Krahé (1998): Peter Krahé, "Rhetorik, Historie und Patriotismus. Tennysons Charge of the Light Brigade", in: *Zeitschrift für Anglistik und Amerikanistik*, 46:2, 114–24.

Kreindler (1986): Isabelle Kreindler, "The Soviet Deported Nationalities. A Summary and an Update", in: *Soviet Studies*, 38:3, 387–405.

Kreiser and Neumann (2008): Klaus Kreiser and Christoph K. Neumann, *Kleine Geschichte der Türkei*, Stuttgart.

Krugosvetov (2016): Sasha Krugosvetov (i.e. Lev Iakovlevich Lapkin), *Svetiashchiesia vorota* [The Glistening Gate], Simferopol' (ebook).

Krymskaia oblast' (1953): "Krymskaia oblast'" [The Crimean Oblast], in: BSE, Volume 23, second edition, Moscow, 552.

Kuchenbecker (2000): Antje Kuchenbecker, *Zionismus ohne Zion. Birobidžan. Idee und Geschichte eines jüdischen Staates in Sowjet-Fernost*, Berlin.

Kulikowski (2007): Michael Kulikowski, *Rome's Gothic Wars. From the Third Century to Alaric*, Cambridge et al.

Külzer (2006): Andreas Külzer, "Die Eroberung von Konstantinopel im Jahre 1204 in der Erinnerung der Byzantiner", in: Gherardo Ortalli, Giorgio Ravegnani and Peter Schreiner (eds.), *Quarta Crociata. Venezia – Bisanzio – Impero Latino*, Volume 2, Venice, 619–32.

Kumke (1993a): Carsten Kumke, *Führer und Geführte bei den Zaporoger Kosaken. Struktur und Geschichte kosakischer Verbände im polnisch-litauischen Grenzland 1550–1648*, Wiesbaden.

Kumke (1993b): Carsten Kumke, "Zwischen der polnischen Adelsrepublik und dem Russischen Reich", in: Golczewski (1993), 56–91.

Kunz (2005): Norbert Kunz, *Die Krim unter deutscher Herrschaft 1941–1944. Germanisierungsutopie und Besatzungsrealität*, Darmstadt (= Veröffentlichungen der Forschungsstelle Ludwigsburg der Universität Stuttgart, 5).

Kurowski (1986): Franz Kurowski, *Genua aber war mächtiger. Geschichte einer Seemacht*, Munich.

Kürşat-Ahlers (1994): Elçin Kürşat-Ahlers, *Zur frühen Staatenbildung von Steppenvölkern. Über die Sozio- und Psychogenese der eurasischen Nomadenreiche am Beispiel der Hsiung-Nu und Göktürken mit einem Exkurs über die Skythen*, Berlin. Also a doctoral thesis, University of Hanover, 1992.
Kusber (1998): Jan Kusber, "Um das Erbe der Goldenen Horde. Das Khanat von Kazan' zwischen Moskauer Staat und Krimtataren", in: Eckhard Hübner, Ekkehard Klug and Jan Kusber (eds.), *Zwischen Christianisierung und Europäisierung. Beiträge zur Geschichte Osteuropas in Mittelalter und Früher Neuzeit*, Stuttgart, 193–312.
Kusber (2007): Jan Kusber, "Zur Einführung", in: Frings and Kusber (2007), 7–16.
Kushko (2014): Nadiya Kushko, "The Birth of the Land of Beauty", in: Magocsi (2014), 9–10.
Latysh (2010): Iurii Latysh, "Antialkohol'na kampaniia v URSR na pochatku Perebudovy" [The Anti-Alcohol Campaign in the Ukrainian Soviet Republic at the Beginning of Perestroika], in: *Pytannia istoriï Ukraïny. Zbirnyk naukovykh statei* [Questions on the History of Ukraine. A Collection of Scholarly Essays], 13, 76–80.
Lavrov (2009): Aleksandr Lavrov, "Russische Gefangene im Osmanischen Reich, tatarische Gefangene im Moskauer Reich. Versuch einer histoire croisée", in: Guido Hausmann and Angela Rustemeyer (eds.), *Imperienvergleich. Beispiele und Ansätze aus osteuropäischer Perspektive*, Wiesbaden, 425–43.
Lazzerini (1973): Edward L. Lazzerini, *Ismail Bey Gasprinskii and Muslim Modernism in Russia* 1878–1914, Ph.D. Dissertation, University of Washington.
Lazzerini (1988): Edward L. Lazzerini, "The Crimea under Russian Rule. 1783 to the Great Reforms", in: Michael Rywkin (ed.), *Russian Colonial Expansion to 1917*, London, 123–38.
Lazzerini (1997): Edward L. Lazzerini, "Local Accommodation and Resistance to Colonialism in Nineteenth-Century Crimea", in: Daniel R. Brower and Edward J. Lazzerini (eds.), *Russia's Orient. Imperial Borderlands and Peoples 1700–1917*, Indianapolis, 169–187.
Lebedev (1990): V.P. Lebedev, "Simvolika i iazyk monet Kryma zolotoordynskogo perioda" [The Symbols and Language of Coins of Crimea from the Period of the Golden Horde], in: V.L. Ianin (ed.): *Numizmaticheskie issledovaniia po istorii iugo-vostochnoi Evropy* [Numismatic Research on the History of Southeastern Europe], Kishinev, 139–156. Englisch translation online: http://byzantinebronzes.ancients.info/page31.html (accessed 19 January 2018).
Leder (2005): Stefan Leder, "Nomaden und Sesshafte in Steppen und Staaten", in: *Scientia Halensis*, 9:1, 19–22.
Leitsch (1981): Walter Leitsch, "Warum wollte Kara Mustafa Wien erobern?", in: *Jahrbücher für die Geschichte Osteuropas*, 29, 494–514.
Lemberg (1985): Hans Lemberg, "Zur Entstehung des Osteuropabegriffs im 19. Jahrhundert. Vom 'Norden' zum 'Osten' Europas", in: *Jahrbücher für Geschichte Osteuropas*, 33, 48–91.
Lemercier-Quelquejay (1967): Chantal Lemercier-Quelquejay, "Les missions orthodoxes en pays musulmans de Moyenne- et Basse-Volga 1552–1865", in: *Cahiers du Monde russe et soviétique*, 8:3, 369–403.
Lemercier-Quelquejay (1968): Chantal Lemercier-Quelquejay, "The Crimean Tatars. A Retrospective Summary", in: *Central Asian Review*, 16:1, 15–25.
Lenhoff (2005): Gail Lenhoff, "The Construction of Russian History in 'Stepennaja kniga'", in: *Revue des Études Slaves*, 76:1, 31–50.

Leontsine (2012): Maria Leontsine, "Justinian II.", in: Alexios G. Savvides, Benjamin Hendrick and Thekla Sansaridou-Hendrickx (eds.), *Encyclopaedic Prosopographical Lexicon of Byzantine History and Civilization*, Volume 3, Turnhout, 422–5.

Lichačev (1970): Dmitrij Lichačev, "The Legend of the Calling of the Varangians, and Political Purposes in Russian Chronicle-Writing from the Second Half of the 11th to the Beginning of the 12th Century", in: Knud Hannestad (ed.), *Varangian Problems. Report on the First International Symposium on the Theme "The Eastern Connections of the Nordic Peoples in the Viking Period and Early Middle Ages"*, Moesgaard-University of Aarhus, 7–11 October 1968, Copenhagen, 170–87.

Likhachëv (1985): D.S. Likhachëv, *Slovo o polku Igoreve i kul'tura ego vremeni* [The Tale of Igor's Campaign and the Culture of its Time], second edition, Leningrad.

Liebich (1997): André Liebich, *From the Other Shore. Russian Social Democracy after 1921*, Cambridge, MA/London.

Lilie (2004): Ralph-Johannes Lilie, *Byzanz und die Kreuzzüge*, Stuttgart.

Litavrin (1967): G.G. Litavrin, "Glava 3: Sotsial'no-ekonomicheskii i politicheskii stroi Nikeiskoi imperii, Epirskogo tsarstva i Trapezundskoi imperii" [Chapter 3: The Socioeconomic and Political Structure of the Empire of Nicaea, the Despotate of Epirus and the Trebizond Empire], in: S.D. Skazkin (ed.), *Istoriia Vizantii* [Byzantium's History], Volume 3, Moscow, 29–49.

Littleton and Malcor (1994): Scott C. Littleton and Linda A. Malcor, *From Scythia to Camelot. A Radical Reassessment of the Legends of King Arthur, the Knights of the Round Table, and the Holy Grail*, New York et al.

Litvin (1995): A.L. Litvin, *Krasnyi i belyi terror v Rossii 1918–1922 gg.* [Red and White Terror in the Russia of the Years 1918–1922], Kazan'.

Liusyi (2003): A.P. Liusyi, *Krymskii tekst v russkoi literature* [The Crimea Text in Russian Culture], St Petersburg.

Löwe (1896): Richard Löwe, *Die Reste der Germanen am Schwarzen Meer*, Halle.

Luchterhandt (2014): Otto Luchterhandt, "Die Krim-Krise von 2014. Staats- und völkerrechtliche Aspekte", in: *Osteuropa*, 64:5–6, 61–86.

Lynch (1965): Donald Francis Lynch, *The Conquest, Settlement and Initial Development of New Russia (The Southern Third of the Ukraine) 1780–1837*, Ph.D. Dissertation, Yale University, New Haven.

Lysenko (2006): N.N. Lysenko, "Iazygi na dunaiskom Limese Rima v 1–2 vv. n. è." [The Iazyges on the Danubian Limes in the 1st and 2nd Centuries CE], in: *Nizhnevolzhskii arkheologicheskii vestnik* [Archaeological Messenger of the Lower Volga Region], 8, 139–153. Online: http://bulgari-istoria-2010.com/booksRu/N_Lysenko_Yazigi_na_Dunay.pdf (accessed 9 August 2017).

Mack and Carter (2003): Glenn R. Mack and Joseph Coleman Carter (eds.), *Crimean Chersonesos. City, Chora, Museum, and Environs*, Austin, Texas.

Magocsi (2014): Paul Robert Magocsi, *This Blessed Land. Crimea and the Crimean Tatars*, Toronto.

Maksymenko (1990): M.M., "Pereselennia v Krym sil's'koho naselennia z inshykh raioniv SSR 1944–1960 gg." [The Resettlement of the Rural Population From Other Areas of the SSR to Crimea 1944–1960], in: *Ukraïns'kyi istorychnyi zhurnal* [Ukrainian Historical Journals], 11, 52–8.

Malek (2017): Martin Malek, "Die krimtatarische Bevölkerung. Von der Repatriierung zur russländischen Besatzung", in: ÖZG, 28:1, 167–206.

Mal'gin (2006): Andrei Mal'gin, *Russkaia Riv'era. Kurorty, turizm i otdykh v Krymu v ėpokhu imperii. Konets 18 – nachalo 20 v.* [The Russian Riviera. Spa Towns, Tourism and Leisure in Crimea in the Imperial Epoch. The Late 18th to the Early 20th Century], Simferopol'.

Marbo (1991): Judith Marbo (ed.), *Veiled Half-Truth. Western Travellers' Perceptions of Middle Eastern Women*, London/New York.

Mark (1993): Rudolf A. Mark, "Die gescheiterten Staatsversuche", in: Golczewski (1993), 172–201.

Marples and Duke (1995): David R. Marples and David F. Duke, "Ukraine, Russia, and the Question of Crimea", in: *Nationalities Papers*, 23:2, 261–87.

Martin (2001): Terry D. Martin, *The Affirmative Action Empire. Nations and Nationalism in the Soviet Union, 1923–1939*, Ithaca, NY.

Mary Holderness (2017): "Mary Holderness", in: Benjamin Colbert (ed.), *Women's Travel Writing, 1780–1840. A Bio-Bibliographical Database*, Wolverhampton 2014–2018. Online: http://www4.wlv.ac.uk/btw/authors/1075 (accessed 1 June 2018).

Maslennikov (1981): Aleksandr A. Maslennikov, *Naselenie bosporskogo gosudarstva v 6–2 vv. do n. ė.* [The Population of the Bosporan State From the 6th to the 2nd Century BCE], Moscow.

Masud (1990): Muhammed Khalid Masud, "The Obligation to Migrate. The Doctrine of hijra in Islamic Law", in: Dale Eickelman and James Piscatori (eds.), *Muslim Travelers. Pilgrimage, Migration, and the Religious Imagination*, London, 131–152.

Matuz (1964): Josef Matuz, "Eine Beschreibung des Khanats der Krim aus dem Jahre 1699", in: *Acta Orientalia*, 28, 129–151.

Matuz (1976): Josef Matuz, *Krimtatarische Urkunden im Reichsarchiv zu Kopenhagen, mit historisch-diplomatischen und sprachlichen Untersuchungen*, Freiburg im Breisgau (= Islamkundliche Untersuchungen, 37).

Matuz (1996): Josef Matuz, *Das Osmanische Reich. Grundlinien seiner Geschichte*, Darmstadt.

McReynolds (2003): Louise McReynolds, *Russia at Play. Leisure Activities at the End of the Tsarist Era*, Ithaca, NY et al.

Meier F. (1991): Fritz Meier, "Über die umstrittene Pflicht des Muslims, bei nichtmuslimischer Besetzung seines Landes auszuwandern", in: *Der Islam*, 68, 65–86.

Meier M. (2005): Mischa Meier, *Pest. Die Geschichte eines Menschheitstraumas*, Stuttgart.

Melman (1992): Billi Melman, *Women's Orient. English Women and the Middle East 1718–1918. Sexuality, Religion and Work*, London.

Melvin (2017): Mungo Melvin, *Sevastopol's Wars. Crimea from Potemkin to Putin*, Oxford.

Messerschmidt (2004): Manfred Messerschmidt, "Karl Dietrich Erdmann, Walter Bußmann und Percy Ernst Schramm, Historiker an der Front und in den Oberkommandos der Wehrmacht und des Heeres", in: Hartmut Lehmann and Otto Gerhard Oexle (eds.), *Nationalsozialismus in den Kulturwissenschaften*, Volume 1: *Fächer – Milieus – Karrieren*, Göttingen, 417–43.

Meuthen (1983): Erich Meuthen, "Der Fall von Konstantinopel und der lateinische Westen", in: *Historische Zeitschrift*, 237:3, 1–35.

Meyer A. (2013): Anne-Rose Meyer (ed.), *Vormärz und Philhellenismus*, Bielefeld.

Meyer J. (2014): James H. Meyer, *Turks Across Empires. Marketing Muslim Identity in the Russian-Ottoman Borderlands, 1856–1914*, Oxford.
Mienert (2000): Marion Mienert, "Krankenschwestern für das Vaterland. Krankenpflege im Krimkrieg und ihre Auswirkungen auf die 'Frauenfrage'" in Rußland", in: Sophia Kemlein (ed.), *Geschlecht und Nationalismus in Mittel- und Osteuropa 1848–1918*, Osnabrück, 181–95.
Molnár and Magyar (2001): Miklós Molnár and Anna Magyar, *A Concise History of Hungary*, Cambridge.
Molnár (2013): Monika Molnár, "Der Friede von Karlowitz und das Osmanische Reich", in: Arno Strohmeyer and Norbert Spannenberger (eds.), *Frieden und Konfliktmanagement in interkulturellen Räumen. Das Osmanische Reich und die Habsburgermonarchie in der Frühen Neuzeit*, Stuttgart, 197–220.
Moon (2001): David Moon, *The Abolition of Serfdom in Russia 1762–1907*, London.
Moreno (2007): Alfonso Moreno, *Feeding the Democracy. The Athenian Grain Supply in the Fifth and Fourth Centuries BC*, Oxford.
Müller L. et al. (1992): Ludolf Müller, Günther Schramm and Andrzej de Vincenz, "Vorschläge für eine einheitliche Terminologie des alten Ostslaventums", in: *Russia mediaevalis*, 7, 5–8.
Müller M. (1984): Michael G. Müller, *Die Teilungen Polens 1772, 1793, 1795*, Munich.
Myeshkov (2008): Dmytro Myeshkov, *Die Schwarzmeerdeutschen und ihre Welten 1781–1871, Düsseldorf* (= Veröffentlichungen zur Kultur und Geschichte im östlichen Europa, 30).
Nagel (1993): Tilman Nagel, *Timur der Eroberer und die islamische Welt des späten Mittelalters*, Munich.
Naimark (2008): Norman M. Naimark, *Fires of Hatred: Ethnic Cleansing in Twentieth-Century Europe*, Cambridge, MA.
Nekrich (1978): Alexander Nekrich, *The Punished Peoples. The Deportation and Fate of Soviet Minorities at the End of the Second World War*, New York.
Nelipovič (2016): Sergej G. Nelipovič, "Die Kriegsbehörde und die Mennoniten Russlands im Ersten Weltkrieg 1914–1918", in: Alfred Eisfeld (ed.), *Deutsche im Schwarzmeergebiet, auf der Krim und im Kaukasus vom 19. Jahrhundert bis 1941*, Hamburg (= Studien zur Geschichtsforschung der Neuzeit, 88), 359–84.
Nepomniashchii (1999): A.A. Nepomniashchii, *Zapiski puteshestvennikov i putevoditeli v razvitii istoricheskogo kraevedeniia Kryma. Posl. tret' 18 – nach. 20 v.* [The Writings of Travellers and Travel Guides in the Development of the Historical Geography of Crimea. The Last Third of the 18th–Early Twentieth Century], Kyiv.
Neubauer H.-J. (1998): Hans-Joachim Neubauer, *Fama. Eine Geschichte des Gerüchts*, Berlin.
Neubauer H. (1960): Helmut Neubauer, "Die griechische Schwarzmeerkolonisation in der sowjetischen Geschichtsschreibung", in: *Saeculum*, 11, 132–56.
Neutatz (1993): Dietmar Neutatz, *Die "deutsche Frage" im Schwarzmeergebiet und in Wolhynien. Politik, Wirtschaft, Mentalität und Alltag im Spannungsfeld von Nationalismus und Modernisierung 1856–1914*, Stuttgart.
Neutatz (2013): Dietmar Neutatz, *Träume und Alpträume. Eine Geschichte Russland im 20. Jahrhundert*, Munich (= Europäische Geschichte im 20. Jahrhundert, ed. by Ulrich Herbert).

Niendorf (2010): Mathias Niendorf, *Das Großfürstentum Litauen. Studien zur Nationsbildung in der frühen Neuzeit (1569–1795)*, second, revised edition, Wiesbaden.

Nieuważny (2011): Andrzej Nieuważny, "La guerre de Crimée. Une guerre 'à l'ancienne', au seuil de la modernité?", in: Jerzy W. Borejsza (ed.), *The Crimean War 1853–1856. Colonial Skirmish or Rehearsal for World War? Empires, Nations, and Individuals*, Warsaw, 491–505.

Noack (2000): Christian Noack, *Muslimischer Nationalismus im Rußländischen Reich. Nationsbildung und Nationalbewegung bei Tataren und Baschkiren 1861–1917*, Stuttgart (= Quellen und Studien zur Geschichte des östlichen Europa, 56).

Nölke (2006): Andreas Nölke, "Weltsystemtheorie", in: Siegfried Schieder (ed.), *Theorien der internationalen Beziehungen*, second edition, Opladen, 325–51.

Noonan (1992): Thomas S. Noonan, "Byzantine and the Khazars. A Special Relationship?", in: J. Shepard and S. Franklin (eds.), *Byzantine Diplomacy. Papers from the 24th Spring Symposium of Byzantine Studies*, Cambridge in March 1990, Aldershot, 213–19.

Noonan (2007): Thomas S. Noonan, *The Economy of the Khazar Khaganate*, in: Golden et al. (2007), 207–44.

Norwich (2000): John Julius Norwich, *Byzanz. Verfall und Untergang 1071–1453*, Augsburg.

O'Neill (2008): Kelly O'Neill, "Bearing Arms for the Empire. Crimean Tatars as Soldiers and Subjects", *Conference Paper: The Russian and Ottoman Interaction, 1650–1920*. Harriman Institute, Columbia University, 13–15. Online: http://harriman.columbia.edu/files/harriman/01165.pdf (accessed 17 May 2018).

O'Neill (2010): Kelly O'Neill, "Rethinking Elite Integration. The Crimean Murzas and the Evolution of Russian Nobility", in: *Cahiers du Monde Russe*, 51:2–3, 397–418.

O'Neill (2017): Kelly O'Neill, *Claiming Crimea: A History of Catherine the Great's Southern Empire*, New Haven/London.

Ostapchuk (1990): Victor Ostapchuk, "An Ottoman Ġazānāme on Ḥalīl Paša's Naval Campaign against the Cossacks (1621)", in: *Harvard Ukrainian Studies*, 14:3/4, 482–521.

Osterhammel (2003): Jürgen Osterhammel, *Kolonialismus. Geschichte – Formen – Folgen*, fourth edition, Munich.

Osterhammel (2008): Jürgen Osterhammel, "Russland und der Vergleich zwischen Imperien. Einige Anknüpfungspunkte", in: *Comparativ. Zeitschrift für Globalgeschichte und vergleichende Gesellschaftsforschung*, 18:2: *Ostmitteleuropa transnational* (ed. by Peter Haslinger), 11–27.

Osterhammel (2009): Jürgen Osterhammel, *Die Verwandlung der Welt. Eine Geschichte des 19. Jahrhunderts*, Munich.

Ostrowski (1998): Donald Ostrowski, *Muscovy and the Mongols. Cross-Cultural Influences on the Steppe Frontier 1304–1589*, Cambridge.

Overmans (2014): Rüdiger Overmans, "Kriegsverluste", in: Gerhard Hirschfeld, Gerd Krumeich and Irina Renz (eds.), *Enzyklopädie Erster Weltkrieg*, Paderborn, 663–6.

Özveren (1997): Eyüp Özveren, "A Framework for the Study of the Black Sea World 1789–1915", in: *Review of the Ferdinand Braudel Center*, 20, 77–113.

Palmer (1987): Alan Palmer, *The Crimean War*, New York.
Papke (1983): Gerhard Papke, *Von der Miliz zum Stehenden Heer. Wehrwesen im Absolutismus*, Munich (= Deutsche Militärgeschichte in sechs Bänden 1648–1939, ed. by Militärgeschichtliches Forschungsamt, 1).
Papp (2012): Sándor Papp, "Die Inaugurationen der Krimkhane durch die Hohe Pforte (16.–18. Jahrhundert)", in: Klein D. (2012a), 75–90.
Parzinger (2004): Hermann Parzinger, *Die Skythen*, Munich.
Patenaude (2002): Bertrand M. Patenaude, *The Big Show in Bololand. The American Relief Expedition to Soviet Russia in the Famine of 1921*, Stanford.
Pausz (2017): Clemens Pausz, "Das Krim-Khanat und der Aufstieg des Zaporoger Kosakentums. Erich Lassotas Mission im diplomatischen Kontext", in: ÖZG, 28:1, 14–40.
Pekesen (2014): Berna Pekesen. "Panturkismus", in: *Europäische Geschichte Online*, ed. by Leibniz-Institut für Europäische Geschichte (IEG), Mainz. Online: http://www.ieg-ego.eu/pekesenb-2014-de (accessed 9 August 2018).
Penter (2000): Tanja Penter, *Odessa 1917. Revolution an der Peripherie*, Cologne et al.
Peter and Wentker (2012): Matthias Peter and Hermann Wentker (eds.), *Die KSZE im Ost-West-Konflikt. Internationale Politik und gesellschaftliche Transformation 1975–1990*, Munich.
Petritsch (1983): Ernst D Petritsch., "Die tatarisch-osmanischen Begleitoperationen in Niederösterreich", in: *Studia Austro-Polonica*, 3, 207–240.
Petrukhin (2007): Vladimir Petrukhin, "Khazaria and Rus'. An Examination of their Historical Relations", in: Golden et al. (2007), 245–68.
Phillips (2004): Jonathan Phillips, *The Fourth Crusade and the Sack of Constantinople*, New York.
Pillinger (1996): Renate Pillinger, "Die Anfänge des Christentums auf der taurischen Chersones (Krim) demonstriert am Beispiel von Pantikapaion/Bospor/Kerč", in: Fritz Blakolmer et al. (eds.), *Fremde Zeiten. Festschrift für Jürgen Borchhardt*, Vienna, 309–17.
Pinson (1970): Mark Pinson, *Demographic Warfare. Aspects of Ottoman and Russian Policy 1854–1866*, Ph.D. Dissertation, Harvard University, Cambridge.
Pipes (1997): Richard Pipes, *The Formation of the Soviet Union. Communism and Nationalism, 1917–1923*, third edition, Cambridge, MA/London.
Pletnjowa (1978): Swetlana A. Pletnjowa, *Die Chasaren. Mittelalterliches Reich an Don und Wolga*, Leipzig.
Plokhy (2000): Serhii Plokhy. "The City of Glory. Sevastopol in Russian Historical Mythology", in: *Journal of Contemporary History*, 35:3, 369–83.
Plokhy (2001): Serhii Plokhy, *The Cossacks and Religion in Early Modern Ukraine*, Oxford.
Plokhy (2017): Serhii Plokhy, *Lost Kingdom. A History of Russian Nationalism from Ivan the Great to Vladimir Putin*, London.
Plontke-Lüning (2012): Annegret Plontke-Lüning, "Christianisierung am Rande des Imperiums. Die Krim", in: Orsolya Heinrich-Tamáska, Niklot Krohn and Sebastian Ristow (eds.), *Die Christianisierung Europas. Entstehung, Entwicklung, Konsolidierung im archäologischen Befund*, Wiesbaden, 343–62.
Pohl (1999): Otto Pohl, *Ethnic cleansing in the USSR. 1937–1949*, Westport.
Polkanov (1936): Aleksandr I. Polkanov, *Sevastopol'skoe vosstanie 1830 goda. Po arkhivnym materialam* [The Sevastopol' Uprising of 1830. According to Archive Material], Simferopol'.

Potichnyj (1975): Peter J. Potichnyj, "The Struggle of the Crimean Tatars", in: *Canadian Slavonic Papers. Revue Canadienne des Slavistes*, 17:2–3, 302–19.
Pratt (1992): Mary Louise Pratt, *Imperial Eyes. Travel Writing and Transculturation*, London/New York.
Pretzel (1987): Ulrich Pretzel, "Löwe, Richard", in: *Neue Deutsche Biographie*, Volume 15, Berlin, 77. Online:https://www.deutsche-biographie.de/pnd117167096.html (accessed 14 March 2018).
Pritsak (1975): Omeljan Pritsak, "The Petchenegs. A Case of Social and Economic Transformation", in: *Archivum Eurasiae Medii Aevi*, 1, 211–35.
Pritsak (1991): Omeljan Pritsak, "Sougdaia", in: Alexander Kazhdan (ed.), *The Oxford Dictionary of Byzantium*, New York/Oxford, 1931.
Pryke (1998): Sam Pryke, "Nationalism and Sexuality. What Are the Issues?", in: *Nations and Nationalism*, 4, 529–46.
Pusat (2017): Atilla Pusat, *Die sowjetisch-osmanischen Beziehungen im "Türkischen Befreiungskrieg" von 1919 bis 1923*, Diplomarbeit, University of Vienna. Online: http://othes.univie.ac.at/48195/1/50504.pdf (accessed 9 September 2018).
Puschner (2013): Uwe Puschner, "Die völkische Bewegung in Deutschland", in: Hannes Heer (ed.), *"Weltanschauung en marche". Die Bayreuther Festspiele und die Juden 1876 bis 1945*, Würzburg, 151–67.
Qualls (2009): Karl D. Qualls, *From Ruins to Reconstruction. Urban Identity in Soviet Sevastopol after World War II*, Ithaca/London.
Quirini-Popławska (2002): Danuta Quirini-Popławska, *Włoski handel czarnomorskimi niewolnikami w późnym średniowieczu* [The Italian Trade With Slaves From the Black Sea Region in the Late Middle Ages], Kraków.
Raab (2017): Nigel A. Raab, *All Shook Up. The Shifting Soviet Response to Catastrophes 1917–1991*, London/Chicago.
Raleigh (1986): Donald Raleigh, *Revolution on the Volga. 1917 in Saratov*, New York.
Rhinelander (1990): A.L.H. Rhinelander, *Prince Michael Voroncov. Viceroy to the Tsar*, London.
Robarts (2017): Andrew Robarts, *Migration and Disease in the Black Sea Region. Ottoman-Russian Relations in the Late Eighteenth and Early Nineteenth Centuries*, London et al.
Röder et al. (1996): Brigitte Röder, Juliane Hummel and Brigitta Kunz (eds.), *Göttinnendämmerung. Das Matriarchat aus archäologischer Sicht*, Munich.
Rodinson (1966): Maxime Rodinson, *Islam et Capitalisme*, Paris.
Rolle (1980): Renate Rolle, *Die Welt der Skythen. Stutenmelker und Pferdebogner. Ein antikes Reitervolk in neuer Sicht*, Lucerne/Frankfurt am Main.
Rolle (1991): Renate Rolle (ed.), *Gold der Steppe. Archäologie der Ukraine*, Neumünster.
Rolle and Brenow (2006): Renate Rolle and Iris von Brenow, "Skythen", in: Hubert Cancik, Helmuth Schneider and Manfred Landfester (eds.), *Der Neue Pauly*. Online: http://referenceworks.brillonline.com/entries/der-neue-pauly/*-e1115640 (accessed 14 March 2018).
Romančuk (2005): Alla I. Romančuk, *Studien zur Geschichte und Archäologie des byzantinischen Cherson*, Leiden.
Roman'ko (2004): Oleg Valentinovich Roman'ko, "Prilozhenie. Biograficheskie svedeniia o nekotorykh upominaiushchikhsia v knige litsakh" [Supplement.

Biographical Information About Some People Mentioned in the Book], in: *idem*, *Musul'manskie legiony vo Vtoroi mirovoi voine* [Muslim Legions in the Second World War], Moscow. Online http://militera.lib.ru/research/romanko_ov/06.html (accessed 18 February 2013).

Roman'ko (2011): Oleg Valentinovich Roman'ko, *Krym pod piatoi Gitlera. Nemetskaia okkupatsionnaia politika v Krymu 1941–1944 gg.* [Crimea Under Hitler's Heel. German Occupation Policy in Crimea 1941–1944], Moscow.

Romashchenko et al. (2018): Mykhailo Ivanovych Romashchenko et al., "About Some Environmental Consequences of Kerch Strait Bridge Construction", in: *Hydrology*, 6:1, 1–9. Online: http://article.sciencepublishinggroup.com/pdf/10.11648.j.hyd.20180601.11.pdf (accessed 19 January 2018).

Rösch (2000): Gerhard Rösch, *Venedig. Geschichte einer Seerepublik*, Stuttgart/Berlin.

Rosen (2007): Klaus Rosen, *Die Völkerwanderung*, seventh edition, Munich.

Rostovtzeff (1922): Michael Rostovtzeff (i.e. Mikhail I. Rostovtsev), *Iranians and Greeks in South Russia*, Oxford.

Rostowzew (1902):, M. Rostowzew (i.e. Mikhail I. Rostovtsev), "Römische Besatzungen in der Krim und das Kastell Charax", in: *Klio*, 2, 80–95.

Roth and Abraham (2011): Karl Heinz Roth and Jan-Peter Abraham, *Reemtsma auf der Krim. Tabakproduktion und Zwangsarbeit unter der deutschen Besatzungsherrschaft 1941–1944*, Hamburg.

Rowell (1994): Stephen C. Rowell, *Lithuania Ascending. A Pagan Empire within East-Central Europe 1295–1345*, Cambridge et al. (= Cambridge Studies in Medieval Life and Thought, 4; 25).

Royle (1987): Trevor Royle, *War Report. The War Correspondent's View of Battle from the Crimea to the Falklands*, London.

Saal (2014): Yuliya von Saal, *KSZE-Prozess und Perestroika in der Sowjetunion. Demokratisierung, Werteumbruch und Auflösung 1985–1991*, Munich.

Said (1978): Edward Said, *Orientalism*, London.

Sapper et al. (2004): Manfred Sapper, Volker Weichsel and Agathe Gebert (eds.), *Vernichtung durch Hunger. Der Holodomor in der Ukraine und der UdSSR*, Berlin (= Osteuropa, 12[2004]).

Sarnowski and Zubar (1996): Tadeusz Sarnowski and Vitalij Mihailovič Zubar, "Römische Besatzungstruppen auf der Südkrim und eine Bauinschrift aus dem Kastell Charax", in: *Zeitschrift für Papyrologie und Epigraphik*, 112, 229–34.

Sasse (2007): Gwendolyn Sasse, *The Crimea Question. Identity, Transition, and Conflict*, Cambridge, MA.

Sasse (2010): Gwendolyn Sasse, "Stabilität durch Heterogenität. Regionale Vielfalt als Stärke der Ukraine", in: *Osteuropa*, 60:2–4, 105–21.

Sauter (2000): Hermann Sauter, *Studien zum Kimmerierproblem*, Bonn (= Saarbrücker Beiträge zur Altertumskunde, 72). Online: http://www.kimmerier.de/start.htm (accessed 11 July 2017).

Scatton (1993): Linda H. Scatton, *Mikhail Zoshchenko. Evolution of a Writer*, Cambridge.

Schäferdiek (1979): Knut Schäferdiek, "Wulfila. Vom Bischof von Gotien zum Gotenbischof", in: *Zeitschrift für Kirchengeschichte*, 90, 253–92.

Schama (1995): Simon Schama, *Landscape and Memory*, New York/London.

Schieder (1977): Theodor Schieder, *Staatensysteme als Vormacht der Welt 1848–1918*, Frankfurt am Main/Berlin/Vienna (= Propyläen Geschichte Europas, 5).

Schimmelpenninck van der Oye (2010): David Schimmelpenninck van der Oye, *Russian Orientalism. Asia in the Russian Mind from Peter the Great to the Emigration*, New Haven et al.

Schmitt J. (2016): Jochen Schmitt, "Der heilige Märtyrerbischof Clemens von Rom. Leben, Martyrium und Werk", in: *Theologisches*, 46:1–2, Columns 71–84.

Schnell (2012): Felix Schnell, *Räume des Schreckens. Gewalt und Gruppenmilitanz in der Ukraine 1905–1933*, Hamburg (= Studien zur Gewaltgeschichte des 20. Jahrhunderts).

Schorkowitz (2008): Dittmar Schorkowitz, *Postkommunismus und verordneter Nationalismus. Gedächtnis, Gewalt und Geschichtspolitik im nördlichen Schwarzmeergebiet*. With collaboration by Vasile Dumbrava and Stefan Wiese, Frankfurt am Main.

Schur (1992): Nathan Schur, *History of the Karaites*, Frankfurt am Main (= Beiträge zur Erforschung des Alten Testaments und des antiken Judentums, 28).

Schwarcz (2017): Iskra Schwarcz, "Das Krim-Khanat zwischen Konstantinopel, Wien und Moskau. Edition eines Dokuments", in: *ÖZG*, 28:1, 207–17.

Seaton (1977): Albert Seaton, *The Crimean War. A Russian Chronicle*, London.

Segal (1995): Ronald Segal, *The Black Diaspora. Five Centuries of the Black Experience Outside Africa*, New York.

Selov-Kovedjaev (1986): Fjodor V. Selov-Kovedjaev, "Die Eroberung Theodosias durch die Spartokiden", in: *Klio*, 68:2, 367–76.

Semin (1955): G.I. Semin, *Sevastopol'. Istoricheskii ocherk* [Sevastopol'. A Historical Outline], Moscow.

Senner (1999): Martin Senner, "Beutekunst und andere Trophäen. Streiflichter aus den französischen Krimkriegsakten", in: *Militärgeschichtliche Mitteilungen*, 58, 137–46.

Siegelbaum (2018): Lewis Siegelbaum, "Famine of 1946–1947", in: *Seventeen Moments in Soviet History. An Online Archive of Primary Sources*. Online: http://soviethistory.msu.edu/1947-2/famine-of-1946-1947/ (accessed 9 August 2018).

Sievernich (2011): Michael Sievernich, "Christliche Mission", in: *Europäische Geschichte Online,* ed. by Institut für Europäische Geschichte (IEG), Mainz. Online: http://ieg-ego.eu/de/threads/europa-und-die-welt/mission (accessed 19 January 2019).

Shirokorad (2006): A.B. Shirokorad, *Chetyre tragedii Kryma* [The Four Tragedies of Crimea], Moscow.

Skorik (1995): A.P. Skorik et al. (ed.), *Vozrozhdenie kazachestva. Istoriia i sovremmenost'* [The Rebirth of Cossackhood: History and Present], Novocherkassk.

Skorupa (1994): Dariusz Skorupa, *Stosunki polsko-tatarskie 1595–1623* [Polish–Tatar Relations 1595–1623], Warsaw.

Slezkine (1994): Yuri Slezkine, "The USSR as a Communal Apartment. Or How a Socialist State Promoted Ethnic Particularism", in: *Slavic Review*, 53:2, 414–52.

Slezkine (1997): Yuri Slezkine, "Naturalists versus Nations. Eighteenth-Century Russian Scholars Confront Ethnic Diversity", in: Daniel R. Brower and Edward J. Lazzerini (eds.), *Russia's Orient. Imperial Borderlands and Peoples 1700–1917*, Indianapolis, 27–57.

Slobin (1992): Greta N. Slobin, "Revolution Must Come First. Reading V. Aksenov's Island of Crimea", in: Andrew Parker et al. (eds.), *Nationalism and Sexualities*, New York/London, 246–62.

Slocum (1998): John W. Slocum, "Who, and When, Were the Inorodtsy? The Evolution of the Category of 'Aliens' in Imperial Russia", in: *Russian Review*, 57:2, 173–90.
Smolin (2012): A.V. Smolin, *Dva admirala. A.I. Nepenin i A.V. Kolchak v 1917 g.* [Two Admirals. A.I. Nepenin and A.V. Kolchak in the Year Jahr 1917], St Petersburg.
Snyder (2010): Timothy Snyder, *Bloodlands. Europe between Stalin and Hitler*, London.
Soucek (2000): Svat Soucek, *A History of Inner Asia*, Cambridge.
Spuler (1965): Bertold Spuler, *Die Goldene Horde. Die Mongolen in Rußland 1223–1502*, second, expanded edition, Wiesbaden.
Stachel and Thomsen (2014): Peter Stachel and Martina Thomsen (eds.), *Zwischen Exotik und Vertrautem. Zur Tourismus in der Habsburgermonarchie und ihren Nachfolgestaaten*, Bielefeld.
Stearns Jr. (2012): MacDonald Stearns Jr., "Das Krimgotische", in: Heinrich Beck (ed.), *Germanische Rest- und Trümmersprachen*, Berlin/Boston (= Ergänzungsbände zum Reallexikon der Germanischen Altertumskunde, 3), 175–94.
Stender-Petersen (1986): Adolf Stender-Petersen, *Geschichte der russischen Literatur*, Munich.
Stepanchuk (1999): V.N. Stepanchuk, "Srednii paleolit Kryma. Industrial'nye traditsii viurmskogo vremeni. Mnogoobrazie proiavleni., vozmozhnye prichiny variabel'nosti" [Crimea's Middle Palaeolithic. Industrial Traditions of the Würm Stage. The Diversity of the Manifestations, Possible Causes of the Variability], in: *Vita Antiqua*, 2. Online: http://archaeology.kiev.ua/pub/stepanchuk.htm (accessed 9 September 2017).
Stickler (2007): Timo Stickler, *Die Hunnen*, Munich.
Stökl (1953): Günther Stökl, *Die Entstehung des Kosakentums*, Munich.
Stökl (1983): Günther Stökl, *Russische Geschichte von den Anfängen bis zur Gegenwart*, fourth edition, Stuttgart.
Strobel (1989): Karl Strobel, *Die Donaukriege Domitians*, Bonn (= Antiquitas. Series 1, 38).
Struve (2015): Kai Struve, *Deutsche Herrschaft, ukrainischer Nationalismus, antijüdische Gewalt. Der Sommer 1941 in der Westukraine*, Berlin et al.
Subtelny (1993): Orest Subtelny, "Die Zeit der Het'mane (17.–18. Jahrhundert)", in: Golczewski (1993), 92–125.
Subtelny (2000): Orest Subtelny, *Ukraine. A History*, third edition, Toronto.
Sulimirski (1970): Tadeusz Sulimirski, *The Sarmatians*, London (= Ancient Peoples and Places, 73).
Suny (1972): Reginald G. Suny, *The Baku Commune 1917–18*, Princeton.
Szyszman (1989): Simon Szyszman, *Les Karaïtes d'Europe*, Uppsala.
Taagepera (1988): Rein Taagepera, "An Overview of the Growth of the Russian Empire", in: Michael Rywkin (ed.), *Russian Colonial Expansion to 1917*, London, 1–7.
Tarle (1954): E.V. Tarle, *Gorod russkoi slavy. Sevastopol' v 1854–1855 gg.* [City of Russian Glory. Sevastopol' 1854–1855], Moscow.
Tarle (1959): E.V. Tarle, *Krymskaia voina* [The Crimean War], two volumes, fourth edition, Moscow.
Tate (2003): Trudi Tate, "On Not Knowing Why. Memorializing the Light Brigade", in: Trudi Tate and Helen Small (eds.), *Literature, Science,*

Psychoanalysis 1830–1970. Essays in Honour of Gillian Beer, New York, 160–80.
Taylor (1982): Anne Taylor, *Laurence Oliphant 1829–1888*, New York.
Telesko (2014): W. Telesko, "Visualisierungsstrategien im Tourismus in der Spätphase der Habsburgermonarchie. Postkarten, Plakate und andere Bildmedien", in: Stachel and Thomsen (2014), 31–46.
Toje (2006): Hege Toje, "Cossack Identity in the New Russia. Kuban Cossack Revival and Local Politics", in: *Europe-Asia Studies*, 58:7, 1057–77.
Treue (1980): Wilhelm Treue, *Der Krimkrieg und die Entstehung der modernen Flotten*, second edition, Göttingen.
Troebst (2002): Stefan Troebst, "'Intermarium' und 'Vermählung mit dem Meer'. Kognitive Karten und Geschichtspolitik in Ostmitteleuropa", in: *Geschichte und Gesellschaft*, 28:3, 435–69.
Troebst (2007): Stefan Troebst, "Le Monde méditerrané – Südosteuropa – Black Sea World. Geschichtsregionen im Süden Europas", in: Frithjof Benjamin Schenk and Martina Winkler (eds.), *Der Süden. Neue Perspektiven auf eine europäische Geschichtsregion*, Frankfurt am Main et al., 49–73 (also in: Stefan Troebst, *Erinnerungskultur. Kulturgeschichte. Geschichtsregion. Ostmitteleuropa in Europa*, Stuttgart 2013, 419–38).
Troebst (2017): Stefan Troebst, "Jalta als europäischer Erinnerungsort?", in: *idem, Zwischen Arktis, Adria und Armenien. Das östliche Europa und seine Ränder*, Cologne/Weimar/Vienna, 343–52.
Trustam (1984): M. Trustam, *Women of the Regiment. Marriage and the Victorian Army*, Cambridge, UK.
Tuna (2015): Mustafa Tuna, *Imperial Russia's Muslims. Islam, Empire, and European Modernity, 1788–1914*, Cambridge.
Tyaglyy (2011): Mikhail Tyaglyy, "Antisemitic Doctrine in the Tatar Newspaper Azat Kirim (1942–1944)", in: *Dapim. Studies on the Holocaust*, 25:1, 161–82.
Tych (1990): Feliks Tych, *Rok 1905* [The Year 1905], Warsaw.
Tyszkiewicz (1989): Jan Tyszkiewicz, *Tatarzy na Litwie iw Polsce. Studia z dziejów XIII–XVIII w.* [Tatars in Lithuania and Poland. Studies on the History of the 13th–18th Century], Warsaw.
Tyszkiewicz (2002): Jan Tyszkiewicz, *Z dziejów Tatarów polskich. 1794–1944* [From the History of the Polish Tatars. 1794–1944], Pułtusk.
Uehling (2004): Greta Uehling, *Beyond Memory. The Crimean Tatars' Deportation and Return*, New York.
Uehling (2015): Greta Uehling, "The Crimean Tatars as Victims of Communism (Part I)", in: *Dissident*, 13 July 2015. Online: http://blog.victimsofcommunism.org/the-crimean-tatars-as-victims-of-communism-part-i/ (accessed 9 August 2017).
Usyskin (2000): G.S. Usyskin, *Ocherki istorii rossiiskogo turizma* [Outline of the History of Russian Tourism], St Petersburg.
Vaneev (1983): G.I. Vaneev, "Predislovie" [Foreword], in: *Glavnoe Arkhivnoe upravlenie* (1983), 5–24.
Vásáry (2012): István Vásáry, "The Crimean Khanate and the Great Horde (1440s–1500s). A Fight for Primacy", in: Klein D. (2012a), 13–26.
Vasiliev (1936): Alexander A. Vasiliev (i.e. Aleksandr A. Vasil'ev), *The Goths in the Crimea*, Cambridge, MA.
Vernadsky (1969): George Vernadsky, *A History of Russia. The Mongols and Russia*, New Haven et al.

Vinogradov (1999): A.Iu. Vinogradov, "Apostol' Andrei i Chërnoe More. Problemy istochnikovedeniia" [Apostel Andrei and the Black Sea. Problems of the Study of Sources], in: A.V. Podosinov (ed.), *Drevneishie gosurdarstva Vostochnoi Evropy. 1996–1997 gg.* [The Oldest States of Eastern Europe. 1996–1997], Moscow, 348–68.

Vinogradov (2010): A.Iu. Vinogradov, "Ioann. Episkop Gotskii" [John. Gothic Bishop], in: *Pravoslavnaia Entsiklopediia. Pod redaktsiei Patriarkha Moskovskogo i vseia Rusi Kirilla* [Orthodox Encyclopaedia. Ed. by the Patriarch of Muscovite and the Entire Rus' Cyril], Moscow. Online: http://www.pravenc.ru/text/468987.html (accessed 4 January 2018).

Vinogradov (2020): Andrei Iurevich Vinogradov, "Khersones - Kherson, Pantikapei: vopros identichnosti ili obshcheimperskii protsessca" [Chersonesus – Cherson, Panticapaeum – Bosporos: A Question of Identity or an Empire-Wide Process?] in: *Vestnik drevnei istorii* [Journal of Ancient History] 80:4 (2020), 995–1006.

Vinogradov and Korobov (2015): A.Iu. Vinogradov and M.I. Korobov, "Gotskie graffiti iz mangupskoi baziliki" [Gothic Graffiti From the Mangup Basilica], in: *Srednie Veka* [The Middle Ages], 76:3–4, 57–75. Online: http://www.gotica.de/boranicum.pdf (accessed 14 March 2017).

Voitovych (2009): Leontii V. Voitovych, *Formuvannia kryms'kotatars'koho narodu. Vstup do etnohenezu* [The Formation of the Crimean Tatar People. An Introduction to the Ethnogenesis], Bila Tserkva.

Völkl (1975): Ekkehard Völkl, *Das rumänische Fürstentum Moldau und die Ostslaven im 15. bis 17. Jahrhundert*, Wiesbaden.

Vozgrin (1992): V.E. Vozgrin, *Istoricheskie sud'by Krymskikh Tatar* [The Historical Fates of the Crimean Tatars], Moscow.

Vozgrin (2013): Valerii Vozgrin, *Istoriia krymskikh tatar. Ocherki etnicheskoi istorii korennogo naseleniia Kryma* [History of the Crimean Tatars. Treatises On the Ethnic History of the Autochthonous Population of Crimea], four volumes, Simferopol'.

Vucinich (1972): Wayne S. Vucinich (ed.), *Russia and Asia. Essays on the Influence of Russia on the Asian Peoples*, Stanford.

Weatherford (2004): Jack Weatherford, *Genghis Khan and the Making of the Modern World*, New York.

Weber (1998): Wolfgang Weber, "Historiographie und Mythographie. Oder: Wie kann und soll der Historiker mit Mythen umgehen?", in: Anette Völker-Rasor and Wolfgang Schmale (eds.), *MythenMächte. Mythen als Argument*, Berlin, 65–97.

Weelis (2002): Mark Weelis, "Biological Warfare at the 1346 Siege of Caffa", in: *Emerging Infectious Diseases*, 8/9: 971–5. Online: https://www.ncbi.nlm.nih.gov/pmc/articles/PMC2732530/ (accessed 11 April 2023).

Wegner (2002): Bernd Wegner, "Einführung. Kriegsbedingung im Spannungsfeld zwischen Gewalt und Frieden", in: *idem* (ed.), *Wie Kriege enden. Wege zum Frieden von der Antike bis zur Gegenwart*, Paderborn et al., XI–XXVIII.

Weisband (1973): Edward Weisband, *Turkish Foreign Policy 1943–1945. Small State Diplomacy and Great Power Politics*, Princeton.

Wendland (1992): Folkwart Wendland, *Peter Simon Pallas (1741–1811). Materialien einer Biographie*, two volumes, Berlin/New York (= Veröffentlichungen der Historischen Kommission zu Berlin, 80).

Wenskus (1973): Reinhard Wenskus, "Alanen", in: *Reallexikon der Germanischen Altertumskunde*, Volume 1, second edition, Berlin/New York, 122–6.

Wenskus (1977): Reinhard Wenskus, *Stammesbildung und Verfassung. Das Werden der frühmittelalterlichen gentes*, second, unaltered edition, Cologne et al.

Werner and Zimmermann (2004): Michael Werner and Bénédicte Zimmermann (eds.), *De la comparaison à l'histoire croisée*, Paris (= Le Genre humain, 42).

Wetzel (1985): David Wetzel, *The Crimean War. A Diplomatic History*, Boulder, CO et al.

Wiederkehr (2007): Stefan Wiederkehr, *Die eurasische Bewegung. Wissenschaft und Politik in der russischen Emigration der Zwischenkriegszeit und im postsowjetischen Russland*, Vienna.

Williams (2001): Brian G. Williams, *The Crimean Tatars. The Diaspora Experience and the Forging of a Nation*, Leiden/Boston/Cologne (= Brill's Inner Asian Library, 2).

Winkelmann (2003): Arne Winkelmann, *Das Pionierlager Artek. Realität und Utopie in der sowjetischen Architektur der sechziger Jahre*, doctoral thesis, Faculty of Architecture, Bauhaus University of Weimar. Online: http://e-pub.uni-weimar.de/opus4/frontdoor/index/index/docId/86 (accessed 14 March 2016).

Wittfogel (1957): Karl Wittfogel, *Oriental Despotism. A Comparative Study of Total Power*, New Haven.

Witzenrath (2016): Christoph Witzenrath (ed.), *Eurasian Slavery, Ransom and Abolition in World History*, Farnham et al.

Wolff (1994): Larry Wolff, *Inventing Eastern Europe. The Map of Civilization in the Mind of the Enlightenment*, Stanford.

Wrochem (2006): Oliver von Wrochem, *Erich von Manstein. Vernichtungskrieg und Geschichtspolitik*, Paderborn.

Yalçiner et al. (2004): Ahmet Yalçiner et al., "Tsunamis in the Black Sea. Comparison of the historical, instrumental, and numerical data", in: *Journal of Geophysical Research*, 109, C12023. Online: https://doi.org/10.1029/2003JC002113 (accessed 9 August 2018).

Yntema (2010): Douwe Yntema, "Die so genannte 'Große griechische Kolonisation' und die Konstruktion einer ehrwürdigen Herkunft, in: Claudia Kraft, Alf Lüdtke and Jürgen Martschukat (eds.), *Kolonialgeschichten. Regionale Perspektiven auf ein globales Phänomen*, Frankfurt/New York, 95–117.

Zaitsev (2003): Iu.P. Zaitsev, *Neapol' Skifskii (II v. do n. é. – III v. n. é.)* [Skythian Neapolis (2nd Century BCE–3rd Century CE)], Simferopol'.

Zalizniak (2008): A.A. Zalizniak, "Problema podlinnosti 'Slova o polku Igoreve'" [The Problem of the Authenticity of the "Tale of Igor's Campaign"], *Mir istorii* [The World of History], 1. Online: http://www.historia.ru/2008/01/slovo.htm (accessed 1 December 2017).

Zaytsev (2010): Ilya Zaytsev, "The Crimean Khanate between Empires. Independence or Submission", in: Plamen Mitev et al. (eds.), *Empires and Peninsulas. Southeastern Europe between Karlowitz and the Peace of Adrianople. 1699–1829*, Berlin, 25–28.

Zelepos (2007): Ionnanis Zelepos, *Griechische Siedler aus dem Schwarzmeerraum in Neurußland seit der Frühen Neuzeit und Pontosgriechen in Griechenland seit dem Ende des Zweiten Weltkriegs*, in: Bade et al. (2007), 617–622.

Zelepos (2015): Ioannis Zelepos, "Griechischer Unabhängigkeitskrieg 1821–1832", in: *Europäische Geschichte Online*, ed. by Leibniz-Institut für Europäische

Geschichte (IEG), Mainz. Online: http://ieg-ego.eu/de/threads/europaeische-medien/europaeische-medienereignisse/ioannis-zelepos-griechischer-unabhaengigkeitskrieg-1821-1829 (accessed 14 March 2018).

Zenkovsky (1960): Serge A. Zenkovsky, *Pan-Turkism and Islam in Russia*, Cambridge, MA.

Zetterberg (1978): Seppo Zetterberg, *Die Liga der Fremdvölker Rußlands 1916–1918. Ein Beitrag zu Deutschlands antirussischem Propagandakrieg unter den Fremdvölkern Rußlands im Ersten Weltkrieg*, Helsinki.

Zhivkov (2015): Boris Zhivkov, *Khazaria in the Ninth and Tenth Centuries*, Leiden/Boston.

Zhiromskaia (2004): V.B Zhiromskaia, "Problema krasnogo i belogo terrora 1917–1920 godov v otechestvennoi istoriografii" [The Problem of the Red and White Terror of 1917–1920 in the Historiography of the Fatherland], in: *Trudy Instituta rossiiskoi istorii* [Works of the Institute for Russian History], 4, 240–5.

Zhukov (1955): E.M. Zhukov (ed.), *Vsemirnaia istoriia* [World History], Volume 2, Moscow.

Zorin (2001): Andrei Zorin, *Kormia dvuglavogo orla ... Literatura i gosudarstvennaia ideologiia v Rossii v poslednei treti XVIII – pervoi treti XIX veka* [Approaching the Double-headed Eagle ... Literature and State Ideology in Russia in the Last Third of the 18th to the First Third of the 19th Century], Moscow.

Newspaper articles

Adler (2016): Sabine Adler, "Politischer Song gewinnt ESC", in: *Deutschlandfunk*, 15 May 2016. Online: https://www.deutschlandfunk.de/jamala-1944-politischer-song-gewinnt-den-esc.1766.de.html?dram:article_id=354204 (accessed 9 September 2018).

Ballin (2018): André Ballin, "Krim-Krise eskaliert. Russland sperrt Straße von Kertsch", in: *Der Standard*, 25 November 2018. Online: https://derstandard.at/2000092245089/Russisches-Schiff-rammt-ukranischen-Marineschlepper (accessed 20 December 2018).

Bayer (2016): Felix Bayer, "ESC-Siegerin Jamala. Die Ukraine und ihr trauriges Lied von der Krim", in: *Spiegel online*, 15 May 2016. Online: http://www.spiegel.de/kultur/musik/eurovision-song-contest-die-ukraine-und-ihr-trauriges-lied-von-der-krim-a-1092448.html (accessed 9 September 2018).

Birger (2015): Oliver Birger, "Kertsch. Eine patriotische Brücke für die Krim", in: *Zeit online*, 13 March 2015. Online: https://www.zeit.de/politik/ausland/2015-03/krim-kertsch-faehre-bruecke (accessed 19 January 2018).

Crimea blockade (2017): "Crimea blockade activists to form volunteer battalion", in: *Ukrinform*. Ukrainian Multimedia Platform for Broadcasting, 26 December 2017. Online: https://www.ukrinform.net/rubric-defense/1937109-crimea-blockade-activists-to-form-volunteer-battalion.html (accessed 19 January 2018).

Eichhofer (2014): André Eichhofer, "Krimtataren auf der Flucht im eigenen Land", in: *Die Welt*, 6 May 2014. Online: https://www.welt.de/politik/ausland/article127659418/Krimtataren-auf-der-Flucht-im-eigenen-Land.html (accessed 19 January 2018).

Esch (2018): Christian Esch, "Luft abgeschnürt", in: *Der Spiegel*, 49, 90–2.

Galustian et al. (2015): Artem Galustian et al., "Krimskotatarskoe ėgo. 'Ъ' v techenie goda sledil za tem, kak krymskie tatary privykaiut k rossiiskoj deistvitel'nosti" [The Crimean Tatar ego. "Ъ" followed over the course of a year how the Crimean Tatars are getting used to the Russian fact], in: *Kommersant* [The Businessman], 23 March 2015. Online: http://kommersant.ru/projects/crimeantatars (accessed 16 February 2016).

Gerke (2022): Laurenz Gerke, "'Zeitenwende ist Wort des Jahres'", in: *Süddeutsche Zeitung*, 9 December 2022. Online: https://www.sueddeutsche.de/panorama/wort-des-jahres-2022-zeitenwende-1.5712321 (accessed 4 June 2023).

Gerste (2004): Ronald D. Gerste, "50 Millionen Europäer starben im Mittelalter an Pest", in: *Ärzte-Zeitung*, 153, 15.

Gnauck (2015): Gerhard Gnauck, "Ukrainische Filmtage. Der Star schmachtet noch in Putins Gefängnis", in: *Die Welt*, 1 July 2015. Online: https://www.welt.de/kultur/kino/article143408263/Der-Star-schmachtet-noch-in-Putins-Gefaengnis.html (accessed 14 March 2017).

Hipp (2014): Dietmar Hipp, "Krim-Krise. 'Der Westen ist scheinheilig'. Der Völkerrechtler Bruno Simma über die Rechtsverstöße Russlands, die Logik Putins und die Fehler der EU", in: *Der Spiegel*, 15, 7 April 2014. Online: http://www.spiegel.de/spiegel/print/d-126393766.html (accessed 9 September 2018).

Höller (2015): Herwig G. Höller: "Russland. Wann die Krim-Annexion wirklich begann", in: *Zeit online*, 16 March 2015. Online: http://www.zeit.de/politik/ausland/2015-03/krim-annexion-leonid-gratsch-putin (accessed 9 December 2017).

Hoppe (2016): Hans-Joachim Hoppe, "Die Brücke von Kertsch", in: *Eurasisches Magazin*, 1 January 2016. Online: https://www.eurasischesmagazin.de/artikel/Russland-will-ueber-die-Strasze-von-Kertsch-eine-Bruecke-zur-Krim-bauen/14007 (accessed 9 August 2017).

Kalnysh and Solov'ev (2008): Valerii Kalnysh and Vladimir Solov'ev, "Iuriiu Luzhkovu perekryli Ukrainu. Mėr Moskvy ob"iavlen personoi non grata" [Iurii Luzhkov remains barred from Ukraine. The Moscow Mayor is declared persona non grata], in: *Kommersant* [The Businessman], 13 May 2008. Online: https://www.kommersant.ru/doc/890983 (accessed 9 September 2018).

Kiew (2014): "Kiew ordnet Kampfbereitschaft an", in: *Neue Zürcher Zeitung*, 3 March 2014. Online: https://www.nzz.ch/kiew-ordnet-kampfbereitschaft-an-1.18254373 (accessed 14 March 2017).

Klußmann (2014): Uwe Klußmann, "Krim-Statut. Warum Russland an Sewastopol festhält", in: *Spiegel online*, 5 March 2014. Online: http://www.spiegel.de/politik/ausland/krim-statut-warum-russland-am-schwarzmeerhafen-sewastopol-festhaelt-a-956815.html (accessed 14 March 2016).

Krekeler (2014): Elmar Krekeler, "Die Russen kommen – und das ist auch gut so", in: *Die Welt*, 17 November 2014. Online: https://www.welt.de/kultur/literarischewelt/article134400463/Die-Russen-kommen-und-das-ist-auch-gut-so.html (accessed 14 March 2017).

Krim (2016): "Krim. Ukraine verurteilt russisches Verbot der Krimtatarenorganisation", in: *Zeit online*, 19 April 2016. Online: https://www.zeit.de/politik/ausland/2016 - 04/krim-selbstverwaltung-russland-verbot-ukraine-proteste (accessed 19 January 2018).

Krim-Krise (2014): "Krim-Krise. Altkanzler Schmidt verteidigt Putins Ukraine-Kurs", in: *Spiegel online*, 26 March 2014. Online: http://www.spiegel.de/politik/

ausland/helmut-schmidt-verteidigt-in-krim-krise-putins-ukraine-kurs-a-960834.html (accessed 19 January 2018).

Krymskii telekanal (2015): "Krymskii telekanal ATR prekratil veshchanie iz-za problem s registratsiei SMI" [Crimean broadcaster ATR cancelled schedule due to problems with media registration], in: *RBK*, 1 April 2015. Online: https://www.rbc.ru/rbcfreenews/5515336a9a7947382b568817 (accessed 19 January 2018).

Kuhn (2001): Nicola Kuhn, "Der Absturz, ein Künstlermythos. Von Joseph Beuys' Schlüsselerlebnis auf der Krim bleibt am Ende wenig. Und dennoch lebt das Erbe der Tataren in seinem Werk", in: *Der Tagesspiegel* (Berlin), 4 May 2001.

Morozov (2016): Dmitrii Morozov, "Ekaterina Bakunina – Gordost' Tverskoi zemli" [Ekaterina Bakunina – Stolz der Erde von Tver'], in: *Krai spravedlivosti. Informatsionno- analiticheskii portal* [Area of Justice. Information-analytical Portal], 3 March 2016,. Online: http://ks-region69.com/easyblog/28401-ekaterina-bakunina-gordost-tverskoj-zemli (accessed 9 August 2017).

Petrov (2004): Sergei Petrov, "Novye vremena Sevastopol'skogo torgovogo" [New times for Sevastopol' trade], in: *Porty Ukrainy* [Ukraine's Ports], 45:1. Online: http://portsukraine.com/node/1319 (accessed 9 August 2016).

Pro-Russia Groups (2010): "Pro-Russia Groups Want Crimean Tatar Bodies Disbanded", in: *Radio Free Europe/Radio Liberty*, 26 April 2010. Online: https://www.rferl.org/a/ProRussia_Groups_Want_Crimean_Tatar_Bodies_Disbanded/2004234.html (accessed 9 August 2016).

Pupchenko and Dremova (2007): Anna Pupchenko and Natal'ia Dremova, "Iurii Luzhkov poobeshchal Krymu milliony" [Iurii Luzhkov promised Crimea millions], in: *KP v Ukraine* [KP in Ukraine], 22 February 2007. Online: https://kp.ua/politics/1228-yuryi-luzhkov-poobeschal-krymu-myllyony (accessed 30 November 2018).

Rubljow (2017): Anatolij Rubljow, "Krimtataren (qırımlı) zwischen Kampf und Überleben. Wie Moskau die Krimtataren bricht. Übersetzt von Annegret Becker", in: *Ukraine-Nachrichten. Die Ukraine im Spiegel ihrer Presse*, 14 March 2017. Online: https://ukraine-nachrichten.de/krimtataren-q%C4%B1r%C4%B1ml%C4%B1-zwischen-kampf-%C3%BCberleben-wie-moskau-krimtataren-bricht_4600 (accessed 19 January 2018).

Russkii Krym (2003): *Russkii Krym* [Russian Crimea], No. 7 (45), April 2003.

Russland-Politik (2014): "Russland-Politik. Ex-SPD-Chef Platzeck will Annexion der Krim anerkennen", in: *Spiegel online*, 18 November 2014. Online: http://www.spiegel.de/politik/deutschland/ukraine-krise-matthias-platzeck-will-legalisierung-krim-annexion-a-1003646.html (accessed 19 January 2018).

Schmidt (2014): Friedrich Schmidt, "Die Krim und die ukrainische Krise. Ruf nach dem großen Bruder", in: *Frankfurter Allgemeine Zeitung*, 20 February 2014.

Schuller (2007): Konrad Schuller, "Tataren im Pfirsichgarten. Die von Stalin deportierten Krimtataren kehren zurück, zum Missfallen der Russen", in: *Frankfurter Allgemeine Zeitung*, 11 September 2007.

Shuster (2014): Simon Shuster, "Putin's Man in Crimea is Ukraine's Worst Nightmare", in: *Time*, 10 March 2014. Online: http://time.com/19097/putin-crimea-russia-ukraine-aksyonov/ (accessed 14 March 2017).

Sochnev (2016): Aleksei Sochnev, "Ot shariata k Evrope. Pochemu Krym voshel v sostav Rossiiskoi imperii v XVIII veke" [From Sharia to Europe. Why Crimea became part of the Russian Empire in the 18th century], in: *Lenta.ru*, 9 April

2016. Online: https://lenta.ru/articles/2016/04/09/krymskoe_khanstvo/ (accessed 20 April 2018).
Spannung (2003): "Spannung am Schwarzen Meer", in: *Der Spiegel*, 33, 93.
Tiuliakov (2014):, Sergei P. Tiuliakov, "Geroi dvukh voin. Komandir 'Potemkina' byl ubit v khode bunta, prichiny kotorogo do sikh por neiasny" [A hero of two wars. The commander of the "Potemkin" was killed during an uprising the reasons for which are still unclear], in: *Nezavisimoe voennoe obozrenie* [Independent Military Review], 20 June 2014. Online: http://nvo.ng.ru/history/2014 - 06 - 20/12_hero.html (accessed 9 August 2018).
Tymchenko (2014): Zinaïda Tymchenko, "Pivnichno-Kryms'kyi kanal. Istoriia budivnytstva" [The North Crimea Canal. History of the construction], in: *Ukraïns'ka Pravda* [Ukrainian Truth], 13 May 2014. Online: http://www.istpravda.com.ua/articles/2014/05/13/142692/view_print/ (accessed 9 August 2016).
Veser (2015): Reinhard Veser, "Hellsichtiger Krim-Roman. Es war einmal eine Insel voller Glück", in: *Frankfurter Allgemeine Zeitung*, 16 March 2015. Online: http://www.faz.net/aktuell/feuilleton/buecher/wassili-aksjonows-prophetischer-roman-die-insel-krim-13484761.html?printPagedArticle=true#pageIndex_0 (accessed 9 December 2017).
Veser (2017): Reinhard Veser, "Abgerissene Verbindungen. Die Krim-Bewohner und wie sie die Welt sehen – drei Jahre nach der russischen Annexion", in: *Frankfurter Allgemeine Zeitung*, 16 November 2017. Online: http://www.faz.net/aktuell/politik/ausland/wie-die-krim-bewohner-nach-der-annexion-die-welt-sehen-15294143.html (accessed 20 February 2018).

Internet sources

Amet-Khan (2018): "Amet-Khan, Sultan", in: *Vikipediia*. Online: https://ru.wikipedia.org/wiki/Амет-Хан,_Султан (accessed 14 March 2017). See the English version: https://en.wikipedia.org/wiki/Amet-khan_Sultan (accessed 14 March 2017).
Artek (2018): Website of the Artek Pioneer camp. Online: https://artek.org/?ID=301101 (accessed 23 November 2018).
Bakhchisaraiski zapovednik (2018): *Ofitsial'nyi sait Bakhchisaraiskogo istoriko-kul'turnogo zapovednika* [Official Site of the Bakhchisarai Historical-Cultural Reserve]. Online: http://handvorec.ru/ (accessed 20 February 2018)
Barth (2022): Barth, Rebecca, "Krimtataren zur Explosion. 'Erste Anzeichen für die Befreiung der Krim'", in: *tagesschau*, 11 August 2022. Online: https://www.tagesschau.de/ausland/europa/krimtataren-101.html (accessed 11 August 2022).
Charter (2021): "Charter of the United Nations", in: *Repertory of Practice of United Nations Organs*. Online: https://legal.un.org/repertory/art2.shtml (accessed 11 April 2023).
Ėndel' (2014): Mariia Ėndel', "Krym i Solomon Krym" [Crimea and Solomon Krym], in: *booknik*, 27 March 2014. Online: http://booknik.ru/yesterday/lost-books/krym-i-solomon-krym/ (acessed 14 March 2018).
Ezhov et al. (2016): V.N. Ezhov, A.N. Buzni and I.G. Matchina, "Vinogradarstvo i vinodelie Kryma. Vchera i segodnia" [Crimea's Viticulture and Wine Production.

Yesterday and Today]. Online http://www.info.crimea.edu/crimea/ac/8/1_1.html (accessed 9 August 2016).
Filélliny (2018): "Filélliny", in: *Vikipediia*. Online: https://ru.wikipedia.org/wiki/Филэллины (accessed 14 March 2018).
Freedom House (2022): Freedom House, "Countries and Territories". Online: https://freedomhouse.org/countries/freedom-world/scores (accessed 30 November 2022).
Gesellschaft für bedrohte Völker (2017): *Drei Jahre Annexion der Krim (2014–2017). Systematische Verfolgung der Krimtataren dauert an. Memorandum der Gesellschaft für bedrohte Völker, Februar 2017*. Online unter https://www.gfbv.de/fileadmin/redaktion/Reporte_Memoranden/2017/Memorandum_Drei_Jahre_Krim.pdf (accessed 19 January 2018).
Haytarma (2015): *Haytarma*, film, 15 May 2015. Online: https://www.youtube.com/watch?v=f181jS4_egs (accessed 9 September 2018).
Iron Maiden (2009): "IRON MAIDEN Like You've Never Heard Them Before!", in: *Blabbermouth.net*, 20 July 2009. Online: http://www.blabbermouth.net/news/iron-maiden-like-you-ve-never-heard-them-before/ (accessed 14 March 2018).
Jamala (2017): Jamala, "1944", translated by BertBrac. Online: https://lyricstranslate.com/de/1944-1944.html-7#songtranslation (accessed 11 April 2023).
Khanskii dvorets (2018): "Khanskii dvorets (Bakhchisarai)", in: *Vikipediia*. Online: https://ru.wikipedia.org/wiki/Ханский_дворец_(Бахчисарай) (accessed 20 February 2018).
Klug (2022): Tetyana Klug, "Faktencheck: Explosion auf der Krimbrücke - was ist real, was ist fake?", in: *Deutsche Welle*, 13 October 2022. Online: https://www.dw.com/de/faktencheck-explosion-auf-der-krimbr%C3%BCcke-was-ist-echt-was-ist-fake/a-63427221 (accessed 4 June 2023).
Koshka (2017): "Koshka, Pëtr Markovich", in: *Wargaming.net*. Wiki, 29 January 2017. Online: http://wiki.wargaming.net/ru/Navy:Кошка,_Пётр_Макович (accessed 9 September 2018).
Krimkhanat (2008): "Das frühneuzeitliche Krimkhanat (15.–18. Jahrhundert) zwischen Orient und Okzident, 31. 03. 2008 – 01. 03. 2008 München", in: *H-Soz-Kult*, 25 March 2008. Online: https://www.hsozkult.de/event/id/termine-8968 (accessed 12 March 2018).
Krym (2017): *Krym Put' na Rodinu* [Crimea. The Path to the Homeland], programme by Andrei Kondrashov. Online: http://russia.tv/brand/show/brand_id/59195 (accessed 14 March 2017).
Krymskii krizis (2018): "Krymskii krizis" [The Crimea Crisis], in: *Vikipediia*. Online: https://ru.wikipedia.org/wiki/Крымский_кризис (accessed 9 September 2018).
Latschan (2022): Thomas Latschan, "Ukraine: Unerreichbares Kriegsziel Krim?", in: Deutsche Welle, 10 August 2022. Online: https://www.dw.com/de/ukraine-unerreichbares-kriegsziel-krim/a-62171676 (accessed 4 June 2023).
Memorandum (2014): "Memorandum on Security Assurances in connection with Ukraine's accession to the Treaty on the Non-Proliferation of Nuclear Weapons", in: *Wikipedia*, 7 March 2014. Online: https://en.wikisource.org/wiki/Ukraine._Memorandum_on_Security_Assurances (accessed 14 March 2014).

Museum (2018): Website of the Museum to Amet Han-Sultan. Online: https://krtmuseum.ru/muzej-dvazhdy-geroya-sovetskogo-soyuza-amet-hana-sultana-galupka/ (accessed 22 February 2023).

Neapolis Scythian (2017): homepage of the Historical and Archeological Reserve NEAPOLIS SCYTHIAN. Online: http://neapolis-scythian.ru/english/history.html (accessed 24 November 2017).

Nikolaus Kleemann (2018): "Nikolaus Ernst Kleemann", in: *CERL Thesaurus. Das Tor zum gedruckten europäischen Kulturerbe*. Online: https://thesaurus.cerl.org/record/cnp01413100 (accessed 2 January 2018).

Putin (2014): Vladimir Putin, "Address by President of the Russian Federation", 18 March 2014, in: *Ofitsial'nyi sait Prezidenta Rossii* [Official Website of the President of Russia]. Online: http://en.kremlin.ru/events/president/news/20603 (accessed 11 April 2023).

Opfer (2014): "Die Opfer des 1. Weltkriegs", in: wiki.sah, 22 October 2014. Online: http://www.science-at-home.de/wiki/index.php/Die_Opfer_des_1._Weltkriegs (accessed 4 September 2018).

Shapoval (2009): Iurii Shapoval, "Krymskaia ėpopeia" [The Crimea Epic], in: *Radio ėkho Moskvy. Dorogoi nash Nikita Sergeevich* [Radio Echo Moskau. Our Dear Nikita Sergeevich], 11 October 2009. Online: https://echo.msk.ru/programs/hrushev/625392-echo (accessed 9 September 2018).

Shmidt (2018): "Shmidt, Pëtr Petrovich", in: *Vikipediia*. Online: https://ru.wikipedia.org/wiki/Шмидт,_Пётр_Петрович (accessed 24 August 2018).

Statistica (2022): Statistica, "Befürworten Sie das Handeln von Wladimir Putin als President?" Online: https://de.statista.com/statistik/daten/studie/1293274/umfrage/umfrage-zu-den-zustimmungswerten-fuer-wladimir-putin-in-russland/ (accessed 20 December 2022).

Steps Scene (2018): "Steps Scene" in Sergei Ėizenshtein's film *Battleship Potemkin*. Online: http://cinema.arte.tv/de/artikel/die-treppenszene-aus-panzerkreuzer-potemkin (accessed 14 March 2018).

Stomporowski (2018): Sava Stomporowski, "Der Vorfall von Kertsch und die Grüne Haltung zur Ukraine. Die Krim-Brücke als Anlass für weitere Militarisierung", in: *planet first. Unabhängige Grüne Linke*, second, revised version of 4 December 2018. Online: https://www.gruene-linke.de/2018/12/01/hintergruende-der-kertsch-krise-russland-ukraine/ (accessed 20 December 2018).

Tagungsbericht (2015): "Tagungsbericht. Der Wiener Kongress und seine Folgen. Großbritannien, Europa und der Friede im 19. und 20. Jahrhundert, 03. 09. 2015 – 05. 09. 2015 Coburg", in: *H-Soz-Kult*, 30 November 2015. Online: https://www.hsozkult.de/conferencereport/id/tagungsberichte-6254 (accessed 19 June 2018).

Treaty of Paris (1856): *Treaty of Paris of 1856. Paris, March 30, 1856. Peace Treaty between Great Britain, France, the Ottoman Empire, Sardinia and Russia*. Online: https://content.ecf.org.il/files/M00934_TreatyOfParis1856English.pdf (accessed 11 April 2023).

Tyshchenko (2017): Yulia Tyshchenko, "Analyse: Die russische Integrationsstrategie für die Krim", in: *Bundeszentrale für Politische Bildung*, 29 May 2017. Online: https://www.bpb.de/themen/europa/ukraine-analysen/249040/analyse-die-russische-integrationsstrategie-fuer-die-krim/ (accessed 21 November 2022).

Ukraine Analytica (2021): "THE CRIMEAN PLATFORM WILL BECOME A FOREIGN POLICY INSTRUMENT OF THE DE-OCCUPATION

STRATEGY", in: *UA: Ukraine Analytica*, 16 March, 2021. Online: https://ukraine-analytica.org/the-crimean-platform-will-become-a-foreign-policy-instrument-of-the-de-occupation-strategy/ (accessed 4 June 2023).

UNESCO (2013): UNESCO. Memory of the World Register, "Evliya Çelebi's 'Book of Travels' in the Topkapi Palace Museum Library and the Süleymaniye Manuscript Library", 2013. Online: http://www.unesco.org/new/en/communication-and-information/flagship-project-activities/memory-of-the-world/register/full-list-of-registered-heritage/registered-heritage-page-3/evliya-celebis-book-of-travels-in-the-topkapi-palace-museum-library-and-the-sueleymaniye-manuscript-library/ (accessed 19 January 2018).

United Nations (2007): *United Nations Declaration on the Rights of Indigenous Peoples*, 13 September 2007. Online: http://www.un.org/esa/socdev/unpfii/documents/DRIPS_en.pdf (accessed 9 August 2017).

United Nations (2013): *The United Nations Declaration on the Rights of Indigenous Peoples. A Manual for National Human Rights Institutions*, August 2013. Online: https://www.ohchr.org/documents/issues/ipeoples/undripmanualfornhris.pdf (accessed 9 September 2017).

Zemletriasenie (2009): "Zemletriasenie 1927 goda i vosstanovlenie Alushty" [The Earthquake of 1927 and the Restoration of Alushta], in: *Sait pro Balaklavu i AR Krym* [Website About Balaklava and the AR of Crimea], 2 November 2009. Online: http://balaklava.ucoz.net/news/zemletrjasenie_1927_goda_i_vosstanovlenie_alushty/2009-11-02-17 (accessed 9 August 2018).

INDEX: PEOPLE

Agamemnon 7–8
Ahmed III 123
Akhmatova, Anna 69
Aksenov, Sergei V. 243, 246
Aksënov, Vasilii P. 2, 251
Albrecht, Stefan 13, 68, 72, 75–6, 265, 267
Aleksei (Alexis) Mikhailovich ("the Quiet", "the Most Gentle", "the Most Peaceful" [Russian: Tishaishii]) 109, 119, 125, 224
Alexander, ruler of Crimean Gothia 85
Alexander I 19, 281
Alexander II 162, 165–7, 170, 172, 176
Alexios Angelos 62–3
Alexios I., Prince of Theodoro 73–74, 77, 267
Amit, Ėmil' 218
Andrew the Apostle 14, 43
Anna Ivanovna 123, 125
Anna Porphyrogenita 16, 54–5
Aqçura, Yosıf (Russian: Iusuf Akchurin) 177
Arctinus of Miletus 32
Artamonov, Mikhail I. 48
Artemis/Diana 7–8
Arthur, King 11
Ascherson, Neal 10, 28–9, 68, 109, 155, 266
Augustynowicz, Christoph xvi, 10, 189,
Aust, Martin 189

Bakunin, Mikhail 162
Bakunina, Ekaterina M. 161–2
Basil II, emperor of Byzantium 16
Batu Khan 58, 92, 264
Bauer, Otto 200

Baumgart, Winfried 167, 279, 286
Baybars 67
Beauplan, Guillaume le Vasseur de 107–8
Belyi, Andrei 17
Bersenev, Ivan, Russian captain 137
Beuys, Joseph 4–5
Bikeç, Dilâra (Russian/Ukrainian: Diliara Bikech), favourite of Kırım Giray 18
Binhack, Franz 117–18, 124, 277
Bixby, character in Tom Clancy's thriller *Command Authority* 241
Bloch, Marc 147
Bogdanov, N. 191
Boniface of Montferrat 62
Brandes, Detlef 284–5
Brandes, Wolfram 50
Brătianu, Gheorghe I. 63, 67, 266
Brezhnev, Leonid 217
Broniewski, Marcin (Martinus Bronovius) 75–6, 79, 90, 98–100, 111, 113, 268
Busbecq, Ogier Ghislain de 12
Busir Glavan (Russian/Ukrainian: Ibuzir Gliavan) 49

Cadot, Michel 21
Camaladinova, Susana (Jamala [Crimean Tatar: Camala; Ukranian/Russian: Dzhamala]) 215–16
Carl XII 122
Casimir, grand duke of Lithuania 77
Catherine II ("the Great") 3, 112, 124–39, 143–4, 150, 154, 171, 223, 281–2, 239
Çelebicihan, Noman 185–6, 192–3, 195, 247, 292

Cemilev, Mustafa (Ukrainian: Mustafa Dzhemiliev; Russian: Mustafa Dzhemilev) 230–1, 236–8, 246
Chalmers, Martin 169–71
Chekhov, Anton P. 17
Chicherin, Georgii V. 197
Churchill, Winston 223–4
Činggis Qaγan (Genghis Khan) 58, 69, 75–7, 84, 90–1, 94
Clancy, Tom 241–2, 244, 301
Clement of Rome (Clemens Romanus) 15, 43–44
Clytemnestra 8
Çobanzade, Bekir 211
Constantine I ("the Great") 44
Constantine (Cyril [i.e. Kirill]), Slav missionary 15, 43, 48
Constantine V 262
Constantine VII 51, 53
Constantine VIII 16
Craven, Elizabeth 135, 141–2
Çubarov, Refat 238, 246
Curtiz, Michael 158
Czerwonnaja, Swetlana 218

Dan, Anca 32
Dasha Aleksandrova "Sevastopol'skaia" (Dar'ia L. Mikhailova) 162
Denikin, Anton I. 188
Derzhavin, Gavrila R. 140
Devlet Giray (cf. also Devlet-Girey) 93, 129, 140
Devlet-Girey 93
Devlet II Giray 122
Devlet IV/III Giray 129, 280
Dimitrov, Georgi 229
Diophantes, Pontic commander 36
Dolgorukov, Vasilii M. 126
Domitian 37, 261
Doroshenko, Dmytro 196
Doroshenko, Petro 120
Dufaud, Grégory 200, 205
Dula, prince of the Alans 11

Edigü (Idiqu) 72, 77, 267
Ėizenshtein, Sergei 182
Electra 8
Elena Pavlovna 161

Elisabeth Petrovna 125
Eminek (Russian, also: Imenek) 83
Ephorus of Cyme 24
Ermanaric 40
Euripides 7–9, 222
Eusebius of Caesarea 14, 261
Evliyâ Çelebi (Mehmed Zilli) 81–2, 90, 113, 269, 272

Feferman, Kiril 213, 297
Fenton, Roger 161
Ferdinand I 12
Figes, Orlando 166–8, 278, 286
Fisher, Alan 77, 83, 84, 93, 95, 99, 113, 116, 129, 131, 185, 203, 268, 273, 274, 276–7, 279–80, 295
Flynn, Errol 158
Ford, Harrison 241

Gagarin, Iurii 229
Gaidukevich, Viktor F. 27
Galakhov, Sergei P. 172
Ğani Beg (Jani Beg) 68
Gaspıralı, İsmail (Russian: Ismail Gasprinskii) 177–9, 183–6, 201
Gaspıralı, Şefiqa (Russian: Shefika Gasprinskaia) 289
Gnauck, Gerhard 218
Goethe, Johann Wolfgang von 7–9, 21, 170, 256
Golden, P.B. 48
Golikov, Evgenii N., Russian captain 182
Golitsyn, Vasilii V. 121
Gorbachev, Mikhail 229, 231–2, 236
Gorizontov, Leonid E. 168
Gorki, Maksim 207
Grigorenko, Petr (Ukrainian: Petro Hryhorenko) 231
Grillparzer, Franz 222
Gumilëv, Lev N. 69

Hacı I Giray 76–9, 82–3, 87
Hadrian II, Pope 43
Hammer-Purgstall, Joseph Freiherr von 121, 123, 269, 278
Havilland, Olivia de 158
Helbig, Georg Adolf von 136
Hentig, Werner Otto von 212

Herdick, Michael 68, 72, 265, 267
Herodotus xvi, 5, 8, 23–4
Herzen, Alexander (Gertsen) 166
Hildermeier, Manfred 189
Himmler, Heinrich 213
Hitler, Adolf 13, 209, 223
Ho Chi Minh 229
Hofmeister, Ulrich xvi, 177
Holderness, Mary 141–3, 149–51, 153–5
Hösch, Edgar 124–5
Hromenko, Serhiy 216
Hunor 11
Hürter, Johannes 211
Hüseynzadə, əli bəy (Russian: Ali-bek Guseinzade) 177

Iakobson, Anatolii L. 113
Ianukovych, Viktor 236, 237, 242
Iaroslav I. ("Mudryi" [the Wise]) 54
Iarovinskii, B.L. 183
Ibn Baṭūṭah 62
İbraimov, Veli (Ibragimov) 204
Igel'strom, Osip A. (Otto Heinrich Igelström) 138
Igor, Prince 57–8
Ilf, Ilia (i.e. Iekhiel Leib Fainzil'berg) 203
Innocent III, Pope 62
Iphigenia (German: Iphigenie) 4, 7–9, 136, 149, 256
Isaac, heir to the throne of Crimea Gothia 62, 84
Islam III Giray 109
İslâmov, Lenur Edem oğlu 246–7
Istomin, Vladimir I. 208
Iushchenko, Viktor 237, 239, 245
Ivan III 94
Ivan IV ("the Terrible") 93–4, 99, 268, 272, 277
Ivanics, Mária 78

Jahn, Hans Henny 222
Jason 222
Jena, Detlef 131, 164
John, bishop of Crimean Gothia 50, 262
Jordanes 39–40, 261
Joseph II 133–4
Joyce, James 36
Justinian II, emperor of Byzantium 48–9

Kadios/Kadmos, bishop of Bosporus (Ukrainian: Kerch, Russian: Kerch') 44
Kapiton, ecclesiast of Chersonesus 44
Kappeler, Andreas xvi, 108, 275, 301
Karamzin, Nikolai M. 93–4, 272
Karl Alexander, Margrave of Ansbach and Bayreuth 135
Kasack, Wolfgang 222
Khartakhai, F. 87
Khmel'nyts'kyi, Bohdan 119
Khodarkovsky, Michael 99
Khrushchev, Nikita 216–17, 224–5, 230
King, Charles 63, 124, 236, 239
Kinsky, Esther 169–70
Kirimal, Edige (cf. Qırımal, Mustafa Edige) 209, 294–6
Kizilov, Mikhail 100
Kleemann, Nikolaus Ernst 90
Klenke, C.L. von 140
Kliuchevskii, Vasilii O. 15, 56, 123, 127
Kniazhevich, Nikolai 191
Kolchak, Aleksandr V. 182
Konstantinov, Vladimir A. 242
Korf, Russian general 166
Kornilov, Vladimir A. 208
Koshka, Pëtr M. 207–8
Kostomarov, Mykola (Russian: Nikolai) 21
Krasin, Viktor 231
Kraus, Hans-Christof 158
Križanić, Juraj 119–20
Krym, Solomon 197
Kuchma, Leonid 238
Kühlmann, Richard von 195
Kun, Béla 188
Kunz, Norbert 13, 209–10, 212, 298
Kurya (also Kuria), prince of the Pechenegs 54

Ladygin, Dmitrii 125
Lazarev, Mikhail P. 208
Lazzerini, Edward L. 130, 147, 176

Lemercier-Quelquejay, Chantal 202
Lenin (Vladimir I. Ul'ianov) 4, 172, 200, 206, 210, 294
Leukon I (also known as Leucon or Leuco) 35
Ligne, Charles Joseph François de 136
Likhachëv, Dmitrii 57
Litavrin, G.G. 64
Littleton, Scott C. 11
Löwe, Richard 86, 270
Luc, Jean de 97–8, 103–4
Luchnikov, Andrei 2
Ludendorff, Erich 193, 195
Luzhkov, Iurii 235
Lyzhychko, Ruslana 215

Magocsi, Paul Robert 115, 255, 259, 264, 276, 277, 284, 290, 292
Magog 11
Magor 11
Maiakovskii, Vladimir V. xv
Malcor, Linda A. 11
Malek, Martin 218
Malenkov, Georgii M. 225
Mamāi 68–9, 72
Mandel'shtam, Osip 17, 169
Manstein, Erich von 209–10
Maria, daughter of the prince of Theodoro 85
Markevich, Arsenii 165
Markov, Evgenii 173
Martin, Terry 200
Martin I, Pope 44
Matthew, hieromonk (Exarch) 71–3
Matuz, Josef 87, 91, 269
Mazepa, Ivan 122
Medvedev, Dmitrii A. 236, 245
Mehdi, Abdurreşit (Russian: Reshid Medievich Mediev) 184–5
Mehmed II ("the Conqueror") 83
Mendez, Medea, figure in Liudmila Ulitskaia's *Medea and her Children* 221
Mengli I Giray 78, 83–4, 87, 90
Menshikov, Aleksandr S. 165
Meshkov, Iurii 239
Methodius, Apostle of the Slavs 15, 43, 48
Meyer, James H. 177

Michael I, king of Romania 210
Michael VIII Palaiologos 63, 67
Mickiewicz, Adam 19–21, 169
Mikhail I, Tsar 121
Mithridates VI 5, 35–6
Mstislav 56
Münnich, Count Burkhard Christoph von 123, 126
Murad Giray 121, 271, 278
Murav'ëv-Karskii, Nikolai N. 167
Mussis, Gabriel de 68
Mustafa III 128
Myeshkov, Dmytro 152–3

Nabokov, Vladimir D. 197
Nabokov, Vladimir V. 197
Naimark, Norman 218
Nakhimov, Pavel 159, 235
Napoleon Bonaparte 124
Neubauer, Helmut 36
Neutatz, Dietmar 152
Nicholas I 155, 165, 281
Nicholas II 181
Nightingale, Florence 161
Nimrod 11
Noack, Christian 178, 185
Nogai, Mongolian commander 105
Noonan, Thomas S. 49
Nur Devlet 83–4, 90
Nürnbergk, Jörg von 86

Ohlendorf, Otto 210, 213
Oliphant, Laurence 171
Orestes 8

Paerisades I 35
Paerisades V 35–6
Pallas, Peter Simon 111, 139, 171, 276
Panin, Nikita I. 125, 279
Papp, Sándor 89–90
Parzinger, Hermann 24, 259
Pasternak, Boris L. 183
Peter I ("the Great") 121–3, 127, 282
Peter III 127
Peter, the Apostle 43
Petrov, Evgenii (i.e. Evgenii Petrovich Kataev) 203
Pinson, Mark 168
Platonov, Nikolai I. 183

Platzeck, Matthias 245
Pliny the Elder 36
Plokhy, Serhii 205, 208, 225, 298
Pompeius 36
Poniatowski, Stanisław 130, 133
Poroshenko, Petro 246, 248, 252
Potemkin, Grigorii A. 131–40, 147, 164, 171, 219, 282
Potocka, Maria (Russian: Mariia Pototska) 18–21
Potocka, Sofia 19
Pritsak, Omeljan 53
Pushkin, Alexander xv, 17–21, 157, 169, 223
Putin, Vladimir V. 1–2, 16, 221, 225, 236, 241, 243–8, 251–2, 301–2
Pylades 8

Qırım Giray (also Geray, "Crimea Giray") 18–19, 89, 124
Qırımal, Mustafa Edige (Edige Kirimal) 209
Qualls, Karl 299

Raab, Nigel A. 203–4
Racine, Jean 36
Rededia (Rededya), Prince 56
Renner, Karl 200
Rhesuporis I, ruler of the Bosporan Kingdom 37
Robertson, James 161
Roosevelt, Franklin D. 223–4
Rosenberg, Alfred 13, 213
Rostovtsev, Mikhail I. (also Michael Rostovtzeff) 27–8, 260
Rubo, Franz A. 160, 162
Rubruk, Wilhelm von 61, 63
Russell, William Howard 161
Ryan, Jack, character in Tom Clancy's thriller *Command Authority* 241

Sahib I Giray 113
Sahib II Giray 128–9
Şahin Giray 129–32
Saint-Arnaud, Armand Jacques Leroy de 165
Sakharov, Andrei 231
Shamil 167
Shapoval, Iurii 225

Sasse, Gwendolyn 225, 227, 239
Saumakos (also Savmak) 36
Sauromates I 37
Sauromates II 37
Schmidt, Helmut 245–6
Schmitt, Carl 65
Schramm, Percy Ernst 210
Ségur, Louis Philippe de 136
Seitablaev, Akhtem 218
Selim I Giray 121
Selim III Giray 131
Seneca 222
Seydahmet, Cafer (Qırımer) 185–6, 192, 194–6, 209, 292
Shaykh Ahmad 78, 269
Shirinskii-Shikhmatov, Platon A. 145
Shmidt, Petr P., Lieutenant 181, 183, 290
Sholem-Beim 155
Simma, Bruno 245
Skilurus, Scythian ruler 33
Skoropads'kyi, Pavlo 195, 293
Skorupa, Dariusz 109
Slashchëv, Ia., officer 188
Smirnov, Vasilii D. 76–8, 92, 108
Sobieski, Jan 119
Soltanğäliev, Mirsäyet (Russian: Mirsaid Sultan-Galiev) 187–8
Spartacus 36
Stalin, Joseph (i.e. Ioseb Besarionis dze Jughashvili) 3, 19, 22, 97, 113, 139, 156, 188–9, 191, 200–1, 204–6, 208, 219, 223–5, 207, 230, 263, 294–5
Ștefan III cel Mare ("Stephen the Great") 85
Stephan Bátory (Hungarian Báthory István; litauisch Steponas Batoras) 75
Stickler, Timo 40
Strabo 32, 35–6
Subtelny, Orest 120
Süleyman I ("the Magnificent" or "the Lawgiver") 84
Sulimirski, Tadeusz 10
Sulkiewicz, Maciej 196
Sultan, Amet-Han (Russian/Ukrainian: Amet-Khan Sultan) 218–19
Surkov, Aleksei A. 207–8

Svyatoslav I (i.e. Sviatoslav), prince of Kyivan Rus' 47, 51, 54

Tarhan, İlyas 206
Tarle, E.V. 164
Taş Timur 76
Tennyson, Alfred 158
Tervel 49
Theophilus of Gothia 44
Thoas, king of Tauris 7, 9
Thunmann, Hans Erich Johann 103
Tiberius II 49
Timur Kuthlug (Timer Qotlığ) 72
Timur (Lenk, the Lame) 69, 77, 267
Tokta (Toktu) 67
Toktamış (Tokhtamy/Toqtamis/ Tohtamysh, also known as Khan Lokhtonus) 69, 72, 76, 77, 267
Tolstoi, Leo (Russian: Lev) N. 17, 157, 163
Troebst, Stefan 223
Tsvetaeva, Marina 17, 169
Twain, Mark (Samuel Langhorne Clemens) 163–4

Uehling, Greta Lynn 230, 294
Ulbricht, Walter 229
Ulitskaia, Liudmila 5, 221–2
Ülküsal, Müstecib 209
Umerov, Ėrvin 218

Vardanis (emperor of Byzantium as Philippucus Bardanes) 49
Vásáry, István 78
Vasil'ev, Aleksandr A. 44, 49–50, 56, 73–4, 77, 261–2, 267, 270

Veselitskii, P.G. 128
Veser, Reinhard 2
Vladimir/Volodymyr, Grand Prince 15–16, 54–56
Volodin, Valeri, character in Tom Clancy's thriller *Command Authority* 241
Voloshin, Maximilian A. 17
Voltaire (i.e. François-Marie Arouet) 128, 130
Vorontsov, Mikhail I. 125–6
Vorontsov, Mikhail S. 145, 155
Vorotynskii, Prince 93
Vozgrin, Valerii 120
Vrangel', Pëtr N., General 188
Vytautas (Witold), Grand Duke of Lithuania 72, 77

Williams, Brian G. 58, 77, 146, 186, 206, 223, 230, 268, 276, 283
Windt, Harry Willes Darell de 104–5, 111
Wolf, Christa 222
Wolff, Larry 140

Young, Arthur 141

Zalizniak, A.A. 57
Zarema 18–19
Zaytsev, Ilya 94
Zelens'kyi, Volodymyr O. 249, 252–3, 302
Zemliachka, Rozaliia S. (Rozaliia S. Zalkind) 188
Zoshchenko, Mikhail M. 199, 204

INDEX: PLACES

Abkhazia 244
Africa 66
Akkerman xiii, 85
Alexandria 62, 67
Algeria 249
Alupka (cf. also Lupico) xii, 63, 218
Amur region 205
Anatolia 107, 159
Andrusovo 109, 120
Ankara xiii, 209
Aqmescit (also Ak-mesjid, cf. also Simferopol') xii, 2, 81, 115, 281
Aqyar (cf. also Sevastopol') xii, 13
Asia 35, 48, 53, 64, 82, 135–6
Asia Minor 5, 36
Astrakhan' (khanate) 78, 87, 93–4, 105, 144
Athens 29, 128
Australia 215
Austria 158, 167
Autonomous Crimean Soviet Socialist Republic (also Crimean ASSR) 97, 190, 201–6, 222, 231–3, 242, 294
Autonomous Republic of Crimea (cf. also Republic of Crimea) 1, 242
Avlita 74
Azerbaijan Democratic Republic 196
Azov (cf. also Tana) xiii, 121, 123, 265, 273–4, 277
Azov, Sea of (cf. also Maeotis, Lake) xii, xiii, 3, 57, 69, 78, 150, 166, 209, 248

Bağçasaray (Russian: Bakhchisarai, Ukrainian: Bakhchysarai, cf. also Pushkinskii) xii, xv, 18–21, 77–8, 82, 84, 89–93, 98, 105, 113–15, 119–21, 12, 129, 133, 142–3, 184, 187, 194, 223, 259, 272

Balaklava (Crimean Tatar: Balıqlava; cf. also Cembalo) xii, 63, 73, 77, 158
Balkans 143, 279
Baltic region 101, 122, 137–8, 173, 183, 191
Baltic Sea 137, 159, 168, 258
Batumi xiii, 204
Belarus (cf. also Byelorussian SSR) 154, 236
Berdians'k xiii, 248
Beresteczko (Ukrainian: Berestechko) 109
Berezan' 181
Berlin 5, 140, 162, 168, 192, 195–7, 208–9, 211–13, 282, 292, 296
Bessarabia 155, 285
Bilohirs'k (Russian: Belogorsk; cf. also Qarasuvbazar) xii, 115, 130
Birobidzhan 205
Bithynia-Pontus 36
Black Sea (cf. also Pontus Euxinus) xii, xiii, 2–6, 10–13, 23–29, 31–2, 36–7, 40–1, 44, 47–50, 53–4, 56, 58, 61–4, 66–9, 72–4, 78–9, 82–3, 85–6, 89, 92–4, 98–101, 103, 107, 109, 113, 117–27, 134, 137, 139–40, 145, 149–52, 154, 159, 168, 181–2, 188, 190, 196, 199, 202, 207–8, 212, 217, 222, 231, 235–6, 258–60, 265–7, 269, 273–4, 285
Bohemia 16, 171
Borysthenes (cf. also Dnipro and Dnieper) 135
Bosporan Kingdom (also Bosporan Empire) 27, 35–7, 40, 44
Bosporus 44, 62, 118
Brandenburg-Prussia 92

Brest-Litovsk 195
Britain (cf. also British Empire, British Isles, Great Britain, United Kingdom, UK, England) 14, 124, 158–9, 161, 279
British Isles (cf. also Britain, British Empire, United Kingdom, UK, England) 11, 160
British Empire 138, 145
Budapest 236
Bulgaria xiii, 73, 229
Buxoro (Russian: Bukhara) 231
Byzantium (also Byzantine Empire) 5, 48–50, 53–5, 58–9, 63–4, 73, 82, 117, 128, 137

Caffa (also Kaffa or Capha; cf. also Feodosiia, Kefe, Theodosia) xii, 25, 64, 66–9, 73–4, 76, 78–9, 82–4, 87, 100–1, 265, 269
Carpatho-Ukraine 255
Caspian Sea 93
Caucasus 18, 48, 50, 61, 122, 146, 167–8, 173, 183–4, 213, 216, 269, 275
Cembalo (cf. also Balaklava) xii, 63, 73–4, 77, 267
Central Asia 3, 40, 97, 177, 179, 216, 218, 229, 231
Central Ukraine 239, 242
Chersónesos Tauriké 8
Chersonesus (cf. too Korsun') 13–14, 16, 25–6, 33, 36–7, 40, 44, 47, 49–50, 53–4, 57, 59, 64, 73–4, 76, 271
China 66
Chornobyl' 232–3
Cimmerian Bosporus (cf. also Kerch Strait) 27
Cossack Het'manate 120
Cossack territories 120
Crimean ASSR (also Autonomous Crimean Soviet Socialist Republic) 97, 190, 201–6, 222, 231–3, 242, 294
Crimean Gothia (cf. also Theodoro, Principality of) 44, 47, 49, 54, 56, 64, 72–3, 85–6
Crimean Khanate 6, 19, 66–7, 73, 75–133, 140, 145, 150, 154, 179, 192, 202, 231, 268–9, 272, 274, 276–8, 280
19 145 268-9 276-8
Crimean Mountains (cf. also mountain region, mountains) 28–9, 41, 59, 218
Crimea oblast' 236
Community of Independent States (CIS) 239
Constantinople (cf. also Istanbul, Tsar'grad) xiii, 44, 48–50, 54–5, 59, 61–3, 73, 79, 82–3, 85, 107, 118, 121, 127, 236
Çufut Qale (Russian/Ukrainian: Chufut-Kale; cf. also Qırq Yer) xii, 155
Cyprus 49

Dagestan 218, 294
Danube, River/region 37, 44, 54, 159, 277
Danubian Principalities (cf. also Moldavia, Walachia) 92, 125, 158–9, 167
Danzig region 152
Delphi 26
Denmark 92
Dnieper, River (cf. also Dnipro, Boristhenes) 14
Dnipro–Buh Estuary 181
Dnipro, River (cf. also Dnieper, Boristhenes) 48, 72, 107–8, 120–1, 126, 133, 135, 181
Don Estuary 150, 265
Don, River/region 10, 57–8, 68, 93, 107, 197, 274
Doros (also Dory, cf. also Mangup-Kale, Theodoro) xii, 40–1, 44, 49–50, 72, 76

Eastern Europe 4, 11, 12–13, 16, 58, 89–95, 99–100, 103, 109, 116, 134, 186, 188, 195, 217, 268, 302
Eastern Galicia 211–12
Eastern Roman Empire 41, 44–5
Eastern Ukraine 4, 216, 237, 239, 242, 246–9, 285
Edirne (Greek: Adrianopolis; Bulgarian: Odrin) xiii, 151

Egypt 29, 159
Ekaterinoslav xiii, 133, 285
England (cf. also Britain, Great Britain, British Isles, United Kingdom, UK) 197
Epirus, Despotate of 64
Eski Qırım (cf. also Solcati, Staryi Krym) xii, 58, 64, 72, 77
Estonia 152, 191, 242
Europe 9, 11–14, 24, 35, 66, 68, 100, 118, 120, 124, 127, 136, 140, 159, 161, 171, 213, 223, 266
European Union (also EU) 4, 239, 243, 245–6, 252
Evpatoriia (cf. also Ievpatoriia, Gözleve, Kezlev) xii, 115, 154, 166

Feodosiia (cf. also Kefe, Caffa, Theodosia) xii, 25, 62, 141, 154, 156, 183
Finland 159, 302
Florence 100
France 14, 124, 136, 145–6, 158–9, 161, 197, 223, 249, 286
Fraydorf (colony) 205

GDR (German Democratic Republic) 229
Genoa 6, 62, 66, 68–9, 73–4, 77, 82, 100, 205
Georgia 190, 222, 244–5, 251
German Empire 152, 195, 197, 207, 292
German Reich 192, 206, 209, 213, 223, 286
Germany (cf. also Germany, Federal Republic of, German Empire, German Reich) 193, 197, 223
Germany, Federal Republic of 210, 296
Golden Horde (cf. also Mongol Empire) 58, 61, 64–5, 68–9, 72, 76–8, 82, 84–5, 91, 93–4, 105, 115, 178, 264–5
Golden Horn 63, 118
Gotenburg (cf. also Simferopol') xii, 13
Gotenland 4, 13
Gözleve (cf. also Kezlev, Evpatoriia, Ievpatoriia) xii, 115

Great Britain (cf. also Britain, British Isles, United Kingdom, UK, England) 224
Greece 128, 149–50, 227

Habsburg Empire 124, 128, 136, 158, 167, 279
Hague, The 245
Halle an der Saale 103
Helsinki 231, 233
Heraclea Pontica xiii, 26, 35
Hermonassa (cf. also Tmutarakan') xiii, 55
Het'manate (cf. also Cossack Het'manate, Cossack territories) 120, 125
Holy Land 14–15, 62
Holy Roman Empire 121, 122
Hungary 11, 16, 91, 97, 243
Hurzuf (Russian: Gurzuf) xii, 4, 228

Ievpatoriia (cf. also Evpatoriia, Gözleve, Kezlev) 115, 154, 166
Inkerman (also known as Ingerman; cf. also Kalamita) 74, 76, 207
Israel 221
Istanbul (cf. also Constantinople, Tsar'grad) xiii, 12, 82–4, 86, 89–94, 98, 100, 113, 118–19, 122–6, 128–9, 131, 134, 159, 165, 177–8, 18–6, 192, 195–7, 209, 272, 274, 278

Japan 233
Jassy (Romanian: Iaşi) xiii, 134, 139

Kahlenberg 119
Kalamita (cf. also Inkerman) 74, 76
Kalka River 58
Kamchatka 159
Karlowitz 122
Karlsbad 172
Kars xiii, 167
Kazakhstan 78, 190, 230, 236, 251
Kazan' 72, 78, 87, 94, 105, 144, 183
Kefe (cf. also Feodosiia, Caffa, Theodosia) xii, 25, 84, 100–1, 108, 115, 129, 141, 273, 276

Kerch (Crimean Tatar: Keriç, Russian: Kerch'; cf. also Panticapaeum) xii, xiii, 25, 44, 55, 126, 129, 166, 210, 226, 229, 247
Kerch Strait (cf. also Cimmerian Bosporus) 27, 39, 56, 247, 248
Kezlev (cf. also Gözleve, Evpatoriia, Ievpatoria) 115
Kharkiv (Russian: Khar'kov) 204, 236
Khazar Khaganate (also Khazar Empire) 48
Kherson xiii, 13–14, 247, 285
Kiliia (Romanian: Chilia [Nouă]) xiii, 85
Kinburn (Turkish: Kılburun) xiii, 126
Kirghiz Soviet Socialist Republic 215
Köktöbel (Russian/Ukrainian: Koktebel') xii, 17
Kolchis 222
Korsun' (cf. also Chersonesus) xii, 14–16, 57
Kuban 78, 131
Küçük Kaynarca (Russian: Kiuchuk-Kainardzha) 127, 128
Kulikovo Pole 69
Kyiv 40, 14, 16, 43, 54–5, 120, 133, 145, 196, 215, 225, 227, 232–3, 236–9, 242–3, 248–9, 299, 300
Kyivan Rus' (also Rus') 3, 6, 14–16, 47, 50, 53–8, 61, 67, 69, 85, 97, 144, 150, 224, 268, 274

Ladoga, Lake 14
Larindorf (colony) 205
Lebanon 209
Leningrad (cf. also St. Petersburg, Petrograd) 164, 183, 199, 227
Lida 76
Lisbon 203
Lithuania (cf. also Grand Duchy of Lithuania, Poland-Lithuania, Polish-Lithuanian Commonwealth, Rzeczpospolita) 77, 85, 154, 192
Lithuania, Grand Duchy of (cf. also Lithuania, Poland-Lithuania, Polish-Lithuanian Commonwealth, Rzeczpospolita) 72, 76, 77, 85

Lublin 99, 270
Lupico (cf. also Alupka) xii, 63
L'viv (Polish: Lwów; German: Lemberg) 246

Macedonia 29
Maeotis, Lake (cf. also Azov, Sea of) 35, 274
Mamluk Empire 82
Mangup-Kale (also Mancopia; cf. also Doros, Theodoro) xii, 41, 72, 76, 85–6, 155
Mari (Republic) 230
Mariupol' xiii, 150, 248
Massandra 229
Matriga (cf. also Phanagoria) xiii, 61
Memmingen 86
Miletus 26–7, 32
Moldavia (cf. also Danubian Principalities) 73–4, 85, 92, 97, 125, 159, 272
Mongol Empire (cf. also Golden Horde) 65–6, 91, 264
Moscow 1–2, 16, 78, 84–5, 92–4, 97–8, 101, 116, 119, 121, 125, 139, 164, 177, 182, 190–1, 200–1, 205, 217, 221, 225, 227, 231–2, 235–6, 239, 242–8, 251, 272, 299, 300, 302
mountain region 72, 103–4, 112, 115
mountains 3, 12, 28, 29, 40–41, 49, 51, 155, 199, 214, 218
Muscovy (cf. also Tsardom) 78, 83–5, 87, 91–4, 99, 101, 105, 108–9, 115, 119–21, 124, 273

Neapolis xii, 33, 37
Neisse, River 223
Neva 183
New Russia (cf. also Russian: Novorossiia) 141, 151
Nicaea 44
Nikaia Empire 64
Nizhnii Novgorod 185
Nogai Horde 78, 105
North Africa 82
Northern Caucasus 167–8, 216
Novorossiia (cf. also New Russia) 145, 151, 153–4

Oder, River 223
Odesa (Russian: Odessa) xiii, 137, 182, 242, 285
Oka, River 47
Olbia xiii, 33, 40
Oreanda 171
Orenburg 183
Ottoman Empire (cf. also Sublime Porte) 10, 14, 66, 76, 79, 81. 83–7, 90–2, 94–5, 98–9, 105, 109, 113, 115–16, 118, 120–6, 128–9, 132, 134, 136, 146, 149, 151, 155, 158–9, 161 166, 168, 177–9, 184–6, 190, 192, 195, 205, 270, 275–6, 279, 286, 289
Özi/Özü (Ukrainian: Ochakiv; Russian: Ochakov) xiii, 273

Palestine ("Russian Palestine") 236
Panticapaeum (cf. also Kerch) 25–6, 35, 37, 40, 55, 260
Pereiaslav 109, 119, 224
Perekop 77, 152, 210, 247, 252
Persia 91, 122, 129
Petrograd (cf. also St. Petersburg, Leningrad) 191, 193–4
Petropavlovsk 159
Phanagoria (cf. also Matriga) xiii, 49, 61
Piacenza 61
Pisa 100
Podolia 92
Poland (cf. also Poland, Kingdom of, Polish-Lithuanian Commonwealth, Poland-Lithuania, Rzeczpospolita) 10, 16, 19, 21, 72, 85, 123, 127, 130, 133, 183, 192, 223, 280, 296
Poland, Kingdom of (cf. also Poland, Poland-Lithuanian Commonwealth, Poland-Lithuania, Rzeczpospolita) 72
Poland-Lithuania (cf. also Polish-Lithuanian Commonwealth, Rzeczpospolita, Poland, Kingdom of, Grand Duchy of Poland Lithuania) 76, 78, 85, 91–2, 98–9, 101, 108, 114–16, 120–2
Poltava 122
Pompeii (cf. also Matriga) 136

Pontic–Caspian steppe 105
Pontus 5, 23, 36
Pontus, Sea of 61
Pontus Euxinus (cf. also Black Sea) 23
Potsdam 223
Prussia 128, 152, 158, 223
Pruth, Treaty of the 122–3
Pskov 69
Pushkinskii (cf. also Bağçasaray) xii, 223

Qarasuvbazar (cf. also Bilohirs'k/ Belogorsk) xii, 115, 130, 142–3, 184, 223
Qırq Yer (cf. also Çufut Qale) xii, 77

Republic of Crimea (cf. also Autonomous Republic of Crimea) 243
Rhodos 123
Roman-Kosh (Crimean Tatar: Roman Qoş) 28
Roman Empire 36–7, 40, 261
Rome 5, 15, 36–7, 40, 43–4
Romania 209
Rostov 69, 93, 150
Russia (cf. also Russian Federation, Russian state; cf. also Russian Empire, tsarist empire) xii, xiii, xvi, 1–2, 3–5, 9, 13–16, 18–19, 48, 53–4, 61, 94, 109, 111, 113, 121–7, 131, 134–5, 137, 141, 152, 155–7, 159, 161, 167–70, 173, 176–8, 183, 185, 191–4, 196–7, 202, 205, 215, 219, 223, 225, 235, 239, 241–53, 255, 257, 263, 279–80, 285, 287, 292, 296–7, 302
Russian Empire 6, 14, 112, 115, 123, 127, 129, 131–4, 137–41, 144–5, 151–6, 158, 161–2, 167, 170–2, 177–9, 183–6, 189–93, 200, 202, 276–7, 269, 283, 284, 286, 289, 299
Russian Federation xvi, 1–4, 7, 164, 208, 215–16, 218, 233, 235–6, 239, 241–6, 251–2
Russian state 14, 93, 128, 150, 152–4, 192–3, 196–7, 246–7, 251

Russian Socialist Federative Soviet Republic (RSFSR) 190, 225, 227, 233
Rzeczpospolita (cf. also Polish-Lithuanian Commonwealth, Poland-Lithuania, Poland, Kingdom of, Grand Duchy of Lithuania) 78, 109, 120

Samarqand (Russian: Samarkand) 231
Sarai 58, 66–7, 77
Saratov 139
Sardinia-Piedmont 14, 158
Scandinavia 12, 140, 152, 261, 268
Scythia (also Scythian Empire) 32–3, 37, 39
Serbia 73
Sevastopol' (cf. also Aqyar, Theoderichshafen) xii, xiii, 14, 17, 25, 134, 137, 156–67, 181–3, 190, 192–6, 207–11, 226–8, 235–7, 239, 243, 281, 286–7, 299
Siberia 18, 119, 188, 216, 276
Sibir', Khanate of 78
Simferopol' (cf. also Aqmescit, Gotenburg) xii, xiii, 2, 13, 33, 81, 115, 175, 183, 187, 193–6, 210, 212, 227, 233, 237, 239, 243, 259, 281, 298
Sinop (also known as Sinope, Sinopolis) xiii, 14, 61, 100, 159–60, 162
Smolensk 120, 133
Sochi xiii, 243
Solcati (cf. also Eski Qırım, Staryi Krym) xii, 58
Soldaia (cf. also Sudak) xii, 61–4, 67–8, 264
Southern Buh (Polish: Boh; Ukrainian: Pivdennyi Buh; Russian Iuzhnyi Bug) 120
Southern Ukraine 28, 48, 120
South Ossetia 239, 244
South Russia 28, 151
South Tyrol 13
Soviet Union (also Soviet Russia; cf. also USSR) 2, 4, 14, 172, 183, 189, 190, 197, 199–211, 213, 216–239, 243–4, 275, 290, 297

Staryi Krym (cf. also Eski Qırım, Solcati) 58
Stockholm 215
St Petersburg (cf. also Leningrad, Petrograd) 14, 16, 19, 112, 123–4, 126, 128–33, 135–7, 143–4, 151, 159, 161, 165, 178, 182–3, 185–6, 283
Sublime Porte (cf. also Ottoman Empire) 79, 81–4, 86, 89–95, 98, 108, 113, 118, 121–4, 126, 128, 134, 139, 143, 159, 161–2, 272
Sudak (Crimean Tatar: Sudaq; cf. also Soldaia) xii, 57–8, 61, 64, 67–8, 231, 264
Suzdal' 69
Sweden 92, 122, 215, 302
Switzerland 140, 152
Syria 247

Taganrog (Ukrainian: Tahanroh/Tahanrih) xiii, 150
Taiwan 2
Taman 49, 55, 61, 69, 129, 247
Tana (cf. also Azov) xiii, 67–9, 101, 212, 265
Taurida Governorate (Tavricheskaia guberniia) 138, 143, 165, 175, 208, 283, 292
Taurida Province (Tavricheskaia oblast') 138
Taurida Soviet Socialist Republic (Russian: Sovetskaia Sotsialistichkeskaia Respublika Tavridy) 188
Tauris (also Taurida, Tauric Peninsula) 3–9, 76, 93–4, 149
Terek 107
Theoderichshafen (cf. also Sevastopol') xii, 13
Theodoro (cf. also Doros, Mangup-Kale) xii, 12, 71–4, 76–8, 82, 85–6, 267
Theodoro, Principality of (cf. also Crimean Gothia) 12, 71–4, 76–8, 82, 86
Theodosia (cf. also Feodosiia, Kefe, Caffa) xii, 25–6, 35

Timurid Empire 69, 267
Tmutarakan' (also Tmutarokan, Tmutorokan; cf. also Hermonassa) xiii, 55–7
Trebizond xiii, 64, 73–4, 107, 267
Troy 8
Tsardom (cf. also Muscovy) 93, 155, 299
Tsar'grad (cf. also Constantinople, Istanbul) xiii, 125
tsarist empire (cf. also Russia, Russian Empire, Russian state) 3, 11, 28, 87, 91, 109, 120, 121–6, 129, 130, 137, 138–40, 143, 153, 158–9, 161, 167, 171, 176–8, 180, 184, 188, 190, 195, 197, 208, 262, 277, 285, 287, 292, 295
Turin 68
Turkey xiii, 86, 123, 127, 190, 204, 209, 231, 246, 270, 301
Tver' 183, 286

UK (also United Kingdom; see also Britain, Great Britain, British Isles, England) 236 252, 302
Ukraine xiii, 1, 3–4, 14, 28, 48, 53, 58, 78, 107, 120, 190, 195–6, 215–16, 224–5, 226, 232–5, 241–53, 273, 285, 293–4, 298, 300, 302
Ukrainian Soviet Republic (Ukrainian SSR) 224–5
Ukrainian State (Ukrainian: Ukraïns'ka Derzhava; also Het'man State) 195–6, 293
Urals 24, 202, 216, 276
USA (also United States) 231, 223, 236, 241, 245, 252, 255, 302

USSR (cf. also Soviet Union) 1–2, 36, 97, 151, 164, 172, 181, 190, 197, 201, 202, 204, 206–7, 218, 221–5, 228, 230–1, 233, 236, 239, 244, 300
Uzbekistan 237, 267
Uzbek SSR 230

Vatican 121–2, 273
Venice 6, 62–3, 65–8, 74, 83, 100, 121–2, 125
Vesuvius 164
Vienna 192, 200, 258, 271–2, 286, 89, 91–2, 119
Vistula region 12
Vladimir 69
Vladivostok 183
Volga, River/region 10, 47, 48, 57–8, 78, 93,–4, 144, 177, 184, 216, 290
Volga-Ural region 145–6
Volhynia 193
Vorskla (tributary of the Dnipro) 72

Walachia (cf. also Danubian Principalities) 73, 92, 125, 159, 272
Waldsassen/Upper Palatinate 117
White Horde 78
Wild Fields (Russian: Dikoe Pole; Polish: Dziki Pola; Ukrainian: Dike Pole) 99, 108

Yalta xii, 5, 17, 156, 171–2, 203, 223–4, 257
Yeñi Qale (Russian: Enikale; Ukrainian Ienikale) 126

Zadar 62
Zbaraż (Ukrainian: Zbarazh) 109
Zborów (Ukrainian: Zboriv) 109